Foundations
— *for* —
Youth Ministry

SECOND EDITION

Foundations
— *for* —
Youth Ministry

*Theological Engagement
with Teen Life and Culture*

DEAN BORGMAN

Baker Academic
a division of Baker Publishing Group
Grand Rapids, Michigan

Published by Baker Academic
a division of Baker Publishing Group
P.O. Box 6287, Grand Rapids, MI 49516-6287
www.bakeracademic.com

Printed in the United States of America

Library of Congress Cataloging-in-Publication Data

Borgman, Dean, 1928–
    [When Kumbaya is not enough]
    Foundations for youth ministry : theological engagement with teen life and culture /Dean
Borgman. — 2nd Edition.
        pages cm
    Rev. ed. of: When Kumbaya is not enough : a practical theology for youth ministry. c1997.
    Includes bibliographical references and index.
    ISBN 978-0-8010-4901-9 (pbk.)
    1. Church work with youth. I. Title.
BV4447.B674 2013
259′.23—dc23   2013013875

13   14   15   16   17   18   19   7 6 5 4 3 2 1

Contents

Preface

[Attend] to wisdom and [incline] your heart to understanding. . . . If you seek it like silver and search for it as for hidden treasures—then you will understand the fear of the LORD and find the knowledge of God. For the LORD gives wisdom.

PROVERBS 2:2, 4–6A

Three loves describe the motivation for writing this book *and* the readers of this book: a consuming love for God, a creative love of culture, and a compassionate love for young people. To love God, culture, and youth implies a desire to understand—as difficult as that may be.

This text, *Foundations for Youth Ministry: Theological Engagement with Teen Life and Culture* takes up where my book *When Kumbaya Is Not Enough: A Practical Theology of Youth Ministry* left off. This work draws on the theories and empirical research of many. It acknowledges divine initiative in all we do and hopes to bring divine revelation and human efforts together. It is written for youth ministers and students who want to think more creatively, critically, and theologically—who want something more than youth group as usual. It is not so much a how-to-do-youth-ministry book as a how-to-think-about-youth-and-family-ministry text.

To my knowledge, *When Kumbaya Is Not Enough* was one of the first youth ministry texts to approach youth ministry from a theological perspective. Since then others have contributed much to this effort.[1] I would describe my theological

1. Examples include Pete Ward, *God at the Mall* (Peabody, MA: Hendrickson, 1999); Kenda Creasy Dean, Chap Clark, and David Rahn, eds., *Starting Right: Thinking Theologically about Youth Ministry* (Grand Rapids: Youth Specialties/Zondervan, 2001); Jeremy Thompson, *Telling*

perspective as historic orthodoxy, based on Scripture and the church's historic creeds. I write hoping this text will be appealing and challenging to youth leaders, whatever their tradition: Eastern Orthodox, Roman Catholic, Anglican, mainstream Protestant, evangelical, Emergent,[2] or Pentecostal.

It is written with longing for a united church or, at the very least, a functionally collaborative one. Our culture and youth demand that we come together with a common vision. Such collaboration calls for a theology that is broad and embracing yet willing to accept God's boundaries and our dividing lines, as we understand them.

I'm grateful for many colleagues who have chosen as a text *When Kumbaya Is Not Enough*, for students who've read and critiqued it, and for others in many parts of the world who have stumbled across it and helped shape this new book. Colleagues in the national Association of Youth Ministry Educators and the International Association for the Study of Youth Ministry have stimulated and taught me. Dan Griswold, Darwin Glassford, and Hillary Danz have been of particular assistance. Please be assured: this new text is much more than a few changes and updates; it represents a new book. These theological reflections have been written over several years while teaching those who care about young people, keeping an eye on culture, and listening to young people. In all this, I've had much to learn—and I continue to learn to this day.

Part 1 is designed to encourage you as a practical theologian to stretch your thinking and refine your skills. You will be asking big questions (that many young students ask) and exegeting (interpreting) the Word, the world, and yourself.

Then, in part 2, we'll consider persons and relationships. This second section addresses a practical theme of youth ministry: it's all about growth. This is the Creator's intention: that the creatures—plants, animals, persons, and communities—grow. In terms of the fall and rebellion of humankind, growth is hindered by oppression (needing liberation) and hurt/anger (needing healing). Many youth leaders become burned out because of unattended wounds from the past or current frustrations. After our examination of self, we'll move to families, peers, relationships, and sexuality.

In part 3 of the book, we begin to theologize about culture in general and youth and popular culture in particular. What are the challenges for students establishing personal identities in societies where values and norms are "up for

the Difference: Developing Theologians for Youth Work and Youth Ministry (Haverhill, UK: YTC Press, 2007); Andrew Root, *Revisiting Relational Youth Ministry: From a Strategy of Influence to a Theology of Incarnation* (Downers Grove, IL: InterVarsity, 2007); and Andrew Root and Kenda Creasy Dean, *The Theological Turn in Youth Ministry* (Downers Grove, IL: InterVarsity, 2011).

2. The Emergent movement (as it is called in the United States) or Fresh Expressions or Pete Ward's Liquid Church (as it is referred to in the United Kingdom).

grabs"? Here, you will be navigating murky cultural waters—but with a positive outlook and hope.

Part 4 of this book seeks a broad vision for youth ministry and its work (*praxis*), applying principles you've already learned in youth ministry and the theological foundation added from this book. If you are beginning youth work or have pressing questions about evaluating your present youth work, you may want to jump immediately to chapter 15.[3] But, for excellence in ministry, don't neglect the theological foundations (described in earlier sections) for a professional discipline of youth ministry.

Only through cross-cultural collaboration and cooperation can we become more effective guides in these complex times.

I hope youth workers, teachers, parents, and pastors will find encouragement, help, and hope in reading. Part of this work, however, will entail becoming aware of our adult crises before (and as) we look at youthful struggles and successes because adolescent problems have adult origins. The dysfunctions of our systems create a toxic environment and have made it difficult for young people to grow up healthy.

This book aims to initiate two conversions: a conversion from the world to Christ, and then a conversion from your Christian comfort zone back into a messy world. Together in this book we engage the world and our various cultures with Christ our leader, in the power of the Holy Spirit, and to the glory of God. For it is with God—Father, Son, and Holy Spirit—that all true theology and ministry begin. Relationship with and reverence for God is the beginning of wisdom.

---

3. See also the articles under the topic "Youth Ministry" (and many other topics) in the "Encyclopedia for Youth Studies" at the Center for Youth Studies website, centerforyouth.org, which covers much of that material and lays the basis for effective ministry. This online encyclopedia is also a rich source for quick information and a start for further studies.

Practical Theological Foundations

— 1 —

Introducing a Theology
for Youth Ministry

Trust in the LORD with all your heart, and do not rely on your own insight. Do not be wise in your own eyes; fear the LORD, and turn away from evil. In all your ways acknowledge him, and he will make straight your [theological] paths.

PROVERBS 3:5, 7, 6 (AUTHOR'S PARAPHRASE)

Personal Starting Point

We all need reminders that practical ministry and practical theology flow from God and are intricately connected to each other. This is an awesome truth beyond proof to the skeptical or distracted mind. The Creator's love and grace initiate the relationship and partnership God desires with humans. Our inclination to love a neighbor and to serve a younger generation is of God; effective ministry is letting God love and bless through us. It is God who has put the compassion and desire to care in our hearts.

Really caring about young people involves spending time with them and responding to their deepest needs and desires. Doing so in the name of Christ has always been the basic and essential characteristic of youth ministers. But this calls into question the motivations and manner of our *relating*. What is the nature of human relationships? Why are we doing youth ministry? How is our attention being perceived? What is the systemic context of our growing relationships? Who has sent us into young people's external and internal spaces? And to what end? These questions, as well as the complicated contexts of adolescence, are what this book is about. So, we begin with God, then we look at ourselves and others in culture, and then we turn our attention to youth.

Changing Families, Youth, and Cultures

Youth, their families, and their peer groups are complicated because of their in-dividualities, their localities, and their associations. Combinations of digital and face-to-face relationships add to the complexity. The impact of cultures and sub-cultures—of systems-within-systems—on the lives of young people is enormous. The digital age has produced a whole new environment. A failure to understand the larger, deeper picture can lead to frustration and burnout for youth ministers.

Back in the 1980s, David Elkind helped us understand how the weakening of families, communities, and schools in our society was forcing young people to turn to media and peers for life, relationships, and instruction. Surrounded by family and media, school and peers, sports and the streets, they began to learn by imitation rather than integration, becoming "patchwork selves." The result was unintegrated compartments in their lives, producing added stress (according to Elkind and those of us who worked with teenagers back then).[1] This pressure was often relieved by chemical stimulants, excessive risk-taking, and sex—which in turn further increased the stress in their lives.

The very titles of studies from the 1990s provide a quick review of what was happening to the young people youth ministry served. They include Peggy Oren-stein's *SchoolGirls: Young Women, Self-Esteem, and the Confidence Gap*[2] and Mary Pipher's *Reviving Ophelia: Saving the Selves of Adolescent Girls*.[3] Experts warned of damage being done to girls by family breakups, the media, advertising, and the gender gap. Other authors found that boys were caught in their own traps. Michael Gurian's *The Wonder of Boys*[4] and William Pollack's *Real Boys*[5] are two of several books explaining the plight of boys in a changing society.

1. David Elkind, *The Hurried Child: Growing Up Too Fast Too Soon* (Reading, MA: Addison-Wesley, 1988); and *All Grown Up and No Place to Go: Teenagers in Crisis* (Reading, MA: Perseus Books, 1998).

2. Peggy Orenstein, *SchoolGirls: Young Women, Self-Esteem, and the Confidence Gap* (New York: Doubleday, 1994).

3. Mary Pipher, *Reviving Ophelia: Saving the Selves of Adolescent Girls* (New York: Bal-lantine Books, 1994).

4. Michael Gurian, *The Wonder of Boys: What Parents, Mentors and Educators Can Do to Shape Boys into Exceptional Men* (New York: Putnam, 1996).

5. William Pollack, *Real Boys: Rescuing Our Sons from the Myths of Boyhood* (New York: Random House, 1998).

Provided a challenge as to how adult leaders could make contact and relate to seemingly disinterested youth, journalists headed into schools at the turn of the century. Their reports affirmed growing concern for the health of the nation's young. Students at Largo High School in Florida at first avoided a middle-aged reporter who started hanging out in and around their school. But soon they opened up to this adult stranger who asked questions and listened attentively. Within a few months students were sharing their discontents, wildness, and anxieties with Thomas French, who described it all in *South of Heaven: Welcome to High School at the End of the Twentieth Century.*[6]

Writer and mother Patricia Hersch followed eight middle and high school students for three years in Reston, Virginia, and wrote a best-selling book whose title describes how we were distancing ourselves and failing our youth: *A Tribe Apart: A Journey into the Heart of American Adolescence.*[7] Another journalist, Elinor Burkett, ventured into the halls and classrooms of Minneapolis's Prior Lake High School and noted the effects of the post-Columbine era, with its zero tolerance of student misbehaviors, school lockdowns, and teaching to the test. The effect of imposing excessive demands, arbitrary school policies, and pedagogical changes on students, while encouraging them to grow up and act creatively and responsibly, is described in Beckett's *Another Planet: A Year in the Life of a Suburban High School.*[8] A few years later Jean Twenge described her own and other studies in the first decade of the twenty-first century: *Generation Me: Why Today's Young Americans Are More Confident, Assertive, Entitled—and More Miserable Than Ever Before.*[9] These titles beg pause for reflection.

Two heralded films further documented what real life was like among twentieth-century students—particularly the stress of school life. *Waiting for Superman* explores the tragedy of poor, especially urban schools and students' stressful hopes of gaining entrance into a charter school, which may or may not provide a better education.[10] *Race to Nowhere*, set in generally more privileged schools, portrays student and teacher/administrator burnout as a result of unrealistic expectations and arbitrary guidelines.[11]

6. Thomas French, *South of Heaven: Welcome to High School at the End of the Twentieth Century* (New York: Doubleday, 1993).

7. Patricia Hersch, *A Tribe Apart: A Journey into the Heart of American Adolescence* (New York: Ballantine Books, 1998).

8. Elinor Burkett, *Another Planet: A Year in the Life of a Suburban High School* (New York: HarperCollins, 2001).

9. Jean M. Twenge, *Generation Me: Why Today's Young Americans Are More Confident, Assertive, Entitled—and More Miserable Than Ever Before* (New York: Free Press, 2006).

10. *Waiting for Superman*, directed by Davis Guggenheim (2010), www.waitingforsuperman.com.

11. *Race to Nowhere*, directed by Vicki Abeles and Jessica Congdon (2009), www.racetonowhere .com/about-film.

A Growing Body of Youth Ministry Research and Theology

Youth ministry writers at the turn of the century were also researching and writing about society's abandonment of youth and, at the same time, the consumption and excess that pushed young people toward autonomy and entitlement. The titles of these books suggest the challenge facing youth ministers, who believe the gospel to be good news for patchwork selves, for the bored or stressed, for overinflated or deflated senses of self.[12]

The most comprehensive study of American youth of the early twenty-first century is the National Study of Youth and Religion by sociologist Christian Smith. It shattered myths of adolescence, at least for the millennial generation—beliefs that adolescents tend to rebel against their parents' beliefs and are spiritual but not religious. This survey of the religious life, values, beliefs, and practices of 3,290 English- and Spanish-speaking thirteen- to seventeen-year-olds (and their parents) yielded notable findings. These young people tended to reflect the opinions of their parents and held a widespread belief in a God who would help them through difficulties but was not particularly interested in the details of their lives. Smith identified a general religious creed (across "mainline Protestant and Catholic youth, but . . . also among black and conservative Protestants, Jewish teens . . . other religious types . . . and even many non-religious teenagers in the U.S."):

1. A God exists who created and orders the world and watches over human life.
2. God wants people to be good, nice, and fair to one another, as taught in the Bible and by most world religions.
3. The central goal of life is to be happy and to feel good about oneself.
4. God does not need to be particularly involved in one's life except when God is needed to resolve a problem.
5. Good people go to heaven when they die.[13]

In short, the study found, across denominations and even religions, a rather shallow belief system that might be described as *moral therapeutic deism*. Such belief in a kindly, not-too-attentive grandfather figure "up there," the researchers concluded, comes to youth primarily from their parents' easygoing, culturally comfortable faith and lack of theological depth.

12. Dean Borgman, *Hear My Story: Understanding the Cries of Troubled Youth* (Peabody, MA: Hendrickson, 2003); Chap Clark, *Hurt: Inside the World of Today's Teenagers* (Grand Rapids: Baker Academic, 2004); Carol Lytch, *Choosing Church: What Makes a Difference for Teens* (Louisville: Westminster John Knox, 2004).

13. Christian Smith with Melinda Lundquist Denton, *Soul Searching: The Religious and Spiritual Lives of American Teenagers* (New York: Oxford University Press, 2005), 162–63.

Youth minister and theologian Pete Ward has made an interesting observation about this and other studies: that youth (and all of us) have both an "espoused theology" and an "operant theology."[14] Such a distinction may question whether "moral therapeutic deism" describes the "operant theology" of teenagers more than their "espoused theology" as Catholics, evangelicals, or members of other faith traditions.

Youthful failures of faith, as expressed by "moral therapeutic deism," point to the failures of parents and churches. An earlier book by Kenda Creasy Dean challenged the church for failing our youth with these words:

> Every stage of the life cycle brings certain human characteristics to the fore; in adolescence, one of these qualities is passion . . . the adolescent brain is wired for passion.
>
> The adolescent quest for passion reveals a theological aneurysm in mainline Protestantism [and I would add, in most of the church]: *We are facing a crisis of passion, a crisis that guts Christian theology of its very core, not to mention its lifeblood for adolescents.* . . . Not only does a church without passion deform Christian theology, it inevitably extinguishes the fire behind Christian practice as well.[15]

There is a rising consensus regarding weaknesses in many youth ministries these days. Many of our youth ministry alums are giving up their connection with churches and often their faith; youth programs are often producing superficial outcomes; and youth ministry sometimes further segregates students from family and intergenerational church. Many of us see these weaknesses as a reflection of a failure to hear young people ethnographically and understand theologically the full meaning of Christ's incarnation, the nature of the church, and our mission to confront culture in the name of Jesus Christ. For the sake of the church today, including those who are young, we are called to further empirical research and rigorous theological engagement.

Our Present Challenge

Making sense of a complicated ministry in a complex world (and church) will require a bold and broad theology, true to its biblical foundation and teachings of the church, careful to include the best insights from the social sciences. We will not attempt to reason our way through culture to God as many do, but instead we seek wisdom from God as our starting point. It is God who has given humans reasoning ability within cultural milieus. We believe God's revelation comes both

14. Personal conversation with Pete Ward, January 2, 2013.
15. Kenda Creasy Dean, *Practicing Passion: Youth and the Quest for a Passionate Church* (Grand Rapids: Eerdmans, 2004), 6–7, emphasis original.

through the written and Living Word of God and through nature and culture. Our challenge is to integrate these two sources of knowledge and wisdom.

Our relationships with (adolescent or adult) others and our relationship with the divine Trinity are twin mysteries. Without God's forgiving and enlightening grace, there is little hope for understanding the origin and nature of culture and obvious dilemmas in culture, and to comprehend the hope of human redemption.

This book seeks God's wisdom to explore the complex and subtle ways culture promotes *and* hinders youthful growth, as well as the ways in which churches and even youth ministries can hinder youthful maturation. Where growth has been hindered, we want to move from recognition of problems to positive assets, to helpful markers, to a clear sense of identity, to purpose and values—all needed for healthy functioning in the passage to adulthood. We will raise bold questions regarding who made culture and how popular culture has it right or has gone wrong. There will be encouragement for a greater collaboration among churches and organizations in supporting families and other social systems that are needed to provide youth with a just and peaceful environment.

An important underlying assumption of this book is that "youth ministry" is a remedial function. If all other systems—families, communities, schools, and churches—were functioning holistically, youth ministry as a profession and an academic discipline would not be needed. A secondary assumption is this: because dysfunctions in families, church, and society will not soon be eliminated, holistic youth ministry is desperately needed in fulfilling the Lord's Prayer: "Thy will [justice or righteousness] be done on earth as it is in heaven." Facing this challenge encourages continuing renewal in the whole discipline and practice of youth and family ministry.

Foundations for Youth Ministry is committed to encouraging and challenging youth ministers, as well as parents, teachers and coaches, social workers, military/prison chaplains, and other adults. What all of these share (or should share) in common are the basics of youth ministry: caring relationships with those passing from childhood to adulthood, relationships inviting youth into the adult world and community of faith. Our text encourages a deeper understanding of our work and its cultural and spiritual contexts.

This book needs your help if it is to work. It needs to interact with your experience, the passions of your heart, and your current ideas. Study questions at the end of each chapter will help, but we need to imagine a constant dialogue as we go along. More than most books, this one demands an interactive reading experience between you and the author, between you and others, even deeper within yourself, and between you and your Lord. Not enough attention has been given to *you* in most youth ministry books. Many of my students and youth leaders confess to deep wounds from the past hindering the way they respond to deep needs in young people. There is sometimes more tension within conflicting parts of ourselves than we realize. Healthy youth workers must attend to self before, or at least *as*, they are giving to others. Hopefully you are willing to look deeply at yourself, alone in private reflection, and with others who can act as social and spiritual mirrors. A later chapter will ask you to do so.

Whether considering our inner lives or outer world, our work begins with God and our communal relationship to God. Out of such relationships God reveals something of divine perspective and intentions. Such theological work is approached in different ways. Self-reflection and ethnographic studies provide basic data regarding the reality of our cultural starting points and subject matter. Biblical theology describes the divine/human drama. Historical theology is the story of the Holy Spirit working through the church.[16] Systematic theology represents a culmination of biblical and historical theology; it serves the church and the world as it is applied in practical theology (ethics and ministry). If practical theology is the integration and implication of ethnography and revelation, it also serves as a critique of questionable assumptions and misplaced emphases. A main theological contention is that "doxological theology"[17] is the necessary antecedent or foundation for all other divisions of theology. Relationship with God enables a productive understanding and expression of divine will.

Wouldn't you agree it is dangerous to *serve*, or even *think* about, God before we *worship* and *relate* to God? Worship and prayer, communally and alone, need to take precedence over our thinking—our considerations and arguments about the important doctrines of God, Christ, culture, the church, and our theories of human behavior and ministry. Theological *process* continues as we apply doctrines to everyday life and to our ministries through practical theology. Historically, leaders of the church expressed this as *lex orandi lex credendi* (loosely: "as we worship, we believe," or, "we believe what we worship").

Practical theology explores our place in the contemporary stage of the divine drama. It seeks God's perspective on current culture—and God is acting in today's world through the church as an extension of Christ's incarnation.[18] Since the climax of the Son of God's incarnation was his death and resurrection, practi-

16. See John 14:26; 16:12–13.

17. We will use this term to refer to our worship and contemplative prayer. The Doxology, as you know, praises God, the Father, Son, and Holy Spirit. "Doxological theology" is theology as it worships the God it will then seek to understand.

18. I agree that the incarnation of Jesus Christ (John 1 and Philippians 3) is a unique historical event. But I see it as a continuation of the grand divine drama—the burning bush; the pillar of fire; the Holy of holies; Emmanuel, the "God-with-us." The gift of the Holy Spirit, the "as the Father has sent me," argues for seeing the church as God's present incarnation. This will be further discussed.

cal theology ponders how the cross meets our world's violence and individual suffering—offering healing and reconciliation.

The Bible is also a story about God's desire for human partnership. It describes how God intervened in a fallen world through Abraham, Moses, Deborah, David, Jesus Christ, and other, sometimes pathetic, followers. In this sense practical theology picks up on the theme of God's seeking human partners to accomplish God's will and the coming kingdom. We do theology to discover our part in the divine narrative. I hope this book suggests such dynamic movement in your life and thinking, helping you and young friends to locate yourselves more fully in this grand drama.

This book will remind you repeatedly that *you* are a theologian and that working with young people demands theological reflection. We cannot expect excellence in youth ministry without effective research and a theology of youth ministry. Few are skilled scientific researchers, but we all build on experiential evidence. You're probably not a biblical, historical, or systematic theologian, but you are a practical theologian; that is, you are thinking about God, God's perspective on our culture, and the place God wants you to have in the larger world around you.

Serving God demands thinking about God; and thinking well about God flows from being communally related to God and to God's world. Doxological theology, as I stated above, precedes biblical/historical/systematic theology. These theological disciplines lead, in turn, into practical theology. We *relate* to God (and others) before we can truly *think* about our Creator (or truly understand our friends). Worshiping God, thinking about God, and serving God are actually interdependent; you can start anywhere in this dynamic process to get to holistic theology and ministry. We want our believing in God to be balanced by our living for God, and we want both to flow from our worship of God.

This book does not pretend to explain how to *do* youth ministry;[19] rather it encourages your preparatory *thinking about* serving God with youth. Its bias considers that those who work over the long haul with young people are heroes deserving the church's and society's high esteem. This book is dedicated to seeing such leaders properly equipped. Part of equipping for youth ministry is a theological task, and the purpose of this book is to encourage a love for, and comfort with, biblically based and experientially extracted theological principles. Doing theology from a youth ministry perspective demands familiarity with the Bible and the church's teaching, with the social sciences, with streets and hangouts, and mostly, with young people and families, with communities and churches.

19. Doug Fields's *Your First Two Years in Youth Ministry* (Grand Rapids: Zondervan, 2002); Len Kageler's *The Volunteer's Field Guide to Youth Ministry* (Loveland, CO: Group, 2011); and other such texts effectively describe the how-tos.

Questions for Reflection and Discussion

1. Does this overview place greater emphasis on young people and youth programs or on you and God?
2. Do you think it is important to talk about theology and social sciences in thinking about youth ministry? Why or why not?
3. Are you comfortable with the terms *empirical* and *ethnographic*?
4. What theological terms did you pick up that deal with our relating to God, thinking about God, and serving God (with young people, for instance)?
5. What did this overview have to say about the church?
6. What did this overview have to say about you?
7. What did you question, or with what did you disagree in this chapter? Can our disagreement be profitable?
8. What did you find most valuable to discuss from this chapter?

—2—

The Art of Interpretation

Ezra . . . was a scribe skilled in the law of Moses that the LORD the God of Israel had given; and the king granted him all that he asked, for the hand of the LORD his God was upon him.

EZRA 7:6

To these four young men God gave knowledge and skill in every aspect of literature and wisdom.

DANIEL 1:17

Take heed to thyself.
DEUTERONOMY
12:13, 19, 30;
1 TIMOTHY
4:16 KJV

When I look within, I find this is the way I operate.
ROMANS 7:21 (AUTHOR'S PARAPHRASE)

Knowing the Word, Your World, and Yourself

The biblical verses above have to do with studying God's Word, society, and self. Where do you consider yourself strongest and weakest—in studying the Bible, culture, or yourself? How would you like to grow in your ability to interpret your own motivations and actions, the culture around you, and Scripture? The interpretation of reality and meaning is neither an absolute science nor haphazard intuition.

Doing theology and developing a practical theology are not easy. In order to follow the model of Jesus and scriptural instruction, we need skills of interpretation. In facing the challenging issue of interpretation, we do well to remember Jesus Christ's warnings to learned scholars and theologians of his time in Matthew 16:3b; 22:29: "You know how to interpret the appearance of the sky, but you cannot interpret the signs of the times," and "You are wrong because you know neither the scriptures nor the power of God."

Openness to young people and their leaders in worldwide cultures further contributes to practical theology and the effectiveness of your ministry. Like Ezra, you want to be knowledgeable and efficient in practice.[1] Like Joseph, Daniel, and Esther you'll seek to understand contemporary culture, and with Paul, you must practice self-discernment. Above all, youth leaders strive for Christ's wisdom and grace. And remember Psalm 111:10a and Proverbs 9:10: "the fear of the LORD is the beginning of wisdom."

Throughout Scripture there is a distinction between the wisdom of this world and the wisdom given to believers from God. God calls people to turn from idolatrous pagan (or today's secular) wisdom to God's heavenly truth. God tells us in Deuteronomy 30:14, "[My] word is very near you; it is in your mouth and your heart to observe it." And a warning comes from Proverbs: "Wisdom cries out in the street; / 'How long, O simple ones, will you love being simple?' / The fear of the LORD is the beginning of knowledge; / fools despise wisdom and instruction" (1:20a, 22a, 7 respectively). The apostle Paul also writes in 1 Corinthians, "Has not God made foolish the wisdom of the world? . . . But we speak God's wisdom, secret and hidden. . . . Now we have received not the spirit of the world, but the Spirit that is from God, so that we might understand" (1:20b; 2:7a, 12 respectively). How can this be? How can our wisdom from God and the wisdom of this world be distinguished—and combined? This is what practical theology attempts to do. In what way do we think differently following the Spirit of God rather than the spirit of this world—since all our understanding seems conditioned by culture?

Our behavior and thinking are performed in cultural ways. Human infants raised solely by animals are called feral children and do not reveal human habits of practice or thought.[2] In favorable situations, parents (as well as grandparents, day care workers, and others) form relationships with infants and begin to model

---

1. "He was a *ready* scribe in the Law," Ezra 7:6 AV; or "a scribe *skilled* in the law," NRSV. The word *mahir* could imply quick, effective, efficient, trustworthy.

2. Douglas Keith Candland, *Feral Children and Clever Animals: Reflections on Human Nature* (New York: Oxford University Press, 1993). See a fuller discussion of this in my *Hear My Story: Understanding the Cries of Troubled Youth* (Peabody, MA: Hendrickson, 2003), 66–69.

human behavior and communication in cultural ways. It appears necessary that humans understand themselves, others, *and* God within a cultural framework. How can knowing God, or knowing anything, escape cultural conditioning? Dealing with this question and apparent dilemma demands careful consideration of language, communication, and meaning.

I suffer a continuing double failure. I ask God to bless *my* thoughts and efforts—as if they were mine, and I just need God's help. And when I'm blessed, I often take subtle credit for it! How ridiculous! Yet changing my ways has been a lifelong process. We cannot proceed on our own. "Without me," Jesus says, "you can do nothing" (John 15:5b NKJV). That must include our sociological and theological thinking.

Exegesis (interpretation) is the Spirit-filled task of the faith community. The critical job for us is allowing this work of the Holy Spirit. We each have a special responsibility in this task, but it is a communal endeavor proceeding from our relationship to God and our worship together. It is part of the learning/teaching (*didachē*) function of Christ's body. It is crucial to remember our communal life and study in the Spirit as we consider interpretation and theology.

Hermeneutics and Exegesis

Some combine these terms into one process; hermeneutics is often seen as the theory of interpretation and exegesis as the principles and practice of interpretation. You might think of hermeneutics as the *philosophy* of interpretation and exegesis as the *skill* of interpretation. Hermeneutics takes into consideration (1) a writer or speaker, (2) a text or message, and (3) a reader or hearer. Beyond writer, text, and reader, we must consider, of course, our culture and community. Without culture and community there can be no language and meaning. The feral children referred to above exhibit the animal culture in which they were nurtured and raised, instead of a human culture. When discovered and tested by social scientists, they don't measure "human" on a social scale and never come to full human maturation.[3] We become human only under human care, learning cultural norms and communication.

Hermeneutics considers the dynamics of our interpretation of meaning. Let's think about that. A group of us are bird-watching; we know birds. We see a robin, a red-winged black bird, and an elusive flicker. We identify a red-tailed hawk and

3. Scientific study of discarded human babies raised by animals reveals they have no capacity for strictly human activities such as walking, talking, or thinking in our cultural ways. See again Candland's *Feral Children and Clever Animals*. I stress this point because we can more vividly appreciate human culture by understanding the consequences of its absence.

later an eagle. In the distance, we count three people crossing a far ridge—that they are humans is all that can be seen. So we have seen several specific kinds of birds and three human figures in the distance. Not much more can be said. We more or less agree we have seen the same things, that they are real, and that our common knowledge is true. We are describing what we all regard as real objects. Our agreement and certainty have been called naive realism, and such realism works up to a point. Cautious philosophers, however, raise objections to our faith and certainty because designations of birds and our knowledge of the animal kingdom, class, order, and species have been learned culturally.

As we begin to study these creatures more closely, questions arise about their characteristics and why they are the way they are. Interpretation of specific characteristics comes slowly and painstakingly. Similarly, in an art museum, questions about our interpretations of signs and symbols would be even more noticeable. A few of us viewing an intriguing work of art suggest different possibilities of interpretation, some true to the artist's intentions, some clearly beyond the intent of the artist. There may be artistic validity to all of our observations.

Walk through any high school, a shopping mall, or an area around town, and you will see different kinds of youth. Socially constructed categories or subcultures classify many. How do you read them, and how do you interpret why they present themselves as they do? You are interpreting signs of fashion and mannerisms meant to convey some kind of meaning. Young people are trying to make sense of their lives and their world, crazy as they may be or feel, creating an identity in order to cope and possibly flourish.[4] Young people's inner makeup, their life situations, their general and particular cultural environments are all part of the way they choose to represent themselves. The effective youth worker realizes that his or her initial interpretation of any young person is just the beginning of a mutual process that can bring about *a meaningful relationship*. That process, and all its conversations and interactions, are acts of interpretation, figuring out who both of us are and what we have to offer each other.

Media *mediate*, or communicate, meaning through signs or images. A skateboarder and a passing preppie both have iPod buds in their ears. It's so much more complex than it seems. Let's say they're listening to the same rap song. The song being played is the result of interactions among artists, producers, and music company executives. An artist's style, the song, and its merchandizing have been established to produce a general and subordinate meanings. (Neither listener in this scenario bought the song; they've gotten it from friends as a result of some

---

4. Lady Gaga and other artists have exploited the vulnerability of young people who feel themselves demeaned. There is evidence worth noticing, however, that she and other pop artists have given dignity and hope to youth struggling with issues of self-worth.

viral buzz.) They attribute quite different meanings to the beat and lyrics of the song. They represent (actually re-present) the music and its meaning in different ways to themselves, their friends, or the public. Such a series of mediations (or conveying of meaning) and representations (reconstructions of signs) goes back and forth, and on and on.

When it comes to interpreting the Bible, we may seem to be trapped in a hermeneutical (interpretive) dilemma. If culture has taught us to interpret, and if churches hold different interpretations of Scripture, is that not evidence our understanding of God and truth is humanly constructed? Related to this is the sequence of *being* and *thinking*. To the natural mind it is logical that thinking precedes being. We are aware of existence because we think about it, and being is according to the way we think about it. This seems to suggest we are lost in a sea of subjectivism.

One solution is to acknowledge our need for mediation from the Triune God—at God's initiative, not ours. Between observer and object, thought and reality, there is always a *tertium quid*, a third factor. The eternal and absolute Word of the almighty God has to be translated into human culture. God decides to reveal the divine self to the created. The task of human interpretation of biblical texts then begins with a relationship, with human participation in the life of the living God. Through select writers, the Creator mediates truth concerning a Triune God, the incarnate Son of God, and the kingdom of heaven. Obviously the inspired texts were gathered and presented to us, first by Hebrew scholars and then by the church.

As Christian philosophers discuss the way we know (epistemology) and believe, cultural experts discuss communication, signs, and meaning (semiotics and cultural studies). We often miss one of three important factors: First, we are at best limited, finite creatures. Second, we can think and converse only out of our own cultural orientation. Finally, we, and our culture, are infected with sin. Naive Christians tend to miss the second crucial point; scholars often miss or minimize the first and third. Young people, meanwhile, are troubled as they discover exceptions to what they are being taught, and their issues often hinge on one of these factors. We need to understand these human limitations because youth deserve an adequate apologetics (that is, thoughtful responses to troubling aspects of the faith).

The Triune God not only created and communicates to us but has established the way we think—including its limitations.[5] We tend to consider ourselves autonomous (independent and self-sufficient) thinkers. By ourselves, or with enough others who think the way we do, we want to get it absolutely right. But only God has absolute knowledge; only God has absolute truth. Absolute truth—which the postmodern world denies—*is* mediated to us through the Holy Spirit using God's

---

5. Besides those mentioned above, we also have limitations within time and space, for instance.

means of nature, culture, conscience, the written Word of God, and preeminently, the *logos* or living Word of God, Jesus Christ incarnate. In this way, the possibility of confident subjective certainty through faith and reason is offered to us—even though dogmatic assertions of objective certainty cannot be sustained. Merold Westphal, a believing postmodern philosopher, expresses his opinion this way:

> We need not think that hermeneutical despair ("anything goes") and hermeneutical arrogance (we have "the" interpretation) are the only alternatives. We can acknowledge that we see and interpret "in a glass darkly" or "in a mirror, dimly" and that we "know only in part" (1 Cor. 13:12), while ever seeking to understand and interpret better by combining the tools of scholarship with the virtues of humbly listening to the interpretations of others and above all to the Holy Spirit.[6]

God's mediated truth is conveyed to all. God makes the rain, sun, and truth to bless all people and cultures of the earth (Matt. 5:45b; Rom. 2:14–15). The divine, creative, and communicative *logos* (John 1:1–5; notice "light, which enlightens everyone," v. 9) gives light to all, regardless of faith response. Paul was undoubtedly speaking of salvation through Christ, the Son of God, when he wrote, "There is also one mediator between God and humankind," but it seems appropriately applied secondarily to the common grace of human thinking (John 1:9). We believe all truth is God's truth, mediated so that all the earth might grasp some common sense of truth and error, right and wrong. This seems necessary if we are to work for justice in the world.

Ultimately those who reject special divine mediation tend to get lost in subjective and relativistic dilemmas. In contrast to secular skeptics, believers in the great Mediator, those who participate in the divine nature, know the origin and final end of all truth and knowledge. Sadly, worldly wisdom lacks critical knowledge of origin and destiny. Humbly we acknowledge our presuppositions of faith and affirm a limited but vital grasp of absolute truth coming to us through the Son and Holy Spirit as it is reinforced by the church as a community of truth and faith. Our passionate desire is for young people to grasp the origin and destiny of our faith, the beginning, climax, and destiny of the gospel, the good news of God's story.

The Abraham and Joseph stories may be viewed differently over time in different cultures, but the meaning and messages derived by ancients and moderns have a constant. The confession, "Christ is Lord," may be reflected upon from different perspectives, but it has similar certainty and assurance throughout the ages.

6. Merold Westphal, *Whose Community? Which Interpretation? Philosophical Hermeneutics for the Church* (Grand Rapids: Baker Academic, 2009), 15.

The bread and wine we share in the Lord's Supper or Eucharist looks and tastes like bread and wine. Christians from many traditions—Eastern Orthodox and Roman Catholic to liberal Protestant, evangelical, Anabaptist, Pentecostal, Holiness, and most Emergents—accept that fact *and at the same time* believe there is something special about what Jesus called his body and blood when he established the rite we now observe until he comes. But, there is no universal agreement as to the precise meaning of the symbols—*how* Christ is present (or absent) in this memorial of his death and resurrection. Some would call this rite a mere social construct, symbols created by church tradition. Are you content to see baptism and Eucharist as products of human convention, or are we dealing with divine realities given the church—though we may understand them differently?

Developing a Theology: A Threefold Interpretive Task

The word *exegesis* signifies the process of understanding—of interpreting and explaining. It implies skill and wisdom. To *exegete* is to interpret a text for teaching and application. Theology begins with an awareness of God and with *exegesis of Scripture*. But we often overlook the necessity of two other interpretive requirements: an *exegesis of the culture* or world in which we were raised and to which we minister, and an *exegesis of self* (whether we are a biblical scholar or theologian, a pastor or youth minister). At the outset it is important to realize three distinct operations in reaching meaning as an interacting process. Our culture gives us the means to understand the world and ourselves. But without God's Word, meaning is allusive and incomplete. We bring cultural tools to the interpretation of Scripture, and none of us can escape our life experience and personal style. It is important, then, to consider the type of skills needed as we seek meaning from these three different "texts" or stories.

In the following chapter we will more closely look at:

- Scriptural exegesis
- Social exegesis
- Self exegesis

In preparation for such exegesis, consider theology as a systematic expression of God's Word in a particular time and space; it formulates the good news within a particular culture. Thus theology always involves contextual exegesis or interpretation of the *Word*, the *world*, and the *self*. Difficulties arise if we forget, or are weak in, any of these skills. Today's students will not accept clichéd teaching, sterile doctrines, or partial knowledge. Working with young people helps us interpret the Bible, the world, and ourselves holistically and more effectively.

An omission may be noted. If we consider exegesis of the world, why not exegesis of the church or churches? There is much to interpret about the church and how we do church. As to the nature and boundaries of the one, holy, catholic, apostolic church, and an appropriate style of worship, we have striking differences. Many feel blessed to be part of what they consider to be the one true denomination, or one preferred above all others. There are also high and low churches, traditional and new churches, denominational and independent churches. *Ecclesiology*[7] is an important and often neglected doctrine of systematic theology. Not enough has been written as to how youth ministers operate differently in different denominations. This book attempts to approach practical theology, youth ministry philosophy, and ministry models in a way applicable to the broadest possible spectrum of churches. I want to acknowledge, though, the need for further serious consideration of the doctrine of the church.

Interpretative errors can arise from a failure to analyze the cultures in which the exegete was raised and to which the theologian speaks. Theological disagreements also stem from the different starting places and premises of their parties as well as from differences in personalities and styles. Breakdowns in theological discussion often arise from a failure to be critical of one's own cultural and personal exegesis (errors of ethnocentrism and egocentrism).[8] Theological controversies will never be eliminated; theologians must agree to disagree on various points of interpretation and doctrine.

Being with all kinds of young people can yield important insights and contributions to the theological endeavor. Just as the theological process among oppressed people has yielded new critiques and emphases, theology done among young people pleads for less egocentrism, ethnocentrism, and dogmatism,[9] for deeper understandings and broader applications.

Change and complexity around us demand a new look at our interpretive skills. They also call for a holistic interpretation wherein our analyses of Word, world, and self are interactive and congruent. Today's world calls for intergenerational approaches to the solutions of current crises. Youth leaders can be helpful bridges between older and younger generations in this endeavor. They can bridge the gap between parents and children, boomers and busters, conservatives and liberals, secularists and believers. Keep in mind that the interpretation of Word, world, and self should point to the transformation of selves and reform of society.

7. *Ecclesiology* is the study of the church.

8. These terms suggest being locked into one's culture or subculture (*ethnocentrism*) or oneself (*egocentrism*).

9. Take a moment to consider how being a European American, or Latina/o American, or African American, or another ethnicity or nationality affects how you relate to the world.

Biblical and Scientific Hermeneutics

Evolution and creationism continue to be controversial issues. Science moves from observation to interpretation and back to further observation. Theological interpretation of Genesis 1 and 2 engages with biblical exegesis, theological anthropology, scientific interpretation, and cultural anthropology. How does the biblical story of human origins and its genealogical tables fit together with scientific calculations regarding the age of the earth and humankind? Those who lead youth need some answers to this dilemma for themselves and youthful questions—that is, for theology and *apologetics*.[10] Biblical and scientific hermeneutics are both at work here, and in this realm we will see biblical believers differing greatly in their methods of interpretation and conclusions.

Students in biology classes often have questions about evolution's challenge to what they've learned at church, temple, or mosque; and they respond in different ways. The unchurched may sense no problem at all because they don't believe God created the earth and humankind. Others place science and religion in different mental compartments. Those serious about their faith and wishing to be good students of science will find, from their religious instructors, what we might classify as four different perspectives in regard to creation and evolution.[11]

First, a traditional, conservative stance interprets Genesis 1–11 quite literally, believing God created heaven and earth in six, twenty-four-hour days—somewhere between six thousand and ten thousand years ago. A global catastrophic flood formed earth's rock formations in a way that has confused geologists. This position argues against scientists' dating methods and the whole idea of biological evolution. Such a viewpoint has been described as *young earth creationism*.[12]

A second position has been called *old earth creationism*.[13] Accepting more scientific dating and evidence of evolution, and with a variety of views, old earth

10. *Apologetics* is the theological discipline seeking to explain and commend the Christian faith. It is in no way "an apology" for our faith. The term has been used since Justin Martyr's *Apologies*, which was written in the second century CE.

11. Here is another example of differing hermeneutics and positions within the Christian church. For consideration of three main views of creation, see J. P. Moreland, *Three Views on Creation and Evolution* (Grand Rapids: Zondervan, 1999).

12. See Donald DeYoung, *Thousands not Billions: Challenging the Icon of Evolution, Questioning the Age of the Earth* (Green Forest, AR: Master Books, 2005); John David Morris, *The Young Earth: The Real History of the Earth—Past, Present and Future* (Green Forest, AR: Master Books, 2007). See also "Biblical Young Earth Creationism," *Northwest Creation Network*, www .nwcreation.net/ageyoung.html.

13. Don Stoner, *A New Look at an Old Earth: Resolving the Conflict between the Bible and Science* (Eugene, OR: Harvest House, 1997); David Snoke, *A Biblical Case for an Old Earth* (Grand Rapids: Baker Books, 2006); David Hagopian, ed., *The Genesis Debate* (Mission Viejo, CA: Crux, 2001).

creationists combine God's creative activity with natural evolutionary process. Some see God's interventions as filling in the "gaps" in natural evolutionary theory.

Intelligent design may be seen as a third position. Its advocates maintain they are offering an acceptable approach for public school curricula—not arguing creationism, but showing how the complexity of the world and universe argues for an intelligent designer rather than blind or random chance. Most advocates of intelligent design believe God created the earth and in some way guided its development.

A fourth position, *theistic evolution*, again of different varieties, accepts most of the work of secular science and evolutionists. Theism implies a God who initiates, loves, and is active in, creation. Theistic evolutionists accept the evolutionary process without necessary divine interventions. One group that promotes this view is BioLogos ("Bio" for human life; "Logos" for Christ the Creator and our divine life).[14]

Despite the terms used to describe these perspectives, it should be emphasized that all Christians are creationists, believing the universe and all life have come from God (Gen. 1:1; John 1:1–3). A helpful book on science, religion, and the origin of the universe for leaders and sharp students, is Andy Fletcher's *Life, the Universe and Everything*.[15] His book—a response to Stephen Hawking's question, "Why does the universe go to all the bother of existing?"—concludes, "No design, no purpose, no good, no evil, nothing but pointless indifference."[16]

Many scientists, both Christian and without particular faith, have come to a much different conclusion. Physicist Paul Davies puts his belief this way: "I belong to a group of scientists who do not subscribe to a conventional religion but nevertheless deny that the universe is a purposeless accident."[17] Another physicist, Freeman Dyson, adds, "The more I examine the universe and study the details of its architecture, the more evidence I find that the universe in some sense must have known we were coming."[18]

Finally, creation is something that should be enjoyed and studied first of all, and only then argued about. Faith has blessed us with conviction about the origin and destiny of it all—the purpose of life. We in the church can agree to disagree on our interpretation of Genesis as long as we believe in God's loving intention in creating nature and humankind. We confess the sad failure of humankind and

14. See Francis S. Collins (founder and previous president of BioLogos), *The Language of God: A Scientist Presents Evidence for Belief* (New York: Free Press, 2007); see also biologos.org.

15. Andy Fletcher, *Life, the Universe and Everything: Investigating God and the New Physics* (Monument, CO: fletchpub at Lulu, 2005). For believers, see his later *Quantum God, Fractal Jesus* (Monument, CO: fletchpub at Lulu, 2012).

16. Fletcher, *Life, the Universe*, 167.

17. Ibid., 189.

18. Ibid.

its terrible consequences, which God, however, refuses to accept as final. Our worship of God sends us out into nature, alone and with young friends, just to walk, observe, and sit in awe.

The Need for Skill and Wisdom

You who serve youth are continually engaging in theological reflection about God's work in young lives, about the nature of the gospel, and about the nurture of faith and the life of the church. Youth leaders receive all kinds of questions from bright, curious, and idealistic young minds. You are confronted by ethical and psychosocial issues, not only from eager and confused young people but also from parents and other adults. Sometimes you are expected to be a family consultant. Schools and other organizations may ask for a presentation or for advice. In many ways youth ministers have more direct access to the heart of community institutions than do most clergy. Together youth ministers, pastors, teachers, parents, and other community leaders seek what we understand as a pastoral theology adequate for today's crises.

Such challenges demand a growing body of information and pastoral skill. We are called to a lifelong study of biblical truth, social systems, and human personalities. As a professional servant to young people, whether you are reading a biography, a newspaper, Scripture, or an article online, you will want to be the best reader you can be. Adler's How to Read a Book can make your reading more efficient and effective.[19] This book urges an aggressive rather than passive approach to any literary work. Engage an author in a dialogue: "I don't have all the time in the world; what are you really trying to say or prove? Why is this important, and what is the purpose of what you've written? What are your assumptions? What are your main arguments or explanations? And how should this affect the world and our lives?" You can apply what Adler says about effective literary interpretation to the analysis of lives and cultures as well. Don't let the digital age obliterate a balance of concentrated focus and solid study.

The questions above can also be asked of persons, culture, and God's Word—for all are stories, texts loaded with symbols and meaning. Interpretation, I repeat, is an ongoing process. Without divine transcendence, without an inkling of our origin and destiny, it would be an interesting yet futile quest for understanding.

These challenges (to be professional, informed, and adopt a style of lifelong thinking and learning) do not mean youth ministers must be brilliant or become scholars. We should want to learn and be thoughtful about our work. Youth

19. Mortimer J. Adler and Douglas Van Doren, How to Read a Book, rev. ed. (New York: Simon & Schuster, 1972).

leaders who take a few minutes a day, a few hours a week, and a number of days or weeks a year to study and to reflect can avoid burnout. Because we want to serve young people with professional skill, it is necessary to read well and think well—to grow in wisdom and favor with God and people (see 1 Sam. 2:26; Luke 2:52). Effective youth leaders are always growing personally and professionally as they serve as social workers and theologians, prophets and pastors, among a youthful generation. Such youth leaders give attention to physical, emotional, intellectual, social, and spiritual growth. The hope is that we display a learning, growing, and fruitful lifestyle to young people who are watching us critically.

Questions for Reflection and Discussion

1. Do you consider this chapter important in today's world? Why or why not?
2. What most impressed you here? With what specifically did you agree or disagree? What would you add or take out?
3. Do you agree that in our culture, we must be aware of assumptions and values underlying the stories and messages barraging students?
4. What do you believe about creation and evolution? Is it important for you to explain and defend your faith in the biblical story? How can you do this most effectively?
5. What from this chapter do you need/want to take into the next chapter (the practice of interpreting Word, world, and self) and the rest of the book (about practical theology and ministry)?

—3—

The Practice of Interpretation

Study eagerly so that you will be approved by God and won't be ashamed
at the way you interpret the Word of God.

2 TIMOTHY 2:15 (AUTHOR'S PARAPHRASE)

Remembering Ezra, whom the King James Version describes as "a ready scribe in
the Law of Moses" (Ezra 7:6), youth leaders must seek skill in interpreting God's
Word and God's will for youth ministry. With the skillful scribe and the promise
of the psalmist about surrendering to God's Word and will (Ps. 119:95–100), we
may come to greater wisdom than scholarly experts. Following God's call to reach
young people in their culture may bring us harder questions, a broader perspective,
and more certainty than some professional theologians and cultural scholars. A
secure practical theology allows us to use keen insights from the social sciences
and make relevant application to youth ministry.

Whatever our perspective, we are humbled by basic assumptions before an
awesome God and encouraged by the promises and presence of the Holy Spirit.
Trusting God, the Father, Son, and Holy Spirit, we embark on our threefold interpretation (or exegesis) of Word, world, and self. And we see our interpretation
as a continuing *process* under God, not a final determination or end product.

General Principles of Interpretation

Exegesis is an art and a science, demanding both individual effort and interaction in community. The theologian (and every Christian is a theologian) needs

24

feedback on the task from the church as the body of Christ and from the world. Exegesis is not a private affair.

Exegesis is often seen as having a single focus—that of getting the meaning of a biblical text. But it can be seen as having a triple focus: interpreting the Bible, ourselves, and our culture. Our ministries may be similarly exegeted. You don't leave your ministry to study theology; your practice provides insights for your theories. Praxis continually feeds theory and understanding. Here is how experience and interpretation can work in ministry:

1. Approach the subject matter from praxis (the mission):
   I sense I'm called by God to work with runaway or throwaway young people who have so little going for them. I am trying to follow the model of Jesus Christ's care for the marginalized in my ministry.

2. Interpret the subject matter (the analysis):
   My own and other studies show a large percentage of these young people have been abused—sexually, emotionally, and physically. Many have learning disabilities and poor school experiences. There is so much pain and denial in them. It's hard for them to trust anyone. Relationships come slowly, but when they do, good things can happen. Our relationships are guided by Scripture, the model of Christ, and the Spirit.

3. Apply the interpretation back into ministry (the test or application):
   Some of these young people have come to trust Christ, and it's changing their lives. Being in this faith community gives opportunities for healing, love, and discipline that reshape broken lives. We are using what we're discovering to establish a program with sound principles of therapy and Christian community. We will evaluate our results and refine our practices.

This process is to be continuous and cyclical. The faith community's need for application urges interpretation. Teaching informs and leads to application. Teaching and living both encourage and affect further interpretation. Fresh from their stories and remembering our own stories, we proceed to interpret biblical stories.

Exegetical Steps

Stories (and our lives) have settings, characters, and plots that include some tension (good and bad) moving toward resolution. Do you have a clear sense of your own personal story? Have you thought much about its being part of your culture's story? And where did God's story meet the intersection of your personal and cultural stories? Our personal story, our cultural story, and God's story all say something about truth; through interpretation they all provide meaning. We interpret all three, in simplest form, when we ask:

- What is the story? What is God saying through Scripture, society, and my life?
- Who, as best as can be known, was the writer/actor and what is her or his situation?
- Who are we as interpreters of this text, story, or instruction? Who am I, the reader, and what needs, hopes, fears, and values do I bring to the text?
- What is its context? What were/are the values and characteristics of the culture in which this story was written or occurred, and how does that compare with our culture today?
- What does it say? What is the plainest sense of this story or message in its original context, and what is it saying to us today?
- What does it mean? Does it have a primary meaning and some secondary meanings? Could they exceed what the original actor or writer intended?
- How does it apply to our stories? What difference does it make? What do our culture, our church, my friends and family, and I need from this story?

Biblical Interpretation

As one who reflects on the situation of young people from God's perspective, you want to do so truthfully and faithfully. You understand young people partially to the extent that you interpret their culture. At the same time you are interpreting the Bible. This task of biblical interpretation or exegesis is not reserved for scholars; it is a privilege and duty of all who read Scripture. Two seminary professors, Gordon Fee and Douglas Stuart, wrote *How to Read the Bible for All Its Worth* to encourage faithful interpretation:

> We recognize that the first task—exegesis—is often considered to be a matter for the expert. At times that is true. But one does not have to be an expert to learn to do the basic tasks of exegesis well. The secret lies in learning to ask the right questions of the text.[1]

Raymond E. Brown adds a caution with which these professors would agree:

> Because Scripture is inspired and presumably this inspiration was for the good of all, there has arisen the fallacy that everyone should be able to pick up the Bible

1. Gordon D. Fee and Douglas Stuart, *How to Read the Bible for All Its Worth: A Guide to Understanding the Bible* (Grand Rapids: Zondervan, 2003), 15.

and read it profitably. If this implies that everyone should be able to find out what the sacred author is saying without preparation or study, it really demands of God in each instance a miraculous dispensation from the limitations imposed by differences of time and circumstance. Of course it is true that considerable portions of Scripture are easily intelligible to all because they voice universal sentiments, e.g., some of the Psalms and some of the simple stories of Jesus. It is also true that spiritual solace and insight may be drawn from the Bible by those who have no technical knowledge and indeed do not understand its literal sense. (Conversely, those who have technical knowledge have at times overlooked the religious depths of the Bible.) Nevertheless, when it is a question of finding out what the human author meant to say, and therefore what God inspired, there is no substitute for educated effort.[2]

As practical theologians, youth ministers study the Bible to the best of their educated abilities while relying on biblical scholars and theologians for exegetical help. Collaboration between biblical and practical theologians will be to the advantage of all. Those who study people may sense cultural or personal lapses in the work of the biblical scholar, who may in turn save the practical theologian from serious technical mistakes. Fee and Stuart admit the need for scholars to be reminded of personal biases:

> The first reason one needs to learn *how* to interpret is that, whether one likes it or not, every reader is at the same time an interpreter. . . . We also tend to think that *our understanding* is the same thing as the Holy Spirit's or human author's *intent*. However, we invariably bring *to* the text all that we are, with all of our experiences, culture, and prior understandings of words and ideas. Sometimes what we bring to the text, unintentionally to be sure, leads us astray, or else causes us to read all kinds of foreign ideas into the text.[3]

These reminders (and others)[4] highlight the importance of understanding ourselves and our culture as we interpret the biblical text. Remembering our own cultural context, we attempt to envision the ancient cultural contexts of particular Scriptures. We consider the times of the patriarchs, the divided kingdom of Israel,

---

2. Raymond E. Brown, "Hermeneutics," in *The Jerome Biblical Commentary*, ed. Raymond E. Brown, Joseph A. Fitzmyer, and Roland E. Murphy (Englewood Cliffs, NJ: Prentice Hall, 1968), 607.

3. Fee and Stuart, *How to Read the Bible*, 16.

4. See Samuel Terrien, "History of the Interpretation of the Bible: Modern Period," in *The Interpreter's Bible*, ed. G. A. Buttrick (New York: Abingdon-Cokesbury, 1952), 1:140. In the conclusion of this article Terrien adds a caution regarding covert presuppositions that influence an exegete's interpretation. Avery Dulles, SJ, *Models of Revelation* (Maryknoll, NY: Orbis Books, 1983) also provides an overview of ways in which different churches have approached Scripture.

the exile in Babylon, the situation of Jesus Christ and his apostles as Hebrew sub-
jects of Rome in a Hellenized world, and then as members of an often persecuted
church. What did any biblical author, from Moses to John, intend to convey, and
how did those early hearers (and gradually those who read the scrolls) understand
the biblical text I am now studying?

All of us have blind spots. The stress of family life, the politics of academia,
and the pressures of our professional work play on our personal egos and weaknesses and make us less than objective—and less tolerant of other perspectives.
Sadly, we do not often have the time or inclination to listen to those who could
point out our subtle biases. Missing vital feedback, we become like someone who
observes his face in a mirror and then forgets what he saw as he goes on living.
We regain perspective when we catch our own reflection in the "perfect law of
liberty" (James 1:25 KJV) or when we profit from heartfelt suggestions of sisters
and brothers who represent different perspectives.

Outline for Exegeting the Word of God

Outlines can help us approach this rather complex process. Using the three general
steps and seven exegetical steps provided earlier in this chapter, you may formulate
your own outline of a book, story, chapter, or brief passage (*pericope*[5]). A very
simple outline uses the questions: (1) What does it say? (2) What does it mean?
(3) How does it apply? Your first question deals with genre, context, and content;
the second, with the original author's intent and what original readers would have
understood. You will also consider how the church historically and today has understood this part of Scripture. Finally, how is this Scripture meant to transform lives
and situations? How can these Scriptures be prayed (*lectio divina*[6]) and journalled?

Further Questions and Suggestions for Working with This Outline

1. What kind of literature am I reading in this book or passage? From what
   kind of societies did this literature arise? In what period of history (of the
   people of Israel or early church) was this particular book or passage written? What is the relation of this section to the rest of the Bible?

   What does this section of the Bible say? What is best understood of its
   words, grammar, and rhetorical style? Use the reporter's questions:

5. A *pericope* is a short saying, story, or passage around a given topic, often suited for public
reading. Luke 4:1–13 might be considered a pericope of Jesus's temptation; his sermon in his
hometown synagogue, Luke 4:16–30, is another.
6. *Lectio divina* is an ancient method of reflection and contemplation—focusing on what the
Spirit seems to be pointing out in a word or phrase; allowing Scripture to penetrate our hearts.

- *Who* is in this passage?
- *What* is said or going on here?
- *Where* is it said or taking place?
- *When* is it said or taking place?
- *Why* is it said or taking place?
- *How* is it said or taking place?

2. What are my presuppositions as to the nature of this book and of God's revelation, and how do I understand the reasons for the various interpretations of Scripture? What were the intentions of the author, the needs of the audience, and their understanding of what they were writing or reading?

As you look for the meaning of Scripture, ask:

- What does this teach me about the nature and ways of God?
- How does this help me relate to Jesus Christ as Lord and Savior?
- What do I see here of the working of the Holy Spirit?
- Who is my neighbor, and how am I to love her or him?
- What do I learn here of corporate responsibility, repentance, and restitution?
- What am I taught to avoid?
- What am I encouraged to pursue?

3. How are these lessons to be incorporated into my life in the world and in the church? What is my strategy? What specific goals do I set and what resources and reinforcements do I need for their accomplishment? How do I evaluate growth and progress?

How can I celebrate my efforts at exegesis and its resulting growth and progress? How am I in need of new beginnings and discoveries in my exegesis? At what new level do I now return to the first step?

A Biblical Example

Though not on the same level of importance as the story of Christ, the story of Joseph, as part of the scriptural canon, "is inspired by God and profitable for teaching, for reproof, for correction, for training in righteousness" (2 Tim. 3:16 NASB). Consider the relevance of Joseph's story in two different contexts.

Chris Hill's[7] way of sharing this story with a group of urban youth workers is a winner. He pictures Joseph as "an urban dude." Coming from a dysfunctional

---

7. Chris Hill is the founder of Chris Hill Ministries International and pastor of The Potter's House of Denver; see chrishill.org.

family, he prizes his sporty jacket and suffers disrespect because of it—and because he snitched. He is put down by his rivals, suffers oppression, and has to perform menial service. Admired by a foxy woman, he receives a bum rap and serves time. But Joseph hangs in there and is finally, finally rewarded by God. Chris uses this lesson to encourage those working among dismissed and disadvantaged members of our society to stay the course. This is an example of a contextualized application of Scripture.

I was told of a boy in a residential treatment program for emotionally disturbed children. Having been abused and rejected, he acted out often and was difficult. He wanted to be told only one story in the Bible—the story of Joseph. He found in Joseph someone with whom he could identify.

We never know what biblical story will touch the heart or pain of a particular person. We do know that Genesis takes just two chapters to tell the story of cosmic creation but thirteen chapters to tell the story of Joseph. And whereas the institution of marriage and family is described in just a few verses of the Genesis account, the reconciliation of a fractured family (Joseph's) covers nine long chapters. Here we can find immediate lessons for ministry.

In his fine study of British youth, Peter Brierley observes: "Only four people are positively identified in the Scriptures as being in their teenage years—and they all had problems!"[8] Of these biblical teenagers, Joseph's is the fullest story. The drama, which is relevant to young people everywhere, may be seen as unfolding in five acts:

1. Joseph has problems with his family.
2. Joseph, rejected by his siblings, serves in Potiphar's house.
3. Joseph is tempted sexually.
4. Joseph is sentenced and serves time in prison.
5. Joseph becomes leader of Egypt and his family.

Each of these scenes is filled with rich lessons for young people struggling with immaturity and misunderstanding at home and elsewhere. Joseph's experiences offer inspiration and instruction to those who live with rejection and abuse. Many feel as if they have done their best, only to be let down by family, friends, society, God. Those who are lonely and discouraged or tempted and misjudged find much in the Joseph story. It raises fruitful questions, such as: Where did Joseph's dreams

8. Peter Brierley, *Reaching and Keeping Teenagers* (Turnbridge Wells, England: MARC, 1993), 89. Besides Ishmael, Joseph, and Kings Uzziah and Jehoiachin, Brierley points out those who would today be classed as early adolescents (twelve-year-olds: Manasseh, Jesus, and Jairus's daughter) and others we can only guess to have been in their teenage years (Isaac, Esther, and Mary, the mother of our Lord).

come from? Should he have shared them? Should he have worn the coat of many colors in front of his brothers? Should he have reported their misdeeds? And how should he have handled their abuse and his being sold as a slave? During his long captive trek to Egypt, what prayers might he have prayed as he went to sleep on the cold ground?

Without family and friends (and with no Bible, Christ, or church), Joseph must have cried out often to a seemingly silent God. This story reveals the God who, through our chaos and flux, and despite our demands for instant solutions and immediate gratification, is still good and just and faithful. The savior of the story is clearly God (Gen. 50:20), and the salvation provided is not only for individuals, families, and tribes but also nations.

Exegeting Sexual Affairs

In one way the temptation of Joseph may be seen as pivotal in the history of redemption. A great deal hinges on every sexual temptation—whether it comes to a pastor, a president, or a high school student. No one has fully explained the power of sexual affairs. People may enter an affair for fun, excitement, or relief, for needed attention or ego satisfaction. Many treat sex as an end in itself. Suddenly they feel nothing else matters; this spontaneous union will make life satisfying and worthwhile. For men, and increasingly for women, the brief encounter expresses some sort of status or exercise of power. In fact, however, a brief liaison can bring disappointment and permanent scars.[9] Joseph could not have known how much hung on his response to this powerful temptation—in a sense, the fate of a nation and the coming of a Savior.

Think of Joseph's situation: the boredom of servitude, presumably years without sex. Lacking a faith community, family, Scripture, or believing friends, Joseph was, as far as we know, single and at the prime of sexual urgency—with seemingly little to lose. He did not yet know the future or God's intentions and providence for his life. We can only imagine an unmarried, hardworking young man who receives little reward, faced by a probably beautiful, available, perhaps half-naked woman—in the inner seclusion of the master bedroom. How much was at stake!

> Now Joseph was handsome and good-looking. And after a time his master's wife cast her eyes on Joseph and said, "Lie with me." But he refused and said . . . , "My master . . . has put everything that he has in my hand. . . . How then could I do this great wickedness, and sin against God?" (Gen. 39:6–9)

9. Witness the fall of prominent politicians and religious leaders—some of whose previous fervent denunciations of sexual aberrations attest to their own lack of wholeness—a lack we all share.

Looking for the Larger Context

To get the most out of this incident, we must see it in the context of the entire Joseph story and the other patriarchal stories of Genesis—as well as in its larger context of all Scripture and the history of Jewish and Christian faith. Joseph tried to put this powerful moment in the context of God's perspective.

1. How is Joseph's situation like so many stories of our times and of history?
   - In what ways is it different in its style and substance?
   - Who were the primary readers of this story?
   - How might the story of Joseph be divided into dramatic acts or stages?
2. With what other stories in the book of Genesis does this one fit?
   - What does this story have to do with God's early covenants?
   - The main point of this story pertains to the history of Israel. How is it significant to that history and to God's whole salvation history?
3. Who, what, where, when, why, and how are all questions that bring this scene to life and clarify its meaning.
   - How old was Joseph when this story begins and when he's finally released from prison and standing before Pharaoh (Gen. 37:2; 41:46)? About how long might he have been a slave? How old was he when he faced the temptation with Potiphar's wife, and how long might he have spent in prison? What difference does all this make?
   - About how far did Joseph walk to find his brothers (Gen. 37:12–17)? How far would you say he walked behind the camel train to get to northern Egypt (Gen. 37:17, 25–28, 36)? (How can students get involved in determining these distances? What can be gained from this information?)
   - What two cultures are meeting in our text?
   - What aspects of Egyptian court and social life, architecture, and other customs might enhance our appreciation of this story?
   - What factors might explain a powerful attraction of Potiphar's wife and Joseph for each other?
   - What word studies and grammatical studies might help to clarify this passage?
4. Why is this story in the Bible? (Expand on what you have seen above.)
   - How was it meant to instruct Israel and promote the growth of its people?
   - How is it meant to instruct the church as a cross-cultural community?
   - How may it promote the growth of readers in all places and times?

- What special impact might this story make on your culture?
- What does this story mean for you?

5. How do you think Israel applied this story? (It would be great to talk to a Jewish friend or rabbi about this.)
   - How might this story be taken differently by Jews, Christians, and Muslims?

6. How can this story be celebrated in the church today?
   - Who can help us understand and appreciate this story more?
   - How has this work of exegesis prepared us to make better use of other passages in the Bible?

Faithfully asking yourself these hard questions will help you field the questions of eager or cynical young people. Why did Joseph taunt his brothers with a dream of his own superiority? Why did God choose Jacob rather than Esau? Why are these stories mostly about men? What about slavery in the Bible? Why is the end of the Joseph story so long and dragged out (Gen. 42–50)? Other questions far from the story of Joseph may come out too, but these can all lead to profitable discussions with the help of a confident leader (who with students is willing to look up what is not known).

Biblical exegesis is obviously hard work, and here I have provided only illustrative principles for the youth worker. Those skilled enough to work from the Hebrew and Greek have an additional advantage, and, fortunately, the works of great exegetes are available for all to read. Although biblical study requires rigorous effort, it can also be fun and satisfying. Above all, skillful interpretation is the necessary foundation for faith, growth, and service.

Being with young people can help one see interpretation—of the Word, culture, and self—from the most exciting perspective possible. At the adolescent stage, many fresh possibilities for analysis and interpretation are suddenly present. The urgency of answers is never stronger; idealism and sensitivity to hypocrisy are heightened; and youth are listening to the leaders who have cared enough for them to earn their trust. That is why you must take exegesis seriously, whether it is the exegesis of the Bible or the exegesis of culture and self.

Exegeting Pop Culture

My *body* hungers for air, food, drink, exercise, and rest. My *soul* at times yearns for a particular kind of music, movie, or sport, for reading, for study and intellectual stimulation, for friends and fun—in other words, for human culture. My *spirit* longs for intimate communion with God, for Scripture, prayer, and

worship. Of course this is a simplistic analysis of a person's holistic and interacting needs and functions. But it shows the role of popular culture. I am body,
soul, and spirit: I have "pop cultural hunger" along with my need for physical
and spiritual satisfactions.

Culture is a complicated and underestimated matter. We define culture as *all
learned behavior*, all the ways humans communicate, manipulate nature, and
produce artifacts. Bear in mind that culture teaches us how to be human, how to
walk, talk, and think, and, therefore, how to interpret life and the Bible itself. In
this sense, cultural exegesis precedes exegesis of the Word. Our senses send images to our brains—images the brain translates into signs or elements of meaning.
Kevin Vanhoozer amends Raymond Williams's definition of culture in this way:

> Culture is the software that determines how things function and how people relate in
> a given society. Culture is both system and practice, a means through which visions
> of the meaning of life (cultural worlds) are expressed, experienced, and explored
> through diverse human products (cultural texts).[10]

To interpret cultural texts we need a basic knowledge of *semiotics*, the study
of the way people interpret meanings from cultural sign systems. One way to understand cultural communication is to speak of a *signifier* (a word or image), and
the *signified* (the meaning inferred or interpreted from the signifier). These two
together produce the *sign* (signifier + signified = sign). The cross around someone's neck is a sign open to many different signifiers (from Madonna to a monk)
and produces a variety of meanings—from death, to redemption, to a particular
style or aesthetic appreciation, or even rebellion against its use by Christians and
church. Along with most of our culture's artifacts, a cross is therefore an ambiguous sign—needing further explanation between wearer and viewer.

This begins to explain why and how reactions to popular culture vary. It's easy
to complain about or condemn pop culture—especially during periods when its
creativity is at a low ebb. One can listen to music, surf TV channels, scan the
web, or pick up a magazine and conclude that all is sex, violence, and dirty gossip controlled by vast corporations brainwashing viewers into obsessive celebrity
gazing and mindless consumption.[11] Such criticisms have some validity but can
miss a larger picture.

---

10. Kevin J. Vanhoozer, Charles A. Anderson, and Michael J. Sleasman, eds., *Everyday
Theology: How to Read Cultural Texts and Interpret Trends* (Grand Rapids: Baker Academic,
2007), 38.

11. See the valid, and balanced, warning from Eric Miller, "Why We Love Football: Grace and
Idolatry Run Crossing Patterns in the New American Pastime," *Christianity Today*, September
2007, 29. Speaking of the power of the $7-billion-a-year corporate NFL, Miller says, "We've
become playthings of the profiteers." More on this in our chapter on consumerism.

In all popular culture, human creativity, the exploration of important themes, public exposure of social foibles and hypocrisies, and provision of relief from the tediously mundane still remain. Creation's beauty is being extolled and vapid lives inspired. The struggle between good and evil is being rehashed—perhaps at times *ad nauseum*. All this is popular culture's positive role. Popular culture surveys and critiques (prophetically) the human landscape; it provides common values by which we can live together. Many practical theologians believe this to be God's intention for popular culture.

Exegesis of popular culture involves enjoyment as well as engagement, discernment, critique, and application. If exegesis is reduced to critical observation and blame, it misses the blessings of popular culture and therefore fails to fulfill our full human responsibility. Strictly negative critiques of media overlook hints of its divine origin and quests for divine union, which are found in all cultures (Acts 17:27).

Popular culture is an arena of competing visions, and those telling the most compelling stories gain significant control. This striking observation brings us to uniquely Christian interpretations of culture. We're asking how the images and messages of popular entertainment stand alongside the person and message of Jesus Christ. God has willed human culture, and Jesus took his place within this culture and enjoyed its social occasions.

Those in control of secular media have vast power, but to infer that kids and women, for instance, are passive objects of media's manipulation—as some secular and religious critics proclaim—is demeaning to children and women and untrue. The consumers of modern media (male and female, young and old—and especially creative teens) add meaning to what they see; they reinterpret products and messages. And they force producers and marketers to respond to their reinterpretations.[12] This process adds to the challenge we face in exegeting pop culture.

Types of Mass Media and Genres of Pop Culture

In this discussion of pop culture, we don't want to lose ourselves in the complexity and controversies surrounding communication, mass media, and the popular arts (we can leave the minutia of pop cultural study to scholars). But we do want to develop skill in discerning what's helpful from what's hurtful in the media—and how so—because we want to encourage such discernment in our students. This does not mean determining the exact line between good and bad, beneficial and detrimental—no one can do that. And if we could, adolescents wouldn't listen until they investigate for themselves and make their own

12. Again, this will be further discussed in the chapter on consumerism.

determinations. Still, without parental advice and thoughtful discussions with us, teenagers can run into serious short-term dangers. So, what further basics do we need to know?

A *medium* is a means of communication (for example, television, radio, internet, magazines, etc., with advertising running across all of these). What separates many youth of the twenty-first century from generations earlier is their life on screens. We need to be careful, however, in accepting myths regarding this technological change, as cautioned by David Buckingham of the University of London:

> The idea of a technological or media-related generation gap is by no means new. One can look back to the 1960s, when the idea of a "television generation" was popularly used as a shorthand means of explaining social change. . . . The contemporary idea of the "Digital Native"—and related formulations such as the "digital generation" and "net generation"—generally place a more positive spin on this basic narrative (of a serious technological generation gap).[13]

Media (plural) use various forms of communication, and within a medium are various types or categories of narrative we call genre. *Genre* is the term used to distinguish the various types of music, fiction, film, television, and so forth, that are generated by the needs and tastes of consumers, as well as the creative styles of artists. Just as the book of Proverbs is interpreted differently than Ecclesiastes or Deuteronomy because of the difference in genre, so we need to make clear what kind of social network, video game, television show, film, song, or book is being discussed.

Sitcoms were an evening staple of TV from its infancy, but by the turn of the century sitcoms were being replaced by various kinds of talent shows and reality TV (supposedly unscripted scenes in real time by nonprofessional actors). Apparently the voyeuristic appeal of television is heightened as audiences watch real people (like themselves) cross conventional standards and get put down, embarrassed, or hurt, or see them succeed in a sensational manner. The many talent shows raise hopes of future fame.[14]

Although television, movies, and the internet are engulfing young people, teenagers, especially younger teens and tweens,[15] are still reading books. Many genres of

13. Michael Thomas, ed., *Deconstructing Digital Natives: Young People, Technology and the New Literacies* (New York: Routledge, 2011), foreword, ix.

14. The TRU (Teenage Research Unlimited) Study, Fall 2006, found that 20 percent of American teens think they will be famous someday.

15. *Tween* is short for *between* and, for our purposes, short for *tweenager*, a term used in marketing and now more broadly to denote prepubescent, almost teenagers and sometimes early teenagers. Tweens are preteenagers.

teen fiction are to be recognized.[16] A huge seller at the beginning of the twenty-first century was the Harry Potter series. Parents and youth ministers have contended over the appropriateness of such reading about witches and dark forces, but such discussions should also question the acceptability of J. R. R. Tolkien's *Hobbit* and *Lord of the Rings* and C. S. Lewis's *Chronicles of Narnia*. Following the success of J. K. Rowling came the *Twilight* series of Stephanie Meyers, and Suzanne Collins's dystopian novel, *Hunger Games*. Discussions about teenagers reading vampire fiction must distinguish "soft vampirism" (where evils of vampirism are overcome by good) from harder core horror and adult vampirism—glorifying erotic gore and even blood drinking.

Our responsibility, again, is not to draw rigid lines between good and bad, between what youth can and cannot read and see; such an effort is of little use. Open discussions with students are more helpful. Through such conversations we learn how media intake is affecting them, how they want to be treated and treat others, how they want to be relieved of fears and healed of hurt, and how they want to grow and relate in healthy ways. Parents, of course, are needed in such discussions, and with them we can discover the wisdom of a positive approach to suitable boundaries. An effective approach allows positive good to overcome seductive evil (Rom. 12:21). We need boundaries, but there are limits to how much of teenage cultural consumption parents and youth ministers can control. Deep down teenagers respect the need for boundaries, and in the best situations youth ministers will find themselves encouraging youthful discernment while respecting parental boundaries. The objective is to overcome negative temptations with youthful desire for and involvement in positive activities.

Outline for Exegetical Study of Pop Culture

1. Do I understand that God created human culture and that it is necessary for socializing humans? Do I see how this includes the necessity and benefits of modern popular culture?
2. How do I understand the tension between Christ and culture, between the sacred and secular, as well as how Christians differ in regard to resolving this tension?
3. Do I understand the fall of culture in human rebellion and the fact that this fall has not obliterated the good, the true, and the beautiful?
4. Do I realize that culture is fallen and is being redeemed—as in "thy kingdom come, thy will be done [here and now] on earth as in heaven"? Do

16. See Diana Tixier Herald, *Teen Genreflecting: A Guide to Reading Interests* (Santa Barbara, CA: Libraries Unlimited, 2003).

I understand that cultures have a divine mandate to help people grow to their full potential (ultimately in Christ), and that any cultural factor that hinders growth is wrong?

5. How am I to study the nature and meaning of our society and popular culture? How can I determine the specific socializing influences of major social systems on young people? How do family, television, school, peers, sports, music, movies, magazines, advertising, and religion influence the teenagers we serve?

6. In regard to a particular cultural artifact, within what kind of system or specific medium am I dealing? How is it related to other (e.g., political and economic, or other group) systems? What are the goals and functions of this medium and how does it influence people? Who has power in making the critical decisions regarding its messages?

7. What is the sign and how is this fashion, song, etc. being interpreted by young people, their parents, and their leaders? Specifically, how are youth re-presenting messages of the media in a way that is not intended by their producers or that is feared by their parents?

8. What is the effect of this message? What factors influence the effect this message has on individuals and groups?

9. How does this message affect the culture overall? What should or can be done about enhancing its benefits or ameliorating its evil?

10. How am I now in a better position to receive and evaluate items within this medium and other media and systems? How can I be a more mature and discerning viewer and consumer, as well as a creator and producer?

11. In general, how does this story (of an ad or film) compare to God's story?

Similar questions guide our exegesis of all popular culture. What is positive and what is negative in current rock music or rap? What movies, music, magazines, games, websites,or TV shows are beyond the limits of good taste? How do we see ourselves—past and present—and how do our students describe the influence of various media and genres upon us? Interpreting culture is such a necessary part of youth ministry that its consideration will fill the greater part of this book.

A later chapter will discuss our need to exegete the place of virtual reality in today's growing-up process and the use of virtual self-marketing, conversations, relationships, sex, and community on the internet.[17] The internet offers fine creative benefits to young people, but it also allows dangerous seductions in terms of

17. Anastasia Goodstein, *Totally Wired: What Teens and Tweens Are Really Doing Online* (New York: St. Martin's Griffin, 2007); and Candice Kelsey, *Generation MySpace: Helping Your Teens Survive Online Adolescence* (New York: Marlowe, 2007) can get us started.

self-promotion, unhealthy disclosures, and powerful portals to pornography. Youth ministers are called to observe, caution, and communicate with youth online. In all such ministry, we must take care of ourselves.

Exegesis of Self

Having discussed the exegesis of Scripture and culture, we come to the important task of analyzing ourselves. Without a knowledge of self we miss some of life's three-dimensional drama (me, another, a world experienced). Narcissists, unable to see themselves from another's perspective, operate in an almost one-dimensional world: the world as *I* see it. Without keen self-awareness, we fail to recognize the effect we have on others; we fail to understand the degree to which we encourage or hinder their personal growth. We may be blissfully unaware of frustrations we cause others and struggle to understand our own frustrations. We may operate as if our truth is the full picture and then end up forcing reality through our over-simplified grid or filter. We interpret life and seek to minister while failing to see the influences of childhood fears or youthful crises that shaped our worldviews and theologies. Our exegesis becomes blind to our own egocentric and eccentric methodologies.[18] Who am I, really? And how deeply does God intend me to know myself? The apostle Paul spoke of "forgetting what lies behind" (Phil. 3:13b), but there may be some hurt in our past that is holding us back.[19]

How can we best take a humble assessment of our lives and the way we work with truth? For some, truth is something to know, facts for passing an exam, data to recite. But truth always transcends our comprehension. We learn about it, study it, practice it, and discuss its nature—all so we may come to know it better.

A prayerful inquiry before God, asking for honest feedback from those we trust, and self-analysis are all helpful. It is important to realize how our personality, upbringing, family, surrounding culture, crises of faith and doubt, spurts of growth, heroes, and mentors have influenced us. On issues such as predestination and free will, authority and personal freedom, evangelization and social action, matters of gender and sex, laws of abstinence and separation versus Christian liberty, and Christ and culture, it is helpful to admit, "Because of who I am, I tend to lean this way."

18. Egocentric or self-centered thinking leads to teaching and leading with inbuilt deviations from what is most helpful to others. Self-centeredness lacks empathy or sensitivity to others' reactions.

19. The 2002 film *Antwone Fisher* tells a story that has helped many of my students remove an old wound, a stumbling block hindering spiritual growth and ministry.

It is good to be able to say, "I am a five-point Calvinist, but I need to be balanced by Arminians." "I'm a Catholic, but it's good for me to work with Protestants." "I'm a suburban Presbyterian, but I need contact with urban African American Baptists." "I am a traditional Episcopalian who needs to understand and appreciate charismatics."

The Greek epigram, "know thyself," and the Hebrew injunction, "watch over your heart with all diligence" (Prov. 4:23 NASB), are twin aphorisms. Both admonitions recognize the danger of ignoring the motivations of our hearts. They imply that brilliant people without self-understanding may hurt themselves and others. Small blind spots can create large errors. These admonitions also encourage a sense of our great potential for personal growth, a necessary foundation for increasing kingdom and community service.

Consider the following end-of-life self-reflection of an Anglican bishop from the twelfth century, whose body is thought to lie in a Westminster Abbey crypt:

> When I was young and free and my imagination had no limits, I dreamed of changing the world.
>
> As I grew older and wiser I discovered the world would not change, so I shortened my sights somewhat and decided to change only my country, but it too seemed immovable.
>
> As I grew into my twilight years, in one last desperate attempt, I settled for changing only my family, those closest to me, but alas, they would have none of it.
>
> And now I realize as I lie on my deathbed, if I had only changed myself first, then by example I might have changed my family. From their inspiration and encouragement I would then have been able to better my country, and who knows, I may have even changed the world.[20]

Self-awareness is a necessary basis for theological life. Self-awareness takes seriously the preciousness of self, the fallenness of self, and the possibilities of grace in one's self. Good theological method should foster the cardinal virtues of wisdom, tolerance, courage, and fairness—as well as the fruit of the Spirit listed by Paul (Gal. 5:22–23). A life that faithfully interprets self, society, and Scripture will produce the humility, vulnerability, strength, and courage desired in a youth leader.

But doesn't this exegesis of self contribute to our Western individualistic tendencies? This is a good question. Only in communal relationships can we find ourselves and discover who we really are—as much as can be known. The tension of knowing ourselves while knowing others and our Lord involves another paradox

---

20. Jack Canfield, *Chicken Soup for the Soul* (Deerfield Beach, FL: Health Communications, 1993), 72. The quote also appears in Steve Wright, *ReThink: Student Ministry* (Wake Forest, NC: Inquest, 2007), 111.

of life. It is similar to the paradox of losing our lives that we might find them, or dying to self that we might live in Christ. If the self I put in community is blind, it becomes a drag and dysfunction in the community. We are asked to know ourselves as individuals in becoming part of a greater body of faithful ones—where we come to know better who we truly are.

Four Basic Questions

When I was doing street work years ago, a young "junkie" might ask me through dazed eyes, "What's hap'nin'?" When our conversation got a little threatening, he'd ask, "Where you comin' from, man?" Then one of us might ask the other, at a superficial or deeper level, "Where're you headed?" But the discussion only really counted if we got realistic: "How're you gonna get there?"

Though obviously dated in wording, these four questions lie at the heart of youth ministry. Youth leaders around the world are using these basic questions as guides to relational conversations, small-group discussions, and curricula. (They will be discussed further in part 4.) In various cultures where I've taught, these questions have been worded differently. They are meant to convey a spirit of relational conversation rather than an interview. Moreover, before these questions can be used effectively with others, we need to apply and use them for ourselves. Consider the wording and range of meaning of the following questions.

1. What's going on?
   - What's going on in my life and how am I doing?
   - Who's important in my life these days?
   - What else has been happening in my world lately?
   - What highs and lows am I experiencing?
2. Where am I coming from?
   - What is my story, my roots, and my history? How has my identity been shaped?
   - How have I been influenced by my family: father, mother, siblings, relatives?
   - How was I influenced by friends, media, school, neighborhood, church, etc.?
   - What inner wounds are not completely healed?
   - How much of my personal story am I comfortable sharing?
   - What are the real stories of my larger family, ethnicity, and nationality?
   - How important do I consider my past?

3. Where am I headed? What dreams do I have?

- What do I see as my purpose in life; why am I here?
- What in life am I most passionate about?
- What is my dream for myself at the apex (or climax) of my life course? What do I most want to be doing? With whom and where would I most like to be living?
- What successes in my past are keys to my future?

4. How can I take responsibility (help myself under Christ's direction and with support from others) to arrive at my life dream?

- How can my future dream be turned into a long-term goal?
- What intermediate and short-term goals will get me there? Are these goals desirable, realistic, and measureable?
- How can I handle positively the obstacles that block these goals?
- Who is going to support and hold me accountable?

Each personal story relates to a communal story and ultimately to God's cosmic story. As you ask yourself the questions above, it will be helpful to share your responses with a trusted partner, a mentor, or a spiritual adviser. A support group and a wise coach will help you use these reflective questions for positive life growth. The faith community is meant to be a storytelling family, and it grows and thrives when rich stories are shared.

With hurting young people, it may be better to go from the first to the third question because their pasts are too painful. Their past stories will come out in due time. The same may be true for you; some wounds call for time.

We ask these questions about our past and future as generally positive reflections, but between our pasts and futures—promising or despairing—is the present, which is a wonderful gift. After some reflection on our past and future we should live primarily in the present. Some live under shame from some dark night of the past. Others struggle in fear of gathering storms. But in Christ we are liberated from the quagmire of guilt (Ps. 40:2; 103:4a)! Jesus took special pains to free us from fears of the future. In his Sermon on the Mount, as recorded in Matthew 6, Jesus says, Don't worry, don't worry, don't worry . . . about your future situation. The Christ who calmed the troubled storm, promises, as the Good Shepherd, to go before us (John 10:4). He is already in the future we worry about. In Christ, we experience the mercy of God "who forgives all your iniquities and heals all your diseases, who crowns you with steadfast love and mercy" (Ps. 103:3–4). Neither shame from our past nor fears for our future should paralyze us in the present. The apostle Paul wrote, "Forgetting those (negative or prideful) things in my past, I use the present to press positively toward all that God has in store for me" (Phil.

3:13–14, author's paraphrase). Liberated from internal obstacles of shame and fear, we can be more fully human, more like Jesus Christ. Letting go of our internal baggage, we are more fit for the race before us (Heb. 12:1). We experience God's gracious freedom—past, future, and present—the secret of the four basic questions.

Many youth workers try to help young people before they have really helped themselves. Answering the above questions honestly is doing exegesis of self and realizing the relationship among biblical, cultural, and self exegesis. Done well, the interpretation of self should take us to Scripture and to our cultural roots. These questions about self are ultimately theological questions. To pursue one's history or future, meaning of life, or ultimate need for guidance and support is to move toward God. Such honest reflection in community is bound to promote healthy growth.

But when and how is self-love a benefit for personal growth and service? Richard Peace pursues such questions.

> What does it mean to love ourselves? This is a concept fraught with difficulties. Improper self-love translates into a lifestyle that is hedonistic, selfish, and self-destructive. But we dare not avoid the subject, because failing to love ourselves properly is also self-destructive. With low (or no) self-esteem, people become doormats for others, fail to use their Christ-given gifts, and have difficulty loving others. Jesus calls us to walk the narrow road between selfishness and selflessness. This involves proper self-understanding, a larger dose of humility, and a healthy sense of who we are.[21]

It is important for us to take time for honest reflection on our present situations, to look at our personal histories and consider the healing of old wounds, then to imagine our dreams for the future and translate those dreams into goals. This process often seems stymied by obstacles and conflicts. I would urge willingness to enter personal counseling. Personal reflections from such counseling need to be integrated into our spirituality. So we ask: How does God—the Father, the Son, and the Holy Spirit—relate to each stage of my life? How have I, and am I, relating to God—the Father, Son, and Holy Spirit—these days? What part do worship, contemplation, and my faith community play in my present growth?

Pursuit of Wholeness

We all seek personal wholeness. The title of Elizabeth O'Connor's book *Our Many Selves* gets right to the point.[22] I am not simply an "I" but a more compli-

---

21. Richard Peace, *Learning to Love Ourselves* (Colorado Springs: NavPress, 1994), 7.
22. Elizabeth O'Connor, *Our Many Selves* (New York: Harper & Row, 1971).

cated "we." It helps to be conscious of the many parts that make up our whole selves—and the tensions that often exist within us.

I am whole only when I know how to *be* as well as how to *do*—I am a human being before a "human doing." The process of self exegesis helps us really *be* before we *do*. Knowing ourselves—as best we can—involves recognizing with O'Connor that we are not singular, but plural in the sense of complicated aspects of ourselves—sometimes even polarizing aspects of the true self. I recognize my traveler in opposition to my settler, the hedonist opposing my monkish aspirations. My Mary tendencies would slow me down and urge withdrawal, while Martha insists on getting it done and tidying it all up. I see a publican in me as well as a Pharisee; I am both a sinner and a saint. The Pharisee keeps me on a spiritual track but can become legalistic and overbearing—even subtly proud and arrogant. The publican helps rescue me from arrogance or defensiveness as it admits and cries out: "Lord, be merciful to me a sinner." We sometimes feel like a motley crew, while God endeavors to bring us into harmony.

Besides my early acquaintance with William Glasser's *Reality Therapy*[23] (from which I somehow got the idea of *tough love* when we were working with New York teenagers caught up in gangs or drugs), my later studies of psychology and training as a counselor were especially helped by the theory and practices of Eric Berne's *Games People Play: The Basic Handbook of Transactional Analysis*.[24] The ways Muriel James and Dorothy Jongeward[25] worked these principles out, for Christian as well as secular contexts, have not only helped me but many students and counselees as well. They combine the Child-Parent-Adult aspect of transactional analysis with a Gestalt method for reconciling our inner polarities.

The Child within me wishes, fantasizes, and imagines creatively while needing help. It cries for more approval and love than my father and mother could ever give, more than my wife and friends can provide. If the Parent within me cannot give me that love and approval, I will tend to place inordinate expectations on others. The Child needs discipline balanced with approval. The Parent cautions and sets limits (when I drive too fast), but its care and approval are also needed. The Adult is meant to keep these needs in balance and to offer "us" necessary reality checks.

These aspects of self have their good points and dangerous extremes. "We" (this family within) need to hold inner meetings to get us all together—and strange things happen in such sessions. My frustrated Parent can learn how it has neglected the

23. William Glasser, *Reality Therapy: A New Approach to Psychiatry* (New York: Harper Perennial, Reissue, 1975).

24. Eric Berne, *Games People Play: The Basic Handbook of Transactional Analysis* (New York: Ballantine Books, 1963, 1996).

25. Muriel James and Dorothy Jongeward, *Born to Win: Transactional Analysis with Gestalt Experiments* (Cambridge, MA: Perseus Books, 1971, 1996).

Child who needs some demonstration of love. An angry Child may discover how the frightened Parent has acted out of fear of rejection by outsiders or by the Child—and is needing reassurance. Mary comes to appreciate and serve Martha, just as Martha recognizes and is inspired by Mary. Salvation may come to our house through repentance of the publican rather than the righteousness of the Pharisee (though we desperately need the Pharisee's knowledge of Scripture). This can all be part of the process of exegeting self in the pursuit of wholeness. Of course, we don't go around thinking about all of this very often, but at times it serves as a helpful exercise.

A good mentor, coach, or counselor hears internal tensions in the other. The mentor may respond, "Part of you is saying you love young people very much, but another part is saying you want to get out of this, get married, settle down, and have kids of your own." Or, "You say you're committed to this church, but there's something pulling you away." Or possibly, "You know you've done good work here and you are needed, but I hear another voice suggesting that it's time to go on for further study—or another position." A seminary student told me, "I'm ready to graduate, and I want a solid prayer life, but instead of praying I end up masturbating." As we discussed this, we hardly talked about sex; it was all about him not finding love for himself within—deep down there was a desperate longing for love and touch. His Parent was having trouble relating to, and conversing with, his Child—and his Pharisee was having trouble relating to his publican. Understanding and dealing with this, he went on to become an outstanding youth leader.

It takes courage and time to face these tensions and to find balance, harmony, and wholeness. To achieve resolution we need an internal arbitrator—or an outside counselor—to get the inner meeting going. Most of us have waited for crisis or brokenness to find an openness and peace that is both realistic and godly.[26] Whatever the cost, self-understanding and commitment to transformation are worth it. Self-knowing and self-healing are difficult tasks, and many of us would benefit from some, at least short-term, counseling in these areas. Many of those who talk with me about a spiritual adviser conclude through conversation that therapy might best precede spiritual direction and mentoring—as important as these are.

We understand ourselves best when we do so theologically. When we understand our lives (our nature) as sacraments of God's love, we experience God's grace in new ways. We may hear more clearly what God is saying through us, appreciate the great meaning of that message, accept the limitations of our existence, and rest in our Lord's gracious application of our lives to a grand divine plan. Ultimately

---

26. For help in the task of self exegesis, see Larry Crabb, *Real Change Is Possible if You're Willing to Start from the Inside Out* (Colorado Springs: NavPress, 1988).

we are not isolated individuals but part of a community of faith praying together, "Our Father. . . ." It is exciting theological work when, in partnership with young people (for their visions are fresh and realistic), we discover the grand significance of God's creative and redemptive activity in these complex vessels of clay.

Theology and ministry, then, begs an exegesis of self. When we make the effort to understand, accept, and tend to our many selves, we will then be much better at tolerating those we've considered unlovable. We can love young people more deeply and effectively as we come to love ourselves in God. Such a love is not self-centered but overflowing—an understanding and healing love. We can love our neighbors as ourselves.

We should also take seriously the criticisms of many current emphases on self. There is a dangerous obsession with self that leads to personal and social narcissism. Morbid introspection or pampered selves can spoil marriages or lead to serious, even deadly, depression. The antidote for self-centeredness is balance, a balance modeled in the blessed Trinity, in a whole life, in life with and for others. It is a balance of self and community, inner prayer and outward service.

This exegesis of self is not meant to be an excursion into navel gazing and vain introspection. If it does not lead to better study of the Bible and culture, if it does not yield better relationships in the faith community, if knowing ourselves does not lead to serving others more effectively and loving God more dearly, then such study is surely in vain.

Questions for Reflection and Discussion

1. What has most impressed you in this discussion of interpretation?
2. Which do you find most difficult: the exegesis of the Bible, of culture, or of self?
3. What in this chapter would you like more fully explained? How could you find such explanation? Do you have any criticisms of, or suggestions for, this chapter?
4. How are you growing these days, and what are your goals for personal growth?
5. Are there any principles here that young people cannot understand? How can you make those principles simpler as you help young people grow in understanding and effective living?
6. How are Christ, the Holy Spirit, and God the Father necessary in all that has been discussed here?
7. What from this chapter can you most immediately use for yourself?
8. What kinds of exegesis can you do best with the young people in your life and care?

—4—

Basic Theology for Youth Ministers

I know, O LORD, that the way of human beings is not in their control,
that mortals as they walk cannot direct their steps.

JEREMIAH 10:23

When you search for me, you will find me; if you seek me with all your
heart, I will let you find me, says the LORD.

JEREMIAH 29:13–14A

Your hands have made and fashioned me; give me understanding.

PSALM 119:73

Theological Paradoxes

The theological quest begins at a human dead end. Our Creator has given us the
ability to ask theological questions about the meaning of life, to delve into the
mysteries of the universe, to test hypotheses about human cultures and behavior,
and to construct theories as to how we know what is true, right, and wrong. Our
ever-changing and revised discoveries, however, can tease us into believing we've
almost figured it all out. But certainty is elusive as we ponder political, economic,
social, church, or individual action. We perceive, think, and live in paradoxes of
endless questions and uncertain conclusions.

Teenagers often catch life's paradoxes more strikingly than adults who have
become accustomed, and perhaps rather numb, to the perplexities of life. We

somehow resist the humility such mysteries should produce. Jesus might have said, "Unless you become as a teenager, or even childlike, you cannot think from a kingdom perspective" (see Matt. 18:2–3).

We adults are slow to admit the futility of our individual and collective wisdom apart from divine intervention. Before we were, God is; before we think, God must give us both thinking ability and a divine key to make sense of it all. It is the key John the evangelist called the *logos*, which enlightens every human (John 1:1–9). Premoderns, moderns, and postmoderns have all been caught in the same human dilemma. The image of God in us seeks infinite meaning, while finite limitations and effects of our fallen spirit mock such effort.

Doing theology involves bringing our lives and thoughts before a living God in awe and fear—the kind of fear the writer of Proverbs had in mind (Prov. 1:7; 9:10; see also Ps. 111:10). We come bringing our questions with a conviction that God alone fully knows us and the world around us. We come *together* because doing theology cannot be a solitary task. We come to God because God first comes to us—even as we love God and others only because God first loved us (1 John 4:19). Pete Ward, youth ministry sage in the United Kingdom, put it this way:

> The Christian story tells of an unknowable God who makes himself known. . . . We cannot make God the object of our study and enquiry. We know God as he chose to come to us. We know God as we are caught up in his knowing us. This aspect of Christian spirituality and experience means that faith is always mystery.[1]

At the dead end of our scientific and philosophical searches comes the possibility of a divine Word. In the midst of our theoretical and social divisions, with all their dreadful consequences, appears a divine incarnation. Upon the mound of human suffering—the consequences of inhumanity and human predation upon the weak and vulnerable, the violence of terrorism and natural disasters—there appears the shadow of a cross: death with the promise of resurrection. Here begins the wisdom of God, where human efforts, the wisdom of this world, have failed us.[2] We can think about God because we have a relationship with God—just as we can truly know only the people with whom we have a relationship. Before studying God, we relate to God in worship, therefore worship (doxology or praise) precedes all forms of "thinking or rational theology."

Spiritual theology (our experiencing God) might be seen at the apex of a triangle. It presides over its lower bases. At one base we might put biblical/historical/

---

1. Pete Ward, *Youthwork and the Mission of God: Frameworks for Relational Outreach* (London: SPCK, 1997), 33.
2. See 1 Cor. 1:18–25. Of course, the apostle goes on to use cultural tools and wisdom as we do. This is all part of the paradox.

systematic theology (our rational formulations of godly concepts and principles). At another base we see all of life as described in practical theology (how our experience and knowledge of God are applied to real life). Topping our imaginary triangle is God, the necessary *tertium quid* or third factor.

One of the great theological paradoxes stems from our understanding of the God who is both among us while far beyond and unfathomable. We have seen the face of God in Jesus Christ; yet, "My face," God says, "no one can see" (see John 14:9b; Exod. 33:20, 23b). We are stuck, you might say, between the familiar God and the unknowable God.

The relationship between believing and understanding is another paradox debated throughout theological history: we cannot understand without believing, and we cannot believe without some understanding. Perhaps more basic is the paradoxical relationship between being and thinking. Ontologically, being comes before thinking, but in our experience and epistemologically, the concept of being is a result of our thinking. We either can become entangled in continuous philosophical debates about being and knowing or avoid what seems to be fruitless controversy. As humans, we tend to resist mysteries we cannot completely resolve.

Because we *are* before we *think*, because reality precedes logic, human thought must begin with a basic assumption or presupposition (which, by definition, cannot be proven). Science accepts only what is observable or rationally demonstrable. But both processes are based on assumptions about human perception and rationality that cannot be proven. Philosophy, science, and cultural studies all necessarily begin with presuppositions regarding human reasoning, communication, texts, and meaning. John Milbank has argued this in depth.[3]

Rather than assuming confidence in human perception and reasoning, we begin with assumptions about God's creativity and revelation. If we say our understanding of God's ways is possible only at God's initiative; if we trust response to that initiative by the Spirit in the community of faith and in ourselves, then these statements become our basic assumptions or presuppositions. Our explanation of the Christian faith, then, cannot be rationally proven to young minds. Our apologetics demonstrates the reasonableness of the gospel and Christian faith; it does not propose to prove creation versus naturalistic evolution or theism against atheism.

From our faith perspective, not only must thinking about God begin through divine grace; our thinking about anything and everything is possible only because God created reality and gave us senses to perceive and minds to conceive a real

3. John Milbank, *Theology and Social Theory: Beyond Secular Reason*, 2nd ed. (London: Blackwell Publishing, 2006) convincingly argues the necessity of admitting presuppositions as prior in all sciences, including theology.

world. This is our basic assumption, the ultimate foundation of our worldview and theology: a self-revealing Triune God calls us into loving relationship through Jesus Christ. Our starting point in all thought and discussion is the fact that God made us to perceive the reality of divine creation and give praise to the Lord. Still, we humbly admit that our faith and certainty contain the obvious paradoxes already mentioned.

Doing Theology among Young People

Youth especially crave contact with transcendence.[4] Our close association with young people helps us theologically. The historic continuity of orthodox theology, which has at times needed revivals[5] and correctives,[6] is another paradox of the Christian faith. The certainty of our faith rests in the fact that a self-revealing, Triune God has spoken above and beyond the clamor of human opinion. Our struggle to hear and understand, and our tendency to oversimplify and become dogmatic, often lead to sad church divisions. The limitations and flaws of any given church are evident to most humble servants of God.

The need for revivals and corrections is historically apparent. The core of our theology, however, as expressed in the Lord's Prayer and in the creeds of a once-united church, has stood the test of time.[7] The Holy Spirit cautions us about overly speculative dogma. As Christian women, blacks, Asians, and those of the southern hemisphere have pointed out weaknesses in Western theology, so youthful realities are also critical in theological reexaminations. Theology from the perspective of youth ministries joins the ranks of corrective theologies.

Young people admire authenticity. In 1843 Karl Marx wrote critically that religion is the "opiate of the people."[8] The same year an Anglican churchman,

---

4. An important "secular" study sponsored by the YMCA, Dartmouth Medical School, and the Institute for American Values in a report to the nation titled "Hardwired To Connect: The New Scientific Case for Authoritative Communities" (New York: Institute for American Values, 2003), concluded that adolescents are hardwired to connect both to caring communities with clear boundaries and to transcendent values and spirituality.

5. No matter our positive or negative opinion of the Protestant Reformation, we should be able to see partially in it a spiritual revival among some people of northwestern Europe at that time.

6. Franciscan theology, Reformed theology, Counter-Reformational theology, Wesleyan and Anabaptist theology, liberation theology, feminist theology, Asian, African, other non-Western theologies, and Emergent theology are examples.

7. Some will object that the church doctrine was always debated and the church never unified. I accept the facts but claim, with others, the overall unity of structure and belief until 1054.

8. "Religion is the sigh of the oppressed culture, the heart of a heartless world, just as it is the spirit of a spiritless situation. It is the opium of the people." *Die Religion . . . ist das Opium des Volkes* from Karl Marx, *Critique of Hegel's Philosophy of Right*, ed. Joseph O'Malley (1843; Cambridge: Cambridge University Press, 1970), 131.

F. D. Maurice, sadly agreed but added a crucial caveat: "We have been dosing our people with religion while what they want is not this but the living God."[9]

There is a deep longing for such authenticity in young hearts. On the surface of their lives they are being seduced, as we all are, striving after false forms of personal pleasure, possessions, and power. The world has invented all manner of shortcuts to ultimate happiness. Behind the mad rush for the quick fix, transient fame, or relative success, young hearts often detect a kind of futility, a certain madness in the race for that which never satisfies, never rings completely true.[10] Their hearts are longing for, if not open to, the perfect humanity of Jesus Christ who introduces us to the living God.

The Gospel Story

Young people share their unique, interesting, and often powerful stories. Other people's stories also matter to them, stories that fill conversations, television shows, movies, Facebook, and Twitter. Why have we often given them clichéd propositions and empty programs—when the sharing of stories in the context of God's story is so dynamic?

The gospel story is a grand and powerful divine drama. All human stories are subscripts, incomplete parts of a whole. Sadly, many churches major in selected parts of the gospel, fragments of the whole story. Theologically, we try to paint a whole canvas of the broad biblical panorama. Let's make sure we satisfy the human longing for completeness with the whole story told to us from creation to re-creation, from beginning to end of God's story.

The whole story is compelling because we are all part of it. Before God interrupts the failed patterns of our life, before faith commitment, our stories are mere fragments floating in confused limbo. Consideration of the whole story, God's story, is a necessary theological enterprise.

Theology of Culture

A final paradox or tension this book explores has to do with the blessings *and* toxicity of our culture. It is the relationship of the gospel to (and in) culture, our

9. F. D. Maurice, *The Life of Frederick Denison Maurice: Chiefly Told in His Own Letters*, ed. Frederick Maurice (London: MacMillan, 1884), 1:369.

10. Pop culture is full of examples of admitted emptiness and futility. Rapper Tyler the Creator radically expresses futility in his song, "Yonkers": "F— everything, man / That's what my conscience said / Then it bunny hopped off my shoulder, now my conscience dead / Now the only guidance that I had is splattered on cement / Actions speak louder than words, let me try this sh . . , dead."

spiritual lives within the church, and our lives in the world (not to suggest that church and culture can be separated). It is the tension between God's city Jerusalem and human cities such as Babylon, Athens, and Rome. An early Christian Father, Tertullian, tended toward a negative view of worldly culture: "What indeed has Athens to do with Jerusalem? What concord is there between the Academy [secular universities] and the Church? What between heretics and Christians?"[11] A Christian philosopher, Merold Westphal, answers:

> It is dangerous for Jerusalem [theology] to turn to Athens [philosophy] for guidance. The word of the cross does not conform to the wisdom of the world (I Corinthians 1:18–2:13). But there are two reasons why the risk is worth taking, especially when one is conscious of the danger.[12]

Westphal explains that theologies denying philosophy have already been unconsciously influenced by a philosophy of their culture, for one thing, and that scientific principles for interpreting anything apply to the Bible as well. Using postmodern critiques, Westphal affirms cultural relativity but asserts: "such relativity is by no means the same as the relativism in which 'anything goes.'"[13]

This paradox/tension between the city of God and city of humankind is not a mistaken modern dualism, as some contend; it is a central biblical theme. The tension and conflict between God's cosmic sovereignty and Satan's rule must be acknowledged. Jesus, in his temptation, accepted the devil's claim over the kingdoms of this world and later referred to "the ruler of this world" (John 12:31; see also Matt. 4:8–9). The apostle Paul calls our adversary "the god of this world" (2 Cor. 4:4) and again "the ruler of the power of the air," linking the enemy with "the course of this world" and "the spirit that is now at work among those who are disobedient" (Eph. 2:2). Paradoxically, in this age, the world is both God's and Satan's—in different ways.

A contrast between God's way and the world's way must be acknowledged. There are in the world, though we cannot ultimately delineate them into clear-cut categories, the ungodly, who seek to manipulate others for personal profit, and the godly, who attempt in God's grace to serve others (Ps. 1; Matt. 25:31–46; John 5:28–29). By extension there are systemic tendencies serving the common good as well as powerful forces fighting against the intent of the Lord's Prayer: "Thy kingdom come; thy will be done."

11. Tertullian (ca. 160–220), *On Prescription against Heretics*, 7, in *The Ante-Nicene Fathers*, ed. Alexander Roberts and James Donaldson, 10 vols. (1885–96; Grand Rapids: Eerdmans, 1986–89), 3:246.
12. Merold Westphal, *Whose Community? Which Interpretation? Philosophical Hermeneutics for the Church* (Grand Rapids: Baker Academic, 2009), 13–14.
13. Ibid. 15.

The church is embedded in God-ordained human culture and benefits from it. In the Bible, God protects Cain and allows his early civilization to flourish. God has Moses educated and trained in Egyptian culture, Daniel and his friends in Babylonian courts. God calls and blesses Nebuchadnezzar the Babylonian (Jer. 25:9; Dan. 1–4) and Cyrus the Persian (Isa. 45:1–7). Esther is called to join herself intimately to a pagan ruler and to Persian culture for a divine purpose (see the book of Esther and especially Esther 4:14).

Serious young Christians have always asked how to be *in the world* and not *of it*. How can we be salt and light in the world if we are to be separate from it (Matt. 5:13–16; 2 Cor. 6:17)? There is no easy answer to this serious tension. I once heard the Reverend Earl Palmer say: "The world is for the learning of the church; the church is for the healing of the world."[14] I hope we will find some explanations of this paradoxical mystery as we proceed.

Theology Generally and Properly

Years back, Pete Ward complained about the profession he loved: "The widespread absence of formal theological training for youth ministry means that Christian youth workers are prone to the latest catchy trends."[15]

Experienced youth minister and scholar Christy Lang writes rather eloquently about our need for theology in youth ministry:

> For the sake of young people, for the sake of the church and for the sake of the world in need of gospel-formed people, figuring out what draws and keeps youth involved in church is part of youth ministry. Often, however, we come up with pragmatic responses, acting without the theological reflection that can ground, guide and critique our action.
>
> A lot of us don't do theological reflection consistently. We're busy; youth group is tonight, and we need a plan, not a doctrine. We are not sufficiently theologically trained, so who are we to "do theology"? Volunteers want direction, not a theology lesson.[16]

But what is theology? And how do we *do* it? Theology is literally the study of God (consider for a moment, the presumptuousness of such an undertaking!). The secular world defines theology as "the study of religion, especially the Christian faith and God's relation to the world."[17] In contrast to this definition, I'd like to

---

14. At a Young Life national conference in California around 1970.

15. Ward, *Youthwork*, 35.

16. Christy Lang, "Communities of Disciples," *Immerse: A Journal of Faith, Life and Youth Ministry* (March/April 2011): 17.

17. *Encarta World English Dictionary* (New York: St. Martin's, 1999), s.v. "theology."

describe theology (and doing theology) as *receiving* God's revelation of the divine self and God's works. The benefits of such an approach are its recognition of God's initiating grace,[18] its acknowledgment of presuppositions or basic assumptions in all human thinking and systems, and its defense against unbiblical rationalisms and deconstructive skepticisms.[19]

Who made God? How could an all-powerful God allow evil, which causes so much suffering? How can God allow earthquakes and tsunamis? Do you mean that good people who don't believe our way go to hell? How do we get to heaven? Should we go to war to prevent people from being massacred by a ruthless dictator? These are more than "wise-guy" questions from young people. For those who are honest, they provoke an uneasy, "I don't fully know, but I believe." Yet, from such realistic humility we are expected to move on *toward* belief, and toward cautious, tentative explanations *from what God has revealed to us*. We recognize that God reveals truth in more than one way (through creation, conscience, natural reason, human culture, Christian tradition and the community of faith, in the written Word, and, supremely, in the Living Word of God). We also recognize that God's revelations do not solve all dilemmas.

Theology is crucial for you who minister among youth. You are doing your best in the name of Christ and the power of the Holy Spirit, but you soon discover that your best, even with these divine resources, is not enough. You don't have to be in youth ministry long before you come across difficult individuals and situations; in time you will meet impossible ones. Such individuals and situations must be left in the hands of God, and for this reason you need to know something about how God works. Theology is important for youth ministers because you are surrounded by views and voices contrary to the historic gospel of Jesus Christ, both from within and beyond today's churches. We need theology because it expands the opening sentence of the Lord's Prayer, which is the ultimate aim of your ministry. What does it mean for God's will and God's kingdom to come to your neighborhood and the world? Above all, theology is important because it explains our relationship to our loving Creator, the God of justice, wisdom, hope, and peace.

We've already said the church needs theology from the perspective of youth ministry—just as it has always benefited in the long run from corrective or complementary theologies. Urban youth ministry calls for a theology from the streets; wilderness ministries emphasize a theology amidst the wilds of nature; ministry among the privileged needs a theology of justice. Youth ministry is generally, and should be, uncomfortable with a theology that is too rigid, exclusive, or dogmatic,

18. For students of theology, this approach leans toward theologians like Augustine and Anselm. It is different than Schleiermacher's move from reason to pietistic "emotion."

19. The "wisdom of this world" against which the apostle Paul posits the foolishness of the cross (1 Cor. 1:22–25; 2:7–13).

too scholarly and out of touch—all of which lose sight of God's concern for the excluded and oppressed, and for a unity as broad as God's love.

Theology as Story

God's revelation to us in Scripture (our starting point) and Scripture's revelation of Jesus Christ (who, with the Holy Spirit, reveals all we can know of God's nature), present us with story first of all. There are principles and propositions, but they come within the context of a grand story of the Creator's relationships with the created. Before God reveals much about the divine nature, God tells us the story of creation. Within that story we begin to notice God's intention for intimate relationships, for justice within loving relationships, for love based on free choice. Before God gives us the Ten Commandments, God tells us the Moses story. The Old Testament prepares us for, and the Gospels reveal to us, Christ the Son in the Jesus story. All this also points to the significance of your story—and the stories of students for whom you care. It points to the stories of families and churches. God's story is one of love, justice, and peace—which we all, and especially those just entering adulthood, crave.

Secular thinkers and some revisionist theologians think *we* have constructed this story, that it is a religious cultural deposit that therefore can and should be deconstructed into naturalistic and progressive explanations. Of course, our words and significations[20] deserve critical questioning and analysis. In the eyes of this world's wise people, God's story of redemption is just *our* metanarrative— something we have constructed on our own.[21] If, on the contrary, Scripture's story comes primarily not from us but from the Creator and Ruler of the universe, it is not the same as the human constructions of Adam Smith, Marx, Darwin, or Freud—and therefore not subject to the same scientific criticism. We do not claim to own this truth as *our* theoretical creation and possession; rather this truth has captivated us who believe, and to it we bear humble witness. Of course, this acceptance is accompanied by thorough questioning and reasoning. It is not, again, a mere cultural metanarrative subject to deconstructive doubt but rather what some have called God's megastory, a story whose truth stands beyond our construction or deconstruction.

God's story begins with God's revelation to us as Creator ("In the beginning, God created the heavens and the earth," Gen. 1:1 ESV) *and* as Lover ("Hear, O

20. *Significations* are what we mean by our words and explanations.
21. *Metanarrative* is a term broadened by Jean-Francois Lyotard to describe scientific, philosophic, historic, religious, etc., theories constructed to provide a comprehensive and complete explanation of our cultural lives. He proposed "incredulity" toward metanarratives such as the theories of Marx and capitalism—the flaws of which history has revealed.

Israel, the LORD our God, the LORD is one. You shall love the LORD your God with all your heart," Deut. 6:4–5 ESV). We begin to see the mystery of God as a divine family or community, as God, three in one, as Father, the Spirit, and chosen servant and Son. Such a Triune God makes all the difference in how we understand ourselves and all human relationships.[22]

Consider how Scripture reveals God as Creator *and* Lover. Then we are better able to see ourselves in God's image, with basic needs to create or achieve, and to love and be loved. We are *homo faber* (human makers) and *homo amans* (human lovers). We have deep and desperate drives to *achieve* and to *love*. Understanding these twin drives is important for all who counsel youth.

From the beginning, God sought creative, loving partners. It is important that we introduce young people to the beginning of the grand story in a garden where human longings and achievements were fulfilled, because their God-instilled longings and drives need validation. God instilled in us desires to be noticed for our creativity and to be loved just as we are. Also God gave us the dramatic risk of free choice—because love and creativity cannot be forced. Our human drives can best be understood in light of a God of ultimate beauty, truth, justice, and loving compassion.

In the garden Adam and Eve were fulfilled with pleasure, possessions, and power; they were in charge of, and enjoying, all they could see. Gospel stories and catechesis[23] do not spend enough time in this garden of human fulfillment. Our culture needs reminders of its golden age, a flourishing of unblemished relationships and therefore truth, justice, and peace. Young people rightfully long for a place of true love, genuine and satisfying relationships, unhampered creativity and accomplishments. Imagine ways to communicate such scenes effectively.

A good friend of mine, Kent McDonald, has often stood before a large Young Life camp audience and asked them: "What was God's first command to Adam and Eve in the garden?" Of course some don't have a clue about the garden, but others yell out, "Not to eat the fruit!" With a sad pause, Kent shakes his head saying, "No, not at all. God's first command was [and here his voice rises]: *Akal . . . takhal* [a strong Hebrew imperative in Gen. 2:16], 'Eat, eat all of it!' But keep one just for Me."

Jesus would later express the Creator's intention, "I came that they may have life, and have it abundantly!" (John 10:10). The world attempts to deceive a youthful

---

22. Each of us is one, yet with body demanding physical nourishment, soul seeking cultural resources and support, and a spirit longing for transcendence. And all our relationships are shaky and vulnerable without a triadic relationship with God, not I-and-Thou, but I-and-Thou-and-God. So also the church and human systems need triadic strength and grounding.

23. *Catechesis* is religious or faith instruction, understanding of baptism and salvation, "discipling."

generation into believing God and the church put negatives first—and churches often fulfill this sad critique. Pop culture and advertising often use the same deception as the mysterious serpent: "Don't listen to those trying to deprive you of real life and experience. . . . Try it, do it now, you'll like it."

We want all to be impressed with the beauty of that garden—and of the world today. God's intention was for our delight and fulfillment in creation and in the culture we would create. God provided beauty, truth, and harmony, offering humanity gifts of godly pleasure, possessions, and power. Over all was the banner of God's love with ringing themes of human community and dignity. We miss so much when we lose sight of God's garden-intention for justice (the right way) and peace (well-being). It is part of our gospel of the kingdom: dignity for all through the common good. May God breathe imaginative creativity into our presentations of the gospel story.

But the crafty serpent knew "a better plan," a shorter path, a shortcut, to the good life. We read the awesome story of Adam and Eve's taking the bait and spoiling everything—as have we all. It's not just theology that demands full emphasis on free will turned wrong and the consequences of rebellion. Whether we are dealing with bullying or terrorism, our very survival calls for an analysis of sin. Adam and Eve hurt each other, they hurt the whole creation, and most of all they hurt the great Creator/Lover. And we have been hurting one another ever since. Our differences fail to move through divinely planned diversity to unity. Rather, a beautiful and possible garden of differences often turns instead toward animosity, prejudice, and a vast landscape of violence.

The sinful fall of humans, as many have said, is the most empirically validated of Christian doctrines. "Nice theologies" may try to avoid what they see as "negative Catholic or Puritan harangues," but realists must deal with this cardinal thesis of orthodoxy.[24] Realistic youth ministry honestly portrays our continued efforts to shortcut God's long-range plan. Young hearts want the real story, just as those who are ill long for true diagnosis. Every day we encounter the results of our obsessions with unnatural pleasure, possessions, and power; they stoke self-aggrandizement, self-harm, greed, corruption, and global violence.

"Nice theology" tries to slide past the biblical doctrine of evil. Secular unbelievers attempt to treat constant reminders of evil as mere, sad aberrations. The evening news heralds stories of murdered women, children, and men as sensational headliners. Later on, prime-time shows spotlight rape and murder mysteries pretending we are in on their solutions. Numbly we brush past the reality of sins against neighbors. The Oklahoma bombing that took the lives of 168 innocent

---

24. Karl Barth, Reinhold Niebuhr, Richard Niebuhr, and others recovered the crucial doctrine of individual *and* corporate (systemic) sin.

people, including nineteen children under six years of age;[25] the bombing and slaughter of youths at a camp in Norway;[26] the slaughter of first graders at Newtown, Connecticut;[27] and the pastoral abuse of children are not just instances of deviant, individual sin (though they are that too). Such atrocities, along with financial swindling and wanton shootings on urban streets, are also indications of evil permeating our social, media, and religious institutions.[28]

Into our rebellion, discord, and violence, God as Son appears: "God shows his love for us in that while we were still sinners, Christ died for us" (Rom. 5:8 ESV). The incarnation (the life and teachings, death, resurrection, and ascension of Jesus Christ) substantiates our culture and offers saving hope. The Christ event is the crux of the whole story.

The brilliant theologian H. Richard Niebuhr called progressive theologians, with their modernist beliefs in the essential goodness of humankind and the inevitability of progress, back to a biblical gospel of human sinfulness and need for the cross. He described their theology as preaching that "a God without wrath brought men without sin into a Kingdom without judgment through the ministrations of a Christ without a Cross."[29] Theologian Miroslav Volf affirms the centrality of the cross: "Indisputably, the self-giving love manifested on the cross and demanded by it lies at the core of the Christian faith."[30]

Responding to youthful suffering and recoiling from youth ministries that use a model of the incarnation merely to justify relationships with young people as means to programmatic ends, Andrew Root, drawing on theologians from Martin Luther to Dietrich Bonhoeffer, calls us to embrace the suffering of young people as he describes the meaning of the cross:

> Suffering is truly suffering; it is as horrible and painful as can be imagined. But it is shared suffering; to know God is to know Jesus Christ who suffers the severity

---

25. Timothy McVeigh's attack on the Alfred P. Murrah Federal Building in Oklahoma City on April 19, 1995.

26. In July 2011, Anders Behring Breivik, 32, carefully planned the bombing to kill and divert attention, while in a police uniform he took control of an island youth camp and began shooting them one by one. Almost a hundred persons lost their lives.

27. James Barron, "Nation Reels After Gunman Massacres 20 Children at School in Connecticut," New York Times, December 14, 2012, www.nytimes.com/2012/12/15/nyregion/shooting-reported-at-connecticut-elementary-school.html?pagewanted=all&_r=0.

28. This by no means argues cause and effect but rather that violent response to personal disputes and systemic/political conflict is part of a culture of violence sometimes prompted by extreme religious groups. Breivik claimed to be a Christian—though in what sense is not known.

29. H. Richard Niebuhr, Kingdom of God in America (1937; Chicago: Willett, Clark, 1988), 193.

30. Miroslav Volf, Exclusion and Embrace: A Theological Exploration of Identity, Otherness, and Reconciliation (Nashville: Abingdon, 1996), 25.

of being human. To encounter the *who* of God is to encounter God on the cross; it is to join God as God takes upon the suffering of the world as God's ministry to the world. There is no reconciliation without the cross, and there is no possibility of being human as God intends by circumventing suffering. . . . We must follow the incarnate Christ as he walks into the center of the world's suffering. When we turn from the suffering of the world, we turn from the cross, which is to turn from the Christ who is found on the cross.[31]

The mysteries of the incarnation and the cross are pictured to us in Scripture as Jesus Christ suffering for us (Ps. 22; Isa. 53; Heb. 2:10; 1 Pet. 2:21), as giving himself as a ransom for us (Mark 10:45; 1 Tim. 2:5–6), as offering himself as a sacrifice for us and our sins (Rom. 3:25; Heb. 7:27; 9:26; 1 Pet. 2:24; 1 John 4:10), as victor over all evil systems, violent principalities, and powers (Col. 2:13–15), and as a moral example, a demonstration of God's love (1 Pet. 2:21; 1 John 4:11–21). The story and its mysteries demand all of these—despite the fact that theologians have argued one over against another. Christians will be more at peace with one another *and* have a fuller gospel as we embrace all of the above biblical emphases in describing the mysteries of the cross and our salvation.

The New Testament is not the end, but the beginning of church history. There are enough human blots across the pages of this history to spoil the persistent introduction of the kingdom. But the story continues with heroes, with victims rescued from oppression and degradation, with the amelioration of systemic terrors. Even now we are bold enough to pray: "thy kingdom come; thy will be done on earth." The stories of saints and servants, of missions and revivals, must continue to be told. Today, *already*, the presence of God is available to be sensed in open hearts. And yet our pain and struggles have *not yet* been ended; our hopes and prayers have *not yet* been answered.

The "already" is the story of the church; the "not yet" is our powerful hope. We need more telling of church stories even though they are not all nice. We need more study and discussion of the church—because so many are giving up on it or imagining that they can start all over again. Admittedly, this book can only allude to our theology of the church (eschatology), and more is needed. But consideration of the "already" is broader than discussion of the church; it includes the story of the kingdom Jesus announced as being already here. When this book refers to justice in today's world or doing the right thing, or the positive benefits of human culture, it is talking about God's kingdom already come. No matter the progress, the beauty in nature and in one another, compassionate hearts weep as they survey the global scene.

31. Andrew Root, *Revisiting Relational Youth Ministry: From a Strategy of Influence to a Theology of Incarnation* (Downers Grove, IL: InterVarsity, 2007), 94.

And so the grand story must be concluded; the metanarrative of divine drama must reach its *denouement* (final resolution of the drama's basic tension). The pain I feel from daily injustices persisting in spite of the church's prayer is relieved by words in beloved black spirituals: "He may not come when you want Him to come, but He comes on time!"[32] God is coming to make all things right! God's story has a beginning, dramatic tension, climax, and a glorious conclusion. "Christ has died, Christ is risen, Christ will come again."

Some will object to the above summary seeing it, not as real theology, but merely the gospel story. I respond: the gospel we preach must faithfully represent our theology, and the whole of our theology be proclaimed as gospel. All theology worth study and discussion must be applicable and in some way understandable to the adolescent mind. Theology, which is not good news to young hearts and minds, is peripheral.

Theology in Our Ministry

Throughout Holy Scripture, God's response to human rebellion and oppression is one of open arms (John 3:16–17, God's love "came not to condemn") and warnings (John 3:18–21, "This is the judgment"). Against self-centered individual and cultural humanism, God seeks to be central. As the divine image in human beings becomes defaced, God pleads for holiness and purity. As greed, animosity, and violence emerge, God is on the side of justice, liberation, and reconciliation. Biblical covenants[33] with blessings and curses, prophecies and types, all point to redemption. The gospel is the good news of God's response to the ills of the human condition.

When young hearts hear the whole story, they can be remarkably open to this drama of good and evil, of redemption from oppression and deliverance from fear. The exodus is the central redemptive act of the Old Testament; its message is one of liberation from all unjust oppression. The life, death, and resurrection of Jesus, the Son of Man, the Son of God, stand at the core of the New Testament, with a message of reconciliation beyond liberation.[34] We are liberated from all that defaces the divine intention; we are reconciled to God and to others. In the stories

32. A black gospel leader tells me these words (or variations of them, such as, "He may not come when we want him, but he's right on time") appear in many black gospel hymns. Above all we remember Mahalia Jackson's "He's Right On Time," www.superlyrics.com/lyrics/ kGRU0hlKGv@c@HG/He%27s_Right_On_Time_lyrics_by_Mahalia Jackson.html.

33. Consider the Noahic covenant (Gen. 9:1–17), the Abrahamic covenants (Gen. 15:1–18; 17:1–8), the Mosaic covenant (Exod. 2:23–24; 6:4–5; 19:5–6; 24:7; 25:22b; Num. 10:33; Deut. 4:13; 5:2–3), and the Davidic covenant (2 Sam. 7:8–16; 23:5).

34. See Volf, *Exclusion and Embrace*, 101–5, 109–10.

of creation and the exodus, and preeminently in that of the cross and empty tomb, we come as close as we can to answering youthful questions (expressed earlier in this chapter) and biblical questions such as Habakkuk's "Why, God?" (see Hab. 1).

The Bible is above all a love story. True love demands the risk of free will, and God is intent on paying the cost of that risk. Suffering with and for us, God's Son, who knew no sin, became sin for us so that we might be right with God (2 Cor. 5:21). This love story stands above all love stories. When religion, theology, and the gospel become primarily guides to proper living, they lose the dynamic of a love story and can be seen as legalistic diversions to youthful hearts. When church is merely proper practice for an expected bookend to a successful week's work, rather than a living love affair, why bother? Somehow God craves our attention, our adoration, our voices, our gifts and touch—the stuff of real love affairs. I don't know why God would. But that is the story. Going to church is returning that love; it's part of the love, if the affair is working.

Teenagers feel and know about love affairs; they just seldom find it at church. They need to discuss how such a love affair with Jesus, with God, couldn't be with puppets or robots. The risk, as we might imagine the Trinity discussing it, must have been incredible. God the Son, God the Father, God the Spirit took that risk with awesome cost. That is the story.

Young people are leaving churches bound in routine formality; they are also leaving churches that are primarily an adult show. They don't feel themselves invited to a love affair. The Last Supper was a loving farewell party. Its guests were invited as friends to partake of their host's body and blood. Many churches who observe Communion only sparingly are rethinking their weekly ritual. From the beginning, the breaking of bread (eventually called the Eucharist) was a weekly, if not daily, celebration. Like youthful love affairs, going to church means being in the presence of the beloved, conversing (hearing the words of a beloved and responding), exchanging gifts, and the holy kiss of peace or a genuine hug. When the real Jesus is presented for the first time by a respected and gifted leader, the response of a youthful audience is usually dramatic. When young people realize that they and their friends have been invited to a love affair called the Eucharist (or the Lord's Table, Holy Communion, the Mass or Divine Liturgy), and when they feel that love all around them, they will respond dramatically and faithfully.

Communion allows us to reenact, to taste, to participate in divine victory and hope. It is crucial for young people to hear the whole story of our theology, the good news of Jesus Christ, and to celebrate this fully in their communities of faith. Many have become bored by constant repetition of favored select portions of the drama (just, for instance, "We're sinners, but Christ died for us"). Therefore, we review and repeat the grand story *from beginning to end*. Then the story with its ancient acclamation, "Christ has died, Christ is risen, Christ will come again," is dramatized in the way the story is told to, modeled to, and received by teen-agers—and by all of us who love drama.

Applying the Story

God's story must become real and exciting, not only to young people, but to their families as well. We are no longer thinking of youth ministry in a vacuum, sepa-rated from families, but as a holistic ministry. There are three levels of stories in the Bible—first the overarching story of God's wonderful works, then stories of people-groups, families, cities, nations, and ethnicities, and finally (and especially important for young people) the stories of individual lives.

You are looking, then, at youth ministry, life, and theology in terms of three stories as mediated from outside and within: your own story; the story of your culture, family, and friends; and the grand story that shapes your faith and brings you to this study. In youth ministry, you are focusing on the stories of your students shaped by cultural stories and their Creator and Redeemer's story. The grand story (the gospel) you share with young people is an expression of your holistic theology.

If this book proves useful, it must travel. And in traveling it will encounter many different theologies—as you will in your ministry. The diversity of today's theologies, to the sorrow of many, differs from the more general consensus of the early fathers[35] in the church's first centuries and in their passionate concern for their Lord. I urge you to take time to ponder this.

Theological Low Points

I think the hearts of most young people are ecumenical. Our most intimate look into the heart of Jesus Christ is in reading his prayer to the Father in John 17. There, Christ prays for the way we do theology, the way we are church, the way we practice youth ministry. He prays that we might be protected—and it is worth-while to consider how we need to be protected *from the world* these days. Then Christ's concern for us, as expressed to the Father, is twofold. First, Christ prayed that we might be kept holy (or sanctified) in the truth, the truth of God's Word (John 17:17). The second petition for us is repeated *four times*: "that they may

---

35. "The Church, though dispersed throughout the whole world . . . has received from the apostles and their disciples this faith . . . as if occupying but one house. She also believes these points (of doctrine) just as if she had but one soul . . . and she proclaims them, and teaches them, and hands them down, with perfect harmony." Irenaeus (2nd century), *Against Heresies*, 1.10, in Roberts and Donaldson, *Ante-Nicene Fathers*, 1:330, 331. Of course, there were always dissenters.

be one, as we [Father] are one . . . that they may all be one . . . that they may be one, as we are one . . . that they may become completely one, so that the world may know that you have sent me" (John 17:11b, 21a, 22, 23).

On this unity hinges, according to Christ, how the world will respond to the gospel—how young people will be drawn to, or repelled from, youth ministry and church. "They will know we are Christians by our love."

To many, the Christian church seems to be stuck theologically between two tragedies: heresy and schism. You are challenged to decide how large and broad a tent the church of Christ, and consequent youth ministries, should be. I hope youth ministry can be broader than the church proper, that youth ministry might bring about collaborations among different churches. How do we navigate among all the historic streams of theology flowing around us and confusing young people? What are the boundaries of truth that include believers and should exclude un-believers and heretics? Whether we like and admit it or not, there are, and have to be, boundaries.

Youth ministry has usually avoided this matter. Better to assume our different denominational traditions and proceed to our practical ministry. This has stifled theological inquiries, though. Amy Jacober observes that youth ministers have "seemed to have a mystical ability to transcend controversial divisions, denomi-national litmus tests, and personal preference in the name of collaborating with others who love God and teenagers as much as they do . . . leaving theological convictions necessarily shallow. . . . Too often, tradition-defining doctrinal posi-tions are abandoned in the name of collaboration."[36] She goes on, urging a balance between necessary convictions and healthy compromise. For your own sake and for those you teach, you must decide how to traverse our present theological landscape.

From the beginning the unity of the Christian church was tested by both her-esies and schisms. The apostles and apostolic fathers faced errors such as legalistic Judaism, gnosticism, docetism, and Arianism. As one can see from the previous footnote on Irenaeus, the church of the first few centuries was very conscious of its catholic[37] unity. Most church history scholars affirm that these early centuries almost providentially provided tests of orthodoxy and unity for the rest of time. Our creeds came from the challenges of heresy. The Apostles' Creed in various forms was apparently used as a basis for early baptismal catechism. The Nicene Creed, formulated to defeat heresy, sets boundaries for us in four key beliefs:

We believe in one God, the Father, the Almighty, maker of heaven and earth. . . .

36. Amy Jacober, *The Adolescent Journey: An Interdisciplinary Approach to Practical Youth Ministry* (Downers Grove, IL: InterVarsity, 2011), 17.
37. *Catholic* is the term early church leaders used for the universal and apostolic church.

> We believe in one Lord, Jesus Christ, the only Son of God . . . incarnate . . .
> crucified . . . risen . . . ascended. . . .
>
> We believe in the Holy Spirit, the Lord, the giver of life. . . .
>
> We believe in one, holy, catholic and apostolic church.

Most Christians in the world accept these statements as theological boundaries expressing a basis for unity—and avoidance of perilous heresies or divisions that weaken the gospel of Jesus Christ. Some will choose the Bible alone (*sola scriptura*) as ultimate authority. Others understand the Bible as originating in, and being canonized by, the church—and therefore coming to us through church tradition. All thinking Christians believe the Bible must be interpreted *and* recognize the fact that Bible believers differ strongly as to its interpretation—on at least what may be considered issues of secondary importance. All in all, it seems fair to say most Christians in the world accept Scripture, tradition, and reason illumined by the Holy Spirit as authoritative sources of Christian truth and unity. Various traditions put different emphases on this threefold authority, but our loyalty to ancient creeds provides a theological base.

After centuries of *relative* unity there came a sad schism between Eastern and Western churches—for reasons seemingly picayune to observers not familiar with the cultures, egos, and church politics of that time. Later came the Reformation, quickly splintering into many diverse churches. English Anglicans killed Catholics, Catholics killed Anglicans, and Cromwell's Puritans killed them both. In the seventeenth century, the Synod of Dort (Dutch Reformed Church) vilified and expelled the followers of Jacob Arminius (the Arminians) for believing that Christ died for the sins of the whole world (rather than just the elect) and that humans possess the power of free choice in response to the gospel. Bitter arguments since that time have erupted over even lesser points of doctrine. Divisions continue; there are now more than forty-two thousand *different* Christian denominations globally,[38] and with contentious divisions and litigations within denominations! The scandal is obvious to the world and to most people of faith.

Youth Ministry's Theological Challenge

The challenge of youth ministries, a small part of Christ's body, is to pray and work for truth and unity, to ameliorate differences, to work in collaborations as broad as possible, and to be on the side of theological peacemaking while

---

38. Todd M. Johnson, David B. Barrett, and Peter F. Crossing, "Christianity 2011," *International Bulletin of Missionary Research* 35, no. 1 (January 2011): 28–29, see table titled "Status of Global Mission, 2011."

keeping our boundaries intact. In this we would do well to remember biblical creeds: "Hear, O Israel: the LORD is our God, the Lord alone" (Deut. 6:4). "Simon Peter replied, 'You are the Christ, the Son of the living God'" (Matt. 16:16 ESV). Thomas responded to Jesus, "My Lord and my God!" (John 20:28). These are unifying creeds.

Theology outlines the gospel we share with young lives. This good news presents Jesus Christ at the center of the biblical story and in the midst of our personal and cultural stories. Christ leads us to the Father and promises the Holy Spirit, gathering us into faith communities to model and bear witness to God's coming kingdom—with power to break through all false news, all the lies and bondage of the world, the flesh, and the devil. The grand story converges with our stories and the story of the church. In Christ, and in the power of the Holy Spirit, we may suffer but will overcome, we may often lose but will eventually gain, we may stumble and doubt but will be upheld by our Lord above and by a faithful community around us. Sowing God's justice, we will reap God's peace.

Christian martyr Jim Eliot reminded us before his death: "He is no fool who gives what he cannot keep to gain what he cannot lose."[39] African American evangelist and prophet Tom Skinner expressed his Christian hope this way: "I would rather be involved and fail at something that is eventually going to succeed than be involved and succeed at something that is eventually going to fail."[40] Such eschatological hope is the basis for our theological persistence—it is the "not yet" that drives our "already."

Questions for Reflection and Discussion

1. Do you see this chapter as providing a broad summary of your theology?
2. What is your main question or criticism of this chapter?
3. What do you consider personally and frankly to be your main theological questions or difficulties?
4. Is the good news you share with young people a summary of your theology?
5. Do you believe young people need to hear the good news of the gospel (God's loving creation) first, before the "bad news" (our sinfulness)?
6. Do you agree that the story of Jesus Christ is the keystone of the biblical story but that people need and deserve to hear the whole of it?

39. Jim Elliot, *Daily Christian Quote*, September 28, 2001, www.dailychristianquote.com/dcqelliotjim.html.
40. I heard this from Tom Skinner in the late 1960s—and since it has been affirmed by others as his words.

7. Has God given us biblical stories as part of a great story before rules and specific instruction? In other words, do you see the biblical narrative (God's stories) taking precedence over theological propositions?

8. Is there any part of the daily news, of current music and entertainment, of business and politics, or of school and social life to which theology does not apply?

—5—

From General Theology to Practical Theology for Youth Ministry

They will call upon me, but I will not answer; . . . because they hated knowledge and did not choose the fear of the LORD. . . . For the Lord gives wisdom. . . . Then you will understand righteousness and justice and equity, every good path.

PROVERBS 1:28–29; 2:6A, 9

See to it that no one takes you captive through philosophy and vain deceit, according to human tradition . . . and not according to Christ. For in him the whole fullness of deity dwells bodily, and you have come to fullness in him.

COLOSSIANS 2:8–10

Abide in me as I abide in you. Just as the branch cannot bear fruit by itself, unless it abides in the vine, neither can you unless you abide in me . . . because apart from me you can do nothing.

JOHN 15:4, 5B

The Nature of Practical Theology

Practical theology seeks God's perspective on our world, the lives of young people, and the growing kingdom of heaven in and among us. Practical theology uses, but should not lose itself in, hermeneutics and cultural studies. It remembers our starting point, that apart from abiding in Christ and without the mind of Christ we are at a loss in figuring out the lives of young people and their culture. Practical theology brings general theology (doxological, biblical, historical, and systematic) into our real world. It works within paradoxes—between the heavenly and worldly, between the ideal and actual, between our highest aspirations and our deepest fears. Practical theology is needed because we, and all around us, are caught in our individual and systemic dysfunctions (in families, education, economics, and politics). Facing the bad news of this world, we aspire for justice and peace.

It's sad that God's call to submission and surrender is sometimes restricted to revival services. Deuteronomy and the Pentateuch call God's people to submit all their individual and corporate lives to the covenant and God's commands—as do the Psalms (especially Psalm 119), Proverbs, and the Prophets. Surrender to Jesus Christ as Lord is a dominant theme of the New Testament. Submission is not just for our "spiritual" lives; it is the starting point for all of life and all aspects of our search for meaning. All practice and theories begin best with the surrender of our senses and critical faculties to God's gracious mediation and enlightenment. It continues as we allow God's light to shine on all aspects of our citizenship in this world and God's kingdom. Practical theology is a call to repent from self- and human-centeredness in order to find truth, justice, and peace in God.

We are again reminded that theology begins in relationships—with God and with others. The Eucharist or Lord's Supper entails a grand relational cycle: communally, we offer ourselves, our love, our service at the altar to our Lord. Our offerings of ourselves and our best—like the bread and wine of the Last Supper—are blessed. We receive Christ's body and blood,[1] a tangible image of our participation in the divine nature, enabling us to face life's challenges in the power of the Holy Spirit. We bring to Communion our selves and firstfruits; we receive in Communion a taste of the future kingdom; we take from Communion what we need for our daily work, and from its fruits the cycle continues.

Practical theology seeks the meaning of God's presence in, and revealed will for, contemporary societies—God's Word for the world. After studying the life of Jesus Christ in first-century Palestine, we imagine Christ (the human, but not just the human side of Jesus) in our world today. We bring the issues of our lives and those for whom we care, the situations of our youth groups and churches, our neighborhoods, and our world into the presence of God. The goal of practical

---

1. In whatever sense we take this, for our Lord Jesus Christ did indeed offer to his disciples his body and blood. And our Lord implied, as the apostle Paul took it (1 Cor. 11:23–26), that we continue this celebration until he comes again.

theology is transformation: individual and corporate, subjective and objective, dramatic or subtle.

We've seen the principles of hermeneutics interpreted somewhat differently by various scholars. So now we will find different perspectives and emphases in approaching practical theology. Ray Anderson has defined practical theology as "critical reflection on the actions of the church in the light of the gospel and Christian traditions." To his own, he adds Don Browning's definition: "the reflective process which the church pursues in its efforts to articulate theological grounds of practical living in a variety of areas such as work, sexuality, marriage, youth, aging, and death."[2] (It's always good to read such definitions more than once.)

Practical theology draws on theological truth and the wisdom of this world as found in the social sciences and cultural and media studies. Christian practical theology should remember its starting point and believe that all truth is God's truth. It accepts "the wisdom of this world" as profitable, but recognizes its prevailing anthropocentricities (human-centeredness) and egocentricities (self-centeredness). Submission to God's gracious revelation ameliorates our autonomous attempts at truth. Part of doing theology is determining how various methodologies and sources (texts) may deny or undermine the Creator's explanations and admonitions.

How do we get it right—when there is so much disagreement among the wise of this world and among Christian thinkers? We've already asserted the importance of a foundation where God's gracious presence meets open human hearts. We've considered it crucial to build our various theories and ministries on the foundation of the revealed Christ. The problem, and some of the fun and frustration, of thinking theologically and culturally comes from the fact that we don't all agree. Reading and listening to the debates, there seems to be a lack of explicit acknowledgment and use of the *key*.

Our basic assumption here, the starting point of this book, is locating that key, not in our minds, but *in our hearts*. The fear of the Lord is the beginning of knowledge, the beginning of wisdom and understanding. Such an assumption or starting point implies that cultural studies, and even theologies, can go astray or become irrelevant without that key.

Media and cultural studies, the social and physical sciences, and revisionist theologies come and go, change and reshape themselves. They seem to lack a fixed starting point, a basic assumption, the ability to supply satisfying truth and certainty. Such a starting point or key is either determined by us or received from our Creator, Revealer, and Redeemer. "Fools say in their hearts, 'There is

2. Ray S. Anderson, *The Shape of Practical Theology* (Downers Grove, IL: InterVarsity, 2001), 26; Don S. Browning, *Practical Theology and Theological Education* (New York: Harper & Row, 1983), 14.

no God'" (Ps. 14:1). God's revelation through sun, moon, and stars doesn't give logical scientists faith; the heart must receive a sense of the Creator (Ps. 19:1–6), and God's law accepted in a person's soul (Ps. 19:7–11). When those outside God's covenant community and God's Word do instinctively "what the Law requires," it is because God's truth is "written in their hearts" (Rom. 2:13–16). God's truth as *logos* enlightens everyone, but acceptance of the Son of God is a matter of the heart (John 1:1, 9, 12–13). This key to faith suggests we humble ourselves as children and seek God's perspective on our world, our lives, and our hopes. Such a starting point may be called "a basic assumption or presupposition," "trusting God," "a leap of faith," or "I believe in order to understand." Such an approach in a scientific age may sound murky. As already mentioned, a technical term for seeking God's face and vision is *spiritual* or *doxological theology*.[3] It begs its place before all other theological disciplines—and all scientific and philosophic endeavors. It makes meeting and hearing from God a necessary priority for all cultural and media studies, for ministry, and for life in general. It is a call to faithful worship.

There are many ways to approach cultural and media studies; let's begin simply with two contrasting approaches. We might, on the one hand, accept with most scholarship that humans are left on their own to figure out how they perceive, how they attach meaning and significance to what they see and hear, and what theories can be deduced from such experience. From there we could take these theories and apply them to theology, church, and youth ministry. Using the principles of worldly wisdom we can try to work our way toward a Christian viewpoint. The brilliance of this analysis may seem satisfactory to many, but such methods remain necessarily subjective and produce only relativistic conclusions.

Or we can, on the other hand, accept the fact that a self-revealing, Triune God has created and revealed to us a correspondence between our loving hearts and our Creator's, our minds and truth, a correspondence between the real world (and what we see of the real world) and our deep sense of meaning, justice, and purpose. This does not mean we possess absolute truth but that, by faith and understanding, we follow the God of absolute truth made immanent in Scripture and in Jesus Christ the Revealer (Heb. 1:1–3). Having been given a divine meta-narrative, we begin to make sense of all our stories. There is now objectivity and certainty about our theologizing.

Theologian John Milbank, who displayed the hidden assumptions of science and cultural studies, put it this way:

> Theology itself purports to give an ultimate narrative, to provide some ultimate depth of description, because the situating of oneself within such a continuing

---

3. *Spiritual* or *doxological theology* is theology through worship and contemplation. *Lex orandi lex credendi* might be roughly translated, "we believe what we realize in worship."

narrative is what it means to belong to the Church, to be a Christian. . . . The *logic* of Christianity involves the claim that the "interruption" of history by Christ and his bride, the Church, is the most fundamental of events, interpreting all other events.[4]

Let's be quick to acknowledge how such a philosophical and theological method can itself be deconstructed and debunked. First of all ("they" will say), in spite of modern and postmodern critical thought, you are *wishing yourselves* truth, certainty, and security. Second, the deep divisions and differences among you who claim such revelation prove the uncertainty of faith methods claiming objective revelation with authoritative certainty. Finally, if you think you can take such faith claims and certainty to young people today, you must be radically out of touch.

Our only response to such objections is a reliance upon the *power* of God's story—within, and historically beyond, the biblical narrative. As the apostle Paul writes, "I am not ashamed of the gospel; it is the power of God for salvation to everyone who has faith" (Rom. 1:16). If the goal of practical theology is transformation, then, by our fruits, the world will identify us and evaluate the claims of our message. These are the basic assumptions of our practical theology; we go on to consider its application and praxis.

Help from Masters of Practical Theology

It would be presumptuous for me, or any of us, to think we can construct our own practical theology without reference to the important foundation that has been laid over the past quarter of a century or so. Don Browning has been called the father or architect of practical theology and the creator of a new genre of theology. Drawing on various streams of theology, Browning sees theology as based in practical reason. His book *A Fundamental Practical Theology: Descriptive and Strategic Proposals* proposes five dimensions (or levels) of practical reasoning, which in the examination of ministry will yield descriptive theology. These dimensions tend to draw on respective social sciences: the *Visional* (cultural anthropology), *Obligational* (social anthropology), *Tendency-Need* (psychology), *Environmental-Social* (ecology/sociology), and *Rule-Role*.[5] Browning uses these dimensions to analyze three different churches. His closing chapter describes how the five dimensions can bring about moral transformation: "Transformation is a multidimensional process following the five dimensions of practical reasoning."[6]

4. John Milbank, *Theology and Social Theory: Beyond Secular Reason* (Oxford, UK: Blackwell, 2006), 253, 390.

5. Donald S. Browning, *A Fundamental Practical Theology: Descriptive and Strategic Proposals* (Minneapolis: Fortress, 1991, 1996), x, 111.

6. Ibid., 280.

Ray S. Anderson attempts to give practical theology a more biblical and dynamic theological foundation and approach.[7] He brings a christopraxis center and trinitarian framework to Browning's useful paradigm of theology's basic movements. Anderson compares modern and postmodern philosophies in terms of the biblical story. He further discusses the church and its ministries, theological ethics, and pastoral care from the standpoint of God's supernatural historical intervention in the incarnation, Christ's death and resurrection, and the gift of the Holy Spirit to the church. He has a strong prophetic and pastoral heart.

Richard Osmer draws from the work of Browning, Chuck Gerkin, and Hans van der Ven.[8] Like Browning and Anderson, Osmer seeks to clarify the thought of many current secular thinkers and theologians, and to use principles from these other fields of knowledge to complement the work of theology. "In short, theology listens to and learns from other fields. But it transforms their insights according to the rules of its own theological grammar."[9] Unlike most other approaches, which move from theology to ministry, Osmer's *Practical Theology* begins in ministry and moves from practice to Christian theology.

Osmer provides four key questions to unravel complex issues in ministry. They seem simple and can be taken rather superficially yet helpfully. Taking these questions deeper, however, demonstrates the necessity and benefit of practical theology:

1. What is going on?
2. Why is this going on?
3. What ought to be going on?
4. How might we respond?[10]

Take a moment to consider some specific problem in your ministry. Imagine some wise person coming alongside you to think through the difficulty. Can you see how, using the four questions above, you ought to be able to see some lesson, or gain benefit, from almost any problem?

Osmer goes on to describe four tasks or perspectives that enlighten each of the four questions above. In each of these tasks, Jesus Christ serves as supreme exemplar.

1. The Descriptive-Empirical Task: Priestly Listening
2. The Interpretive Task: Sagely Wisdom

7. Anderson, *Shape of Practical Theology*.
8. Richard R. Osmer, *Practical Theology: An Introduction* (Grand Rapids: Eerdmans, 2008), viii.
9. Ibid., 169.
10. Ibid., 4.

3. The Normative Task: Prophetic Discernment
4. The Pragmatic Task: Servant Leadership

You might pause to reflect on the way Osmer's four tasks deal with his four questions, and then, how Christ demonstrated these roles. Finally, consider how you can use this process in your ministry. Further study of Osmer's text can help us reflect theologically on our ministry.

Another helpful book, *The Theological Turn in Youth Ministry*, comes from two important leaders in youth ministry and practical theology—Kenda Creasy Dean and Andrew Root.[11] Their book describes the past demeaning of youth ministry through uncritical use of entertainment and instruction. True relationships with young people, who are discovering who they are in the midst of life's ambiguities and suffering, will reveal our need for a rich theology to answer their deep questions. It will also demonstrate the church's need for youth's prophetic passion.

Practical theology for Dean begins in practice. "Practical theology is . . . reflection on Christian life. . . . Practical theology studies those moments, contexts, situations and practices in which God's action intersects with our actions, and transforms paltry human effort into something holy and lifegiving."[12] Insightfully, Dean sees adolescent identity formation as a search for meaning and salvation. Youthful questions prophetically inspire the church, and their passion is a challenge and rebuke to a church too absorbed in self-preservation.[13]

Root also stretches youth ministry's theological boundaries in a rich and thoughtful way. His hermeneutics and method of theologizing have produced guidelines and issues that need serious discussion in youth ministry circles. With Dean, he believes practical theology begins in ministry itself—for God *is* the Great Minister. We join the divine encounter with human suffering. Ministry leads theology through experience, reflection, and action. Theology cannot act alone; it must be interdisciplinary operating between the norms of scriptural/theological tradition on one side, and social science and communal experience on the other.

Root encourages our use of relevant theological voices, which he calls "theological companions." Feeling the suffering in his own youth and in that of young friends, he begins with the crisis of human existence. His resulting crisis theology finds theological companions such as Søren Kierkegaard, Karl Barth, Dietrich Bonhoeffer, and Douglas John Hall. Root also finds reference to existential crisis in the theology of Martin Luther—and more particularly, in Luther's striking theology

11. Andrew Root and Kenda Creasy Dean, *The Theological Turn in Youth Ministry* (Downers Grove, IL: InterVarsity, 2011).
12. Ibid., 17.
13. See also Kenda Creasy Dean, *Practicing Passion: Youth and the Quest for a Passionate Church* (Grand Rapids: Eerdmans, 2004).

of the cross. Youth ministers enter the place where human angst and absurdity are met by divine intervention. Following the way of Christ, the way of the cross, we enter the existential line of tragedy and death with one another. This is the area of christopraxis, ministry between our tragic existence and eschatological hope.

As theology begins with human crisis, its attempt to understand God involves a dialectical method breaching the divide between infinite and finite, the transcendent, unknown God and the works and words of God in our story. A dialectic of faith and truth-building is a result of life's paradoxes between being and nonbeing, God's hidden transcendence and immanent unveiling, and the objectivity and the subjectivity of our faith. Young people need to be aware of both the hiddenness and unveiling of God.

Root describes four methodological approaches to practical theology. He labels the first "neo-Aristotelian." The practical life is good in itself and beneficially contributes to the health of the community (both faith and larger secular communities). "Dorothy Bass and Craig Dykstra have been two of its greatest proponents, reflecting deeply on the practices of communities as *the* task of practical theology."[14] In *Practicing Passion* Kenda Creasy Dean richly places youth ministry within a neo-Aristotelian perspective.

> (Although) Dean is adamant about the independant and dynamic activity of God . . . (she) turns to human action, believing the church can reignite its passion by reviving its practices, thereby inviting young people to practice their passionate faith in an accepting community.[15]

The second methodology, "Critical social theory," draws on early Marx and others who focus on unjust social systems. Sensing the oppressive aspects of fallen systems, youth ministry writers like David White[16] (and Michael Warren,[17] though not mentioned by Root) use historical critique and cultural studies to point out the social quandary of adolescents in this late capitalistic age. Church and youth are called to discern oppressive systems and to radically address adverse social structures for positive change.

A third perspective for Root is "pragmatism." Pragmatists are similarly aware of oppressive social systems but judge them to be not entirely evil. They call for education and reformation rather than "revolution." Christian pragmatists see challenging the system as a gospel imperative. "One of the greatest *implicit* pragmatist

14. Root and Dean, *Theological Turn*, 223.

15. Ibid., 223.

16. David F. White, *Practicing Discernment with Youth: A Transformative Youth Ministry Approach* (Cleveland: Pilgrim, 2005).

17. Michael Warren, *Youth, Gospel, Liberation* (New York: Harper & Row, 1987).

thinkers may be Chap Clark. His work has a significant ethical dimension. . . . He sees youth ministry working to 'right wrongs. . . .' For Clark then, the job of the youth worker is to help young people act in a manner congruent with the Bible so that they might, in their individual lives and for the good of society, glorify God."[18]

Finally, Blair Bertrand (taking over the writing of Root and Dean's postscript) places Root in the position of a "Kierkegaardian," the book's fourth perspective or methodological approach.

> Kierkegaard believed that his perspective followed the tradition of Luther, who saw human action as an impossibility to save itself, and sought for God, the very activity of God, in and through impossibility (the cross) as our hope. Therefore, Kierkegaard contends that divine and human action are completely distinct, one in heaven and the other on earth. The only action the human agent can take is to face the abyss, to admit the impossibility of action and, in the midst of the impossibility, to trust in the utterly absurd. . . . Therefore, the only action possible from the human side is the action . . . of faith; it is to trust in God's action in the midst of the futility of human action. . . . Andrew Root . . . draws on the words of Dietrich Bonhoeffer to tease out what it means to be in relationship with another human being in light of the absurdity of the human condition.
>
> Following Kierkegaard, Root contends human action is an impossibility; it cannot be a means of transformation or salvation . . . that adolescents are awakening to the existential state of their existence—awakening to the tragic core of human existence—and seeking to discover who they are next to impossibility and limitation. Yet, unlike a strictly Kierkegaardian perspective . . . Root still believes that humans need to act . . . action that reveals and dwells in impossibility . . . that unveils what we already know: that we are stuck and that death is operative in our lives. This action of articulating and facing a reality of impossibility, Root contends, is where divine and human action associate. When we invite young people to face their impossibility, the God of the cross encounters them.[19]

Quotations and reviews never do justice to original writers, and this summary misses the contribution of Douglas John Hall to Root's practical theology. If Root's theology sometimes seems too pessimistic and dark, even though corresponding to so much of our experience, the optimism and brightness of Kenda Creasy Dean serves to balance Root's analysis.

Questions will remain for youth ministers to discuss. Does practical theology begin in experienced ministry or in prayer and adoration (doxological theology): "Our Father in heaven, hallowed be your Name"? In this theology do the dilemmas of our present existence tend to overshadow youthful positive exuberance

---

18. Root and Dean, *Theological Turn*, 230, 232.
19. Ibid., 233–34.

and history's highs and lows? Are the negative aspects of our present struggles and anxieties emphasized to the exclusion of life's joys and successes? Are we taken to the cross without a chance to scan nature's wonder: "The heavens are telling the glory of God; and the firmament proclaims his handiwork. . . . Their voice goes out through all the earth, and their words to the end of the world" (Ps. 19:1, 4)? May young people working to change their world and their neighborhoods be discouraged by the impossibility of it all? Might youth workers, who don't understand Hegel, Heidegger, Kierkegaard, and Douglas John Hall, become discouraged with meager efforts to share their lives and influence those for whom they care—or feel that their efforts to attract and instruct youth in rather traditional ways are demeaned?

We academic practical theologians are asking and attempting to respond to these questions so that youth ministry may be deepened and enriched. We hope we are being humbled in this task. It is also our responsibility to make our work a joint effort with practitioners and youth themselves. Additionally, we must take seriously the whole sweep of theology, ecclesiology, and missiology.

Jeremy Thomson, national leader of the Oasis College Youth Work and Ministry course in the United Kingdom (UK) provides another challenging and helpful practical theology. His theology proceeds from a house church perspective (influenced by Australian theologian Rob Banks) and from his Anabaptist persuasion (he acknowledges the influence of James McClendon). Thomson explains the crucial difference between youth work and youth ministries. He works carefully from Scripture as his theological foundation, beginning with distinctions drawn from the patristic writings and tracing difficulties arising from the Constantinian church/state arrangement and any notion of a universal invisible church.

Thomson has studied and is well acquainted with a broad spectrum of theologies; he concludes: "The notion that there is just one 'correct' theological system or philosophical approach to theology is historically naive. There is no neutral standpoint from which a detached presentation of various positions can be made, although it is important to be as fair as possible in presenting others' views."[20] Reading other theologies has made Thomson "very conscious that I also come from a particular tradition and witness to a minority Christian viewpoint."[21]

The final chapter and last few pages of his book, *Telling the Difference*, suggest that "some proposals for helping youth workers develop theologically begin by encouraging critical interaction with films, music, TV programmes, sub-cultural icons and other accessible cultural elements familiar to young people."[22] Reacting

20. Jeremy Thomson, *Telling the Difference* (England: YTC Press, 2007), 17.
21. Ibid.
22. Ibid., 282–83.

to what he sees as an over-participation in popular culture, Thomson encourages more effective faith development in family and house church discussions. Thomson leaves readers with this important question: "How can we nurture the critical skills that are necessary to help churches and young people become theologically alert?"[23]

Practical Theology of Popular Culture

What some of these well-recognized texts of practical theology have missed or minimized is theology's responsibility for interpreting popular culture. Kevin Vanhoozer and colleagues have produced a work of cultural and media literacy from a Christian viewpoint titled *Everyday Theology*. It fills the pop cultural void without calling itself practical theology. Vanhoozer rather speaks of "every day theology . . . faith seeking understanding of every day life."[24] This text follows work done by John Wiley Nelson, Steve Lawhead, William Romanowski, Quentin Schultze, Walt Mueller, Pete Ward, myself, and others.[25] *Everyday Theology* considers the nature of culture and conflicting viewpoints as to how culture and media are to be interpreted. Chapter titles illustrate this book's discussions of pop culture: "Despair and Redemption: A Theological Account of Eminem," "Between City and Steeple: Looking at Megachurch Architecture," "Swords, Sandals, and Saviors: Visions of Hope in Ridley Scott's *Gladiator*," and "Welcome to Blogosphere."[26]

Pete Ward holds a significant place in the field of youth ministry and practical theology—especially in the UK, but globally as well. His many books reflect a keen understanding of cultural studies. Ward identifies himself as having experienced evangelical conversion and charismatic blessing. His particular passion for youth outside the church and the faith has brought him to cross-cultural insights from works such as those of Charles Kraft. He also admits strong influence from Eastern Orthodox patristic writers (with their emphasis on Christian theosis or

---

23. Ibid., 288.

24. Kevin J. Vanhoozer, Charles A. Anderson, and Michael J. Sleasman, eds., *Everyday Theology: How to Read Cultural Texts and Interpret Trends* (Grand Rapids: Baker Academic, 2007), 17.

25. John Wiley Nelson, *Your God Is Alive and Well and Appearing in Popular Culture* (Philadelphia: Westminster, 1976); Stephen R. Lawhead, *Turn Back the Night: A Christian Response to Popular Culture* (Westchester, IL: Crossway Books, 1985); Quentin J. Schultze, Roy M. Anker, James D. Bratt, William D. Romanowski, John W. Worst, and Lambert Zuidervaart, *Dancing in the Dark: Youth, Popular Culture and the Electronic Media* (Grand Rapids: Eerdmans, 1991); Walt Mueller, *Engaging the Soul of Youth Culture: Bridging Teen World Views and Christian Truth* (Downers Grove, IL: InterVarsity, 2006); Dean Borgman, *When Kumbaya Is Not Enough: A Practical Theology for Youth Ministry* (Peabody, MA: Hendrickson, 1997); Peter Ward, *Gods Behaving Badly: Media, Religion, and Celebrity Culture* (Waco: Baylor University Press, 2011).

26. Sidebars summarizing important "Book Links," "Toolkits," and "Reflections" are also helpful. Vanhoozer, Anderson, and Sleasman, *Everyday Theology*.

divinization[27]). With an eclectic style, he is a leading thinker in the movement called Fresh Expressions in the UK (what he has called the "Liquid Church," known in the United States as the Emergent movement). Along with the already mentioned *Youthwork and the Mission of God*, his *Participation and Mediation: A Practical Theology for the Liquid Church* is a most pertinent contribution to the field of practical theology. This book is a rich challenge to our thinking about popular culture and youth ministry. Ward offers a subtle challenge to previous practical theologies:

> The cultural study of a congregation, or the investigation of how faith develops, are not in and of themselves "theology." Neither should it be assumed that it is the judicious inclusion of systematic theology that makes practical theology "theology." Practical theology is theological because it is reflection. Reflection is the mediation of and a participation in the Trinitarian life of God. . . . In reflection practical theology becomes transforming participation in glory.[28]

Ward wants us to benefit from the insights of cultural studies. Mediation is obviously a crucial factor in our consideration of media—yet it is an elusive and complicated word and idea. Ward attempts to explain how we receive and reflect divine grace and glory, using scholars from Raymond Williams to Karl Barth to Athanasius.

I hope I'm interpreting Ward simply and correctly when I explain that no one has *immediately* seen God, the source of all being. We know God through a series of communications or mediations. These mediations are culturally conditioned; mediation has sometimes been called remediation—as the medium adds meaning in the transmission. God draws us to participation in the divine through Jesus Christ and the Holy Spirit, using the media of Scripture, the Eucharist or Communion, and contemplation within the Christian community.

Ward calls us to a more complicated working out of our faith than most have imagined it—as he explains:

> Theology is "theology" because it is a participation in God, and so mediation has a Trinitarian structure. Yet this patterning must be discerned in and by means of a reflective practice that is itself cultural. So mediation serves to "muddy the waters" and produce a practical theology that is without guarantees.[29]

27. *Divinization* is the general idea that God became man so that man might become God, in Irenaeus, Athanasius, and others. Biblically, it's the idea that believers are one in Christ, partakers of the divine nature.

28. Pete Ward, *Participation and Mediation: A Practical Theology for the Liquid Church* (London: SCM, 2008), 104.

29. Ibid., 120.

This theology without objective absolutes or subjective certainty does not leave Ward in theological no-man's-land, but with real convictions about his relationship to his Lord and liquid church. Taizé[30] is the book's final example of a Christian community or church that is ecumenical, eclectic, and dynamic in the flow of life and the Spirit.

Your Responsibility as a Practical Theologian

As one who cares about young people, you are in God's sight a shepherd. As you study how culture is shaping young students, you need integrity of life (as a good model) and an inquiring mind (to lead discussions about the changes and challenges of culture). This calls for a theological foundation and professional skills. Seeking God's best for youth, and praying for our Father's kingdom and will to be done, is theological work. Godly shepherding assumes practical theology. Although not a scholarly theologian or cultural expert, you are a "practical" practical theologian—more in touch in many ways than we, your professors (Ps. 119:99).

Although our review of practical theologians in this chapter may have been tedious and confusing, hopefully you have gained some valuable perspectives and will take from this chapter these key questions of practical theology:

1. What's going on in the world these days?
2. What is God's perspective on our world?
3. What is God doing in the world these days?
4. What should I and my community be doing to fulfill the Lord's Prayer these days?

It is important to take what we can and move on. The rest of this book pursues practical or everyday theology—hopefully from the love of God, in the grace of Jesus Christ, and with the illumination of the Holy Spirit.

Questions for Reflection and Discussion

1. What makes the most sense to you in this chapter? With what do you take exception? What questions do you have, and how can they be answered?
2. Does it make sense to you that theology best begins in our hearts rather than in our minds—that we relate to God, in worship and contemplation, before being able to think rightly about our Creator and Redeemer?

30. Taizé is a famous monastic-style community in France—Catholic, Protestant, and ecumenical, liturgical in practice, using a unique style of music and chant.

3. If you do assent to these two questions, can you accept the paradoxical fact that all our thinking and receiving of truth is culturally mediated?

4. Do you agree that a lot of philosophy, cultural studies, and perhaps theologies themselves lack a sure sense of origin and destiny because they do not root themselves in a relationship with the Creator?

5. Why do you need to be able to explain these ideas to students? From what do you see them gaining their values and sense of purpose—and how important are values and purpose in clarifying an adolescent's identity?

PART 2

Theology of Persons

—6—

Theology of Growth and Development

And so, brothers and sisters, I'm sorry I couldn't speak to you as mature people, but rather as . . . infants. . . . I fed you with milk, not solid food, for you were not ready for solid food.

1 Corinthians 3:1–2a (author's paraphrase)

The boy Samuel and the boy Jesus grew in wisdom and stature and favor with God and people.

1 Samuel 2:26; Luke 2:52 (author's paraphrase)

The Importance of Growth in Culture

As a teenager and the oldest of eight siblings, I watched my mother's belly grow a number of times (and I watched with embarrassment because of kidding from my neighborhood friends). Within the space of two years, came my twin brothers, and then two more brothers—while I was still in high school! I learned to change the old cloth diapers, then to feed and burp the twins—at the same time, one in the crook of my arm, the other in the crook of my leg. My family and I watched each of them through various stages of growth.

Years later, in greater awe, I witnessed the births of my own four children and their amazing early growth. Later still, into our empty nest came our youngest daughter and her family (four children, eight years old to early infancy). I again witnessed the miracle of pregnancy, birth, and day-by-day growth—from grasping and sucking, to struggling to hold up her small head, to intermittently focusing her eyes, to the little smiles—at first, mere reflex or gas pains, and then, to our delight, her gradual recognition of our eager faces. It was the beginning of a smiling human relationship. Growth is surely God-ordained.

Humans grow as individuals, yet necessarily as social beings. Science demonstrates that a human creature cannot grow on its own. Theology explains our relational nature, our need for connection to the Creator, to the natural world, and to one another. God has put humans in cultures and in covenantal or relational contexts within societies. This chapter will examine the necessary contextual or cultural settings for human growth and flourishing.

Noting how *growth* and *culture* are interrelated, we bring theological perspective to both. In comparison to animals, human infants have very few instinctual abilities. Babies are very dependent and have to learn *everything*. Therefore it takes a culture to raise a child.

As mentioned above, Douglas Candland's fascinating study, *Feral Children and Clever Animals*, looks at children raised outside a human environment. Candland studied Peter the Wild Boy of Germany, Victor of France, Kaspar Hauser of Nuremberg, and especially Amala and Kamala of India.[1] The latter two were found living with wolves in a subterranean cave under an abandoned anthill and brought to the Rev. J. A. L. Singh. Their ages were estimated at about eight and two. At first they could not stand, walk, communicate, or be continent; they were like animals in every way. Raised and taught by wolves, these girls could only display the cultural behavior of animals until they were gradually taught limited and rudimentary human words and behavior. Candland, a professor of psychology and animal behavior, uses these cases to test the contemporary understanding of human intelligence. Human culture calls for the socialization of children by social systems including families, towns, schools, peers, media, internet, and more. Strikingly, without family and cultural support a child cannot walk or talk or behave as a human! Without human models and instruction, human babies are unable to think and act in a human fashion.

Human growth, then, is dependent on culture; the group comes before any individual human. But just as we tend to take *culture* for granted, so we glibly assume *growth*. Imagine the joy of a young family with a newborn child; everyone is beaming and eager to show off this beautiful newcomer. We enjoy and comment on its infant innocence. Then imagine coming back in several months or a year to

---

1. Douglas Keith Candland, *Feral Children and Clever Animals: Reflections on Human Nature* (New York: Oxford University Press, 1993), ch. 2.

a family incredibly sad because that cute little baby is in the same state and has evidenced no sign of growth.[2] Nature demands growth, and failure to grow is a tragedy! Continue hypothetically to imagine a young lobster trapped within a shell that won't shed. Consider how its flesh would become hardened and gnarled as its growth is restricted. That picture hints at what society is doing to many young people, emotionally and spiritually.

Science instructs us regarding human physical, emotional, cognitive, and social growth. Faith enlarges the picture as it looks at the awesome potential of the self for good or evil. Embedded in all persons is the image of the Creator, and that image seeks to fulfill divine intentions of relational growth, creativity, and reproduction.

We want to consider hindrances to growth seriously, as Jesus did when he pronounced woe on any who would cause a little one to stumble (Luke 17:2). This book takes seriously the stumbling blocks and the toxicity of culture hindering youthful human potential. Growth failure violates a basic law of nature.

> In the beginning . . . God created . . . vegetation: plants yielding seed . . . swarms of living creatures, . . . [to] be fruitful and multiply. . . . [And] God created humankind in his image . . . male and female he created them . . . and God said to them, "Be fruitful and multiply, and fill the earth and subdue it; and have dominion." (Gen. 1:1, 11, 20, 22, 27–28)

Can you conceive of this powerful scene without growth? Certainly implied in this beautiful landscape is God crying out to creation, "Grow, grow, grow!" Theologically we can imagine sin as a horrible restriction of growth, a desecration of God's intention for a healthy, growing creation. Fallen society produces retardation of all kinds, as well as unnatural cancerous growth.[3]

Many high school teachers and youth workers, and perhaps you yourself, find the challenge of life between puberty and adulthood so intriguing and complex that dealing with a larger framework than the classroom or youth group seems daunting. If we can keep students learning the task at hand (passing SATs or understanding a rudimentary gospel), that seems to be enough. When we are convinced that God is watching each student with a view to his or her whole life trajectory and potential, we are more holistically future-oriented. We begin with a God concerned about all the past frustrations and wounds that hinder one's

2. This is not to insinuate real examples of radical physical retardation, but imaginary zero growth.

3. From original perfection, over generations of perverted society, have come all manner of dysfunction and abnormal growth. This was not God's original and intentional will before evil entered creation. Parents and all who suffer and endure the consequences of any kind of dysfunction may be considered heroes and deserve communal support.

growth in life. We take time to deal, for instance, with an extremely quiet or excessively troublesome student. (In doing so who knows what future rampage we may prevent.)[4] From there we seek a clearer theology of growth and development. Doing justice to such a theological topic, as we've seen previously, requires both Scripture and social science.

Our theology of growth begins, as does all theology, in worship of the great unchanging Lord of all. God alone is—ultimately and beyond comprehension—*mature*. The Creator is the source and model of all growth and being. God is the great I AM, "as it was in the beginning, is now, and will be forever."[5] God is not just above and beyond us; God is at the core of our being and our growth potential. Worship *and* understanding call for awe and imagination before divine and cosmic mysteries. As with all theological mysteries, we experience God without complete comprehension. In worship, and participating in the divine, we are transformed—being grown into the image of God. Ultimately all growth is progress toward God and all lack of growth, a process of death and decay.

Real Life Growth and Development

How can we comprehend and apply the mysteries of human growth? Imagine yourself with a class or group of youth—hearts and minds eager for information about how humans grow. (One important aspect of youth ministry is getting them to a point of common eagerness.) Imagine having an expert embryologist come and talk to your students with a graphic and fascinating video of initial conception through all stages of uterine growth, culminating in an actual birth—the drama of conception, the intricacies of the blastula,[6] the dynamic growth of organ systems, and the climax of birth. Consider the possible implications of such a mystery—as well as appreciation for the very process of growth. (Besides lessons in human growth and potential, your students would be receiving some important sex education.)

4. Social scientists are concluding that some of the shooters are not necessarily "loners" but frustrated "joiners," longing to belong but unable because of mental/social issues. Katherine Newman, "Why we miss school shooting warning signs," *CNN.com*, February 28, 2012, www .globalpublicsquare.blogs.cnn.com/2012/02/28/school-shooting-warning-signs/. And Katherine Newman, *Rampage: The Social Roots of School Shootings* (New York: Basic Books, 2005).

5. From the liturgically often-repeated "*Gloria Patri*," the contemporary English version of the Latin: "Glory be to the Father, and to the Son, and to the Holy Spirit. As it was in the beginning is now and will be forever." The Greek Orthodox version concludes: "Both now and always, unto the ages of ages." And a Syrian version: "From everlasting and for ever and ever."

6. A *blastula* is "an early stage of animal or human development through which a zygote develops into an embryo, characterized by a fluid-filled sphere formed by a single layer of cells." *The Free Dictionary*, s.v. "blastula," www.medical-dictionary.thefreedictionary.com/blastula.

Then, we take our group to a newborn clinic where a psychologist explains how infant IQs are measured in the first twenty-four hours and first few weeks (response to sound, touch, and light) and explains recent and exciting research on infant brain development. A pediatric specialist describes infant ills and how they are treated—nature's remarkable resilience.

As a group, we spend some hours another day watching a nursery of one- to two-year-olds before discussing their behavior and developmental tasks—hand-eye coordination, their relationships with one another, their words (perhaps an emphatic "No!," "My," and "Mine"). Then, similarly, we observe a day care of two- to five-year-olds—growing mobility and dexterity, social skills, appreciation of stories, learning, and memory. Imagine what we've learned so far and how that might be extended with a morning among six- to eleven-year-old elementary students—in classrooms, cafeteria, and on playgrounds.

Now comes what is especially significant for us—imagining your group to be a class of college or seminary students. You and your group take all you have learned and observed so far, including a presentation on adolescent brain development, into a four-year secondary school (with permission from public or private school administrators). High school is more familiar ground, but ponder how recent experiences and discussions enable you to notice fundamental developmental tasks and behaviors differently. In classes and hallways, cafeteria, bathrooms, and outside, you note demonstrations of youth's development stage we often miss or take for granted—actions that suggest nuances of identity and relationship formation, impulsive behaviors, seeking or avoiding attention and touch, the use of defensive humor, and so much more. This series on human development could go on to discuss life after high school[7] through old age and death.[8]

(As part of this exercise you could ask your students to condense their findings and discussions to a one-page chart of human development and a second page of notes.)

Theories of Human Growth and Development

Imagine then that our seminar continues with a developmental professor's animated lecture on various theories of human development. With brief historical

---

7. This reminds me of the old but significant book by Ralph Keyes, *Is There Life after High School?* (Boston: Little, Brown, 1976)—and books with similar titles.

8. Paul Van Ness's film, "A Good Death" can produce a rich discussion of cancer at too young an age and the interface of medical science, health care, and faith and family support in the death of Howie Rich, a former Young Life leader, public school teacher, and pastor. See www.agooddeathdocumentary.com, accessed January 28, 2013.

background and references to mythology, Confucius and Aristotle, Locke and Rousseau, our compelling presenter gives a favorable, if slightly apologetic, explanation of Freud's Psychosexual Theory of human development. We hear about Erik Erikson, who studied under Freud's daughter, Anna, with her own idea of adolescent personality development. Erikson was also influenced by his own youthful experience, being taunted in a German school yard. As a teenager, he grappled with his real identity. Not content with "I am German . . . or Danish, a Jew . . . or a Gentile" (all true), he struggled with the issue of identity throughout his life. His mother was a Danish Jew in denial, his father a mystery never resolved. And, was he at heart an artist or a psychoanalyst? There is much more to Erikson's fascinating story, reminding us of the importance of autobiographical stories behind scientific and theological theories. Out of Erikson's adolescent struggles came his important emphasis on identity. He extends Freud's five stages of life, ending in adulthood, to his famous eight stages of human development—from cradle to grave.

Physiology, psychology, sociology—and perhaps anthropology—are all needed to grasp how a young person grows. Jean Piaget's cognitive-developmental theory, Albert Bandura's social learning theory, Lawrence Kohlberg's and Carol Gilligan's moral development theories, and James Fowler's stages of faith development all add important dimensions to our understanding of human growth. As Gilligan challenges male biases in developmental theory, so writers like Diane T. Slaughter and Jawanza Kunjufu provide insights regarding the growth of African American children.[9] More studies are needed among other ethnic groups (touching on unique problems in various Hispanic, African, and Asian American second and third generations, for instance). An important text looking at faith development from a scientific perspective is *The Handbook of Spiritual Development in Childhood and Adolescence.*[10]

Research psychologist Alison Gopnik has produced evidence that children, at a very early age, reason and come to moral decisions beyond the scope of Piaget's and Kohlberg's nicely ordered conclusions. Her studies observed infant discrimination between "nice" and "mean" persons and toys. Her book titles indicate the direction of her studies and conclusions: *The Scientist in the Crib: What Early Learning Tells Us about the Mind,* and *The Philosophical Baby: What Children's*

9. Carol Gilligan, *In a Different Voice: Psychological Theory and Woman's Development* (Cambridge: Harvard University Press, 1982); Diane T. Slaughter, *Black Children and Poverty: A Developmental Perspective* (San Francisco: Jossey-Bass, 1988); Jawanza Kunjufu, *Developing Positive Self-Images and Discipline in Black Children* (Chicago: African-American Images, 1984).

10. Eugene C. Roehlkepartain, Pamela E. King, Linda Wagener, and Peter L. Benson, eds., *The Handbook of Spiritual Development in Childhood and Adolescence* (Thousand Oaks, CA: Sage, 2006).

Minds Tell Us about Truth, Love, and the Meaning of Life.[11] We are left to ponder new riches in the words of Jesus: "Truly I tell you, whoever does not receive the kingdom of God as a little child will never enter it" (Mark 10:15). Such insights also increase our sorrow for those who, instead of experiencing childhood nurture, have suffered childhood abuse and neglect (see Luke 17:2). So far, we have combined research and theory, Scripture and imagination, in considering the nature and importance of human growth.

Adolescent Growth and Development

Understandably we don't remember the shock of leaving the womb for the outside world, or the "terrible twos and threes" as we began to claim our own place in the world. Less understandable is the way we forget one of life's biggest changes: trading in childhood for an adult body, mind, and soul. It's like stepping out of a cheap, aging, two-cylinder car, into a powerful new vehicle. The natural inclination for adolescents is to assume that their new bodies and emotions are *made to be tested*—sometimes to their limits.[12]

We know the age of puberty has declined over the last centuries to about ten to fourteen for girls and twelve to sixteen for boys. New studies provide insights into precocious puberty at even earlier years—and with attending problems.[13] Puberty can bring embarrassment or pride as swift hormonal and physical changes point toward adulthood. Early puberty in girls, and to a lesser extent boys, and late maturity for boys and girls can result in negative long-term consequences. Basic tasks at this stage of growth involve "dramatic changes in identity, self-consciousness and cognitive flexibility."[14]

We will continue to consider the important task of clarifying one's identity—a particularly noticeable aim for two-year-olds and teens. Here we are more interested in issues of overall human development.

Until the 1990s, we thought brains were pretty much developed by puberty, that high school students were quicker with facts, just slower on wisdom, or as

---

11. Alison Gopnik, Andrew N. Meltzoff, and Patricia K. Kuhl, *The Scientist in the Crib: What Early Learning Tells Us about the Mind* (New York: Harper Paperbacks, 2000); Allison Gopnik, *The Philosophical Baby: What Children's Minds Tell Us about Truth, Love, and the Meaning of Life* (New York: Farrar, Straus & Giroux, 2009).

12. Lynn E. Ponton, *The Romance of Risk: Why Teenagers Do the Things They Do* (New York: Basic Books, 1997).

13. "Precocious Puberty," *Kids Health*, Nemours website, www.kidshealth.org/parent /medical/sexual/precocious.html, accessed January 28, 2013.

14. Sarah-Jayne Blakemore and Suparna Choudhury, "Development of the Adolescent Brain: Implications for Executive Function and Social Cognition," *Journal of Child Psychology and Psychiatry* 47, no. 3/4 (Mar/Apr 2006): 296.

neurologist Frances Jensen describes previous notions, that "a teenage brain is just an adult brain with fewer miles on it."[15] But we now know better.[16]

Neurologists have found an early overproduction of the brain's gray matter (basic neuronal cells, the communication means of our brain and central nervous system) in infants, from latter months in the womb until about eighteen months. As the infant begins to observe, interpret, and develop language skills, junctions of neurons are formed to allow for effective functioning. A pruning effect also occurs, described as a "use it or lose it" principle. Brain potential not used tends to decline. Unused gray matter diminishes, which is why early childhood stimulation is so important.[17] And that is why early childhood, professionally run day care centers in disadvantaged neighborhoods are important—for the long-term life expectancies of such infants, for their communities, and for our entire society. This is a justice issue.

Research from the 1990s has established the fact of another growth spurt of gray matter beginning just before puberty. Important skills and abilities are developed with increased gray matter in the brain's frontal lobe. As with children, a similar overproduction of gray matter and pruning ("use it or lose it") are taking place in teenagers. Meanwhile, another important development is occurring with the brain's white matter. This white matter consists of long, wire-like fibers connecting the prefrontal cortex (the anterior "executive" functioning section of the frontal lobe) to other parts of the brain. A coating of myelin[18] insulates these fibers, making almost instant communications within the brain more efficient (as insulation of electric wires improves conductivity).[19] The pruning of frontal lobe functions and development of white matter is now known to go on throughout the teenage years and well into the twenties.

Teenagers, then, do not have *full capacity* of executive functions of the prefrontal cortex: reasoning, discrimination of emotions in themselves and others, planning, impulse control, delayed gratification, awareness of future consequences of immediate actions, determining clear paths to future goals.

---

15. Richard Knox, "The Teen Brain: It's Just Not Grown Up Yet," *National Public Radio*, March 1, 2010, npr.org/templates/story/story.php?storyid=124119468.

16. Researchers have been able to study the brain through autopsy microscopic exams, Magnetic Resonance Imaging (MRI, which reveals vivid pictures of the brain), and newer modalities such as Magnetic Resonance Spectroscopy and Positron Emision Tomography, which give functional information about neurotransmitters and centers of elevated brain activity (Matthew Borgman, MD, email to author, June 13, 2011).

17. See the work of Fraser Mustard and The Founders' Network, www.founders.net, such as *Early Years Study 3: Early Childhood Education Report* (2011).

18. *Myelin* is a white substance rich in lipid fats and proteins that sheaths or protects the long extensions of nerve cells called axons.

19. "The Teen Brain: Still Under Construction" fact sheet, National Institute of Mental Health, nimh.nih.gov/health/publications/the-teen-brain-still-under-construction/index.shtml, accessed March 12, 2013.

It's amazing to consider how God cares about cells and the cosmos, nations and sparrows, you and each detail of our students' lives. It's exciting when teenagers allow us to enter the challenge of physical and emotional growth with them. Our task in youth ministry and as theologians is to follow the research and integrate all we're learning from young people themselves and from other sources into our theological theory and practice. Blakemore and Choudhury's conclusion implies as much:

> The study of the development of executive function and social cognition beyond childhood is a new but rapidly evolving field with applications for medical diagnosis, education and social policy. In this paper, we have focused on research in developmental cognitive neuroscience, but a richer account of changes in adolescent learning, and strategic and social behaviour requires a multi-disciplinary approach that recognises the complex interactions between genetics, brain structure, physiology and chemistry and the environment.[20]

Nature, Nurture, and Differences

Advances in the cognitive sciences have placed new emphasis on early childhood development. (Studies have alternated between emphasis on *nature*—genes—and *nurture*—environmental care—in the matter of growth and development.) The work of neuroscientists like Lise Eliot (neuroscientist and mother of three) takes the Human Genome Project and its implications seriously but finds balance in evidence proving the amazing plasticity of the brain.

> Of course genes are important, but everyone who has ever studied nerve cells can tell you how remarkably plastic they are. The brain itself is literally molded by experience: every sight, sound, and thought leaves an imprint on specific neural circuits, modifying the way future sights, sounds, and thoughts will be registered. Brain hardware is not fixed, but living, dynamic tissue that is constantly updating itself to meet the sensory, motor, emotional, and intellectual demands at hand.[21]

Experienced and sophisticated youth workers also discover the reality of multiple intelligences and character and cultural issues in evaluating the growth of students and dropouts.

Not only urban and rural youth workers, and those in squalid sections of developing countries, but all of us should be informed and concerned about the shaping

20. Sarah-Jayne Blakemore and Suparna Choudhury, "Development of the Adolescent Brain," *Journal of Child Psychological Psychiatry* 47 (Mar/Apr 2006): 308.

21. Lise Eliot, *What's Going on in There? How the Brain and Mind Develop in the First Five Years of Life* (New York: Bantam Books, 1999), 4.

of a child in the womb, at birth, and during very early years.[22] Neural scientist Fraser Mustard and The Founders' Network in Canada have demonstrated the incredible difference it makes if parents and infants are guided into special sensory stimulation (looks, touch, sounds and words, etc.). Their international and longitudinal studies show how such care increases chances for educational success and diminishes teenage pregnancies, bullying, and aggressive behavior.[23] It is sad to see such studies overlooked, especially by urban workers and government planners. Consider the difference in mental stimulation between one child with an attentive father and mother, grandparents, siblings, professional day care, and schools with small classrooms, and another child, whose single mother is somehow working a full-time job, who is being "tended" by a nonprofessional busy neighbor and a TV, and who is headed for schools unable to do much teaching.

The Commission on Children at Risk (a panel of thirty-three leading children's doctors, neuroscientists, research scholars, and mental health and youth service professionals) drew on a comprehensive literature review and the evaluation of eighteen commissioned papers to produce a report that should be studied and discussed by all who are interested in relieving the distress of children and building positive character for a successful life.

> Science (and especially neuroscience) is increasingly demonstrating that the human person is hardwired to connect (hardwired for relationships). First . . . we are hardwired for close attachments to other people, beginning with our mothers, fathers, and extended family, and then moving out to the broader community. Second, a less definite but still definitive body of evidence suggests that we are hardwired for meaning, born with a built-in capacity and drive to search for purpose and reflect on life's ultimate ends.
>
> Primary nurturing relationships influence early spiritual development—call it the spiritualization of attachment—and spiritual development can influence us biologically in the same ways that primary nurturing relationships do. . . . Religiosity and spirituality significantly influence well-being. . . . The human brain appears to be organized to ask ultimate questions and seek ultimate answers.[24]

Brain functions that signify moral and spiritual growth in children and youth are being watched with brain imaging. The lessening of anxiety and antisocial

---

22. Consider the impact of declining marriage in the United States in Kay S. Hymowitz, *Marriage and Caste in America: Separate and Unequal Families in a Post-marital Age* (Chicago: Ivan R. Dee, 2007); W. Bradford Wilcox and Elizabeth Marquardt, eds., *State of Our Unions 2010: When Marriage Disappears: The New Middle America* (New York: Broadway Publications, 2011); and David Blankenhorn, *Fatherless America: Confronting Our Most Urgent Social Problem* (New York: Harper Perennial, 1996).

23. Fraser Mustard and The Founders' Network (www.founders.net).

24. Commission on Children at Risk, "Hardwired to Connect: The New Scientific Case for Authoritative Communities" (New York: Institute for American Values, 2003), 14–15.

behavior, and the increase in positive behaviors, are being recorded with scientific evidence. This report has coined a term, *authoritative communities* (not authoritarian), to describe environments with warmth and structure in which children and youth thrive. In terms of the growing crisis of "rising mental problems and emotional distress among U.S. children," this report acknowledges the importance of "at risk" models of special programs but suggests the greater importance of an "ecological model" dealing with environmental *causes* rather than just *symptoms*. Developing practical theology, with special concern for the young, continually points us toward social systems and holistic thinking.

Developmental theories have not always given adequate attention to the crucial influence of the primary systems around young people (family, community, school, peers, and media). Kurt Lewin's change theory not only describes three stages of learning—unfreeze-change-refreeze (the process of prior learning being replaced)—but suggests attention to the context of development and behavior.[25]

In terms of context, too little note has been given to the systems approach of Urie Bronfenbrenner, [26] which helps us understand that context. This renowned psychologist approached developmental study with systems thinking and a holistic perspective, developing an approach he called "ecological systems theory." His observations indicated the presence of cognitive development, along with physical and emotional dynamics, in the context of a person's immediate environment: the family, the neighborhood or community, school, peers, and religious institutions.[27]

These immediate social systems Bronfenbrenner called the *microsystem*. Global and national institutions, far removed from the young person, yet still affecting this person, are termed the *macrosystem*. The interaction of the larger and further removed social institutions with those persons and systems with which a child or youth is in immediate contact, are named the *mesosystem* (when the individual is present) and *exosystem* (when a person is not present to the interaction yet still affected by it). To these four systems, Bronfenbrenner later added a fifth, the *chronosystem*, to describe important change or evolution of systems over time. I consider the internal systemic operations of any particular individual important enough to be considered the *endosystem*. (Try, as you read all this, to select some broad and general pattern of principles you will use in ministry and in training others.)

25. www.change-management-coach.com/kurt_lewin.html.

26. Urie Bronfenbrenner, *The Ecology of Human Development: Experiments by Nature and Design* (Cambridge, MA: Harvard University Press, 2006). See also Bronfenbrenner, *Making Human Beings Human: Bioecological Perspectives on Human Development* (Thousand Oaks, CA: Sage, 2004).

27. I had been stressing the five primary growth contexts of young people for twenty some years without knowledge of Bronfenbrenner's 1979 text (reprinted in 2006). Nor did I know Bronfenbrenner was a cofounder of the US Head Start program for underprivileged children.

A Practical Theologian of Human Growth and Development

No other practical theologian has given such specific and deep attention to human growth and development as James Loder. Loder locates his analysis of human growth and development in the subspecies of theology called theological anthropology. To understand his profound work, one needs to read and reread Loder's *The Transforming Moment* and *The Logic of the Spirit*.[28] Loder works with two theological assumptions; he says, "The two classical doctrines central to any discussion of theological anthropology are the *image of God*, or human likeness to God, and *original sin*, or human distance from God."[29] He is well aware of other developmentalists but insists that the divine Spirit is not bound to classically formulated stages, that Spirit has its own logic.

Listen to Loder's eloquent words:

> We will work, rather [in contrast to other developmental theories] with development as an emergent resultant of the interaction between the person and her environment, with that interaction giving rise and shape to structural potentials within the personality. How do environments and persons interact to give rise to the personality?[30]
>
> I . . . propose to take theology, particularly the theology of the spirit, seriously as a way to assess and interpret scientific findings about human nature.[31]
>
> What is a lifetime . . . in a vast, apparently empty universe . . . and why do I live it . . . when time and space so far outreach our grasp? The answer . . . can only be grasped humanly as a total, existential response to the way in which the Creator Spirit takes and transforms the negation, the nothingness, the frightening abyss that pervades and haunts human development as a whole.[32]
>
> In each person the search is for a longing for the eternal intimacy of a love that may be grasped only unclearly and proleptically,[33] but nevertheless profoundly. . . . When the longing for that intimacy is satisfied in the Spiritual Presence of Christ, the Face of God, then answers to our basic questions may dawn on us . . . by returning ourselves to God, directly and through others in love. . . . As each life unfolds, gets torn open, stripped of its survival techniques and passing pleasures, and discovers

28. James Loder, *The Transforming Moment* (Colorado Springs: Helmers & Howard, 1989); and *The Logic of the Spirit: Human Development in Theological Perspective* (San Francisco: Jossey-Bass, 1998); as well as erudite commentary such as Dana R. Wright, ed., *Redemptive Transformation in Practical Theology: Essays in Honor of James E. Loder* (Grand Rapids: Eerdmans, 2004); and Eolene Boyd-MacMillan, *Transformation: James Loder, Mystical Spirituality, and James Hillman* (New York: Peter Lang, 2006) .

29. Loder, *Logic of the Spirit*, 109, emphasis added.

30. Ibid., 20.

31. Ibid., xiii.

32. Ibid., see book's cover, x, and 14.

33. *Proleptically* means with future anticipation.

itself as spirit, then it appears from under the surface that we have been created for nothing less than the pure love of God, whose universe is our home.[34]

More than any other, James Loder is the quintessential theologian of growth. Through interdisciplinary reflection, he studied the trajectory of human development, and he takes us deeply into the human spirit while reminding us of surrounding interconnected systems. Loder explains growth from human and transcendent perspectives. He accepts the necessity of divine initiating grace, the glory of the divine image in humankind, our wayward sinfulness, the analogy of the human spirit to the divine Spirit—and above all, the transforming power of that Spirit as the goal of human growth. Building on the work of Freud, Erikson, Piaget, and others, Loder describes the stages of human development from this spiritual perspective.

> When the fetus grows too large for the womb, it pushes out into the world and begins to forge its own definition of itself and of the world into which it has come. . . . Having grown too large for the space available at home, the young adolescent begins to move out to make room for herself, or at least to have a room of her own. . . .
>
> Adolescence is the first time anyone can ask . . . with some awareness of what is at stake, "What is a lifetime?" and "Why do I live it?"[35]

As a Christian neo-Freudian, Loder is interested in ego development from a theological perspective. The *ego* is seen as the self's integrating principle, interpreting and integrating our subconscious desires and restrictive cautions, attempting to regulate our inner lives in terms of external realities, and guiding us through life's perilous journey. Even in birth, and before the ego has been developed, the fetus faces the negation of separation from the womb's safety and threat of death.[36] As the child begins to understand parental "Nos," she may respond with her emerging ego's own "Nos." These may be reactive responses—not to be taken literally (as when a no to a meal does not mean she wants the meal to be taken away, or a no to a kiss does not mean that she doesn't want attention and love). The negation to an outside world is establishing the structure of an internal self. Later a child may reflect on death, realizing there was a time, and can come a time, when he won't be alive—a "sudden awareness of one's own non-being." Loder picks up on Erikson's description of this as *"ego chill."*[37]

Up to the time of adolescence, "the human spirit, primarily through its construction of the ego and superego, has consistently created forms of order designed

---

34. Loder, *Logic of the Spirit*, 341–42.
35. Ibid., 203, 124.
36. Ibid., 83, 87–95.
37. Ibid., 115.

to sustain the developing person in the face of incipient destruction."[38] These themes of universal human development are "(1) the inevitability of order, (2) the eventual emergence of disorder, (3) the possibility of new order, and (4) the relationality that underlies all forms of order and their explanation."[39] Now with puberty and beyond, adolescents are able to see themselves in light of abstract universals.

> The spirit, restless with its limited successes and its corresponding failure to liberate itself without entailing further entrapment, now breaks free in the strange new powers of adolescence. . . . The overall topic for this period in the context of this book is the release of the spirit and its discovery of its eternal ground.[40]

Relationality has to do with our relationship to God, the universe, and one another. This book seeks to expand your understanding of the relational nature of life. As we have already stated, before truth and knowledge comes our relationship with God the Creator, Christ the Redeemer, and the Holy Spirit—God as life and light giver. Before redemption and transformation comes relationship; before conviction of our fallenness comes grace—as Loder beautifully points out. Examples of such principles fill his book, and reading his stories and description of confused young lives being transformed will put spiritual handles on our own struggles to help young people. Here is one of his conclusions:

> One of Erikson's major contributions to resolving the dilemmas of adolescent identity is his reference to the category of the "adult guarantor [literal definition: a person who guarantees something]. . . ." Usually such persons are not the parent; this person is close enough to the adolescent . . . to participate in his world, but at the same time guarantees that authentic adulthood is possible. . . . My impression is that adult guarantors are called; they manifest a transformation of authority into authenticity. . . . It is not just that you change your world; you change it in accordance with the way Christ is changing it and in conformity to his nature.[41]

As you share in adolescent suffering in the spirit of the cross,[42] you are able to share resurrection hope.

38. Ibid., 203.
39. Ibid.
40. Ibid., 204.
41. Ibid., 227, 228.
42. A theme of Andrew Root's *Revisiting Relational Youth Ministry: From a Strategy of Influence to a Theology of Incarnation* (Downers Grove, IL: InterVarsity, 2007) and *Relationships Unfiltered* (Grand Rapids: Zondervan, 2009) is a willingness to suffer with youth for their sake in the model of our crucified Lord.

An Often Missed Obstacle to Growth

Imagine a section of highway so dangerous you can no longer consider your future destination; your only goal is to survive the hazards of this stretch of roadway. Many teenagers are so caught up in the fun and difficulties of high school life (or early college) they can hardly look further ahead than the very next step. Our goal is to be more clearly concerned about their short- and long-term growth, and their futures, than they themselves can be.

Neglected in our discussion so far (and in most developmental theories, excepting Loder) is consideration of what most hinders healthy growth and maturity: our fallen sinfulness. Whether we call sin mistakes, carelessness, weakness, dysfunction, or hurt, we find ourselves conscious, even across religions and serious secularism, of something hindering us from within. The apostle Paul, in a touching, personal confession, admits his own struggles as a Christian.

> I do not understand my own actions. For I do not do what I want, but I do the very thing I hate. . . . I have the desire to do what is right, but not the ability to carry it out. For I do not do the good I want, but the evil I do not want is what I keep on doing. (Rom. 7:15, 17–18 ESV)

Another famous confession comes from Augustine's memory of stealing pears from a neighbor's tree with boyhood friends one night.

> I had a desire to steal, and did so, not because of hunger or poverty, but to rebel against the right and enjoy my impulse for wrong. . . . We hauled off a load of pears, not to eat ourselves, but to throw to the hogs, barely tasting them ourselves. Our delight was in doing it just because it was forbidden.[43]

Christians, realizing their internal struggle against ungodly tendencies, continually confess they have sinned against God "in thought, word and deed."[44] We also seek forgiveness from others ("forgive us our sins *as we forgive those who sin against us*").[45] And finally we seek forgiveness even from ourselves, for God is more ready to forgive us than we are to relinquish our guilt and shame. After humble and honest confession, and without final resolution of the cycles of hurt (being hurt, hurting others and ourselves, which hurts God), we claim, with Paul, victory in Christ and freedom in the Holy Spirit (Rom. 7:25; 8:1–2).

43. Augustine, *Confessions* 2.4.9, in *Great Books of the Western World*, edited by Robert Maynard Hutchins and Mortimer J. Adler (Chicago: Encyclopedia Britannica, 1952), 18:10–11 (author's paraphrase).
44. *The Book of Common Prayer* (New York: Seabury Press, 1977), 79, 360.
45. See Matt. 5:23–24, emphasis added.

The pagan and secular worlds, without respect for Scripture and God's law, still have a general sense of their sin—though they may go to great lengths to excuse or smile at it. In the same passage quoted above, Augustine refers to the law of God written in the hearts of men. Like Paul, the Roman poet Ovid remarked, "I see the better things, and I approve them, but I follow the worse."[46] There is a universal and common sense of right and wrong, an admission of a common *dark side* to our personalities. Though morality can be mocked and justice twisted, as peacemakers and kingdom builders we make our best appeal to that underlying sense of the right in all but the most extreme psychopaths.

You who minister to youth traveling the most dramatic stage of human development, in a complex and challenging era, come to know their wounds suffered in the past. Their present growth is often weakened by previous emotional injuries, sometimes from childhood. God's intention of growth to full human maturity can be hindered by conscious or unconscious stress from past traumas. Injustice toward individuals or groups is the antithesis of God's will for all. It is a terrible crime before God to relegate groups to inferior status, or to treat men as boys—or women as girls—and either as objects.[47] The goal of healthy growth to maturity is a criterion on which people of various faiths, theological perspectives, and humanistic points of view ought to agree in a secular society. Justice, a pursuit of the common good, is a glue holding contemporary secular societies together.

The gospel of Jesus Christ promises liberation, healing, growth, justice, and peace to individuals as well as to families, towns, and nations. Inner subjective struggles reflect tensions without, in the various levels of our social systems. Cycles of revenge call for reconciliation within families and among people in violent neighborhoods, barrios and shantytowns, and everywhere. Peaceful alternatives among tribes, religions, and nations are desperately needed if we are going to survive as a planet. Miroslav Volf unpacks what this might look like as he explains the theological and psychological challenges entailed in ethnic reconciliation.[48] Donald Shriver describes historic examples of reconciliation between nations in *An Ethic for Enemies: Forgiveness in Politics.*[49]

---

46. Ovid, *Metamorphoses* 7.20.

47. Both hardcore pornography and soft or "normalized pornography" of commercials and screen hinder the maturity of observers and those objectified.

48. Miroslav Volf, *Exclusion and Embrace: A Theological Exploration of Identity, Otherness, and Reconciliation* (Nashville: Abingdon, 1996).

49. Donald W. Shriver Jr., *An Ethic for Enemies: Forgiveness in Politics* (New York: Oxford University Press, 1995). See also his *Honest Patriots: Loving a Country Enough to Remember Its Misdeeds* (New York: Oxford University Press, 2005); and Raymond G. Helmick, SJ, and Rodney L. Petersen, eds., *Forgiveness and Reconciliation: Religion, Public Policy and Conflict Transformation* (Philadelphia: Templeton Foundation Press, 2001).

Rising generations of youth are open to being involved in helping to bring our world together. They will look to leaders for meaningful discussions and vital learning experiences.

Community and National Growth and Development

When we describe the gospel as relevant and holistic, we refer to its applicability—and not just to the spiritual side of youth, but to their physical, emotional, academic, and social lives as well. But individual growth and development are not enough. Despite our Western tendencies, the gospel is to peoples and nations as well as to individuals. Our God-inspired concern for growth and development gives us a heart for corporate redemption and communal growth.

The gospel, Scripture, and the Lord's Prayer call us to commitment for the growth and development of underdeveloped communities and nations. Community and national development involve collaboration across boundaries of faith and ethnicity. Christ's blessing on the peacemakers, Moses's commitment to liberation, Nehemiah's challenge to rebuild the city walls, and God's intention for a fruitful and productive world urge all citizens of the world to work for the common good. Christians take the best principles of community organization and development and add a relational element, in which both helper and receivers learn from each other and grow. This has been called "transformational development."[50]

Consumed with efforts to keep ourselves and our children up with the times, suburban communities can overlook struggles taking place in disadvantaged inner-city neighborhoods. It then becomes easy to blame the inhabitants for woes of violence. On a larger scale, technologically advanced nations may be engaged so competitively that they lack the energy to help nations struggling to survive. It's understandable how we may feel overwhelmed by the complexity of needs in our communities. Such anxiety can turn us into protective isolationists, or it can bring humble vulnerability, openness to the mysteries of God, commitment to helping all sorts of neighbors. It's easy to retreat into a Christian subcultural ghetto, to work inside parochial walls, to become so involved with our institutional problems and affairs that we never venture into the mainstream of life where salt and light are desperately needed. Whatever our context, God challenges us to work for a kingdom characterized by personal and communal healing and growth, justice, and peace.

50. This is a whole additional study, and I highly recommend Bryant Myers, *Walking with the Poor: Principles and Practices of Transformational Development* (Maryknoll, NY: Orbis Books, 1999).

Conclusion

Nature pushes all species to fullness of growth or maturity. Peter and Paul pray that "their" churches might grow into the full measure of Christ (1 Pet. 2:2; 2 Pet. 3:18; Eph. 1:15–19; 3:16–19; 4:12–16). The grand story of God's creative and redemptive work did not begin with a finished product; Eden was a starting point. Though laced with pain, the story of redemption points to the full glory of God's creative and redemptive process. The alleluias of the apocalypse reflect victory over all enemies of growth, the triumph of a mature creation, and the reconciliation of all manner of people to the glory of God.

As we gain insight into stages of human growth, it is important to keep three things in mind: the systemic context for human development, the mysterious uniqueness of each human being, and the unpredictable power and grace of God.

Our theology of growth (and justice) holds that

1. The image of God promises dignity to all persons and cannot be erased in this lifetime.
2. The presence of evil cannot be denied, theologically or empirically; it not only hinders individual growth but it causes systemic dysfunction and calls out for healing and restoration through God's transforming grace.
3. The development of human culture and growth of all individuals within diverse cultures is ordained by God and a given responsibility to all cultures, communities, families, and churches.
4. Children are born dependent on human caretakers, and all social systems nurturing them are shepherds judged by God.[51]
5. Relations and interactions among any humans, societies, and the living God are complex and dynamic.
6. Adolescence is the most radical development in a person's life and a most opportune time to meet God's transforming grace.
7. Youth ministry is a remedial ministry, supporting and filling in the fissures apparent in families, communities, and church structures.

The challenge and responsibility of contributing to adolescent and communal growth surely suggest humble worship before Jesus Christ, who has called us to be servants and shepherds among young people, and builders of a better world. Loder describes such humble worship:

> When the longing for (eternal) intimacy is satisfied by the Spiritual Presence of Christ, the Face of God, then the answers to our basic questions may dawn upon

51. See Ezek. 34.

us. A lifetime is an unfinished act of God's love; it is intended that we complete that act by returning ourselves to God, directly and through others, in love. . . . It appears that we have been created for nothing less than the pure love of God, whose universe is our home.[52]

Questions for Reflection and Discussion

1. Prior to reading this chapter, how much time have you spent considering a theology of growth?
2. Do you feel you have some notion of growth theories and some basic principles of growth to take with you into practice?
3. Has this chapter helped you to measure your own growth? Have you identified any past hurts that may hinder such growth? How is God growing you these days?
4. Are you satisfied that the gospel you share is relevant and holistic? Does it speak to physical, emotional, social, intellectual, financial, and spiritual realities?
5. Is the gospel you believe and proclaim good news to communities and nations? Is God concerned for their healing and growth?

52. Loder, *Logic of the Spirit*, 341–42.

—7—

Theology of Personhood
and Community

Thank you for making me so wonderfully complex!

Psalm 139:14 NLT

For thus says the high and lofty One who inhabits eternity, whose name is Holy: "I dwell in the high and holy place, and also with him who is of a contrite and humble spirit."

Isaiah 57:15a RSV

Introduction

Controversial writer William Deresiewicz, in an essay containing some questionable generalizations and analyses, nevertheless offers a tantalizing observation about a rising generation's creation of selfhood:

> We're always selling ourselves. We use social media to create a product—to create a brand—and the product is us. We treat ourselves like little businesses, something to be managed and promoted. The self today is an entrepreneurial self, a self that's packaged to be sold.[1]

The question of selfhood is age-old. Contemplating the marvels of nature a psalmist asked, "What is man that thou art mindful of him," and in worship of

1. William Deresiewicz, "Generation Sell: The New Zeitgeist: We're All Peddling Ourselves and Managing Our Own Brands," *New York Times*, Sunday Review, November 13, 2011, 1, 7.

the Creator continued, "and the son of man that thou dost care for him?" (Ps. 8:4 RSV). The emphasis in this part of practical theology is on humanity, human beings as individual selves and as community. The psalmist considered the whole of humanity, but the paradoxical reality of unique individuality is picked up by Moses asking God, "Who am I?" in terms of liberating the children of Israel from Egyptian bondage (Exod. 3:11), and David asking God, "Who am I?" to be ruler over your people (2 Sam. 7:18), and Solomon's "Who am I?" that I should build a temple of God (1 Chron. 29:14). Who would claim ultimate knowledge of the mystery of self?

"Who am I?" is intimately connected with "Who are we?" Despite the power of networks and connectedness, northwestern Europeans and North Americans have imbibed from their culture a striking and pervasive sense of individualism. We even read Scripture subconsciously from an individualistic standpoint. A "you" or "we" in the Pauline Epistles is casually taken as a message to us as individuals.[2] It is profitable, as we read the biblical text, to notice how most of us take Paul's plural "you" primarily personally. But only in our relationship to our Creator and others can we know ourselves as individuals. The paradox is that we are unique individuals, with all reality surrounding our personal viewpoint, and yet a human self exists only as part of a whole that depends—in terms of origin, life, and destiny—on others.

Even the physical universe appears to be relationally constructed—down to the mysteries of quantum physics. Nature operates with a kind of attraction and repulsion down to its tiniest elements—element to element, and systems in relationships to systems. Wikipedia and some scientists tell me that an elemental particle, a quark, is never found in isolation, but always in combination with others in groups of three known as hadrons.[3] The whole physical and biological universe operates on the basis of networks.

Two scientists from the field of public health and social science began studying the power of human connectedness out of their research of contagious diseases. In their study of the endless networking of human beings, Nicholas Christakis and James Fowler were struck by the relational nature of the universe.

> As we began to study human connections, we encountered engineers studying networks of power stations, neuroscientists studying networks of neurons, geneticists studying networks of genes, and physicists studying networks of darn near everything.[4]

2. A point made strikingly clear in a presentation and unpublished paper of Sharon Ketchum, "Incarnational Praxis and Community: A Person's Relationship to the Community of Faith," AYME Conference, Seattle, October 2011.
3. See wikipedia.org/wiki/Quark.
4. Nicholas A. Christakis and James H. Fowler, *Connected: The Surprising Power of Our Social Networks and How They Shape Our Lives* (New York: Little, Brown, 2009), xv.

Christakis and Fowler were amazed to find the power of influence among humans, not only friend to friend, but to friends of friends to the third and fourth distance, and beyond. The internet has made human connectivity even more striking. Operating from a nontheistic evolutionary perspective with its "survival of the fittest" assumptions, social scientists have been puzzled by the paradox between selfishness and cooperation. New theories of human altruism have been needed. Without acknowledging the relational and communal nature of the Triune Creator, and restricted to empirical evidence, scientists like Christakis and Fowler puzzle over the ultimate origin and mystery of altruism and compassion. They make their case as to the importance of human networks, however, and conclude their book with hope that

> the whole of humanity comes to be greater than the sum of its parts. Like an awakening child, the human superorganism is become self-aware and this will surely help us achieve our goals. But the greatest gift of this awareness will be the sheer joy of self-discovery and the realization that to truly know ourselves, we must first understand how and why we are all connected.[5]

From the most basic and primitive relationships in the physical world, we find a principle of emergence—relational combinations of elements to form higher-level, more complex entities. Necessary human relationships then reflect the relational quality of the physical universe, both of which are a reflection of the relational nature of the Creator. Therefore, I can know myself only as I know and am known by my Creator, and in relationship to my fellow creatures.

Our personal growth, then, involves a balance in our concern for self and for others. At one extreme are those who have lost themselves in busy care for others, perhaps even as enabling codependents, and on the other, those who are so self-absorbed that in missing attention to others, they lose themselves. Cautioning against self-inflation or self-diminishing, and continuing the third chapter's "interpretation of self," this chapter considers the importance and mystery of self.

The Mystery of Self

The profound mystery of self is recognized but seldom pondered by most of us. The person or self is a product of culture, whether shaped by tribal primitive culture, urban premodern culture, industrial modern culture, or digital postmodern

---

5. Nicholas A. Christakis and James H. Fowler, *Connected: How Your Friends' Friends' Friends Affect Everything You Feel, Think, and Do,* paperback ed. (New York: Back Bay Books, 2009), 305, concluding paragraph and sentence.

culture. Yet, besides being a *product*, every person is also a *creature*—and that is part of our mystery and paradox. Culture shapes our soul and thinking, while the image of God and the Spirit draws our hearts, including our emotions and reasoning, toward the transcendent, to the heart of the Creator.

The questions, What is humankind? and Who am I? are considered almost imponderables. A psalm attributed to David reflects on the first question: Who, in God's vast universe, are we?

The second question, Who am I?, was asked biblically (as already noted) by Moses, David, and Solomon, more functionally than philosophically. That you and I *are* defies incalculable odds. So easily we could not have been. The subconscious confidence in our inevitability is folly. With some thought we should realize that our nonexistence was quite possible. When we ponder the relationship between the creature and the Creator, the finite and the infinite, the absolute and the relative, we sense what philosophers describe as the anxiety of our being.

Adolescents appreciate adults who are sensitive and open to their struggle for personhood, the teenage anxiety that accompanies their quest for identity and personal meaning. Youth are still open to the capacity for wonder. The brightest researchers of the human body tell us they've only fathomed a bit of how we are made and how we function. What we do know is amazing. And amazement is an important aspect of spirituality. (How exciting to witness the amazement of young people—and watch them grow spiritually.)

Let's continue to ponder the personal question: Who am I? Consider first the mysteries of self-consciousness and perception; reflect a moment on the delights of our sensations. We *see* the beauty of a flower, ferns, lofty trees, majestic mountains, a peaceful meadow, a placid lake, expansive ocean, sparkling stars, the human body. We *hear* insects, birds, crashing waves, inspiring music, a loving voice. We take pleasure in *touching* smooth surfaces, warm sand, soft grass, and in greeting others through touch in a variety of ways. Our sense of *smell* brings delight as we walk past the lilacs or the rose hips, or breathe the fragrance of the sea. Nor would we want to lose the *taste* of our favorite meal, dessert, or drink. A 2011 global study by the McCann Worldgroup Singapore found an additional *tech sense* among sixteen- to twenty-two-year-olds, 53 percent of whom say they would give up their sense of smell and taste rather than their social media skills.[6] Our perceptions reflect our consciousness.

A Christian sociologist asks the question we are considering in *What Is a Person?* A highly respected social scientist, Christian Smith argues against undeclared

---

6. McCann Worldgroup, "Today's Global Youth Would Give Up Their Sense of Smell to Keep Their Technology," May 25, 2011, www.prnewswire.com/news-releases/todays-global-youth -would-give-up-their-sense-of-smell-to-keep-their-technology-122605643.html.

naturalist and relativist assumptions at the base of much social science—in a way that continues the critique of John Milbank (see chapter 5). Smith's empirical research has found a resurgence, rather than expected demise, of religious faith—suggesting we might call our times a "postsecular" age.

Smith's profound text goes on to suggest a critical *realist-personalism* in contrast to naturalistic and reductive and determinist views of the self or the subjective and relativistic views of self that are prevalent in many sociological discussions. He opens up the possibility that both secular and religious scientists might see self as a reflection of ultimate reality, destined for justice and moral ends. Smith raises a series of questions for fellow social scientists and all of us:

> Are we simply self-conscious animals improbably appearing for a moment in a cosmos without purpose or significance? . . . Or are we rather illusions of individuality destined to dissolve into the ultimately real Absolute? . . . Or maybe only bodies with capacities to define by means of the exercise of the will and discourse our identities through self-description and re-description? Or perhaps are we children of a personal God, whose perfect love is determined to rescue us from our self-destruction in order to bring us into the perfect happiness of divine knowledge and worship?[7]

All this mystery of self is just a part of what you are called to meet and to love. It is through relationships and stories that you will have the privilege of sharing unique mysteries in the lives of real people.

Finding Self

I've had friends who seemed to enjoy an isolated life. One is happy at sea in his fishing boat and off-season hunting in the woods with his dog. Another was an artist who never gained renown but still remained happy working alone at his craft. There is a musician, who enjoys performing and can enjoy a party somewhat, but seems most content at home with his music. Just *being* brings contentment to these friends, and they have something to teach me. I enjoy my own company but usually need to be accomplishing something. It's taken me years just to enjoy relationship with myself, with nature, with God, for long lengths of time.

For most teenagers, solitude is boring if not frightening. But many can be coaxed into one or more days spent solo as part of a wilderness experience. They most often come back revitalized by what they have discovered, alone, about nature and

---

7. Christian Smith, *What Is a Person? Rethinking Humanity, Social Life, and the Moral Good from the Person Up* (Chicago: University of Chicago Press, 2010), 7.

themselves. The adolescent identity quest is carried out with the help of mirrors. Young people use peers and special friends as social mirrors on self. Besides the benefits of teenage cohorts, we recognize the tyranny of conformity, pressures to fit in, to produce personages acceptable to the current fad or style. Alone in the wilderness, a new relationship with nature provides a fresh mirror and new clarity from the natural world and from within ourselves.[8] There is much to discover about selfhood and the sheer appreciation of life itself.

Paul Tournier, noted Swiss physician, counselor, and writer, learned, as he grew up, about his father's death, which happened when he was only three months old. Then, at the age of six, he experienced the death of his mother. As orphans, he and his older sister were raised by relatives. Paul grew into a shy and insecure Swiss teenager, and to compensate he hid behind academic success, eventually becoming a successful physician. He professed faith in Christ at age twelve, but a second spiritual experience, "a face-to-face encounter with God," led to introducing psychotherapy into his medical practice. Rich counseling experiences brought him a deep appreciation of personhood, as his many books display. In *The Meaning of Persons*, Tournier shares profound, yet always relative, insights he gained about the *personages* of those who came for advice. Personage, for Tournier, is that view of self, imposed on us by society and by ourselves, that tends to obscure the person we really are.

> There remains in every (one), even for (oneself), something of impenetrable mystery. . . .
>
> I become increasingly aware that the *person*, pure and unvarnished, will always escape us. Doubtless only God knows it. I can never grasp the true reality, of myself or anybody else, but only an image; a fragmentary and deformed image, an appearance; the "*personage.*"
>
> How can we discover the true person when we see only distorted and varied images of it, and when these images derive their origin not only in the (person) himself, but also from ourselves, and from the whole environment to which he belongs? . . . Nevertheless . . . this search is not fruitless.[9]

Tournier's distinction between person and personage can be instructive. God's prediction, "You shall die" if you disobey, surely refers to the degeneration of the self. *Self* retreats in shame from holy reality—as did Adam and Eve after their disobedience. The self becomes vulnerable like Abel, and the soul needs to protect

8. See Andrew J. Bobilya, "Wilderness, Solitude, and Monastic Traditions," in *Exploring the Power of Solo, Silence and Solitude*, ed. Clifford E. Knupp and Thomas E. Smith (Boulder, CO: Association for Experiential Education, 2005). Also, Richard Louv, *Last Child in the Woods: Saving Our Children from Nature-Deficit Disorder* (Chapel Hill, NC: Algonquin Books, 2006).

9. Paul Tournier, *The Meaning of Persons* (New York: Harper & Row, 1957), 13, 15, 21.

itself, as Cain's mark was for his protection. At youth camps with a spirit of loving trust, we watch the protective masks of students, their defensive fronts needed in the threatening halls of high school, melt away until their real persons are exposed. Personages are the self-*protection* and self-*promotion* we need as fallen creatures.

We may see an acceptance and glorification of what Tournier called the personage, "an image fragmentary and deformed," in celebrities like David Bowie, Madonna, Lady Gaga, and others.[10] And, of course, we see similar tendencies in ourselves. We are given the task of accepting our own and other personages as mere images of God's positive intentions. This task involves rejecting the world's manipulation of personages and pressing on to higher, holy ground, where self can open social protective fronts to share inner secrets with another. As Tournier puts it in the closing paragraph of this book:

> It is a mysterious spiritual reality, mysteriously linked to God, mysteriously linked to our fellows. We are aware of these links at those privileged moments when there springs up a fresh current of life, bursting the fatal fetters of the personage, asserting its freedom and breaking out into love.[11]

Deep and thoughtful interactions with young people can facilitate the opening of self to self in appropriate ways.

Losing Self: An Example

Part of my own story can be taken as an example of carelessness with regard to self. Looking back, I could consider the 1950s the heyday of my years in youth ministry—although the 1960s in New York City were more formative, and there's been much to learn from and experience with youth and their leaders since. Try to imagine my life back in the 1950s. I was a zealous bachelor in my twenties, just out of the paratroopers, on a red Triumph motorcycle (my only all-season vehicle). I was a full-time teacher, an assistant coach; I was running a New Canaan (Connecticut) Young Life Club and assisting in starting up another in neighboring Darien. Weeknights through Saturday morning (in football season), I was cycling around New Canaan finding students, at club itself, or visiting homes. Somehow teaching preparation got done during free periods, late at night, or in early mornings.

After Friday night basketball games, Saturday football or track meets, I'd pack dirty laundry and student papers into my backpack and take off for responsibilities

10. Ibid., 15.
11. Ibid., 234.

as a senior leader of the Black Rock Teenagers (Black Rock Church) in Bridgeport, fifteen miles down the Merritt Parkway (or Route 1). Bill Koerner and I had a wonderful team of volunteers, and there was great musical and humorist talent among the high school students themselves. Loads of kids would arrive Saturday nights by cars, vans, and even a small bus. I was a driver and often the speaker. We thought we'd really succeeded when attendance passed two hundred. The evening wasn't finished until we visited a miniature golf or driving range, a pizza parlor or diner—depending on our carload's decision. Rarely did we get to bed before 1:00 a.m. Still, the next morning I'd be teaching teenage Sunday school. After church and a good meal, I and a tired brother or friend would "pass out" on our living room floor—before going off for afternoon tag-football, basketball, ice-skating, or sledding. By late afternoon we were picking up students for what we called Follow-Up (discipleship with Bible study and prayer). After the evening church service, we'd go upstairs for more prayer, and finally a few "faithfuls" would help me grade my papers—to be returned the next day. By midnight, with clean clothes and corrected papers, I was on my bike headed back for another week.

I was getting just enough sleep, eating fairly well, working out by running and pickup basketball games during the late afternoons after practice. Intellectually, I was reading and studying enough to get by in classes. My spirituality was evangelical piety as I understood it: Bible study for speaking or teaching and prayers for the work and individual young people.

All my friends were younger than myself and ministry-related. I had no older mentor, adviser, or supervisor—and no peer accountability group. Dates with a serious girlfriend merely consisted of driving her home from meetings. When that relationship broke up, I never grieved or missed a step. I was a fanatic functionalist! There was no such thing as a vacation or spiritual retreat for me—such were replaced by taking kids to camp. Socially and spiritually, I must have been flunking. After a few more years, I think I burned out—but never recognized or admitted it. I simply moved on to further graduate study—relinquishing the work to able younger leaders. I had drifted into youth ministry without a clear sense of calling and continued to drift toward a vague goal of college teaching and more youth ministry. My dissertation was interrupted by an invitation to help Young Life begin a new urban venture on Manhattan's Lower East Side.

My failure in loving and nurturing myself resulted in a failure of intimacy, an inability to love others for I hardly loved myself. Such failure lacks spiritual depth in God's love—intimate receptivity to God's love. I had little idea about a balanced life—except as it happened upon me by chance or providence. The *work* was everything. I was a "human doing," not a full human being. It would take years, failures, and a broken heart to teach me what I never learned about myself. Maybe this is why I'm so concerned about my students' attention to self, emotional health, and spiritual growth, and their ability to reflect upon and understand themselves.

Taking Care of Our Forgotten Selves

Care for ourselves may begin with asking how we (and those we recruit and train) are dealing with relationships, time, money, sex, and other responsibilities. In the period of my life described above I was doing pretty well in those basics, at least to general appearances, but my life could easily have become disastrous. It is important to take an honest look at our weekly schedule, as well as our wallet, personal budget, and credit rating. It may be more difficult to assess one's sexual identity, fantasy life, and behavior—and, finally, how well others and our Lord can depend on us. This is all the beginning of self-evaluation.

Also important is an honest assessment of our calling and motivations. Some are drawn into youth work because they don't know what else to do; seminarians may find it the only job available. For others, without knowing it, there is an attraction to avoiding the responsibilities of a nine-to-five job or typical adult life in general. There may be an unconscious desire to extend adolescent highs or capture high school experiences missed the first time around.[12] It's healthy to be honest about all of this.

Dan Ponsetto was a popular participant in our training program at Gordon-Conwell Theological Seminary during the 1980s. He went on to become youth ministry coordinator in the Catholic Archdiocese of Boston. Listen to his observations and wisdom:

> Parish leaders and adults often heap enormous expectation on youth ministers. . . .
> I am becoming more and more aware of the lack of recognition and support experienced by many . . . youth ministers. . . . My sense is that this problem is not unique to parishes. During my years with Young Life, I often felt alone. I yearned to be more recognized and accepted, both with the organization itself and especially within the communities where I was ministering. Too many of my friends are out there going it alone and honestly I don't know how they are surviving.
>
> I was struck by the fact that there weren't many devotional or reflective resources for youth workers—the overwhelming emphasis in youth ministry publishing was on programmatic materials.[13]

12. Dean Trulear tells of a workshop at a youth ministries conference where he spoke of such poor motivations for youth ministry, making several in the room walk out in anger.
13. Dan Ponsetto, *Praying Our Stories: Reflections for Youth Ministers* (Winona, MN: Saint Mary's Press, 1992), 32–33, 10.

Ponsetto further encourages youth ministers to share and pray their stories in a way that helps them see God's perspective on their lives and work.

Paul Borthwick, while a youth minister, lost the two most important men in his life—his father, who died, and his pastor, who was removed from ministry.

> I found myself dealing with my sense of purpose, my call to youth ministry: *Why was I in the ministry—and in youth ministry—in the first place?* Asking questions about the influence these men had on me led to increased evaluation, doubting, and self-interrogation. I began to wrestle with questions such as: Am I in youth ministry to serve God? Or do I just like the status and power it gives me over those younger than I? Did I take the job simply because no one else wanted it . . . ? Could it be that I undertook youth-ministry leadership to fulfill a latent desire to obtain the popularity I always wanted in high school?[14]

Borthwick goes on to discuss flaws in the character and style of two leaders (actually composites from his experience in ministry). Leader One, Al, is mainly motivated by success in youth ministry; he's caught in a "performance trap." Growing up under a nonaffirming father pushed Al to seek success at all costs. "He is trying to be all things to all people but feels like he is burning out and cannot keep up." Leader Two, Mike, is more of "a relational person . . . strongly motivated to be liked by his students. . . . Since he measures effectiveness by closeness to his students, his spiritual growth (as well as ability to relate to adults—as his wife will testify) has been stunted."[15]

Fortunately there are further resources providing encouragement for the souls of youth ministers. Gordon MacDonald's *Ordering Your Private World* has gone through many printings. Applicable to all Christian ministry, it begins with the metaphor of a sinkhole.

> It is likely that at one time or another many of us have perceived ourselves to be on the verge of a sinkhole-like cave-in. In the feelings of numbing fatigue, a taste of apparent failure, or the bitter experience of disillusionment about goals or purposes, we may have sensed something within us about to give way. We feel we are just about a moment from a collapse that will threaten to sweep our entire world into a bottomless pit.[16]

Borthwick's book can help you in terms of your motivations, general organization, use of time, gaining wisdom and knowledge, growing spiritually, and

---

14. Paul Borthwick, *Feeding Your Forgotten Soul: Spiritual Growth for Youthworkers* (El Cajon, CA: Youth Specialties, 1990), 21.

15. Ibid., 23–24.

16. Gordon MacDonald, *Ordering Your Private World* (Nashville: Thomas Nelson, 1984, 2007), 13.

restoring yourself through significant rest. Other resources such as David Chow's *The Perfect Program and Other Fairy Tales*,[17] spiritual mentors, life coaches, and counselors can help you avoid pitfalls many of us have experienced.

Concluding Thoughts on Self

This chapter is meant to be complementary to our "Exegesis of Self" section in chapter 3. There we saw from another perspective the complexity of self and possible tensions within—we situated the self between the world and God's Word. Here we are looking at the self in its relationship to God and to others. Our understanding of self is rooted in our relationship to, and worship of, God. We are struck by paradoxes between losing ourselves to Christ and gaining ourselves as servants, between sacrifice and achievement, between faithfulness and success. Appreciating the great mystery of self, we seek balances between introspection and self-care on the one hand, and service to others on the other. Our goal is a healthy self for its own sake, for the sake of others, and to the glory of God. We are engaged with young people we care about in the challenge of unraveling the mystery of self for healthy growth and community.

Youth workers and many others have received critical help and encouragement from Brennan Manning's *Abba's Child: The Cry of the Heart for Intimate Belonging*,[18] in which he deals with the Imposter within us all—the guilty or repressed feelings creating an inner adversary that sabotages some of our best efforts and our desire for deep appreciation and love. I like this book's conclusion:

> The vulnerability of God in permitting Himself to be affected by our response, the heartbreak of Jesus as He wept over Jerusalem for not receiving Him, are utterly astounding. When God comes streaming into our lives in the power of His Word, all He asks is that we be stunned and surprised. . . .
>
> The recovery of passion is intimately connected with astonishment. We are swept up by the overwhelming force of mystery.
>
> In worship we move into the tremendous poverty that is the adoration of God. We have moved from the Upper Room where John laid his head on the breast of Jesus to the book of Revelation where the beloved disciple fell prostrate before the Lamb of God.

17. David Chow, *The Perfect Program and Other Fairy Tales: Confessions of a Well Intentioned Youth Worker* (Colorado Springs: Think, 2005). This traces failures similar to my own—with helpful and humble acceptance of God's grace.

18. This book may carry us a bit beyond Paul Tournier's deep analysis. Or, you may find it parallel to that work.

Wise men and women have long held that happiness lies in being yourself without inhibitions. Let the Great Rabbi hold you silently against His heart. In learning who He is, you will find out who you are: Abba's child in Christ our Lord.[19]

We find in Tournier and Manning helpful pastoral theology, which is an aspect of practical theology. Effectiveness in youth ministry will be increased as we give closer attention to our own lives and the inner lives of those we train.

Questions for Reflection and Discussion

1. Considering the image of celebrities and the rest of us, how do you respond to the question: "What is humankind that God should care for us?"
2. How do you respond to the question, "Who am I?"
3. How helpful was this discussion of selfhood to you? Did you take exception to some of its explanation? Does it leave you with questions, and if so, with whom could you discuss them?
4. Together with the discussion of self in chapter 3, do you understand the relationships within self, the complex nature of a person?
5. Do you accept the relational emphasis of this book? Do you see your relationships as three-dimensional: to yourself, to God, and to others?
6. Considering also the analysis of self and the four questions of chapter 3, what grade would you give your own care of self?

19. Brennan Manning, *Abba's Child: The Cry of the Heart for Intimate Belonging* (Colorado Springs: NavPress, 1994, 2002), 165–66.

—8—

Theology of Family and Peers

[Jesus said, God] made them male and female. . . . For this reason a man shall leave his father and mother and be joined to his wife, and the two shall become one flesh.

MATTHEW 19:4–5

Put these words of mine in your heart and soul. . . . Teach them to your children, talking about them when you are at home and when you are away.

DEUTERONOMY 11:18A, 19A

There are friends who point the way to ruin, others are closer than a brother.

PROVERBS 18:24 JB

Introduction

Youth ministry must be youth *and* family ministry, or moving toward that goal. Some today are calling for the elimination of youth ministry (and Sunday school) in order to integrate young people into the larger church with their families. Against such a view, I propose a "both/and" approach. Youth ministry should be more integrated into families and the adult church, but at the same time families and churches need specialists in popular culture and deep adolescent issues.

Young people need security and support from home and church. But they also need a peer family and outside instructors who complement positive teaching at home. Youth look for what they consider healthy models of personhood, family life, and real friendship. They want to talk with those who appreciate the mysteries of self, marriage, and friendship. It is not just modern adolescents who need individuation and rites of passage; these have been around for a long time and are part of most traditional cultures. This chapter discusses the special interrelationship of families and peers.

The self is intricately related to its family throughout its life, positively and negatively. As our lives are intimately connected with family, so families are also connected with expanding concentric circles of systems and influences. In the dynamic creation of a relational God, we see a dynamic *interrelationship* among all human cultural systems. The amazing work of two professors from the disciplines of sociology, political science, and medicine has established statistical charts of broad and "contagious" human networks.[1] They found us to be influenced, positively and negatively, as to our attitudes, beliefs, and behaviors, such as obesity and addictions, and choice of a life mate, by three degrees of influence: our immediate friends, their friends, and the much larger circle of their friends' friends. We are strongly influenced, in ways beyond our knowledge, by those we don't even know. The family, then, is an internal system intertwined with external systems. Is there any question, then, that our ministry must involve families and church communities, being relational in all ways and at all levels?

Complexity and Confusion Regarding Marriage and Families

In discussions about youthful violence and other problems, I often hear seminarians, pastors, and others quip, "It is all the fault of the parents." While parents do bear serious responsibility for their children, the problems that young persons face stem from faults of all adults, from society at large. Parents are just part of the dysfunction in all social systems. Many parents themselves were neglected or abused as children, perhaps damaged by war, trauma in the workforce, or breakdowns in society's "safety net." Since the family is a critical base for all cultures, we must pay it this special attention.

Though I've always done home visits, I admit to neglecting family ministry in my own youth ministry—and in my teaching. Fortunately writers like Ginny Ward Holderness, *Youth Ministry: The New Team Approach*, Mark DeVries,

---

1. Nicholas A. Christakis and James H. Fowler, *Connected: How Your Friends' Friends' Friends Affect Everything You Feel, Think, and Do* (New York: Back Bay Books, 2011).

Family-Based Youth Ministry, and Pamela Erwin, *The Family Powered Church*, came along to remind me of this crucial dimension of our theology and ministry.[2] There will be many answers, but none final, to the balance of age-distinct and family-ministry approaches for a church—both are needed, with different emphases in various church situations. But whatever our philosophic approach, churches and communities are called upon to support the threatened family social system as it raises children in a bewildering age.

In their constituency, their mealtime habits, their mores and boundaries, and their use of media in the home, families have greatly changed in the past century—and even the past few decades. A 2007 Pew research report surveyed US public opinion about marriage and parenthood.

> Younger adults attach far less moral stigma than do their elders to out-of-wedlock births and cohabitation without marriage. They engage in both at rates unprecedented in U.S. history. Nearly four-in-ten births in this country are to an unmarried woman. Nearly half of adults in their 30s and 40s have spent a portion of their lives in cohabiting relationship. Adults of all ages consider unwed parenting to be a big problem in society, but only 41% say that children are very important to a successful marriage, compared to 65% of the public who felt this way as recently as 1990.
>
> Americans by lopsided margins endorse the mom-and-dad home as the best setting in which to raise children. But by equally lopsided margins, they believe that if married parents are unhappy with one another, divorce is the best option, both for them and the children.[3]

Commentators on marriage in the twenty-first century are pointing to changes that make neither the Right nor the Left happy. In spite of criticisms of the traditional family by feminists and others, some marriages today provide evidence of happier and more fulfilled women and men than ever before.[4] These same writers, however, see marriage as more fragile, more postponed, and even more ignored than expected. Others go further to predict marriage passing out of existence.[5] Some studies show marriage surviving better among the educated and wealthy,

2. Ginny Ward Holderness, *Youth Ministry: The New Team Approach* (Atlanta: John Knox, 1981); Mark DeVries, *Family-Based Youth Ministry* (Downers Grove, IL: InterVarsity, 1994); Pamela E. Erwin, *The Family Powered Church* (Loveland, CO: Group, 2000).

3. Pew Research Center, "Generation Gap in Values, Behaviors: As Marriage and Parenthood Drift Apart, Public Is Concerned about Social Impact," July 1, 2007, pewresearch.org/assets/social/pdf/Marriage.pdf.

4. See Stephanie Coontz, *Marriage, A History: How Love Conquered Marriage* (New York: Penguin, 2006).

5. Maggie Gallagher, *The Abolition of Marriage: How We Destroy Lasting Love* (Washington, DC: Regnery, 1996).

disappearing in lower classes, and moving us toward a "two-caste" society.[6] The changing roles of mothers and fathers, the absent father,[7] and the prevalence of divorce[8] are all having profound effects on children (even thirty years after divorce) and on society in general.

A Pew report in 2011, "A Tale of Two Fathers: More Active, but More Are Absent," describes the changing "role of fathers in the modern American family . . . changing in important and countervailing ways. Fathers who live with their children have become more intensely involved in their lives (as more mothers are working), spending more time with them and taking part in a greater variety of activities. However, the share of fathers who are residing with their children has fallen significantly in the past half century."[9]

The definition of family is being stretched by social realities and progressive social science. The *New York Times* featured a full three-page story: "And Baby Makes Four: How a Woman, Her Son, Her Sperm Donor and His Lover Are Helping to Redefine the American Family." A deep longing for a child/family, financial realities, and practical needs brought these four together. Carol lost her father at a young age, never found the right person to marry, and had run into and struck up a new friendship with an old high school classmate—who turned out to be gay. Hearing her deep longing for a child, he volunteered to donate sperm, and from economic necessity accepted a four-day-live-in babysitting job/relationship for a baby he couldn't accept as a son. As the child began to talk, he called his babysitter Uncle George. George spent the other three nights in the apartment with a man he loves—they're not sure about a long-term commitment.

> Two addresses, three adults, a winsome toddler and a mixed-breed dog. . . . None of this was the familial configuration any of them had imagined, but it was for the moment their family. It was something they had stumbled into, yet had a certain revisionist logic.
>
> Such is the hiccupping fluidity of the family in the modern world. Six years running now, according to census data, more households consist of the unmarried than

---

6. Kay S. Hymowitz, *Marriage and Caste in America: Separate and Unequal Families in a Post-Marital Age* (Chicago: Ivan R. Dee, 2006); W. Bradford Wilcox and Elizabeth Marquardt, eds., *State of Our Unions 2010: When Marriage Disappears: The New Middle America* (Charlottesville, VA: National Marriage Project and the Institute for American Values, 2010).

7. David Blankenhorn, *Fatherless America: Confronting the Most Urgent Social Problem* (New York: Harper Perennial, 1996).

8. Craig Everett, ed., *The Consequences of Divorce: Economic and Custodial Impact on Children and Adults* (New York: Routledge, 1992); Julia M. Lewis, Sandra Blakeslee, and Judith S. Wallerstein, *The Unexpected Legacy of Divorce: The 25 Year Landmark Study* (New York: Hyperion, 2000).

9. Pew Research Center, "A Tale of Two Fathers: More Active, but More Are Absent," June 15, 2011, pewsocialtrends.org/2011/06/15/a-tale-of-two-fathers/.

the married. More people seem to be deciding that the contours of the traditional nuclear family do not work for them, spawning a profusion of cobbled-together networks in need of nomenclature. Unrelated parents living together share chores and child-rearing. Friends who occupy separate homes but rely on each other for holidays, health care proxies, financial support. "What matters to us," many are saying, "is the health of the relationships, not the form of the relationships."[10]

When the definition "a father and mother and their children" no longer described current realities, academics and social workers began to define family as "any household group." Certainly children benefit from loving attention, support, and encouragement from the partnered caring of a mother *and* father. But we know children can still thrive, with some assumed gaps, when raised by an attentive mother or father alone, or with loving gay parents.

Along with summarizing theories of changing families, it is valuable to hear observations and opinions of teenagers from a study like the National Study of Youth and Religion. Christian Smith's report on extensive interviews of thirteen- to nineteen-year-olds is found in *Soul Searching*.[11] Follow the topics "Marriage" and "Family" from its index, and you will get a sense of what youth have experienced and are hoping for in regard to family.

> The majority of U.S. teenagers tend to be quite like their parents when it comes to religion. They tend to share similar beliefs . . . , tend to be situated in the same general religious traditions . . . , and tend to attend religious services with one or both of their parents.[12]

This massive study concludes families are producing children who shape their beliefs by the lived out faith of their parents—that the family model of beliefs and practices is the largest determinant in a youth's own beliefs and practices.[13]

The Mystery of Marriage and Family

We believe the mystery of marriage begins in the mystery of the triune, covenant-making God. The God-in-relationship we worship has made us relational creatures and, from the beginning, declared that we should not be alone (Gen. 2:18). So

10. N. R. Kleinfield, "And Baby Makes Four," *New York Times*, June 19, 2011, 25–27. On the related subject of early and easy divorce, see Pamela Paul's *The Starter Marriage and the Future of Matrimony* (New York: Random House, 2003).

11. Christian Smith with Melinda Lundquist Denton, *Soul Searching: The Religious and Spiritual Lives of American Teenagers* (New York: Oxford University Press, 2005).

12. Ibid., 68.

13. Ibid.

God made humankind (Gen. 5:1–2) male and female to be, as was the Trinity, humans-in-relationship. Genesis, with the rest of Scripture, also conveys the idea that human relationships must be triadic—man-woman-God—anything else is highly vulnerable. The marital union was one of God's first covenants.

I doubt you can find a really healthy and successful family in the Bible, unless you take the Holy Family of Joseph, Mary, and Jesus as the prime example.[14] Still, we read of family distress when Jesus stayed in the temple without his parents' knowledge,[15] and we assume the death of Joseph before Jesus's ministry begins. Then, as Jesus begins his ministry, his mother and family seem unable to understand and support him.[16]

The biblical story and description of the origin and intent of marriage is cryptically expressed in Genesis 2:24. "Therefore a man leaves his father and his mother and clings to his wife, and they become one flesh." This explanation was first read (or heard) in the context of God's covenantal revelation and intentions, on the one hand, and, on the other, the social mores of that time. Of course the Bible has much more to say about marriage—especially from the apostle Paul. In Matthew 19:3–9 and Mark 10:2–12, Jesus describes the sanctity of marriage in clear reaffirmation of Genesis. Marriage and the family are not, however, a large part of Jesus's teachings.

After Scripture itself, one is helped in turning to the church fathers,[17] to begin with Chrysostom's *On Marriage and Family Life* (probably written between 386 and 397). For Chrysostom, according to his translator and commentator, Catherine Roth, "marriage is like monasticism . . . a sign of God's kingdom. Thus marriage is both a great mystery in itself and represents a greater mystery, the unity of redeemed mankind in Christ."[18] Although an ascetic monk early on and then a lifetime celibate, John Chrysostom became a compassionate preacher on marriage and family, drawing freely and richly from Paul's Epistles to the Ephesians and Colossians. Although women and children were addressed, the golden-tongued Chrysostom particularly challenged men.

> Husbands . . . you have heard how important obedience is . . . now hear about the amount of love necessary. . . . Even if it becomes necessary for you to give your life

14. Joseph is highlighted in Matthew's account of the nativity (Ch. 1–2). He is a noble and supportive husband and a protective step-father to Jesus.

15. Luke 2:41–50.

16. Mark 3:31–35.

17. Theology requires study as to how the earliest church leaders interpreted and used Scripture. Here, two great contemporaries in the late fourth and early fifth centuries are examples of theologians who must be carefully interpreted in terms of their historical context (which we cannot do carefully here) and their fallibilities (e.g., regarding their bias against sex in itself and attitudes towards Jews).

18. *St. John Chrysostom: On Marriage and Family Life*, trans. Catherine P. Roth (Crestwood, NY: St. Vladimir's Seminary Press, 1986), 10.

for her, yes even to endure and undergo suffering of any kind, do not refuse. Even though you undergo all this, you will never have done anything equal to what Christ has done. You are sacrificing yourself for someone to whom you are already joined, but He offered Himself up for one who . . . hated him. . . . Even if you see her belittling you, or despising and mocking you, still you will be able to subject her to yourself, through affection, kindness, and your great love for her. There is no influence more powerful than the bond of love, especially for husband and wife.[19]

The early church fathers were pastoral theologians (we might say practical theologians)—and here is practical advice. How many marriages might be saved if wives and husbands were able, by God's grace, to love as Christ loves? And, contrary to what many consider to be the teaching of the church, Chrysostom taught that God instituted marriage *first* for the holiness and encouragement provided one another, and only *secondarily* for the procreation of children.

Augustine's practical theology of marriage is dynamic, developing over the course of many years. Younger and living longer than Chrysostom, Augustine wrote quite influentially in the Western church, as Chrysostom did in the Eastern Church. In his treatise *The Excellence of Marriage* (ca. 401), Augustine argues that marriage is good (though not as good as celibacy) for three reasons. The threefold divine purpose of marriage, according to Augustine, is the procreation of children, fidelity between its partners, and its sacramental purpose as a prophetic sign to the world. From this, some church leaders have emphasized the procreation of children as the only justification for marriage. Augustine has a broader, though complicated, view of marriage, beginning as the first bond of society:

> Every human being is part of the human race, and human nature is a social entity, and has naturally the great benefit of friendship. . . . God wished to produce all persons out of one, so that they would be held together in their social relationships, not only by similarity of race, but also by the bond of kinship [i.e., all humans related]. The first natural bond of human society, therefore, is that of husband and wife. . . . The result is the bonding of society in its children.[20]

Although for Augustine procreation is the first and evident purpose for marriage in human society, he goes on to describe fidelity as another adequate purpose. It justifies marriage for partners who cannot have children. Marital sex should help keep partners faithful to one another; what Augustine is commending here is sex for the sake of your partner, your intention to keep your partner satisfied and

19. Ibid., Homily 20, 46.
20. Avid G. Hunter and John E. Rotelle, eds., Ray Kearney, trans., *Saint Augustine: Marriage and Virginity* (Hyde Park, NY: New City Press, 1999), 33.

free from adultery. Augustine's final sacramental purpose for marriage is more than making it one of the seven sacraments (as articulated later in history). He is thinking of it in terms of Greek *mysterion*, a sacred sign or symbol of Christ and the church, the bride of Christ. Viewing biblical history, Augustine saw differing notions of marital propriety. His theology of marriage accepted some moral relativity while holding to mysterious transcendence in all human relationships.[21] Here in these early theologians we find a deep sense of compassion and emphasis on the dignity of human nature.

A traditional and important statement of marriage in the *Book of Common Prayer* declares three reasons for marriage: "The union of husband and wife in heart, body, and mind is intended by God (1) for their mutual joy; (2) for the help and comfort given one another in prosperity and adversity; and, when it is God's will, (3) for the procreation of children and their nurture in the knowledge and love of the Lord."[22]

The Nature of Marriage and Family

Regarding conflicting views on the quintessential quality of marriage, Ray Anderson and Dennis Guernsey see, on the one hand, those who make the family an unchangeable structure built into the created biological nature of humankind (*determinism*) and, on the other, those who see marriage in terms of cultural *indeterminism*, allowing "the human person to form relationships that are mutually fulfilling . . . (so) that which is mutually satisfying . . . cannot violate the law of God and nature."[23] Unsatisfied with both perspectives, these writers envision a solution they call *created contingent order*, standing beyond these two views:

> We can view the natural world as contingent upon a source beyond its own structures and laws. When applied to the natural world, a contingent order (such as marriage) is a created order; that is, it exists in such a way that its own natural order is established by a higher order. . . .
>
> It seems, therefore, that there *is* a quintessential order for the family as a social structure. However, the quintessence is not located within the natural order as the determinist would have it, nor in the freedom of the individual to create a social order, as the indeterminist would have it. The quintessence of the social structure we

21. See David G. Hunter, "Sex, Sin and Salvation: What Augustine Really Said," www.jknirp.com/aug3.htm.

22. *The Book of Common Prayer* (New York: Seabury Press, 1977), 423.

23. Ray S. Anderson and Dennis B. Guernsey, *On Being Family: A Social Theology of the Family* (Grand Rapids: Eerdmans, 1985), 15–16.

call family is rooted in the creative Word of God and its purpose, which expresses itself through the order of creation.[24]

Marriage, in our Western world and increasingly worldwide, usually begins in the mystery of courtship.[25] As Agur, a contributor to the book of Proverbs, put it: "Three things are too wonderful for me; four I do not understand," the final and most mystical being "the way of a man with a girl" (Prov. 30:18, 19b). If it was complicated for men and women back then, it is more so today. Too often we dream or fantasize *personages* (see chapter 7) without the patience or persistence to discover a real *person*.

Anderson and Guernsey go on to describe real marriage and family as "grounded in the intentionality and practice of love."[26] (Tournier might suggest a permanent relationship committed to continual rediscovery of the real person in spouse and children.) They conclude:

> We seek to set forth the basic structure of the quintessential order of the family as grounded in God's covenant love, experienced in good parenting, expressed through marriage, and culminating in spiritual maturity and the freedom of fellowship and participation in the church as the new family of God. And we do this with full confidence that the old commandment [the Law] is also the new commandment [Love].[27]

Jack and Judith Balswick have produced what is often regarded as the best Christian textbook on the family. From sociological and biblical insights, they develop a nonlinear, nonhierarchical model of family, tracing the interaction of four divine intentions for marriage: *covenant*, *grace*, *empowerment*, and *intimacy*. This text does not neglect careful consideration of the family's challenges and difficulties in our times.[28]

> We initially wrote *The Family* . . . to present an integrated view of contemporary family life based on current social-science research, clinical insights, and biblical truth. . . . This new edition incorporates the most current research to date and includes

24. Ibid., 17.
25. I say usually. I met and became friends with a *lost boy*, an emigrant from troubled Sudan. He came to me excited one day asking me to stand up for him in his coming wedding. He had not met or ever seen the woman; his family assured him she was a wonderful match. So, for many cows, he became married. Some weeks later, we received hours of wedding videotape in which he got to see her for the first time. She eventually arrived from Sudan, and they now have a family with three boys.
26. Anderson and Guernsey, *On Being Family*, 22.
27. Ibid., 26.
28. Jack O. Balswick and Judith Balswick, *The Family: A Christian Perspective on the Contemporary Home*, 3rd ed. (Grand Rapids: Baker Academic, 2007).

two new chapters: "Family Spirituality" and "Complex Families in Contemporary Society." We also include a new focus on Trinitarian theology of relationship to enhance the biblical themes . . . in earlier editions.[29]

Since so many families are struggling, many with the addictions of a family member, it seems important to mention a book with practical helps. John Bradshaw has been a leader in recovery programs and his *Bradshaw on the Family: A New Way for Creating Solid Self-Esteem* has helped many damaged in dysfunctional families to gain a new sense of freedom and self-confidence.[30] Bradshaw writes as a psychological coach and theologian in the broad sense. His book is filled with helpful diagrams to explain the dynamics of family systems and emotional issues.

> While we've always known that our families influence us, we're now discovering that the influence is beyond what we had imagined. We now understand that families are dynamic social systems having structural laws, components and rules . . . [that affect] the formation of solid self-esteem.[31]

The Practice of Family

Youth ministry has a responsibility to families as families do to youth ministry. How families work in a fallen and broken world is, of course, complicated, filled with good intentions and paradoxes, dysfunctions and redeeming love. A functional family is a system committed and contributing to the healing, growth, and long-term goals of all its members. In considering the family as system, we're not dealing with the workings of bicycles, cars, or even computers but intricate interactions of an individual's inner systems, within a family's system(s), among still larger social systems.[32]

As a church or community leader, you interact with and are often asked to offer counsel to perplexed parents. A helpful scheme to understand differences in family styles of control comes out of studies from the University of Minnesota Extension Center for Family Development. Their research produced a matrix using high and low parental control with high and low parental responsiveness/warmth. A four-cornered diagram demonstrates four styles of parenting: the Authoritative (with high control and high responsiveness), the Autocratic (with

---

29. Ibid., 11.
30. John Bradshaw, *Bradshaw on the Family: A New Way for Creating Solid Self-Esteem* (Deerfield Beach, FL: Health Communications, Inc., 1996).
31. Ibid., 1.
32. For Christian systems thinking, see Douglas Hall, *The Cat and the Toaster: Living System Ministry in a Technological Age* (Eugene, OR: Wipf & Stock, 2010).

high control and low responsiveness), the Unengaged or Laissez-Faire (with low control and low responsiveness), and the Permissive (with low control and high responsiveness). You will find explanations of this, a survey to identify parental styles, and more at their website.[33] Their research into the importance of family mealtimes revealed ten significant reductions in detrimental behaviors among young people in families who frequently eat together.[34] Pamela Blewitt and Patricia Broderick present similar parenting patterns in an article and their textbook. Drawing on the research of parenting styles in Baumrind and others, they describe two dimensions of parenting: responsiveness and demandingness. Parents that are authoritarian (not autocratic), high on responsiveness and demandingness, have the best outcomes in their children's later lives.[35]

A helpful and provocative religious resource for families is *Parenting in the Pew: Guiding Your Children into the Joy of Worship*. Author Robbie Castleman is assistant professor of biblical studies at John Brown University and national director for the Religious and Theological Studies Fellowship with InterVarsity Christian Fellowship. She is also the wife of a pastor and mother of two sons. This book is not about keeping kids quiet in church; it's about the joy of worship beginning with leisurely Sunday morning preparation—and church worship without doodling gimmicks for children. Because the author's challenge may seem daunting, the book's study guide is especially helpful. With so many complaints about parental failures, about the weak spiritual life of families, and about kids not wanting to go to church, this book seems timely.[36]

Care for the Unmarried

We've acknowledged humans as created in the image of the Triune God. We are made for triadic intimacy with special others *and* a loving God. Married couples are incomplete without a third partner, a loving and merciful God. Trouble begins when intimacy with God, and therefore self, is neglected. Marriage works when it is part of a new family, the church of Jesus Christ. This "two-way street" between

---

33. University of Minnesota Extension, "Parenting Education Resources," www.extension.umn .edu/parenting/.

34. University of Minnesota Extension, "The Importance of Family Mealtimes," extension .umn.edu/projects/family/parenting/components/mealtime.html.

35. Pamela Blewitt and Patricia Broderick, "Adolescent Identity: Peers, Parents, Culture and the Counselor," *Counseling and Human Development*, April 1, 1999, http://business.highbeam .com/104229/article-1G1-68913449/adolescent-identity-peers-parents-culture-and-counselor. See also Patricia C. Broderick and Pamela Blewitt, *The Life Span: Human Development for Helping Professionals*, 3rd ed. (Boston: Pearson, 2009).

36. Robbie F. Castleman, *Parenting in the Pew: Guiding Your Children into the Joy of Worship* (Downers Grove, IL: InterVarsity, 2002).

church and families is rightly emphasized. What has been terribly neglected in many circles is the attention needed and deserved by those outside the bonds of holy matrimony. Jesus Christ, the apostle Paul, and many of the great saints of church history, were *not* fathers or mothers of happy families. Without neglecting families, both Christ (implicitly) and Paul (explicitly) affirmed a higher calling, a life denying nuptial and domestic joys for single commitment to kingdom work. John Stott is a noble example of a Protestant evangelical who turned from more than one attractive and willing woman to consciously follow the path of celibacy. It is the strong responsibility (don't you agree?) of Christians and the church to actively support and encourage those who are celibate by choice or single by any kind of circumstance. I wish every church could follow the example of churches with orders[37] or deaconates of singles who are called to special ministries (such as youth ministry). Single youth leaders (and other Christians) need and deserve special communal support.

From consideration of families and single adults, we move on to consider our understanding and theology of peer groups. If there is too little theology of marriage and the single state in the church, there is even less theology of peer groups. I would suggest that in this transition we are moving from a consideration of "family of orgin" to "the transitional peer family."

Peer Families and the Origin of Adolescence

"What can you mean by a theology of peer groups?" you might ask. Again, this takes an integration of science and biblical insight. We know sociologically that adolescence emerged in the Western industrial age, took on clear form with compulsory education in the 1920s, and that the term *teenager* was first used soon after, during World War II. It's true that Shakespeare's *Romeo and Juliet* and *Hamlet* in the sixteenth century foreshadowed adolescent struggles and emotions. Rousseau romanticized emotional and mental changes at puberty in his 1762 scandalous tract, *Emile*. But it was G. Stanley Hall's *Adolescence* in 1904 (with emphasis on "storm and stress") and Erik Erikson's *Childhood and Society* in 1950, and later *Identity, Youth, and Crisis* (emphasizing adolescents' identity crises) that solidified our naming and thinking about a life stage called adolescence. In this sense adolescence is a social construct. But by nature and culture, puberty and the transition from childhood to adulthood have always existed.

The "houseboys," who worked our campus homes for school fees when I taught at Liberia's Cuttington College in the mid-1960s, were "taken away" to bush school

---

37. A group taking vows toward a particular religious purpose or function under supervision of a sponsoring church.

for a rite of passage. In the manner of universal puberty rites, they were separated from family and all females, isolated with male elders, instructed in the ways of adult life, subjected to some pain (circumcision and/or scarification—decorative scarring of the skin), and then returned to an exuberant celebration. They would now be treated as "potential" adults—no longer children.

Elkind points out how we have in this age stripped growing youth of important social markers.[38] Frank Fasick explains what social scientists consider the causes of modern adolescence:

> Compulsory secondary education is clearly the core of adolescence as we know it, but we should not neglect the role played by the broader society in its "invention." Adolescence is deeply embedded in the whole fabric of industrial urbanism. In turn, many of the structural features that characterize modern day North America have been generated by three major developments: (a) the application of technology to increase productivity, (b) the affluence created through this process, and (c) the demographic transition that accompanied it. Each of these factors contributed to the "invention" of adolescence in North America.[39]

Peer Groups

It stands to reason the Bible doesn't talk about teenagers or adolescence as such. But it contains rich insights as to youth and the transition from childhood to adulthood. Neither does Scripture teach us about peer groups, although we find helpful encouragement for making and maintaining friendships.

A peer group, in modern times, is "a social group consisting of people who are equal in such respects as age, education, or social class."[40] Peer and special friendship groups exist at every age, but they serve a special function in adolescence.

Smith and Denton have described the rise of adolescent peer groups in this way:

> Macroeconomic changes after 1970 accelerated the entry of women, including mothers of adolescents, into the paid labor force. The no-fault divorce revolution of the 1970s and other social forces significantly increased the number of single-parent households in which teenagers lived and live. These and other related factors left youth increasingly on their own, both alone and with other youth, for growing numbers

38. "Vanishing Markers," ch. 5 in David Elkind, *All Grown Up and No Place to Go* (Reading, MA: Perseus Books, 1998).

39. Frank A. Fasick, "On the 'Invention' of Adolescence," *Journal of Early Adolescence* 14, no. 1 (February 1994): 7.

40. *Encarta World English Dictionary* (New York: St. Martin's, 1999), s.v. "peer group."

of hours of the day and night. This high degree of youth autonomy has become the normalized reality for many adolescents [among all classes alike].[41]

I like to put this in the context of five primary social systems of influence around adolescents: family, community, schools, media, and peers. As family, community, and schools began to lose their influence on youth in the post–World War II era, media and peers began to take up the functions of family, community, and education. Over time, collaboration between media and adolescent (and preadolescent) peer groups has grown closer and stronger.

The phenomenon of bullying has provoked studies of the structure and hierarchies in early childhood peer groups. Sociologist William Corsaro published *Friendship and Peer Culture in the Early Years* in 1985.[42] We've all observed young children *playing* adult roles (in contrast to adolescents, as we'll discuss). Corsaro describes how school-age children play at ages and situations just older than themselves. Studies at this time picked up little taunting or bullying among the young at this age. Corsaro points out the importance of adult intervention in conflicts arising from three sources of disputes: (1) excluded children attempting to get access to playgroups, (2) sharing of play materials, and (3) overly aggressive play.[43]

A decade or so later, Patricia and Peter Adler produced a fascinating study of somewhat older peer groups. For their *Peer Power: Preadolescent Culture and Identity* (1998), they observed eight- to twelve-year-olds (grades three through six) over a period of eight years. Their methodology emphasized entering into the culture of the young students, interacting with them, and learning from them.

> Working only loosely within the context of the major institutions of family, school, and after-school programs, we observed, interacted with, and asked children questions about the free time they constructed for themselves within these realms. It was within their social lives that they found the freedom to create and express themselves. This was where they forged the peer culture that set the standards against which they both evaluated the outside world and measured themselves.[44]

The Adlers observed elaborate strategies for leadership (power) and shrewd manipulation of roles in children as young as nine years old, in fourth grade.[45]

41. Smith and Denton, *Soul Searching*, 184.
42. William A. Corsaro, *Friendship and Peer Culture in the Early Years* (Norwood, NJ: Ablex, 1985).
43. Ibid., 302.
44. Patricia A. Adler and Peter Adler, *Peer Power: Preadolescent Culture and Identity* (New Brunswick, NJ: Rutgers University Press, 1998), 194.
45. Note, in the wake of bullying, the spate of books in the first decade of this century: Charlene C. Giannetti and Margaret Sagarese, *Cliques: 8 Steps to Help Your Child Survive the Social Jungle* (New York: Broadway Books, 2001); Rosalind Wiseman, *Queen Bees and*

More important, they found preadolescent and adolescent culture to mediate and shape the way young people clarify their identities and represent themselves within society.

> From these discussions, we see the power of peer culture, setting both the content and timing of preadolescent cultural norms and values. From their subculture, children learned the culturally acceptable behavioral guidelines and the consequences of violating them. They saw the positive and negative sanctions, social status and ridicule applied to individuals based on their power, position, attitudes, and behavior. They learned and experienced the identity outcomes of their placement in relation to peer culture. . . . Their peer culture . . . united and divided them, supported and destroyed them, gave them structure and process, and fit them as a distinctive subunit within the broader American culture.[46]

Adolescent Peer Groups

Theologically speaking, God has placed us and speaks to us in various kinds of peer groups—extended family groups, tribes, and kingdoms in the Old Testament, faith communities and outsiders in the New. Social scientists and public health experts Christakis and Fowler (see chapter 7) demonstrate how behaviors from obesity to oral sex are "spread" not only by immediate friends and friends of friends but also from friendships six degrees removed.[47]

Looking at a young person's peer group, then, is very important but inadequate. We need to consider the broader age cohort. Its earlier (and later) age stages should also be taken into consideration. Why begin with prepubescent peer groups? I admit my lack of concern, as a high school teacher and youth leader, for the subculture from which my teenage students had come—or for the subcultures and life to which they were headed. What has just been observed about preadolescent (generally middle-class) subcultures carries over into adolescent culture and peer groups as well. Teenagers have long left childhood with its *playing* of adult roles and life. Now, in very specific ways, though with self-centered lack of understanding, they are *practicing* adult roles, opportunities, and responsibilities. This emphasis points to the critical importance of peer groups as preparation for adult business, social relations, courtship and marriage, family life, worldviews, values, and decisions.

Wannabes: Helping Your Daughter Survive Cliques, Gossip, Boyfriends and Other Realities of Adolescence (New York: Three Rivers, 2002); Hayley DiMarco, *Mean Girls: Facing Your Beauty Turned Beast* (Grand Rapids: Revell, 2008).

46. Adler and Adler, *Peer Power*, 217 (concluding paragraph of book).

47. Christakis and Fowler, *Connected*.

For this reason I believe churches do well to maintain a healthy balance between family-integrated youth ministry *and* differentiated age groups. Understanding the power of peer groups (of various kinds and structures) leads to recognition of our responsibility for peer evangelism, peer discipleship, and varieties of peer leadership. Exclusively family-integrated churches are hardly able to carry on peer evangelism or peer discipleship. I also watch segregated Sunday school classes and youth groups where members have not bonded. Their primary and secondary friendship groups are outside their faith communities. In all such cases I am convinced that little teaching or spiritual growth has taken place. Young people learn and grow in groups to which they are bonded—where they can trust the sharing of deep questions and struggles.

Part of what we are discussing here is friendship, and the Bible has quite a bit to say about it. Jesus appears to be more active and interested in friendship than family. "Who are my mother and brothers? . . . Here are my mother and my brothers!"—as he turns to his followers and listeners (Mark 3:31–35). "No one has greater love than this, to lay down one's life for his friends. You are my friends" (John 15:13–14).

Consider also all the families described carefully in the Bible. From Adam and Eve's family, to Noah's and Jacob's (taking up so many chapters in Genesis) to King David's, most are honestly portrayed as having serious problems. Then, notice important friendships and partnerships emphasized in Scripture.[48] Moses and Aaron were probably friends. A poignant story from the book of Judges describes an impulsive vow taken by the judge Jephthah. As a result his innocent and only daughter had to be killed. She willingly acquiesced to her doom but asked to be given two months "that I may go and wander on the mountains, and bewail my virginity, *my companions* and I" (Judg. 11:34–40, quote at v. 37, emphasis added). David and Jonathan, Barzillai and David, Paul and Barnabas, Paul and Silas, Paul and Luke and others, demonstrate the power of friendships. I also consider anyone who would sit with a stinking, diseased, and depressed man for seven days, offering presence without words, to be a caring friend. Such were Job's three friends . . . until they got into their rational diagnoses.

A proverb declares, "Some friends play at friendship, but a true friend sticks closer than one's nearest kin" (Prov. 18:24). And Proverbs also reminds us that iron sharpens iron and that we need advice from others (Prov. 27:17).[49] The 1994 movie *The Shawshank Redemption* beautifully illuminates the verses from Ecclesiastes: "Two are better than one, because they have a good reward for their toil. For if

48. The Hebrew word for *neighbor* can sometimes be translated as "friend." Deuteronomy 13:6 refers to the intimacy of friendship.
49. Consider the difference between peer and adult iron in confronting and holding teenagers accountable—the importance of peer advice: Prov. 11:14; 15:22; 24:6.

they fall, one will lift up the other; but woe to one who is alone and falls and does not have another to help" (Eccl. 4:9–10). You might have some wonderful student discussions of that verse, along with a verse to the contrary: "Even my best friend, the one I always told everything—he ate meals at my house all the time!—has bitten my hand" (Ps. 41:9 Message). Many teenagers are experts on rejection—and need to talk about it.

I reemphasize: the first task of any Sunday school class or youth group is that of *bonding*, the emergence or renewal of friendship. Without the bonding of teacher/ leader to the group, and without the bonding of students to one another within a group, there can be little learning and growth. How many classes or groups would have gone somewhere, or at least further, if they had just gone out in the woods together or painted some poor person's house—and processed their interactions *before* Bible studies and catechesis?[50] From real experiences, we are able to foster real discussions and genuine learning among them. To put this in the words of Kara Powell and Chap Clark, "sticky faith"[51] takes teenagers beyond high school and youth groups. It begins with positive relationships between students and their parents, and students and their friends in the fellowship of the church and Jesus Christ.

This means thinking theologically about marriage and families, about friendships and community. As Osmer put it:

> What is happening in this family or peer group?
> Why is this going on in this family or peer group?
> What ought to be going on in this family or peer group?
> How might we youth leaders respond to this family or peer group?[52]

Where there is tension, dysfunction, or hurt may we be healing and enabling ministers of God—the Father, the Son, and the Holy Spirit.

Questions for Reflection and Discussion

1. What questions do you have about the dynamic relationships among individuals, families, and friendship groups?

50. The process of experiential or service learning in short: What's going on or what happened? How did you feel about it and how did you respond? What can we learn from this and why is that important? Finally, what's next or where can we go from here?
51. Kara E. Powell and Chap Clark, *Sticky Faith: Everyday Ideas to Build Lasting Faith in Your Kids* (Grand Rapids: Zondervan, 2011).
52. Richard R. Osmer, *Practical Theology: An Introduction* (Grand Rapids: Eerdmans, 2008), 4. See chap. 3.

2. Do you sense mystery in regard to the origin, complexity, and functioning of families and peer groups?

3. Does this chapter, in your opinion, bring social science and biblical principles together for theologies of families and peer groups?

4. What do you see as your task in regard to supporting, and drawing on the resources and support of, families and friendship groups?

5. Where do you consider yourself to be weakest in understanding and supporting families and peer groups?

6. Does this chapter help us to discuss a theology of culture and prepare for a discussion of sexuality?

—9—

Theology of Sexuality

I've always been told that sex is like candy: once you're introduced to it, you never get enough. And boy, is that the truth.

SOPHOMORE FEMALE

Come on, sex has nothing to do with love or friendship. It's as meaningless as eating. Sometimes it's wonderful, other times it's gross and no fun. Lighten up on this relationship stuff. The phrase "to death do us part" means nothing anymore. All we can do in this world is get as much pleasure as possible. If that means risking AIDS or pregnancy, so be it. Where is all this love you're talking about?

TEENAGE LETTER TO "ASK BETH," BOSTON GLOBE, JANUARY 14, 1993

Today's teenagers have sex first, and date later.

EVOLUTIONARY BIOLOGIST JUSTIN R. GARCIA[1]

From the beginning of creation, God made them male and female . . . and the two shall become one flesh; consequently they are no longer two, but one flesh.

MARK 10:6, 8 NASB

---

1. Quoted in Karen Weintraub, "Looking for Love: How Science Is Revealing the Roots of Romance and Debunking Myths," *Boston Globe*, February 6, 2012, G12. Garcia is a postdoctoral fellow at the Kinsey Institute for Research in Sex, Gender, and Reproduction at Indiana University.

Introduction to a Theology of Sexuality

No practical theology of youth ministry can neglect a theology of sexuality. Sex is built into human nature and culture. It flows out of the very nature of the Triune God and parallels our spiritual quest for union with God. In awe of God we approach the mystery of sexuality.

Teenagers think about sex in many different ways, depending on family situation and training, their friends' values and style, and their personal disposition and values. How often boys think about sex, in contrast to girls, is open to debate. There is general agreement that boys have sexual thoughts and urges more frequently than girls, but there is also evidence the gap is closing. Accepting the estimated three thousand ads they see in a day, besides the actual people they see often who dress or act to attract, we know teen thoughts about sex are quite frequent—they admit as much to us. It's been estimated that males in our society think some sexual thought or fantasy every few minutes.

Facts about Adolescent Sexuality

According to the reliable Guttmacher Institute: "Teens in the United States and European teens have similar levels of sexual activity. However, the latter are more likely to use contraceptives and to use effective contraceptive methods; they therefore have substantially lower pregnancy rates."[2] Other statistics from this fact sheet on American teens' sexual and reproductive health include the following:

- Although only 13 percent of teens have had vaginal sex by age fifteen, sexual intercourse is common by the late teen years. By their nineteenth birthday, seven in ten teens of both sexes have had intercourse.

- On average, young people have sex for the first time at about age seventeen, but they do not marry until their mid-twenties. This means that young adults are at increased risk of unintended pregnancy and STIs [sexually transmitted infections] for nearly a decade.

- Teens have been waiting longer to have sex than they did in the recent past. In 2006–2008, some 11 percent of never-married females ages fifteen to nineteen and 14 percent of never-married males that age had had sex before age fifteen, compared with 19 percent and 21 percent, respectively, in 1995.

2. Guttmacher Institute, "Facts on American Teens' Sexual and Reproductive Health," guttmacher.org/sections/adolescents.php.

- However, after declining substantially between 1995 and 2002, the proportion of teens who had ever had sex did not change significantly from 2002 to 2006–2008.

- In 2006–2010, the most common reason that sexually inexperienced teens gave for not having had sex was that it was "against religion or morals" (38 percent among females and 31 percent among males). The second and third most common reasons for females were "don't want to get pregnant" and "haven't found the right person yet."

- Among sexually experienced teens, 70 percent of females and 56 percent of males report that their first sexual experience was with a steady partner, while 16 percent of females and 28 percent of males report a first sexual experience with someone whom they had just met or who was just a friend.

- Seven percent of young women ages eighteen to twenty-four who had had sex before age twenty report that their first sexual experience was involuntary. Those whose first partner was three or more years their senior were more likely to report this than were other women in the same age-group.[3]

It would seem from this there is both good news and bad—for young people themselves, and for parents, youth leaders, and society in general. There *are* positive trends, yet still, facts representing detrimental consequences of sexual promiscuity provide a basis for reflection and discussion among young people. Quantitative research must also be balanced by qualitative interviews and focus groups. Such social research can then be integrated with biblical principles in shaping our theology of sexuality.

The Need for a Theology of Sexuality

In the beginning, God—can we imagine a smiling face—invented sex. And God said, "Enjoy." (That's not exactly how the biblical account goes, and not all would agree it approximates its truth.) I reject all notions that the forbidden fruit was an apple . . . or sex. Certainly not the latter. For overall, God's Word says sex is, or should be, beautiful, good, and fun. "Rejoice in the wife of your youth. . . . May her breasts satisfy you at all times; may you be intoxicated always by her love" (Prov. 5:18–19).[4]

Sex came from the heart of God, and though we don't fully know what we're talking about, it came out of the experience of the Triune God. The *essence* of sex,

3. Ibid.
4. See also Eccl. 9:9 and the Song of Songs. Karl Barth apparently missed this verse in Proverbs when he spoke of only two biblical passages on erotic love.

if we can use that term, is *mystical union*, unity of being—and the communion of the Trinity is reflected in human communion, most deeply in the intimacy of marriage.

If we are to produce a practical theology of sexuality (as we have described practical theology), it begins at the altar of God, where we present our best to God and God returns the divine presence to us. We've called this doxological theology, spiritual communion with God. From there we develop a biblical theology of sexuality, reflect on commentary throughout the ages (historical theology), test it in the waters of culture and social science as we work out a practical theology *in* ministry, and prepare ourselves for a pastoral theology that will help those confused or hurt by sex.

Although surrounded by sexual images and innuendos, many youth ministers don't reflect theologically about sexuality. When the subject is addressed, it is often discussed more in terms of standards than underlying principles. Ethicists Stanley Hauerwas and William Willimon help chart a course for dealing with sexuality in our times.

> When Christians discuss sex, it often sounds as if we are somehow "against sex." What we fail to make clear is that sexual passion (the good gifts of God's creation) is now subservient to the demanding business of maintaining a revolutionary (Christian) community in a world that often uses sex as a means of momentarily anesthetizing or distracting people from the basic vacuity of their lives. When the only contemporary means of self-transcendence is orgasm, we Christians are going to have a tough time convincing people that it would be nicer if they would not be promiscuous.
>
> We believe it is only when our attentions are directed toward a demanding and exciting account of life that we have any way of handling something so powerful, so distracting, so creative, so deadly as sex.[5]

A prerequisite for theological reflection on the mystery of this mighty force is an honest consideration of our own sexuality. Few of us are without some kind of gender or sexual confusion, frustrations, or struggles. Having been honest with ourselves about our own struggles, we can more effectively help adolescents work through their own issues around gender and sexuality.

Young people in modern societies are sexually aroused through media and peers at a remarkably young age—with marriage an extremely remote possibility (for some, even referred to as a dead end). Youth leaders should be aware of early or precocious puberty. The signs of such puberty are typical, but the onset

5. Stanley Hauerwas and William H. Willimon, *Resident Aliens: A Provocative Christian Assessment of Culture and Ministry for People Who Know That Something Is Wrong* (Nashville: Abingdon, 1989), 63–64.

of secondary sexual characteristics in this case begin at age seven or eight in girls and nine in boys—even younger ages have been recorded. In addition to the general trend of diminishing age for puberty, advertising has attempted to shock and attract by featuring childhood eroticism. Contemporary youth culture seems like a social science laboratory in which society has decided to study adolescent frustration by maximizing sexual stimulus and postponing the economic and emotional viability for marriage.

While we were driving home from a family vacation years ago, Whitney Houston's "Saving All My Love for You" came on the radio. (You might check it out from iTunes or your favorite source before reading on.) It's an old and pretty song—attractive, technically well done, and capable of sticking in your mind for days. You have probably heard it as background music in an elevator, restaurant, or dentist's office—perhaps even hummed it yourself. On that particular drive, I heard my fourth-grade daughter singing along in the backseat—before her older brother convinced her to be quiet. The tune was familiar, but I didn't know the song well then, and snatches of the lyrics my daughter was singing piqued my interest. When we arrived home, I asked her if she could write out the words for me so I could use them in a class. She did—word for word from memory.

The song starts out sweetly, describing a few moments shared by two lovers. Then, in the next line, the lover reminds her guy that he has a family and is needed there. Although she realizes she must always be last on his list, no other can ever fulfill her longings—so, "I'm saving all my love for you." The song goes on to speak of tonight as the night when all her feelings, longings, and frustrations are going to be fulfilled—all night long.

What happened next with my daughter is a lesson in itself. We talked about the song; my daughter had not noticed the implications of the words. When she took a good look at them, she agreed with me that the song involves a case of adultery. She saw it, and did not approve of it but was not particularly bothered by it. Most of us have gotten such responses, "Of course it's not right, but what's the big deal?" Still, the conversation seemed profitable for both of us. Youth ministry includes youth numb to a promiscuous society, others cautiously testing its delights—and even some engaged in its extremes.

We should take note, not only of the general and changing norms of rising generations in our secondary schools, but also of possible extremes. Victoria Gill interviewed Jonni about sex for the *Irish Times*.

"It's something that I know really well. I've been having sex since I was 12 years old. I just always seem to attract it," this 18-year-old singer from Hertford (says). Threesomes, sixsomes, bondage, married mums: it would be easier to tell you about what Jonni hasn't done. Does he think his generation is different? "Yes. It's just the amount of sex they're having from a young age. There's no shock factor in sex any more. People are very promiscuous at my age. There's a lot of casual sex now. It's all become much simpler."[6]

Jonni's mother says she knew he was sexually active from about the age of thirteen and tried to discuss it with him, but then "he kept much more quiet about it. I'd rather not know too much. I don't think it's good to be their friend." The writer of this article went on to visit Sophie in Surrey just before her seventeenth birthday party. The party was themed (unknown to her parents) "Rock Stars and Porn Stars."

> "It's not like in the olden days when it was like, 'Oh, please tell me what it's like to have sex?' If I wanted to know I could just go online and talk to someone random. . . . When you're 10 they tell you how to have sex, what drugs give you which effects and what alcohol does to you."
>
> At Sophie's party, "Everyone ended up stripping and getting off with each other— whether they were gay or straight, they were changing their personalities." Sophie estimates that she "got off with at least a hundred" boys last year. "I just like meeting guys and making out with guys. It doesn't matter if I'm at a party, if I'm on the Underground, it's wherever I feel like it."[7]

Concerned about rising promiscuity at that time, the English government developed, with help from Exeter University, a program called "A Pause." According to the *London Times*, it "encouraged pupils under 16 to experiment with oral sex, as part of a drive to cut rates of teenage pregnancy—training teachers to discuss various pre-sex 'stopping points.'"[8] The United States has more than its share of sensational stories. One of these documents regular orgies among teens in Conyers, Georgia, during the summer of 1996. Their clandestine escapades took place in the afternoon or after busy parents had gone to sleep. An unusual outbreak of syphilis finally caught the attention of health workers and enabled them to track the carnage. According to a public health nurse: "You don't expect to see a 14-year-old with 20, 30, 40, 50 or 100 sex partners." This story was covered in a significant PBS Frontline special, "The Lost Children of Rockdale County."[9] The documentary includes discussions with two high school generations (four

6. Victoria Gill, "What's Love Got to Do with It?" *Irish Times*, Sunday Magazine, March 23, 2008, 51–52.

7. Ibid., 52, 53.

8. Glen Owen, "Government Urges Under-16s to Experiment with Oral Sex," *London Times* online, February 21, 2003.

9. The story is summarized and the source cited in Dean Borgman, *Hear My Story: Understanding the Cries of Troubled Youth* (Peabody, MA: Hendrickson, 2003), 341–47.

or five school years apart) of young girls discussing the inevitability of sexual activity—and expressing regret about how early, and sometimes crudely, they lost their virginity.

The desire for peer approval, attention, relationship, and touch seem to be key factors leading girls toward sexual activity. For boys, the urge for a high, relief, adventure, conquest, and peer approval all motivate. Then there are media inducements. An assortment of adult and adolescent television shows promotes and sanctions spur-of-the-moment, recreational sex. Music videos vie for "over-the-edge" sexual impact. The incessant, erotic, urgent beat (and it's the beat that most attracts teenagers to a song) of rap music includes lyrics (which they know by heart) admonishing them: "How ya doin' young lady. . . . What's the problem? I don't see no ring on your hand. . . . I be the first to admit it, I'm curious about you, you seem so innocent. . . . Let your guard down ain't nobody gotta know."[10] A Rand Study found that adolescents who listen to a great deal of music with heavy sexual lyrics have sex sooner.[11]

Cultural history has moved from the 1960s as "The Sexual Revolution," in which rules and taboos were broken, to the "Immediacy of Sex" in the 1980s and '90s when progressing through the four stages from first base to home was discarded for meeting with mouths wide open and clothes magically evaporating until it's done (with no after-mess to clean or consequences to pay), to "Consumptive Sex" in the new century as the internet fostered normalization of "soft" and "harder" pornography and digital/virtual sex. In fact there are signs of society's moving toward "tired sex" where recreational hook-ups have become boring.

Teen Pregnancies and Sexually Transmitted Diseases

According to the Guttmacher Institute, three-quarters of a million young women under twenty in the United States became pregnant in 2006—by far the highest rate in the industrialized world. Eight of ten of these pregnancies were unintended, and almost a third were terminated by abortions. More than four out of ten teenagers get pregnant before reaching the age of twenty. The cost of teenage pregnancies to the United States is estimated at more than $7 billion annually. After a decline in pregnancy and abortion rates from a peak in 1991, the rates began to increase in 2006. The decline from a million pregnancies a year for that age group is attributed both to delayed sexual activity and more careful use of

10. Nelly Furtado, "Promiscuous," from the album *Loose*, Geffen, 2006.
11. S. C. Martino, R. L. Collins, M. N. Elliott, A. Strachman, D. E. Kanouse, and S. H. Berry, "Exposure to Degrading Versus Nondegrading Music Lyrics and Sexual Behavior among Youth," *Pediatrics* 118, no. 2 (August 2006): 3430–41.

contraceptives. Despite positive effects from abstinence education and the availability of contraceptives, teenage sexuality and pregnancies halted their decline in this first decade of the twenty-first century. The rise in teen pregnancies, beginning in 2006, is causing concern.[12]

Another danger in teenage sexual activity is a dramatic rise in sexually transmitted diseases (STDs). Many studies suggest that only half of sexually active teenagers in the United States use protective devices.[13] Too little attention has been brought to the severity and long-term consequences of STDs. Meg Meeker, MD, has raised an alarm in *Epidemic: How Teen Sex Is Killing Our Kids*.

> Every day, this silent epidemic strikes 8,000 teens. Consider that this year alone, 15.3 million Americans will contract a new sexually transmitted disease. More to the point, 2 million to 4 million of those infected will be teenagers Nearly one out of four sexually active teens is living with a sexually transmitted disease at this moment. . . . Because most STDs have no symptoms, experts can only estimate the scope of this epidemic.[14]
>
> In 1960, physicians contended with two major sexual diseases: gonorrhea and syphilis. . . . The STD epidemic is not a single epidemic. [Now] the Centers of Disease Control and Prevention (CDC) consider it a *multiple* epidemic of at least 25 diseases— nearly 50 if you count the various strains of virus groups. . . . In the 1960s, a simple shot of penicillin could cure the two known STDs: syphilis and gonorrhea. Today, there are no simple cures and *in many cases there are no cures at all* (e.g., herpes).[15]
>
> Here's another way to look at it: Picture a football stadium filled with teenagers. Start counting. One out of five of those cheering kids has herpes (at least that we know of). Every third girl in the stands has human papilloma virus (HPV), and one out of ten has chlamydia. If we pulled all the healthy kids out of there, leaving just those teens infected with an STD, the stadium would still be nearly full.[16]

We know that herpes is incurable, embarrassing, and painful; that HPV, one of the most prevalent of STDs, causes 99.7 percent of cervical cancers, killing

12. The Guttmacher Institute, "U.S. Teenage Pregnancies, Births and Abortions: National and State Trends and Trends by Race and Ethnicity," January 2010, guttmacher.org/pubs/USTP trends.pdf; and the National Campaign to Prevent Teen and Unplanned Pregnancy, thenation alcampaign.org.

13. See, for instance, "Teens' Failure to Use Condoms Linked to Partner Disapproval, Fear of Less Sexual Pleasure," *Science Daily*, September 12, 2008, www.sciencedaily.com/releases/2008/09/080909122757.htm.

14. Meg Meeker, *Epidemic: How Teen Sex Is Killing Our Kids* (Washington, DC: LifeLine, 2002), 3, 11. See also Hillard Weinstock, Stuart Berman, and Willard Cates Jr., "Sexually Transmitted Diseases among American Youth: Incidence and Prevalence Estimates, 2000," *Perspectives on Sexual and Reproductive Health* 36, no. 1 (January 2004): 6.

15. Meeker, *Epidemic*, 31, 14–15.

16. Ibid., 13–14.

more than five thousand women a year; and that chlamydia (half of all new cases are in girls ages fifteen to nineteen) can, without symptoms, bring on extreme cervical infection and may lead to infertility. Boys and men are not immune to these diseases. Chlamydia can bring on infections of internal genital organs and make urination difficult. And men with HPV are candidates for penile and anal cancer—and possibly some head and neck cancers.

We have a problem here: teenagers (including Christians) are having oral and vaginal sex—and hurting themselves. Many churches and Christian youth organizations are either doing little about it or are approaching it in a way that excludes those needing guidance the most. The teaching may be fine for those who have decided or are open to wait, but those already sexually involved, or on the brink of sexual activity, may not hear anything that makes sense for them. Most parents are not sure what to do; many simply tend to hope for the best.

Approaching Sexuality in Our Times

Parents and youth leaders need to be able to relate with compassion and a positive approach to sons, daughters, or young friends who are having sex before marriage. It is very difficult when you find out your young daughter is already having sex with her boyfriend, or when a young man you have led to faith becomes sexually active. As Christians we feel differently about promiscuous sex among young people than many others do; we think it *is* a big deal. Emotional damage, early pregnancies, abortions, and incurable diseases can do immediate damage and last a lifetime.[17] And beyond that, spiritual and eternal issues can be at stake. The theology of sexuality contains a warning that although sexual sins can be forgiven, some consequences may remain.

Parents and youth ministers have different relationships to young people, but they need to work together—and can, if they trust each other. In love and with firmness, parents set and explain the rules and boundaries of their home—and their concern for the long-term welfare of their children. Youth workers approach the situation with interest, respect, and concern. Both parents and youth ministers can convey to young persons strong rationale and practical guidelines for sexual abstinence before marriage. Some young people *are waiting* until they are married to have sex; we're there to support and prepare them in godly standards. Still, the studies and our experience with youth show that many are not waiting (a good estimate might be a third among conservative Christians—half of the *general teen*

17. Robert Rector, Kirk Johnson, and Lauren Noyes, "Sexually Active Teenagers Are More Likely to Be Depressed and to Attempt Suicide," *Heritage Foundation*, June 3, 2003. From a large national survey, AdHealth Center for Data Analysis, www.heritage.org.

generation). Some sexually active youth have been able to modify or restrain their sexual activities—sometimes by separation. In a postmodern, media-influenced age, abstinence works only by the grace of God and with strong encouragement on the grounds of a solid and relevant theology of sexuality shared among peers.[18]

Most of us in youth ministry are on the side of abstinence,[19] yet we want to be realistic and unconditionally compassionate with all young people. We want to understand the relative difference between promiscuous teenage sex, sex between loving, committed late teen couples and cohabitation of a Christian couple in their twenties or thirties, planning to marry. Whatever our read on these different situations, pastoral theology calls for such distinctions. Finally, we deal most effectively with sex as we help young people work out their own personal identities, their worldviews and values, and healthy relationships with others.

Many experts on adolescent sex in the 1960s and 1970s followed the sexual revolution toward permissive freedom. "Have fun, but be responsible"—whatever that meant in specific situations. During the 1980s, however, many secular specialists took a more conservative stance. They came to question whether teenagers were emotionally mature enough for sexual intimacy, for keeping themselves from unwanted pregnancies, and for avoiding STDs. But from the 1990s on, "experts" seemed to capitulate and accepted the fact that *most* young adults from high school seniors to college students are sexually active. Some suggest strategies for saying yes or no, and thoughtful gradualism. "It's good to postpone, but we know you can't, so be emotionally ready." This more permissive attitude has left young people understandably confused or content just to follow the flow.

For many youth, we have in some ways passed the age of restraint. Progressive stages from hand-holding, to kissing, to necking, to petting no longer appear to work. We are in an age of instant sexual expression. Media depictions move from warm attraction to almost immediate sexual meltdown. And though some young people of faith are postponing sexual activity, they are not immune to acting out their sexual drives in the long wait for appropriate adulthood. In regard to sexual norms, cultural norms seem very influential.

Rules are inadequate when they do not rest on a strong theological foundation and positive models. If negative restraints have not protected our young folk sexually, we must seek an approach that is positive and powerful. "Just *saying*

18. Music and other media should be brought into these discussions. Presented in the late 1990s by Motown Records with a vibrant and sexy image, The Shades still believed loving to be much more than sex. Their song "I Believe" rejects one-night stands, talks about slowing it down, and looks forward to a love that lasts. Christian pop music goes further still: see the 1994 *True Love Waits* album with strong messages from DC Talk, Michael W. Smith, Newsboys, Petra, DeGarmo & Key, and others.

19. Lauren F. Winner, *Real Sex: The Naked Truth about Chastity* (Grand Rapids: Brazos, 2005), is a thoughtful book from the conservative side of this discussion.

no" is not a strong enough way to handle overwhelming temptations for three reasons. First, sex is too powerful for "just." Second, if you wait until you have to say something ("no"), it's probably already too late. Finally, as Paul reminds us, positive and offensive measures against the easy path of temptation are stronger than any defensive means: "Don't allow yourself to be overpowered with what's wrong. Take the offensive—overpower the wrong with good!" (Rom. 12:21, author's paraphrase). Young people seek a way to live an exciting and affirmative life—a way of life that says yes rather than no.

The town of Gloucester, Massachusetts, attracted international attention when its pregnancy rate shot from four or so a year to eighteen in 2007–2008.[20] Understandable community defensiveness and shifting of blame took place. At first we heard nothing from the girls and their parents. Money was appropriated for outside consultants and facilitators to help. Meanwhile, budget constraints had cut sports, music, drama, and peer counseling programs—all positive and preventive measures. (Because of high entry fees for sports, music, and drama at this high school, it was easier for a student to get herself and her baby enrolled in the school's child care unit than to go out for music, art, drama, or sports.) Attention seemed to be more on negative image and consequences than on positive ways to give teenagers the attention and love they can find from babies.[21] "Hardwired to Connect" (mentioned in chap. 6) calls for *authoritative communities* of warmth and structure that most young people are missing, but its lessons have hardly been heard.[22]

We need to understand more of what it is like for a young person who needs to say no and *why* "just say no" is usually not enough. As we contemplate the emptiness of consumer society and the power of hormones, media, and peers in the experience of a young person, we will better appreciate how difficult it is for a mere no to overcome passion. As adults, we lack a clear picture of what it is to live in today's youth culture. We do want to see young men and women living out a dynamic yes to their own sexuality, to the fullness of life, to challenging activities,

20. Stephanie Marsh, "Gloucester High School: After the Pregnancy Pact, the Blame Game," *The (London) Times* online, July 14, 2008. Residents of Gloucester heard from friends in Japan, Korea, South Africa, and other places when this hit international news. In 2010 a quite thoughtful documentary was made of the stories behind this story: "The Gloucester 18: The Realities of Teen Pregnancy," Media Education Foundation (www.mediaed.org).

21. Jim Munn (Gloucester track coach and writer), "Maybe Outside 'Facilitators' Can Handle All Our Problems," *Gloucester Daily Times*, August 8, 2008, 6: "How come School Committee members haven't gone out and gotten any money from the state to help reduce, not raise, the cost of participation in much needed after-school pregnancy-and-drug prevention activities—such as music, drama and sports?"

22. Commission on Children at Risk, "Hardwired to Connect: The New Scientific Case for Authoritative Communities" (New York: Institute for America Values, 2003), 35.

to supportive community, to the law of God, and to God's loving presence in and for them. We adults need a more dynamic connection with young people—for the benefit of both generations.

Before we can help young people deal with their sexuality in a society bombarding them with highly titillating messages and icons, we must deal with our own sexuality and come to a sound theology of sexuality by addressing the following questions.

- How are we handling our own sexual temptations and fantasies, and the powerful images and messages that influence us in subtle ways?
- How do we define sex and sexuality?
- What is the nature of sex and the sexual drive?
- How does God intend the sexual drive to operate in a single person, and how should married people appreciate and love their partners and those outside their married relationship?

Then, we must go on to deal honestly with our responsibility to teenagers who are awash in sexual come-ons and powerful peer pressures.

- How can today's teenagers develop a healthy sexual identity? What are God's intentions for males and females?
- How should young people deal with their sexual energies? Why has God endowed them with such powerful passions?
- How can we tell teenagers and those in their twenties that sexual activity should wait until marriage?
- What guidelines can we give them as to the level of sexual intimacy they should have before marriage?

Underneath all the information and questions about sex, we have a sense that whereas rules are failing, relationships last. We wish to anchor young people in healthy relationships with their parents, adult leaders, and friends. Beyond that we encourage their vital relationship with the Lord of sex rather than idols of sex.

Developing a Theology of Sexuality

Any theology of sexuality begins with God, the divine model, exemplar, and instructor of all we are and should be. God created humans with drives for *union* and *significance*. We are meant to *love* and to *serve*, and we do so with a divine energy surging within us for connection and creativity. We long to be at one with

God and one another (communion) and to serve and be affirmed by one another (service). In this we find love and worth. This is the first step in working out our understanding of sexuality.

Our next step is to understand the mystery of the Trinity as a model for human life. The eternal flow of love and light (or wisdom) is the bond of perfect unity. From a Christian perspective, God's *unity* (as emphasized in Judaism) is reflected in the *diversity* of roles within the Trinity (as emphasized in Christianity): Father, Son, and Holy Spirit. The Father is revealed through the Son, while the Son defers to the Father and promises the Holy Spirit. The eternal Triune God gives no hint of superiority or discontent. Father, Son, and Holy Spirit enjoy perfect union and significance. The holy Trinity is supreme love and worthiness (unity and significance). God has placed these holy drives toward union and significance in human nature. They are what loving and living are all about.

The Genesis accounts of creation make clear it was good for Adam and Eve to be created. It was not good for Adam to be alone and incomplete—goodness came in Adam and Eve being joined together. Aside from the idea of holy celibacy, there is an incompleteness about manhood apart from womanhood and womanhood apart from manhood. Each one is an incomplete reflection of the divine. (Hear the struggles online in our secular culture as persons without faith wrestle with random connections and autonomous incompleteness.) The bond of marriage provides what might be called "redemptive completion," a completion and wholeness reflecting divinity. Still, marital bliss is a pale reflection of heavenly glory and union we will experience in God. The human incompleteness of celibacy is compensated by beautiful rewards of special divine grace, loving relationships, and gracious service.

Human marriages, moreover, find security as a communion and partnership of three: man, woman, and God. The Lord is the crucial third partner in all healthy relationships. Those who are single are promised a special "marriage" to, and unusual support from, the Lord. Separated from our source, we flounder and fade as mere shadows of ultimate reality. We seek all kinds of shortcuts and grasp all manner of substitutes. Following the Creator's plan for sex and marriage, humans find fulfillment of their drives for union and significance.

It is in this sense the church speaks of matrimony as a sacrament. Marriage is a visible expression of unseen realities: love within the holy Trinity and Christ's love for the church. In this light we begin to understand sex theologically. At first it sounds strange to speak of the sacrament of sex, but as we work on this theology of sexuality, we slowly come to understand sex as a visible expression of the invisible union and glory enjoyed in the blessed Trinity. Sex is a part of a larger creative drive—our loving and creative power.

The Russian theologian Nikolai Berdyaev describes the possible slavery of sex (unfortunately using generic masculine language):

The erotic lure is a lure that is particularly widespread, and slavery to sex is one of the very deepest sources of human slavery. The physiological sexual need rarely appears in man in an unmixed form, it is always accompanied by psychological complications, by erotic illusions. . . .

Erotic love (by itself) always presupposes deficiency, unfulfilledness, yearning for fulfilment, attraction towards that which can enrich. There is *eros* as a demon, and man can be possessed by him. . . .

With sex, which is a sign of deficiency in man, is connected a particular longing. And this longing is always stronger in youth. . . . The greatest triviality may be connected with sex. Not only the physical aspect of sex, but also the psychical is profaned.[23]

Augustine, a great philanderer before his conversion, finally came to say: "Our souls are restless until they find their rest in Thee." Among his problems in accepting Christianity was trying to imagine going to bed without some woman. In Augustine's dictum we find the secret of our sexuality. The Creator has placed in humans a restless and surging passion for God. Thank God it is there! It is the drive for *knowing* and *communicating*, receiving attention and touch—all related to sexual intercourse. To have sex with someone is the ultimate form of human communication; it is literally entering into each other's being; it is "knowing" in the biblical sense. That is why the Creator has guarded sex so carefully within marriage. "The one who made them at the beginning 'made them male and female.' . . . '[A] man shall . . . be joined to his wife, and the two shall become one flesh.' . . . So they are no longer two, but one flesh" (Matt. 19:4–6).

Berdyaev further describes sex in this way:

Man is a sexual being, that is to say, he is a divided half, he is incomplete and he feels an urge towards fulfillment, not only in his physical nature, but psychologically also. Sex is not merely a special function in man, connected with his sexual organs, it flows through the whole organism of a man. . . .

Sexual energy is life energy and may be the source of the urge of creative life. A sexless creature is a creature of lowered life energy. Sexual energy may be sublimated, it may be detached from specifically sexual functions and be directed towards creativeness.[24]

Toward a Definition of Sex

Pondering Berdyaev's exploration of this mystery, we begin to see the weakness of thinking of sex merely in a genital way and recognize our need for a broader,

23. Nikolai Berdyaev, *Slavery and Freedom* (New York: Scribner, 1944), 222–23, 225, 231.
24. Ibid., 223, 231.

deeper definition. The impulse to seek a vision of God, to find union with the Most High, flows out of the same passion we have for communion with significant others around us. It *may* involve sexual intimacy with a lifetime partner. Or, it may be beautifully expressed by those who are single—in freedom for a special relationship to God from which to express their creativity—caring for themselves and others in a special way.

It is important to understand how single people are to express their sexuality. Families in contemporary society barely find enough support from the church, and single persons find even less. The frustration, even the anger, of single Christians, who hear support given to the married but seldom to singles, is understandable. How are the unmarried to understand and use their sexual energies? Must they simply repress their sexuality? Can they separate it from the energy needed to pursue ultimate union and significance? Were Jesus and the saints devoid of sexual energy?

Such questions demand a broad view of sexual energy—one related to love. Christ loves the church *as* husbands and wives love each other (Eph. 5:1–2, 25). The sexual language in the Song of Songs has been used from ancient times as a metaphor for our striving after and attaining union with God. How are we to understand, and explain to young hearts, the divine energy that seems to drive both human sexuality and spirituality?

A Deeper, Broader Understanding of Sex

Hopefully we have begun to see the impossibility of defining sex apart from love and union. Love, the passion to belong, to communicate, and to serve, is related to erotic energy, which one must keep in its proper place. A nursing mother feels love for her infant and may enjoy pleasure in its sucking at her breast; fathers may feel fleeting sensual pleasure from contact with their small children. Youth workers can admire the beauty of young people of the opposite sex, an attraction that can move toward holistic compassion or be easily diverted to sexual fantasy and even inappropriate behavior. Pleasant sensual feelings of mothers, fathers, and youth ministers are, and should be, different from those experienced in lovemaking. Erotic love is properly highly specialized in marriage. General friendship and spiritual love should be going on all the time. What are we saying? Emotions leading us toward union go beyond genital attraction. They are part of a larger energy. To deal with sexuality we must have a sense of this larger drive toward communion.

Our Lord Jesus Christ in his humanity was a sexual person; in his incarnation Christ did not empty himself of sexuality. At puberty he must have felt sexual awakenings—or else the incarnation was not complete. Sexuality can hardly be conceived as a totally dormant energy in Jesus as he walked our way of life and was "in every respect . . . tested as we are, yet without sin" (Heb. 4:15b). Rather, his sexuality, without genital expression, animated his life in pure and positive expressions of love and compassion. Jesus Christ is the great example, for single and married alike, of the healthy use of those energies that produce a longing for union with God and friends.

With a similar understanding of sexual energy, Kenda Creasy Dean provides a fine example of Jesus's sexuality.[25] She shares a simple story that takes place on a crowded street in a busy day in the life of our Lord. He is on his way to help an anxious father whose daughter is desperately ill and who is urging him to hurry. Suddenly Jesus stops and asks a ridiculous question: "Who touched me?" Quietly, an embarrassed woman from the crowd confesses; she has touched the Master and is healed. Dean uses this story to show what we've missed in Mark 5:21–43 over the years. The exchange of physical, emotional, and spiritual energies (with added reference to bodily fluids) between Jesus and the unnamed woman illustrates the relationship between sexuality and spirituality, a broader sense of sex beyond the genital.

The Creator has not wasted sexuality by depriving its energy from single or celibate persons. I've asked students, Who's sexier: Madonna, Lil' Kim, Lady Gaga, Beyonce, or . . . Mother Teresa? Mother Teresa was not sexless—she radiated powerful presence! Even when she felt cut off from her Beloved, Mother Teresa conveyed a compelling aura of love as she touched the dying and well, the poor and rich. A silent Lord gave Mother Teresa a healthier and more powerful sexuality than any mere celebrity sex object or boy toy. At first glance a current sex goddess may appear sexier, but finally she (like Madonna in *Truth or Dare*) admits to being sexually bored! And her viewers, saturated by cheapened sexual images, may finally succumb to effects of their own visual tedium. All who seek satisfaction in her sexual delights will eventually become bored—and have to move on—hence, Madonna's (and Lady Gaga's) extreme efforts to reinvent persona and image. Young people (and all of us) need to realize how their greatest sexual fantasies, if separated from love and lived out apart from the fullness of life, finally become boring, nauseating, and fatal. No healthy human could watch extremely sexy rock videos for an hour or so without feeling a deep sadness and regret for their use and abuse of those who appear in them and the degradation of those who watch. Theologically, it is a sin to trivialize sex.

Passionate singing and speaking draw on sexual energies. I have talked with many gifted Christian communicators and musicians. Those highly spotlighted

25. Andrew Root and Kenda Creasy Dean, *The Theological Turn in Youth Ministry* (Downers Grove, IL: InterVarsity, 2011).

before audiences experience a special rush of creative flow, and after great performances many feel sexually vulnerable. Rock stars have commented on the same phenomenon. Powerful spiritual and artistic communication seems to flow from the same energy as sexual desires. Creative energy should drive us in the direction of ultimate union with the Creator—and from there to deeper, godly relationships with others. Any substitution of mere physical union for that ultimate spiritual union is disastrous at worst, and at best trivializes our human existence.

Agnes Sanford, once a popular Christian speaker and author, in lectures on sexuality would recommend what may sound odd or simplistic. In regard to frustrated sexual energy, she advised people to "lift and shift" the creative force. Whether we call this sublimation or whatever, God has provided alternatives for the use of erotic energy.

The title of Madeleine L'Engle's *A Severed Wasp* suggests a disturbing image taken up in discussion among her characters—an image that provides a clue to the novel's theme.[26] Her title's use of this image came from an earlier book review by George Orwell, who described

> a wasp . . . sucking jam on my plate, and I cut him in half. He paid no attention, merely went on with his meal, while a tiny stream of jam trickled out of his severed esophagus. Only when he tried to fly away did he grasp the dreadful thing that had happened to him. It is the same with modern man. The thing that has been cut away is his soul. [27]

Bragging celebrities who flaunt sexual conquests and leaders who try to sneak sex as a means to selfish ends are like the wasp. Their enjoyment of the pleasures of sex may be similar, in its euphoric feelings, to sex within the bounds of a loving, committed relationship. Indeed, outside liaisons can be more exciting. But the momentary enjoyment is a fragmented joy, and the end of sexual infidelities is death rather than life. We're all subject to the lure of such diversions, so all are warned: "The adulteress . . . forsakes the partner of her youth . . . her way leads down to death" (Prov. 2:16b–18a; see also Prov. 5:5; 7:17–27).

Contemporary cultures reject divine dimensions of love and provisions for sex. A cover of the *New York Times Magazine* portrays a red heart with fuzzy borders, inscribed with the black headline: "Infidelity Keeps Us Together."[28] The author of this lead article quotes "America's leading sex-advice columnist," Dan Savage, who believes monogamy, while possible for some, is for many a confining

26. Madeline L'Engle, *A Severed Wasp* (New York: Farrar, Straus, Giroux, 1982), 59–60.

27. Sonia Orwell and Ian Angus, eds., *The Collected Essays, Journalism and Letters of George Orwell*, vol. 2, *My Country Right or Left* (New York: HarcourtBrace, 1968), 15. See www.georgeorwellnovels.com/journalism/notes-on-the-way/.

28. Mark Openheimer, "Married, with Infidelities," *New York Times Magazine*, July 3, 2011, 22.

principle—better to have affairs and be honest about them. Not only twisted sex but pederasty, even bestiality, are being affirmed by some sophisticated teachers. Lust takes us down a path of diminishing returns, to vulnerable victims, to S&M, bizarre fetishes, robotic love[29] and even to necrophilia.[30] The value of age-old norms in marital commitment, and the sense that marriage is much more than sex, are being lost. Any breaking of the Ten Commandments is wrong, not primarily because it violates a law, but because it violates relationships and diminishes human dignity. Socially approved "consensual sex" is usually consensual self-centeredness—hardly ever leading to wholesome human relationships.

Sexual promiscuity finally ends in using others—as a means for one's own personal relief or excitement—in a way that moves toward destruction for oneself and the objects of one's lust. Idolatrous sex, exploited sex, and sexual abuse lead to degeneration, not only of the unlawful or careless, but also of the innocent. The weak and innocent (such as children of AIDS or of divorce) suffer along with— and often before—those who transgress. No matter how we interpret them, rape, abortion, and AIDS are paradigms of something gone wrong in nature; they are not just; they are not what the Creator intended. And the fact that rape victims are often so traumatized is evidence of the sanctity of sexual intercourse.

In short, sex is part of our vibrant, creative energy. It is relational—a vital aspect of our communicating and communion with others. This is why it is useless to try to subdue sexuality merely by restraints or by denial. Those who are crippled in their communicating, their knowing, or in the way they relate to others—be they great leader, counselor, teacher, or whoever—are often sexually frustrated. Those who neglect their God, their neighbors, or themselves often experience sexual unrest. More and more young people are pursuing purity and positive group experiences rather than appeasement in their sexual lives. They are becoming integrated rather than "patchwork selves."

Defining Sex in a Broader Scope

Can we then define sex in this way? "Sex is one part of the passion that drives us toward union. That drive may be directed in genital, artistic, altruistic, or spiritual

29. See David Levy, *Love and Sex with Robots: The Evolution of Human-Robot Relationships* (New York: Harper Perennial, 2008); and Jeffrey R. Young on Sherry Turkle's experience and warning, "Programmed for Love: Turkle warns of the dangers of social technology," *The Chronicle of Higher Education,* January 14, 2011, www.chronicle.com/article/Programmed-for-Love-The/125922/.

30. "Necrophilia is a paraphilia [a psychosexual disorder] whereby the perpetrator gets sexual pleasure in having sex with the dead. Most jurisdictions have laws against this practice." Anil Aggrawal, "A New Classification of Necrophilia," *Journal of Forensic and Legal Medicine,* December 23, 2008, www.scribd.com/doc/19156122/A-new-classification-of-necrophilia. For some, sex with corpses is an addiction and a reason for seeking employment in mortuaries.

directions—its goals are attention, belonging, and communion." We are trying to see sex as a sacrament of ultimate union with God. Sex is a visible manifestation of our soul's need to be sought after and joined in meaningful relationships. Exquisitely experienced in marriage and the marriage bed, its source and deeper drive is our creative energy toward union with God, nature, and our human community.

Sex is therefore related to spirituality. The erotic impulses of a lover can hardly be excised from the Song of Songs. It is an ancient love poem. Still, many of the greatest saints, the deepest students and practitioners of prayer, have found the book to be the Bible's "Holy of Holies," speaking to the heart's longing for our Beloved. The Song of Songs is both a prayer book and love manual, and the human energy it describes, both spiritual and sensual, enriches our spiritual lives and our relations with all others. It feeds our creative potential.

As earlier mentioned, God has placed two fundamental drives in human beings: the drive to love and be loved in communion that we have been discussing, *and* the drive to produce and achieve. Love (no matter how exciting) without productivity is incomplete and becomes boring (a honeymoon cannot last more than a few weeks before we need to get back to work). And achievement and great accomplishments without love are dry and empty. William Glasser (in *Reality Therapy*)[31] has helped many who counsel youth by reminding us that all people need to love and be loved, while also feeling worthwhile in their accomplishments.

The principles of this chapter can be adapted or translated into public life apart from faith. In the secular realm as well as in the Christian arena, we would promote responsible human relationships. Anything that hinders the growth and dignity of individuals, as well as the justice and the peace of community, is not acceptable. We cannot accept a moral philosophy based on the way things are; we must strive toward a higher view of the common good. Recreational sex violates human relationships and demeans personal identity. Indeed, it is a confusion about personal identity that leads many young people into reckless sexual experiences. If I do not know who I am, I am not sure of my personal boundaries. Good parenting, education, and youth ministry focus not so much on negative cautions as on the building up of positive identities and relationships. In contrast to those who exploit sex for pleasure and profit, saints are fulfilled through human relationships and service. The excitement and profundity of sex make us eager to discuss all its ramifications with young people.

Our sexuality defines us as one of God's created genders. Furthermore, our sexual drive includes the following:

31. William Glasser, *Reality Therapy: A New Approach to Psychiatry* (New York: Harper Paperbacks, 1975).

- an extremely pleasurable aspect of love,
- a bonding between husband and wife,
- the origin of family in childbearing,
- an energy that nurtures our own souls,
- a creative flow that fosters artistic beauty, healthy relationships, and human communities,
- and above all, part of a holy passion for divine union.

The Contentious Issue of Homosexuality

With all of the noncontroversial aspects of our sexuality, we also need to look at a currently very controversial aspect. How can practical theology ignore the LGBT community,[32] or youth ministry avoid its responsibility to gay teens? How can we take a pass on this issue even if it means walking into a no-win matter? We know we are bound for disagreements, but our common goal should be truthfulness to God's Word *and* to the experience of humans.

From the streets to the pulpit, from politics to domestic crises, the issue demands consideration, contentious as it is. Alongside a banner, "God made us Queer," hecklers wield a sign, "God hates fags." Sermons addressing the subject in a conservative church are strikingly opposed to those in a liberal church. Teaching on the subject, from conservative seminaries to liberal schools, is radically at odds—and often avoided in conservative circles. Between the extremes, moderate positions are sought by pro-gay evangelicals, liberal conservatives, and liberal moderates, who stand by biblical and traditional views of sexuality and marriage.

Heterosexuals can begin this consideration by studying the key biblical passages or by listening to a good friend, relative, son, or daughter who is gay. It makes a difference whether you are interpreting the Bible in order to judge someone who is gay, or if you are relating to someone you care about with Scripture as your guide.

The conservative position[33] against homosexuality finds the five or more biblical passages usually associated with this issue conclusive (notably the Sodom and Gomorrah story in Gen. 19, the Holiness Code prohibiting same-sex behavior

32. *LGBT* stands for Lesbian, Gay, Bisexual, and Transgendered (sometimes referred to as GLBT). LGBTQ adds those questioning their sexual identity.
33. See Christopher Yuan and Angela Yuan, *Out of a Far Country: A Gay Son's Journey to God, A Broken Mother's Search for Hope* (Colorado Springs: Waterbrook, 2011); Mark A. Yarhouse, *Homosexuality and the Christian: A Guide for Parents, Pastors and Friends* (Bloomington, MN: Bethany House, 2010); William J. Webb, *Slaves, Women and Homosexuals: Exploring the Hermeneutics of Cultural Analysis* (Downers Grove, IL: IVP Academic, 2001); John A. J. Gagnon, *The Bible and Homosexual Practice: Texts and Hermeneutics* (Nashville: Abingdon, 2002).

in Lev. 18:22 and 20:13, Paul's examples of God's judgment on unnatural sex in Rom. 1:27, same-sex behavior's exclusion from the kingdom of God in 1 Cor. 6:9–11, and its condemnation among other behaviors in 1 Tim. 1:9–11). Added to this is the long tradition of the church and opinion of a majority of global Christians. This perspective finds obnoxious and demeaning the comparison of the gay movement to earlier civil rights movements. Its motto is "to love the sinner but hate the sin." Except for outright homophobes (and sadly some Christians are so disposed), they condemn not the orientation but homosexual behavior. Since they cannot believe homosexuality is genetic, it must be a matter of choice somewhere along the line. Many believe LGBT orientation can be rectified by conversion, therapy, and spiritual healing. This perspective bolsters its position by anatomical,[34] psychological,[35] social, and religious arguments.

The liberal or progressive Christian view[36] is more nuanced. Broadly speaking, the LGBT position is that sexual identities are not a matter of choice—many tell of struggling against the idea and their same-sex attraction knowing how difficult it is to grow up and live as a disadvantaged minority. For the progressive Christian, this *is* a matter of civil rights. Gay persons find it very difficult to separate identity from behavior. Theirs is a struggle to be accepted, not as gay, but as persons. "Your motto tells me," many say, "that you hate me as well as my sin—your attitudes and actions tend to back that up." As to the Bible, those with religious faith emphasize that there was no gay culture in biblical times and no long-term committed partnerships to which the biblical passages could apply. The scriptural injunctions (cited above) are viewed as condemning inhospitality, pagan orgiastic rites, rape, or pederasty—not today's committed relationships. Besides, they point out that biblical passages on this issue are few, and the great themes of Scripture are the dignity of all persons and compassionate love. Jesus stands as the great model of accepting sinners and those on the margins of society. As one who welcomed lepers and prostitutes in his day, he would be accepting of gays today. Homosexuals should be afforded all privileges afforded heterosexuals: to marry a person of the same sex or be ordained for Christian ministry.

A problem for this progressive, revisionist perspective remains in the words of Jesus in Mark 10:6–8: "from the beginning of creation 'God made them male and

---

34. For instance, that vaginal muscles are receptive, anal muscles expulsive.

35. That there is a progression of sexual development in human growth, from auto-eroticism to homo-eroticism to hetero-eroticism.

36. See Jack Rogers, *Jesus, the Bible and Homosexuality* (Louisville: Westminster John Knox, 2009); Mel White, *Stranger at the Gate: To Be Gay and Christian in America* (New York: Plume, 1995); Candace Chellew-Hodge, *Bulletproof Faith: A Spiritual Guide for Gay and Lesbian Christians* (San Francisco: Jossey-Bass, 2008); Daniel A. Helminiak, *What the Bible Really Says about Homosexuality* (San Francisco: Alamo Square, 2000).

female.' 'For this reason a man shall leave his father and mother and be joined to his wife, and the two shall become one flesh.'"[37]

There are biblical problems for traditional conservatives as well. The passage above immediately admits to an exception: Moses's bill of divorce, confirmed by Jesus (Matt. 19:8–9). This brings up the problematic issue of God's permissive will (as opposed to God's intentional will). More difficult is the apparent divine acceptance of polygamy in the Old Testament in patriarchal and early kingdom times—another example of God's permissive will.[38] Second Samuel 12:8, demanding explanation of kingly cultural rights, would seem to be an example of God's permissive will trumping God's intentional will for sexual unions.

Arguing that all homosexuals are so by choice is a weak argument when tested by our gay friends' life experiences. More objectively, we have to deal with infants born with ambiguous gender (hermaphrodites). Nature produces "abnormalities." In the case of confusing genitalia, we're faced with decisions about who should choose (and on what basis) their surgical "repair." Beyond the issue of confusing genitalia, a growing number of boys and girls feel trapped in a body opposite to their emotional and psychic orientation; these are called transgendered children. Many of their parents and some schools are helping them make the transition, through hormonal treatment and surgeries, to what they feel to be their true gender. How are such ambiguities to be theologically explained, pastorally tended, and communally accepted?

Having a good friend or family member confide in you that he or she is gay can be extremely difficult. Or perhaps teenagers share with you their painful struggle with same-sex attraction—whether they openly accept their situation or dare come to you as the only person in the world who can be trusted. In such cases, do we see these persons as inherently damaged goods? Are their only options to struggle with celibacy or to sin as they live out what they feel to be their identities? There are answers to these questions, but they are not easy.

Andrew Marin has a remarkable story to tell. He was a gay-bashing high school athlete who grew spiritually into a Bible study leader in college. During the summer after his freshman year, three friends separately drew him aside in consecutive months to confess their gay orientation. He was stunned and had no ready response. His background made this a spiritual crisis from which came a drastic decision. He would immerse himself in Boystown Chicago's gay culture.

---

37. See also Matt. 19:4–6.

38. It seems clear from Scripture and history that God uses and blesses many individuals, situations, and people groups that are not in God's best or perfect will. Some theologians have admitted the idea of God's permissive will to be a "can of worms" best avoided if possible. Allowing Israel to have a king and the anointing of Saul have been seen as God's permissive will. It is obvious how this concept is here applicable.

His radical commitment as a Bible-believing Christian was to move beyond the controversy, to establish communication—befriending, listening, discussing, and letting the Spirit of God help those on their particular journeys to wholeness.

To that end Marin has written a striking book being studied at Christian colleges and in small discussion groups: *Love Is an Orientation: Elevating the Conversation with the Gay Community*. If we appreciate Marin's evangelical position, we can hear him say: "we need to put ourselves, as much as heterosexual Christians can, into the cloudy circumstances and daily life of what it is to live attracted to people of the same sex."[39] He asks us to "acknowledge the LGBT community's perception of evangelicalism." Secular and religious LGBT community members wonder if they can relate to us in our church environments, whether we will always see them as just gay, whether they can join in church activities and groups, whether we see homosexuality as a special sin, whether we believe they chose their orientation, and whether we're afraid they'll hit on us or our children. Finally, they wonder if they may be rejected at some point and be kicked out—as many have been.[40] Marin does not have clear biblical and theological answers to all this, nor does he urge his readers to respond with answers that seemingly only God can provide.

Marin might rightly and humbly object to the way I, as a professor and writer, laid out two or three categories of responses to the homosexual issue, putting labels before persons. (It is my occupational hazard.) Marin's personal calling is to relate and to listen. His teaching, he found, was attractive to gay persons because he "unapologetically focused on how to have a better, more intimate relationship with God apart from any LGBT issues."[41] His exegesis of "The Big Five" (key biblical passages on the issue of homosexuality) is unusual as he seeks for the broader meaning of Scripture—and in that broader context finds God's grace for all.

I have gay friends who have moved through therapy (sometimes called "restorative"), have experienced spiritual deliverance or healing, have married and raised their children, and still admit to me an underlying attraction to the same sex. In my limited experience, I'm not aware of any strongly homosexual persons completely changed into heterosexual orientation. I do know, however, some with underlying same-sex attraction who are doing their best in strong two-gender marriages, and happily so—despite weaknesses we all share. And I know those who are living out their gay lives in healthy celibacy. We should pay special tribute to those throughout history and today, who with same-sex attraction, have been called to lives of celibacy and extraordinary Christian service. Meanwhile the issue of gay partnerships, civil unions, and marriages continues to divide church and society.

39. Andrew Marin, *Love Is an Orientation: Elevating the Conversation with the Gay Community* (Downers Grove, IL: InterVarsity, 2009), 23.
40. Ibid. 31–32. See also The Marin Foundation, www.themarinfoundation.org.
41. Ibid., 105.

Ritch Savin-Williams's *The New Gay Teenager*[42] provides qualitative research that may add to our confusion. His interviews with many gays in their teens and twenties reveal a rejection of categories and nomenclature. As the LGBT community finds the term "homosexual" derogatory, many young people, for various reasons, are rejecting "gay" or "lesbian" labels, wanting a more fluid gender or sexual identity. Among other things, they are asking to be considered persons rather than a category. We have, however, the warning from "Hardwired to Connect": "*the need to attach social significance and meaning to gender appears to be a human universal. . . .* [T]he risk of not attending to real differences that exist between males and females can have dangerous consequences."[43] The gays who spoke to Savin-Williams were on to something we can learn. Sexual orientation is an important part of our personal identities that cannot be denied, but our identities are much more than hetero- or homosexual. As people of faith, all parts of our identities are overshadowed by our identity in Christ as God's beloved.

We need both a *practical* theology and a *pastoral* theology for this issue—such a distinction is important. Practical theology deals with our understanding of the issue, and pastoral theology, with how we treat individuals. Our discussion has aimed at demonstrating our need for both a practical theology of homosexuality and a pastoral theology to guide our ministry with individuals. For me, this is not a "done deal" but a challenging work in progress. Hopefully we can all respect those who stand dogmatic in strict traditional beliefs, as well as those who have moved into progressive, revisionist thinking—and many struggling somewhere in middle ground. I see strengths and values in all these positions. As a moderate conservative, I see weak spots in my position and my need to learn from, and collaborate with, those who differ from me. Where I don't have clear-cut answers to offer, I do have an all-caring, all-powerful Lord.

The overarching message of Scripture, and our theology's apologetic, is this: that our hearts are restless until they are centered in God and until God comes first. That is the essence of the great commandments given us by Jesus. All sex apart from God is idolatry; and idolatry's antidote is accepting and passing on the love of God. Every human, regardless of orientation or situation, is meant to be on a path toward that love of God. At a given time, we have all wandered off the path. We are called to be encouragers along the path.

---

42. Ritch C. Savin-Williams, *The New Gay Teenager* (Cambridge, MA: Harvard University Press, 2005). See also his article, "The New Gay Teen: Shunning Labels," *Gay and Lesbian Review Worldwide*, November–December 2005, www.glreview.com/issues/12.6/12.6-williams.php.

43. Commission on Children at Risk, "Hardwired to Connect: The New Scientific Case of Authoritative Communities" (New York: Institute for American Values, 2003), 24–25, emphasis original.

I spend some time reading serious blogs among those experimenting with heterosexual or same-sex attractions. Strong cultural voices declare "just doing it" as the only path to personal truth and happiness. I hear, however, a sound of sadness, loss, and futility in many online confessions and conversations. I realize no digital comment will do. As Marin found, it takes hours of listening and relationship building to respond effectively with empathetic concern to those seeking personal resolution. His call for bridge building is a needed challenge for us all. Our task is to strengthen the many teenagers who are grounded and more or less clear about their sexual identities, while reaching out and being available to all who need a listening ear and caring heart.

Dealing Practically with Wholesome Living and Sexuality

As you approach the subject of sexuality with teenagers, consider the following:

1. Understand sexuality. Be able to define and describe sex in your own words. Consider how you and your adolescent friends are dealing with sex physically, emotionally, relationally, socially, and spiritually.

2. Deal with your own sexuality: your own gender issues; your sexual fantasies, temptations, repression, etc.; your embarrassment about the topic in public; and the way you process this issue with your leadership team and friends.

3. Know where your faith community stands on important issues. Be aware also of the attitude of your town or city, class, or ethnic group. Know the concerns of the parents of your young people; discuss any units on this topic with your adult committee and key parents. Be sure that you and the senior pastor, or your immediate director in an organization, have discussed these issues and that they approve of what you intend to teach.

4. With well-guarded exceptions, let male leaders deal with boys, and female leaders with girls. Be sure your church or organization has subscribed to safe church practices. Do background checks on all volunteers and staff.[44] Some group sessions should be for girls and boys separately; others as coed discussions with shared male/female leadership.

5. Respond openly and appropriately to all inquiries from young people. Do so on the spot, in your next session together, or privately.

6. Develop a teaching unit on sexuality convincing youth of its importance and enlisting their help and input. Begin with an understanding of sexuality

---

44. Your church or organization should have resources such as can easily be obtained online from Safe Church (www.safechurch.com/Pages/Default.aspx) and other safe church training from your denomination.

and emphasize its relational aspects. Familiarize yourself with some of the resources that describe the damage sexual images can do to teenagers[45] and with popular music that counters cultural currents and suggests restraint.[46]

- Be sure to use materials from the type of media teens engage.
- Use brief video clips or songs to initiate discussion.
- Clear these discussion starters with the senior pastor and adult/parental committee.
- Bring in appropriate professional resources.
- Be sure you and your leaders are not projecting your own issues on young people. Let them be involved in setting the agenda and emphases.
- Always use help from leaders among the youth.

7. When you do not feel fully prepared to deal with some aspect of sexuality, bring in some experts cleared by the senior pastor and your committee.
8. Don't overemphasize the topic. Teach and model the fact that there is much more to life than sex. Emphasize creative group activities and dynamics.

Imagine asking some ninth or tenth graders what issues they would like to discuss in their group. Instantly, a bright mischief-maker yells out, "Sex!" And everyone laughs or smiles with a look of "We've got you!" on their faces. You might pause for a long moment. Then look them squarely in the eyes and, with love and respect, ask them: "And do you want to talk about the *biological mechanics* or the *relational* aspects of sex?" Most often they will tell you they are tired of hearing about penises and vaginas in gym or health classes. They want to know more about the relational side of sex (meaning when and how to do it).

You might begin with collecting information from them on relationships. Stand at a whiteboard (or large pad of paper) and have them list how they've been hurt or seen people hurt in relationships. Then, on another board ask and record what they would most like in a true friend. Stepping back, create another dramatic pause, and ask them if they see anything in those two lists. All the hurts are common consequences of teen sex without commitment; true love is exhibited on the

---

45. The secular and fairly liberal Media Education Foundation (www.mediaed.org) has powerful videos showing music videos, video games, commercials, and music's toxic influence on young male and female images, which I've used to good advantage for discussions.

46. Bringing this list up-to-date could be a fruitful project for your group. Here are some oldies. On the secular side, Sense Field, "Save Yourself"; Death Cab for Cutie, "Soul Meets Body"; and Lenny Kravitz's album, *It's Time for a Revolution*. Maybe even Tupac's "Brenda's Got a Baby," using the YouTube video. For Christian music: Ransom, "Not That Kind of Girl"; Lust Control, "Virginity Disease"; The Procussions, "Miss January" and "For the Camera"; Rebecca St. James, "Wait for Me"; and Paul Wright, "Fly Away." See especially Bill Mallonee and the Vigilantes of Love, "Love Cocoon," with its explicit description of sex saved for marriage. Thanks to Walt Mueller and Center for Parent and Youth Understanding for help here (cpyu.org).

board that unites sexual attraction, genuine friendship, and love with marriage commitment. Leaders (male and female) can go on to discuss:

- What do you want or need in a relationship?
- What are some of the best relationships you have seen?
- How can people hurt each other in a relationship?
- What is wrong with some of the adult relationships you have seen?
- What hurts you or your friends most in relationships?
- Can you think of any way in which you have failed in a relationship? What can you do about such failures?
- How do you think God might help young men and women get ready for healthy relationships? How does a relationship with Jesus Christ help in dealing with all this?

These questions are an outline for a theological discussion about sex for junior or senior high students. Next, the group can try to find practical and profitable agreement in the following statements.

- Sex is God's gift to us (we might say it was invented for our pleasure).
- Sex is a natural and beautiful human function.
- Like anything else, sex can be distorted out of its appropriate context.
- Sex isn't everything; just think—really think—of trying to make sex the main thing or the whole thing in your life.
- Sex can be used in a way that deeply hurts people.
- Sex should be enjoyable and significant for a whole lifetime.
- Sex is about love and relationships.

It helps to discuss our sexuality in a group that cares about friendship, fun, community, and service. Adolescent issues of identity and values can be clarified by interaction with friends. Out of such discussions we may find ourselves asking questions such as:

- Can a group of friends sometimes be more fun and more supportive than a date?
- Where do we see ourselves now, and how do we want to grow?

These discussions provide a sense that we're contributing to the cutting edge of growth in young lives. Having been honest about our own sexuality and vulnerable as to our own struggles—and admitting that we do not have all the answers—we can be of great help to those young people searching for real answers in their own lives. After sessions on this topic, it's important for leaders to process and discuss what they've heard:

- If I know some of my young people are having sex, should I encourage them toward safer sex? Should I ever inquire about these matters?
- How can we best help teens who are questioning their sexual identities and dealing with same-sex attraction? If a teenager confides in you that they are gay, how can we further the discussion regarding their coming out (often happening at about age seventeen)? Can students who are open about their same-sex attraction still be an active part of this group? If I have a strong sense of someone's orientation in this direction, should I ever bring up the issue?
- How, to what extent, and what Scriptures should I use in dealing with these issues?

The answers to these questions rest mainly in the situation, in our relationship to young people, and in the standards and style of our faith community. Our understanding of Scripture, our experience of human life, our self-understanding, and our relationship to our church or organization are critical factors. Equally important is our relationship with the young people involved. Do we feel deep compassion toward and have high hopes for these young friends? Do we understand their view of life, the world, and themselves? Are we willing to let them help us answer the questions above? Remember their faith is always more important than sexual standards at a particular point in their lives. And yet, let our teaching be clear and boundaries understood. Such a style and approach will be more beneficial than dogmatic answers and negative judgments.

Our approach to sex and sexuality as we instruct young people works best in the spirit of true celebration—an assured sense of the delights and holy possibilities of this vital life force. Sex is part of what God described as good—and, we might add, it is fun. Young people want in us an unembarrassed and frank approach to sexuality as we explain biblical principles from a positive and confident posture. Seeing these qualities in us will help them sense the relevance of Christ's teaching about sex.

Concluding Reflections

Pastoral theology deals with complex issues, and in many ways, sexuality is the most difficult. How is a young Christian supposed to handle overwhelming sexual desires through society's greatly extended adolescence? If two Christians are living together, must they separate before being married in a Christian ceremony?

When and how does a girl respond to what she considers an inappropriate remark or touch from a prominent and respected church leader? How can we ensure the safety of all children and youth? How can a Christian live with a spouse who is not a believer or who they do not love anymore? When does a woman leave an abusive husband? Life is not all yes or no; much of it can be gray and complex. Solutions to moral problems are not always clear. Youth ministers also serve young people with loyalty to the positions held by their church or organization. All this is the challenge of pastoral theology.

Pastoral counselors and youth ministers are called to exhibit the holiness of God and the compassion of Christ. Our times call for both high beliefs *and* a deep sense of grace. With our Lord we stand firm against sin, yet we are gentle in tending the flickering wick or the broken reed (Isa. 42:3, a beautiful depiction of God's servant shepherd).

As we approach the subject of sexuality with young people, let us have a very high view of sex. It is great, it is beautiful, it is a sacrament! We look young folk in their eyes and plead, "Don't get cheated by illusions that lead over a cliff or by shortcuts that lead to dead ends. Don't let the media or peer pressure rip you off. Don't miss any of the joys God has for you in this life and through all eternity. 'Delight yourself in the LORD; and He will give you the desires of your heart'" (Ps. 37:4 NASB). What a powerful promise that takes a lifetime to test!

If you are still trying to find ways to *control* the sexual behavior of the young people in your ministry or of your own sons and daughters, you have not gotten much help here. But if your desire is to help young people grow toward their full potential, if you are willing to give them freedom to fail, if you are able to forgive, and if, above all, you are willing to learn from young people as any effective parent and youth leader must do—then perhaps there is hope for us all in a world filled with pitfalls. From the darkest night comes the brightest dawn. "Where sin abounds, grace does much more abound" (Rom. 5:20, my change of tense from KJV). Or as we might paraphrase Paul's declaration: "When this world's sinfulness seems completely overwhelming, God's grace is triumphant still."

Questions for Reflection and Discussion

1. In what ways are you happy about your sexuality? How comfortable are you in your manhood or womanhood? Are you able to express attraction and love to others in a powerful and free way? What kind of lover are you? How does this work out for you on genital and nongenital levels?

2. In what ways are you not happy with your sexuality? To what extent do you feel unsure of what it means for you to be a woman or a man? To

what extent are your genital drives a distraction and difficulty for you? To what extent is the flow of love and creativity restricted in expressing itself to others? Where can you turn for help and who might assist you in any of these issues?

3. If a straight person, are you comfortable with gay people? If gay, are you comfortable with straight people and yourself? (If perplexed, it is important to talk with someone about this—someone who's wise, someone you trust.)

4. How would you like to grow sexually and spiritually? How are the sexual and spiritual aspects of your life related as you pursue holistic growth? Might counseling or spiritual direction be of help to your growing?

5. How effective have you been in teaching or counseling teenagers about their sexuality and sexual behavior? What frustrations have you or they had? What might help you become more natural and effective?

6. What kind of help do young people in your group need from you, your team, and possible resource persons? How can you improve your curriculum and experience of sexual education?

7. What can you do to move from negative to positive in sex education and the social life of your group?

8. Are the young people to whom you minister given enough opportunity for celebration and intimacy in their worship and play? What more could be done?

PART 3

Practical
Theology
Engaging
Culture

—10—

Theologizing about Culture and Cultures

You are worthy, our Lord and God . . . for you created all things, and by your will they existed and were created.

REVELATION 4:11

The God who made the world and everything in it, . . . from one ancestor he made all nations [cultures] to inhabit the whole earth, and he allotted the times of their existence . . . so that they would search for God and perhaps grope for him and find him.

ACTS 17:24–27

The Nature of Culture

We have come a long way in our discussions of practical theology and a theology of persons, but the richness of practical theology urges us to take all we have pondered and consider further our relationship to culture and contemporary society. We've already considered God and human culture—as created by God. But, more precisely, what is this culture we have been talking about?

As has often been said, fish are not aware of water until they're brought out into the air. We humans grow up taking both air and culture for granted. Moving into a completely different culture can make us aware, as if for the first time, of specific aspects in our home culture. Beyond matters of cultural difference, the underlying reality of all human culture is an intriguing enigma.

Raymond Williams's often quoted dictum that "culture" is one of "the two or three most complicated words in the English language"[1] expresses some of the paradox. Culture is one of the most obvious, yet one of the most complex, features of human reality. Avoiding the intricacies of highly theoretical discussions and controversies, let's attempt to make the idea of culture, pop culture, and youth culture clear for practitioners of youth ministry.

We hardly need say that culture is not "a thing," like a tree or a city. We know culture as an underlying, all-pervasive process by which humans become human, learn to think, and make small and large choices about their lives and the lives of those around them. It describes our whole and various "ways of life." How do we make sense out of our lives and situations? What does it all mean, and how do we arrive at meaning?

There are various definitions of culture; one of them is simply "all learned behavior." Culture is all that humans learn in community and pass on to future generations; it is all that we have learned to make out of our physical environment to improve human existence. Theologically, culture is the God-allowed extension of our living context.

In contrast to animals, humans are extremely dependent at birth, needing to be taught all content of human culture. We considered in chapter 6 children raised in the wild, in animal rather than human culture. It made us conscious of how dependent on culture we are. Through culture God provides gifts of language, self-consciousness, consciousness of death, and opportunity for belief in God. Language, oral and written, allows for the flowering of civilization, the accumulation of learned behavior. Animals can only mimic bits of these human abilities.[2]

People of faith can view culture as that which humans create between the physical world and the heavenly spiritual world. My body is part of nature, but my clothes, glasses, dental work, and the way I wear my hair are culture. T. S. Eliot discusses culture as the interaction among philosophy, the arts, politics, and religion (he slights economics). Eliot comments on culture as a whole way of life, seeing in English culture of his time "all the characteristic activities and interests of a people. Derby Day, Henley Regatta, Cowes, the 12th of August, a cup final, the dog races, the pin table, the dartboard, Wensleydale cheese, boiled

---

1. Raymond Williams, *Keywords: A Vocabulary of Culture and Society* (London: Fontana, 1976), 87.

2. Project Nim describes the attempt to raise an infant chimpanzee as a human and teach it sign language. The entire project has raised objections, and the results are highly controversial. The most substantial conclusion: "a chimp is a chimp." You can find many sources of information about Project Nim online, including www.torontosun.com/2011/07/21/project-nim-fascinating-profound.

cabbage cut into sections, beetroot in vinegar, 19th century Gothic churches, the music of Elgar."[3]

Culture affects us, then, in terms of

- the way we perceive things,
- the way we feel about things,
- the way we think about things,
- and how we respond to things, and make decisions and act.

God, ultimate reality, and absolute truth are mediated to us through culture. Holy Scripture is both inspired by God and part of culture. The incarnate Christ is God revealed in and through culture. Some have argued: "So, if you admit to the cultural mediation of Scripture and absolute truth, that means all truth is subjective and relativistic, and there really is no objective *truth*." Even most agnostic philosophers ultimately rejected such reasoning. Truth is validated in many ways, and the Christian faith is just this: a *faith* that is reasonable. Most of us do not claim our faith as a dogmatic possession of absolute truth with postulates that can be proven. It is our God-given "meta-narrative,"[4] a gospel that we see as above the realm of scientific proof but hold in full confidence (whether we lean toward modernism or postmodernism). To claim that our grand story of redemption can be proven, or made the basis for all society, holds us up to understandable ridicule. Such considerations might take us further into the area of epistemology (how we know) and how truth is received.

Studying Culture and Meaning (Semiotics)

Youth leaders need a basic communication theory, which in simplest terms involves sender, message, and receiver. We will develop our understanding of the nuances of this simple formula in order to improve our communication to students—and to help them improve their communicating skills. In doing so we need semiotic theory, which deals with the meaning of a message.

Let's look more closely at this cultural, semiotic process. We teach children the names of things and help them learn to read by using pictures of things. A picture of a dog is different than any dog. In fact, neither a real dog, a picture, nor a definition of a dog gets us to the ultimate idea of dogs, or *dogness*. Plato

3. T. S. Eliot, *Notes Towards a Definition of Culture* (London: Faber, 1948, 1963), quoted in Dick Hebdige, *Subculture: The Meaning of Style* (London: Routledge, 1979, 1993), 7.

4. Merold Westphal, *Overcoming Onto-Theology: Toward a Postmodern Christian Faith* (New York: Fordham University Press, 2001), xiii.

describes our distance from ultimate reality through the analogy or parable of the cave[5]; the apostle Paul does so by the metaphor of an ancient mirror, "now we see in a mirror, dimly" (1 Cor. 13:12). Children understand abstract ideas in terms of the concrete: they imagine that God has a body somewhere "up" in heaven or see their priest or pastor as Jesus or God—they haven't separated representation or signs from reality.

We all learn through signs, which are representations of things and practices. Words are signs, as are pictures, or even gestures. Life in a postmodern world is a rapid reflexive exchange of signs and meanings, with reinterpretations or representations going on all the time. Usually we hardly notice how we, and others, are participating in this process of re-creating and re-presenting meanings.

Cultures are cohesive because of their shared social meanings. Cultural studies investigate how meaning is transmitted to those who share a common culture. The study of culture may be seen as observing and analyzing how representation takes place. An Australian scholar explains:

> A good deal of cultural studies is centered on questions of representation. That is, on how the world is socially constructed and represented to and by us in meaningful ways. Indeed, the central strand of cultural studies can be understood as the study of culture as the signifying practices of representation. This requires us to explore the textual generation of meaning. It also demands investigation of the modes by which meaning is produced in a variety of contexts. Further, cultural representations and meanings have a certain materiality. That is, they are embedded in sounds, inscriptions, objects, images, books, magazines and television programmes. They are produced, enacted, used and understood in specific social contexts.[6]

Semiotics is the study of signs and how meanings are generated in texts in which they appear. Consider attempts to discern the "real" from the "unreal." Thomas De Zengotita warns that: "Some people refuse to accept the fact that reality is becoming indistinguishable from representation in a qualitatively new way. They find permanent refuge in the belief that nothing is new under the sun."[7] (There is a sense that human life is repeating itself on different levels, as the writer of Ecclesiastes implied.) Cultural studies demonstrate complications in understanding "reality." De Zengotita breaks down our daily experience among "Real real" (what happens to us), "Observed real" (what is happening to someone else), "In-between real real and observed real," and so forth. Here are his further examples:

5. Plato's *Republic*, beginning of book VII.
6. Chris Barker, *Cultural Studies*, 3rd ed. (Los Angeles: Sage, 2000, 2008), 7–8.
7. Thomas De Zengotita, *Mediated: How the Media Shapes Your World and the Way You Live in It* (New York: Bloomsbury, 2005), 18.

Staged realistic: Movies and TV shows like *The English Patient* and *NYPD*.

Staged hyperreal: Oliver Stone movies and *Malcolm in the Middle*.

Overtly unreal realistic: SUVs climbing up the sides of buildings. Digitized special effects in general, except when they are more or less undetectable.

Covertly unreal realistic: The models' hair in shampoo ads. More or less undetectable digital effects, of which there are more and more every day.

In-between overtly and covertly unreal realistic: John Wayne in a contemporary beer ad (because you have to know he's dead in order to know he isn't "really" in the ad, whatever that means).

Real unreal: Robo-pets.

Unreal real: Strawberries that won't freeze because they have fish genes in them.[8]

Reference to these distinctions can help students learn to practice discernment with regard to culture. We are bombarded by music, movies, television, ads, billboards, emails, comments at various levels of seriousness and humor from family and friends, instructions from professors and bosses, phone calls and text messages, and much more. All come to us in signs and move toward shared meaning. We participate in this dynamic process as we interpret and reinterpret signs sent our way. We re-signify meaning as we send messages on to friends.

What, then, is culture doing to us as leaders, to our students, and to the general public? How is it shaping a rising digital generation? Darwin Glassford of Calvin Theological Seminary suggests that "culture does not really teach; rather as human beings we 'catch' what culture is communicating."[9] How would you express our socialization process and the influence of culture on society and all of us?

Kinds of Culture

Even though we have begun to think of culture as a dynamic process rather than as a thing, we can still speak of human culture (generally) in contrast to animal culture, and youth culture as distinguished from adult culture. We further realize that human culture is actually plural; nations and ethnicities have their own distinct cultures. In most countries today, because of cultural diffusion, immigration, and so forth, cultures are meeting one another and responding in one of three ways. There may be cultural *conflict* as we see among tribal and immigrant groups in some places, or *assimilation* as one culture takes on more or less the norms and mores of the majority cultural group. Finally, we may find *accommodation* in

8. Ibid., 19–20.
9. Darwin Glassford, email to author, August 9, 2011.

which the dominant culture accepts values and norms, somewhat contrary to its own, for certain groups like the Amish or Hasidic Jews in the United States. We can identify a dominant culture in most countries. We are learning, and rising generations perhaps more quickly, to live in some degree of harmony with those much different than ourselves—with Jesus and Scripture encouraging us to do so.

Drawing on principles from our Judeo-Christian tradition, we might imagine God intending just (or righteous) human cultures to (1) promote the economic and general prosperity of their people so all can live with dignity, (2) protect families and the growth of children to maturity, (3) support and nurture the environment, (4) defend citizens from internal and external injustice and violence, and (5) allow people to seek for a higher power, groping toward the Creator of all (whom Christians know to be our Redeemer). These five principles might be considered as a biblical basis for a theology of justice. Hopefully these five goals are generally agreeable to people of faith, to secularists, and to the growing number of persons somewhere in between. Curricula and catechesis for youth should aspire to these goals.

Youth Culture and Subcultural Dynamics

Cultural processes, then, are meant to serve the just needs of the constituents of that process. When the dominant culture neglects the needs of a given constituent group, members of that minority group begin to take things into their own hands, consciously or subconsciously, to form what has been called a subculture (or *special* culture if "sub" seems demeaning). When youth or an ethnic minority, for instance, sense their identities are not being respected nor their needs attended to, they begin naturally to construct a language, sense of ironic humor, behaviors, music, and so forth that constitute a special or subculture and binds them together. Semiotics helps us understand the working out of this process as new meaning and styles are created.

The reasons for a youth culture and the historic occasions of youth culture are two different things. Having explained the reason for a youth culture, we go on to consider its historic occasions. At one time many of us thought of youth culture as emerging in the latter half, or at least latter two-thirds, of the twentieth century. Several studies, however, have illustrated antecedents of youth culture that arose much earlier. Thomas Hine notes intimations of "adolescent" aspirations and rebellion in Rousseau's eighteenth-century *Emile*:

> This stormy revolution is proclaimed by the murmur of nascent passions. . . . A change in humor, frequent anger, a mind in constant agitation. . . . He disregards

his guide; he no longer wishes to be governed. . . . This is the second birth of which I have spoken. It is now that man is truly born to life and now nothing human is foreign to him.[10]

Joseph Kett has been taken as a special historian of adolescence in America. His *Rites of Passage: Adolescence in America from 1790 to the Present* describes "the uprooting of young people from agriculture, their immigration to cities, a dramatic rise in . . . occupational and intellectual choice . . . and increasing disorderliness and violence that marked their educational and social institutions"[11] in the period from 1790 to 1840. He further points to a growing divide between middle and lower classes in the latter part of the nineteenth century. Juvenile delinquency in the nineteenth century is clearly documented. Industrialization, immigration, and economic necessity drove some urban boys to scavenging gangs and some girls into prostitution. Extending compulsory education and raising the age of accepted adulthood marked a further isolation of teenagers and students in their early twenties.

A new understanding of youth or adolescence came at the beginning of the twentieth century. Although the term *teenagers* emerged only in the 1940s, adolescence as we know it was studied and written about earlier by sociologists and psychologists like G. Stanley Hall (his two-volume *Adolescence* was published in 1904). Kett observes, "The era of the adolescent dawned in Europe and America in the two decades after 1900."[12]

Jon Savage has written a 549-page book on "prehistory of the Teenager," arguing that, "between 1875 and 1945, every single theme now associated with the modern Teenager had a vivid, volatile precedent."[13] Hine also traces the growth and influence of dance halls, movies, and automobiles on teenagers in the first half of the twentieth century.

A classic in cultural studies, Dick Hebdige's *Subculture: The Meaning of Style*,[14] makes use of previous sociological studies and semiotics[15] to demonstrate what can be learned from the British after the war, especially 1970s working class groups, such as mods, teddy boys, and punks. Drawing on the works of cultural critics and sociological studies of youth,[16] Hebdige relates youthful subcultures to their

---

10. Jean-Jacques Rousseau, *Emile* or *On Education* (1762), as quoted in Thomas Hine, *The Rise and Fall of the American Teenager* (New York: Avon Books, 1999), 34.

11. Joseph Kett, *Rites of Passage: Adolescence in America from 1790 to the Present* (New York: Basic Books, 1977), 5.

12. Ibid., 215.

13. Jon Savage, *Teenage: The Creation of Youth Culture* (New York: Viking, 2007), xv.

14. Dick Hebdige, *Subculture: The Meaning of Style* (London: Routledge, 1979).

15. As previously noted, *semiotics* is a way of reading and interpreting cultural signs.

16. Such as Roland Barthes, Karl Marx, Stuart Hall, Albert Cohen, and Phil Cohen.

parent cultures while asserting their autonomy, displaying both their own social contributions and their rebellions against adult cultural hegemony (or dominance). As the media of dominant cultures

> progressively colonized the cultural and ideological spheres, youthful groups would create a credible image of social cohesion . . . maintained through the appropriation and redefinition of cultures of resistance. In this way, the media not only provide groups with substantive images of other groups, they also relay back to working-class youth a "picture" of their own lives which is "contained" or "framed" by the ideological discourses which surround and situate it. Understanding this process of representation provides insight into "the reflexive circuitry of production and reproduction."[17]

We see the dynamic reciprocity between adults and youth, between media and youth in the continuing creation of youth cultures. There is continuous tension of values and meaning between power structures, the media, and youthful recipients, who become producers of their own signs and meaning.

Youth take for granted this process of receiving mediated signifiers and manipulating them in company with their friends; they don't have to think about it. But *we* do need to study mediation and signs, representation and participation, in order to better understand the complicated dynamics involved when young people try to work out their identities in an often inhospitable social context. In doing so it is important for us to appreciate youthful resilience and creativity. Thinking about how youth receive signs and messages, and interpret and re-present meaning, is incredibly helpful for those who work in multicultural or disadvantaged communities.[18] Their hostility toward our dominant culture and their use of vulgarity will leave us dismayed and confused if we do not understand their struggle for dignity. Those working in more privileged settings also need to understand this dynamic because youth of all classes at times feel adult adversarial restraint. Besides parental pressure, all teenagers face the challenge of media and peer pressures working against their interests—and those of a healthy community. According to their context and peer associations, they will work out expressive styles and meaning in different ways. Appreciation of culture generally, and subcultures in particular, will help any leader intending to be more effective in living and conversing with youth.[19]

17. Hebdige, *Subculture*, 85.
18. For instance, in the study and deep understanding of hip-hop.
19. For further reading on youth subcultures: Michael Brake, *Comparative Youth Culture: The Sociology of Youth Culture and Youth Subcultures in America, Britain, and Canada* (New York: Routledge, 1985); Ken Gelder and Sarah Thornton, eds., *The Subcultures Reader* (New York: Routledge, 1997); and Arielle Greenberg, *Youth Subcultures: Exploring Underground America* (New York: Pearson Longman, 2006).

Thomas Hine has made a very perceptive remark about America's construction of adolescence: "America created the teenager in its own image—brash, unfinished, ebullient, idealistic, crude, energetic, innocent, greedy, changing in all sorts of unsettling ways."[20] For better and worse, adolescents are more like their parents and our culture than we usually think.

We have seen, then, generally though superficially, how cultural changes give rise to youth cultures as separated and subordinate demographic groups, and we have noted how in response youth create their own meaning, differently in particular historical times and places. Understanding the process of meaning-creation underlies many of our discussions with youth—the whats, hows, and whys behind many of their (and our) concerns and questions.

We have also seen how subcultures of youth are bound to proliferate into further subcultures when the needs of particular groups (alternatives, nerds, gays, etc.) are not being met. This is important because issues around identity, so crucial in the transition to adulthood, are an important part of our ministry.

Gradually, youth not only claim their own particular niches, but collectively, as an increasingly important market, they begin to influence, if not dominate, adult society. In other words, adolescent autonomy is breaking adult hegemony. Kenda Creasy Dean insightfully puts it this way:

> Fifty years ago, it was possible to speak of an emerging "youth culture" (that needed to be reached as a new "unreached peoples group"). . . . No more. Youth ministry is still missionary work, and adolescents still need Jesus. But the "adolescent society" no longer exists, not because it has vanished but because it had devoured everything around it. Today, *all* popular culture is youth culture, and vice versa, and *all* age groups participate in it—forcing young people to turn to increasingly marginal and dangerous alternatives in order to distinguish themselves from adults. Youth ministry no longer focuses on the cultural idiosyncrasies of the young as a homogeneous group simply because youth culture is no longer idiosyncratic and because adolescents are not (and have never been) homogeneous.[21]

Even if such a cultural conquest by youth is here slightly overstated (and it may not be), the point is crucial indeed. In fact, in the late 1960s and 1970s it was not uncommon to mistake mothers for daughters and fathers for sons by their fashions. Joseph Kett concluded his book in the mid-70s with this quotation: "These observations suggest that if young people have become more like adults, adults have become more like young people."[22] We see, then, the juvenilization of adult

---

20. Thomas Hine, *The Rise and Fall of the American Teenager* (New York: Avon Books, 1999).

21. Andrew Root and Kenda Creasy Dean, *The Theological Turn in Youth Ministry* (Downers Grove, IL: InterVarsity, 2011), 32–33.

22. Kett, *Rites of Passage*, 272.

society, adults whose materialistic and hedonistic longings covet the passion and freedom of young generations. This adult return to adolescence, with their interest in teen flicks and popular styles, anticipates our next topic.

What Is Popular Culture?

If culture generally has been described as "the air we breathe" and "the water we swim in," we might consider pop culture as the part of overall culture mass produced for us, the way in which we buy and sell, are entertained, and normally communicate with one another. Pop culture has been contrasted to "high culture," although high culture can, at times, become popularly acclaimed (as with the operatic tenors). Neither pop culture nor high culture is easily or conclusively defined. Pop culture can also be contrasted to the folk art of traditional cultures or contemporary subcultures.

John Storey in his *Cultural Theory and Popular Culture* has this to say about the difficulty of defining pop culture:

> There are various ways to define popular culture. This book is of course in part about that very process, about the different ways in which various critical approaches have attempted to fix the meaning of popular culture. Therefore, all I intend to do for the remainder of this chapter is to sketch out six definitions of popular culture, which in their different, general ways, inform the study of popular culture.[23]

Punk and grunge rock were first of all a kind of folk art of a subculture, as was the first hip-hop music of young, New York African Americans. But soon the music of these groups went mainstream, becoming mass produced for a mass market; it was no longer folk art but pop art. Dominic Strinati, if I can extract just a bit of his quotation, says, "Popular culture is produced by mass production industrial techniques and is marketed for a profit to a mass market of consumers. It is commercial culture, mass produced for a mass market."[24]

The symbiotic relationship between youth cultures and pop culture should be clear by now. The more extreme and sensational aspects of youth cultures, which are often associated with excess or rebellion, have special influence. For example, the questioning of authority, widespread use of drugs, and open mores on sexual activities have generally affected adult and pop culture. Iain Chambers takes note of some of these changes.

23. John Storey, *Cultural Theory and Popular Culture* (Athens, GA: University of Georgia Press, 2006), 4.
24. Dominic Strinati, *An Introduction to Theories of Popular Culture* (London: Routledge, 1996), 10.

Spectacular subcultures, commercial popular culture, America, the triumph of record and television, by the time of the 1960s these were all uniting to announce the death of an aesthetics based on the stable referents of the "authentic," the "unique," the "irreplaceable." . . . With the rise of Pop Art in the 1950s, the distinctions between advertising, design and painting become increasingly blurred. . . . Pop Art employed the despised, more frequently simply ignored, commercial iconography of popular experience.[25]

What then is popular culture? Resisting conclusive definition, popular culture is often seen in contrast to such classifications as high culture and folk culture. Popular culture needs a mass culture produced by mass communication feeding an industrialized consumer society. Wikipedia gives this definition: "Popular culture (or, pop culture) is the totality of ideas, perspectives, attitudes, images and other phenomena that are deemed preferred through an informal consensus within the mainstream of any given society"—and goes on to note that it has been called "the culture that is 'left over' when we have decided what high culture is."[26] Popular culture is produced in many ways. The needs and issues of a subculture, race, class, and gender may play an important role. Subcultures like urban blacks or punk whites may create music that is their folk music but then goes mainstream to a mass market, becoming the latest pop-cultural trend.

In general, mass art as popular culture is produced among three parties: the marketing industry (music, television, and film industries, for instance, and high level producers), artists (performers with their agents),[27] and the audience and fan base. (Of course, the internet is democratizing this hierarchy.) Critics argue as to which of these hold primary control, but the creation of popular culture can be seen as dynamic interaction. The changing tastes of the public are researched and measured; the industry discovers, creates, and promotes artists who have relative power in expressing their talents and ideas—with business reaping primary profits. But the manipulation of artists and the exploitation of the public can go only so far. For every extreme or imbalance, there are corrective responses from the public, artists, and the industry itself.

The first decade of the twenty-first century saw many significant changes in popular art. Among them was a decline of the music industry, due in large part to legal and illegal digital downloading of music. Contributing to the changing music scene is what we might call populist art. Earlier, hip-hop's rappers and

25. Iain Chambers, *Popular Culture: The Metropolitan Experience* (New York: Methuen, 1986), 8.

26. Wikipedia, "Popular Culture," wikipedia.org/wiki/Popular_Culture. In my opinion Wikipedia is at its best in the realm of pop culture (see various music groups, television, sitcoms, satire, and such)—a good source for ready reference.

27. Writer and mixer Lex Luger and his small studio managers, for instance, working with Jay-Z, Kanye West, and others.

graffiti artists were examples of pure *folk art*; rap then went mainstream to become a *mass popular art*. The internet has facilitated a democratization of the music and art scenes. Anyone can create the latest online sensation; sudden interest in a YouTube video can create a viral buzz leading an amateur performer to sudden professional fame. A double rainbow[28] along with the consequent song, "Double Rainbow Song"[29] provided many laughs among YouTube viewers.

Self-promotion on YouTube is one of two innovations that can bring almost instant fame to those who earlier were mere home or street-corner artists. The other is the sudden, global popularity of television talent shows. Television's talent shows go back to *The Original Amateur Hour* and *Arthur Godfrey's Talent Scouts*, beginning in 1948. But *American Idol, America's Got Talent, The Voice*, and a host of other shows, with international equivalents, spread the spotlight of fame to a much broader base of performers. Simon Cowell put it succinctly: "We live in a fame epidemic now, don't we? Everyone wants to be famous, and to me that's part of the charm of these shows . . . whether they're good or bad, they genuinely believe they're the best undiscovered talent."[30] Of these two new platforms, YouTube is the most democratic. With a home camcorder, or even a smart phone, anyone has a chance of becoming an international hit.

Christ and Popular Culture

From earliest Christian times, as we have noted, there have been controversies as to how Christians should live in and interpret pagan or secular "ungodly" culture. Canadian pastor John Van Sloten became more and more convinced that God's revelation has come to us both through the Bible and through revelation of truth and conflict in nature, in technology, in arts and music. His sermons began exploring God's truth in popular culture—in movies such as *Crash* and music like Metallica's "Dirty Window" from the album *St. Anger*. Van Sloten concludes that the unfathomable God, the hidden God of spiritual theologians, is everywhere trying to tell us about our lives and divine redemption; there are two bibles: Holy Scripture and God's revelations through nature and all human arts. The relationship of Christ and culture continues to be a controversial issue, as Amazon reviews of Van Sloten's *The Day Metallica Came to Church* reveal:[31]

28. "Yosemitebear Mountain Giant Double Rainbow," YouTube video, January 8, 2010, www .youtube.com/watch?v=OQSNhk5ICTI, if you will excuse the Lord's name in vain.

29. "Double Rainbow Song," YouTube video, July 17, 2010, www.youtube.com/watch?v=gi WtAQKREk8&feature=related.

30. Ann Oldenburg, "Talent Show Fever," *USA Today*, June 16, 2006, www.usatoday.com /life/television/news/2006-06-15-talent-shows_x.htm#.

31. John Van Sloten, *The Day Metallica Came to Church: Searching for the Everywhere God in Everything* (Grand Rapids: Square Inch Books, 2010).

It is full of subjective "spiritual" observations that have little to do with Christianity as revealed in Scriptures . . . [and] has much more to do with pantheistic thought than it does with anything in the New Testament. (S. Peek)

What would you say about a message that completely misses the main point. How would you feel if you went to an emergency room with a broken leg and the doctor there gave you hair tonic to make you feel better. . . . This book is empty, meaning-less and gives no hope nor solution for spiritual need. (Valerie)

Other reviewers had opposite reactions:

The idea that God can be found in all things is nothing new in Christianity. (editorial review)

I was introduced to a concept I had never considered before: the concept that there are two different texts of scripture—the Holy Bible and the world itself. (terdsie)

Finding the redemption story and seeing God's hand at work in songs, books, movies, rock stars, architects and a host of other things was quite an eye-opener for me. (Virgil Michael)

This is a MUST read for all youth workers as well as teenagers and their parents! (Gwen)[32]

Van Sloten encourages our "learning how to discern, to see and love God in *all things*" so we can "realize that what's happening inside (our) hearts is also happening in all creation, for *everyone* and *everything* in the cosmos . . . [so that we will] fall on our knees and join the song: 'Praise the Lord, all his works everywhere in his dominion' (Ps. 103:22)."[33] Here is a practical theology of popular culture needing to be discussed if we are to discern and deal rightly with God's revelation and will in our times and in our cultures.

Theology and Popular Culture

Craig Detweiler and Barry Taylor give four reasons that Christians should study popular culture: (1) it "both reflects who we are as people and also helps shape us as people," (2) it "must be investigated theologically because . . . [it is] the

---

32. Reviews of *The Day Metallica Came to Church*, by John Van Sloten, *Amazon.com*, www.amazon .com/Day-Metallica-Came-Church-Everywhere/dp/1592554954/ref=sr_1_1?s=books&ie=UT F8&qid=1327942791&sr=1-1.
33. Van Sloten, *Day Metallica Came to Church*, 235, 238, emphasis added.

primary forum for disseminating values, ideas and ethics . . . [and] is already studied by the broader culture," (3) "pop culture serves as the lingua franca of the postmodern world [and despite warnings, such as those from Allan Bloom,[34] has become] a new 'canon' of literacy" for a younger generation, and (4) the "divide between the academy and the populace leaves modern Christianity, which took its theological cues from the academy, with a lamentable theological grid. . . . There is a conversation about God going on in popular culture that the church is not engaged in and is often unaware of."[35]

If God planned human culture, does popular culture also have a divine origin? As we come to see the human origins and dynamics of human cultures generally, we ask if popular culture is strictly a human endeavor, or a work of human and divine collaboration. Or is it, as some imply, a human rebellion against the Lord, their Creator? Since we're all deeply engaged in popular culture, what can we make of God's perspective on today's music, movies, television, and internet? How can people today, young and old, discern what is helpful and what is harmful in popular culture?

To scan popular culture is an enormous task—greater than this book can bear. So, imagine that you and your youth group, or you and your academic class, have been awarded a sizeable grant for a semester's study of current popular culture. You are to reach some tentative conclusions about pop culture's images, messages, values, perhaps worldview, and its attempts to influence for good, or exploit for profit, the general public. Each week, or perhaps on weekends, you will come to a special room outfitted with computers and television sets. There is a huge rack of magazines along the wall, magazines of all types. Also available are listings of television programs and movies now showing, and a rack of recent film DVDs. On the walls are examples of pop art. Most of all there are computers with fast Wi-Fi and tablets with countless apps. You organize your project into sections and divide into small working groups. By the third session you want to have a working plan and some general hypotheses. Three-quarters of the way through the project, you aim to produce an initial report. The last two sessions will consider God's perspective on it all with suggested working plans for church and youth study groups. Your overall objective: "to work toward a theology of popular culture."

Even minus such rich resources, my students come to certain conclusions about God's intention for popular culture. Aside from God's desire to save the world through the Son, God may also want, along with the sun and rain promised for

34. Allan Bloom, *The Closing of the American Mind* (New York: Simon and Schuster, 1987).
35. Craig Detweiler and Barry Taylor, *A Matrix of Meaning: Finding God in Pop Culture* (Grand Rapids: Baker Academic, 2003), 19–21.

all (Matt. 5:45), to allow people the common grace of popular culture. About God and popular culture, here are our conclusions:

1. Popular culture may be intended to survey the cultural landscape of any particular people and bring unity and a sense of human community. (Sports like the World Cup and the Olympics operate in this way.)
2. Music, too vast and varied to elaborate, can add dimension or supply meaning and support to lives missing some important ingredient. (From folk to country, rock to punk, the blues to hip-hop to funk, dance to glam, or just pop, music energizes people to get on with their lives.)
3. God may be pleased to see those who spend their lives in tedious jobs find some entertainment and relief in sitcoms and talent shows. And God must take some pleasure in the expression of human artistic talent. (Examples among countless illustrations might be an inauspicious middle-aged woman, Susan Boyle, on "Britain's Got Talent,"[36] to a little girl, Anna Graceman, on "America's Got Talent,"[37] both with tremendous voices. Wherever they go next in their careers, on those nights they took audience, judges, and television viewers from blah to cloud nine in minutes—and they were watched on YouTube much longer.)
4. God may want to bring inspiration to those beaten down through abuse or fighting terminal illnesses with stories of those who have overcome and achieved. Among many dramas bringing hope and encouragement to millions, we could mention the story of Jaycee Dugard, a kidnapped girl imprisoned and sexually molested for almost two decades,[38] or the TV documentary *Teenagers Fighting Cancer*.[39] Note also the critical potential of the church as an instrument of God's grace, supplementing the inadequacies and correcting the misdirections of popular culture. The apostle Paul's second letter to the Corinthians begins with recognition of special, graceful comfort that can come from God alone.
5. God must be discouraged by a country that has not acknowledged its responsibility for racism, sexism, or classism, hidden plagues that hinder growth for so many. God may be pleased with a documentary or series exposing

36. "Original Version. Susan Boyle, "I Dreamed A Dream." YouTube video, April 11, 2009, www.youtube.com/watch?v=wnmbJzH93NU.

37. Michael Slezak, "*America's Got Talent*: Precocious Child Singing," *TV Line*, June 22, 2011, www.tvline.com/2011/06/americas-got-talent-recap-season-6-atlanta-auditions-anna-graceman/.

38. The Jaycee Dugard documentary portrays this dramatic story of a girl who was kidnapped when she was eleven and held as sexual slave for eighteen years. ABC *2020*, "Exclusive: Dugard's Home Video," March 3, 2010, www.abcnews.go.com/2020/exclusive-jaycee-dugards-home-video/story?id=10002110.

39. The documentary tells the poignant stories of teenagers Rebecca, Alex, and Adam, now twenty-four, but first diagnosed with cancer at age fifteen: www.uhb.nhs.uk/teenagers-fighting-cancer-c4.htm.

such injustices. (Examples include television series or documentaries like *Eyes on the Prize*; *Roots*; *Harlan County, U.S.A.*; *Bowling for Columbine*; *Hearts and Minds*; *The Fog of War*; *An Inconvenient Truth*; and *Shoah*.)

6. Christ's anger toward hypocrisy, and especially religious dissembling and evils, seems to justify some of the social criticism we find in pop culture. (In songs like Arrested Development's "Fishin' 4 Religion" or the prophetic protests of Talib Kweli in his album *Eardrum*, in films and television sitcoms like *Monty Python* and *Saturday Night Live*, *The Simpsons* or *South Park*, our civic foibles and religious failures are satirized—subtly suggesting positive change.)

7. God may be pleased with the many songs, movies, and shows pointing through life's emptiness toward divine and scriptural themes. Such can lead unbelievers to (in the words of Paul, the missionary) "search for God and perhaps grope for him and find him" (Acts 17:27). (Songs like Kansas's "Dust in the Wind" and "Wayward Son," Tupac's "Ghetto Gospel" and "So Many Tears," and BIG's "Ready to Die" make us think. The works of King's X and U2 are more clearly aimed to promote spiritual considerations. Bette Midler's "From a Distance" and Joan Osborn's "God Is One of Us" have theological implications—if taken seriously. Films like *Evan Almighty, Bruce Almighty*, Steve Martin's *Leap of Faith*, *The Matrix*, *Magnolia*, and *Dogma* provoke thought and discussion in godly directions.) As Robert Johnson put it, "Conversation about God—what we have traditionally called theology—is increasingly found outside the church as well as within it. One of the chief venues for such conversation is the movie theater and its adjacent cafés."[40]

Weeds and Wheat

We've traced the origins and dynamic of popular culture and suggested examples of its positive possibilities, but how are we to distinguish the good from the bad? We have no biblical texts dealing specifically with modern music, video games, or reality shows. Not even experts can distinguish the exact boundary between soft- and hard-core porn. We question our response to sexual scenes in R-rated films. Is gory violence preferable to explicit sex? When does popular culture cross the line between helpful and hurtful for different age levels? And what do we consider appropriate in the secular sphere though it may not be for the family of God? Most will agree there are no cut-and-dried answers to these questions—though they are important.

40. Robert K. Johnston, *Reel Spirituality: Theology and Film in Dialogue*, 2nd ed. (Grand Rapids: Baker Academic, 2006), 22.

As background for dealing with these questions, we might turn to a parable. Jesus may have taught in parables for more reasons than even he realized (Christ did not claim omniscience while on earth [Matt. 24:36], nor foreknowledge of our times). Parables were a well-known teaching genre before Jesus's time, as seen in Nathan's confronting King David with the story of the ewe lamb (2 Sam. 12), in Plato and other teachers before Jesus's time, and among Jewish rabbis. Jesus certainly knew how stories attract—and how they could be used effectively for different levels of receptivity and understanding. Parables may contain a single point or a broader response to complicated issues—and the issue of God's perspective on postmodern media is certainly complex. An important feature of parables is that they give no pat answers, no final conclusion. That is left to the hearers. Similarly, we will be left, after this discussion, with unfinished and continuous work of interpretation and application.

In the parable of the wheat and the tares (or weeds) in Matthew 13, a farmer finishes sowing what we take to be a fairly large field and returns home to rest. During his sleep, an enemy comes and sows weeds. (Most probably poisonous darnel, which resembles wheat, often grows with it, and does so intertwined, especially in its root system. And apparently, hostile neighbors in Jesus's time might take such revenge.) As the mixture of weeds and wheat becomes evident, servants cry out to the farmer, "Shall we root out the weeds?" The response is significant for the purpose of our discussion: "No; for in gathering the weeds you would uproot the wheat along with them. Let both grow together until the harvest. . . . I will tell the reapers, Collect the weeds first . . . to be burned, but gather the wheat into my barn" (Matt. 13:29–30).

After two more parables in this chapter and a brief rationale for parables, Jesus leaves the crowd for shelter in a house where he explains this parable to his disciples.

> The one who sows the good seed is the Son of Man; the field is the world, and the good seed are the children of the kingdom; the weeds are the children of the evil one, and the enemy who sowed them is the devil; the harvest is the end of the age, and the reapers are angels. Just as the weeds are collected and burned up with fire, so will it be at the end of the age. The Son of Man will send his angels, and they will collect out of his kingdom all causes of sin and all evildoers. . . . Let anyone with ears, listen! (Matt. 13:37–41, 43)

Augustine, bishop of Hippo, once preached on this parable:

> O you Christians, . . . I tell you of a truth, . . . even in these high seats [of the clergy] there is both wheat and tares, and among the laity there is wheat and tares. Let the good tolerate the bad; let the bad change themselves, and imitate the good. Let us

all, if it may be so, attain to God; let us all through His mercy escape the evil of this world.[41]

Surely the parable of the wheat and weeds can apply to the mixture of good and bad in the church, as in Augustine's application. In answer to scholars who admit to only a single point taught in a parable, Jesus's declaration that the Son of Man will send his angels implies his deity—certainly an important subpoint of the parable. And though this story is applicable to the unfortunate mixtures in churches, its primary focus is toward the whole world (*kosmos*). Martin Luther lamented Christian torture and murder of Turks, heretics, and Jews as being against the principle of this parable—not within, but outside the church. Similarly, leaders such as Roger Williams, John Milton, and others have applied this parable to civic (secular) life. At the last day, according to Christ's interpretation, God will collect (out of the earthly kingdom of heaven) all causes of sin *and* all evildoers (who will not repent of their evil ways). If this parable can guide Christian discernment in the world of popular culture, it suggests difficulty in ascertaining the exact distinction of good and bad. It also speaks to the fact that God's final kingdom on earth must be free from all evildoers *and* all systemic causes of sin— of oppression, dysfunction, and hurt. In regard to our judging popular culture, I would take the final lessons of the parable to be encouragement for *patience* in regard to the delay of God's judgment upon ungodliness, and for *discernment* between what is righteous (or just) and what is unrighteous.

Although passing ultimate or absolute judgment on any cultural image or text is impossible, there are principles, biblically based, that people of faith can use. Here are suggested principles for separating the wheat and the chaff of popular culture in a just or righteous way.

1. As Van Sloten has written,[42] the fullness of God's kingdom intentions, God's full will, and the paradoxes involved in human responses to God's sovereign love and grace, need both Holy Scripture and the complementary expressions from general revelation and the image of God in all persons. Psalm 19 clearly portrays the bible of nature and God's Holy Word. The apostle Paul referred more than once to human cultural truth (Acts 17:22–31; Titus 1:12–13). God used moral principles and patterns from earlier Sumerian and Egyptian culture in divine instructions found in the Pentateuch. All truth is God's and valuable for us as long as it is judged by God's supreme revelations in written Word and living Word: the Bible and our Lord Jesus Christ.

41. Augustine, Sermon 23.4, www.newadvent.org/fathers/160323.htm.
42. Van Sloten, *Day Metallica Came to Church*.

2. What promotes healthy growth and dignity of children is to be affirmed; all that hinders or twists the growth of children and youth is to be condemned. The abuse or neglect of the young by parents/caretakers or society is contrary to nature and God's will. "Children are an heritage of the LORD" (Ps. 127:3 KJV) and "Train up a child in the way he should go" (Prov. 22:6 KJV). That there will be differences of opinion in application of this principle is admitted. That it therefore is of no effect is denied; it is still a useful principle.

3. God's heart is set on people living together in just societies, in communities committed to the common good. All that oppresses, dehumanizes, marginalizes, and denies the dignity of individuals, families, and groups is unjust, is not right. As abstract and vague as this may sound, it should not be discarded. "[God] has showed you [Israel, Moab, and all people on earth], what is good; and what does the LORD require of you but to do justice, and to love kindness [compassionate mercy], and to walk humbly with your God?" (Mic. 6:8 RSV). God's kingdom comes as believers live out these principles, talk and vote these principles, preach and teach the same, and depend on the work of God's Spirit.

4. God's aim is an end to violence, and peace through justice. "[God] shall judge between the nations, and shall arbitrate for many peoples; they shall beat their swords into plowshares, and their spears into pruning hooks; nation shall not lift up sword against nation, neither shall they learn war any more" (Isa. 2:4). There is room, in this present age, within the biblical record and Christian tradition, for pacifism and cautious just-war practices, but not for militaristic exercises in power or warmongering. Pacifists well argue the absolute futility of suicidal war in a nuclear age; believers in just war point to Bosnia, Uganda, and Darfur as incidences of maniacal slaughter calling for forcible intervention. The weaknesses of peacemakers at all levels increase opportunities for militarists. Similarly, God hates all distortions of sex—in sexism and all other distortions of this powerful gift. We need strong collaboration, in our disagreement, toward the common goal: by God's grace and as God's partners, sowing justice (proper functioning) that we may reap peace.

5. God intends divine creatures to treat their environment as the Creator's handiwork and as our legacy for future generations. "The LORD God took the man and put him in the garden of Eden to till it and to keep it" (Gen. 2:15). "The land is mine . . . you are but aliens and tenants" (Lev. 25:23).

6. Finally, we uphold the freedom of all people to seek out divine perspective and help. Even here, most agree. Secularists respect the principle of freedom of religion; only tyrannies deny the right of free conscience and public worship. It is important to uphold what we see as the Creator's intention that all cultures seek the true and living God, and that divine judgment is upon all forms of human idolatry and suppression of spiritual life. "God . . . made

the world and everything in it . . . made from one [common stock] every [culture on earth] . . . so that they should seek God, and perhaps grope for him and find him—though he is not far from each one of us" (Acts 17:24, 26–27).

A majority of the world's population can accept the wording of the above—and almost all accept the principles. That some intellectuals and those with small party interests quibble over details should not hinder us from making these principles a basis for our practical theology and youth ministry.

These principles are important for three reasons: we live in increasingly multicultural societies, we seek to make a difference in the world, and discussions about popular culture are needed. We can encourage students to become "expert" in popular culture as citizens of another world. Such principles are not cold propositions; they are just—characteristics of the divine nature and healthy human relationships. They flow as warm principles out of genuine worship of the Triune God.

Questions for Reflection and Discussion

1. Do you find reflection on your own personal identity profitable? What kind of effect have family, ethnicity and nationality, school and friends, social trends and media, had on your sense of personal identity and value system?

2. Had you reflected much on how you were socialized into human society before reading this chapter? Or on the effect on babies who have not had human contact and nurture?

3. How do you understand and apply the idea of subcultures? Can you identify the subculture to which you belonged when you were a teenager? How is knowledge of subcultural dynamics helpful in youth ministry?

4. Can you see ways in which your culture has influenced your theology? Has this chapter convinced you of the complexities and nuances in practical theology and in cultural discernment? How do you see God's grace protecting you and your church from harmful cultural compromise?

5. Are you content to minister without all the answers and with an understanding that many important issues are relative? Can youth ministry be "successful" when we are learning with students rather than trying to give them all the answers?

6. Are you committed to being a lifetime learner with the help of others? And does such learning come from your worship of God and love for neighbors?

—11—

Relating to Christ in Culture

Render to Caesar the things that are Caesar's, and to God the things that are God's.

MARK 12:17 KJV

God so loved the world . . .

JOHN 3:16A KJV

Love not the world, neither the things that are in the world. If [anyone] love[s] the world the love of the Father is not in him.

1 JOHN 2:15 KJV

Followers of Christ who proclaim the gospel announce the kingdom for today's cultures. Consider the Gospel accounts: "Jesus began to proclaim, 'Repent, for the kingdom of heaven has come near'" (Matt. 4:17), or "Jesus came . . . preaching the gospel of the kingdom of God" (Mark 1:14 KJV), or Luke's account of Christ announcing himself as anointed to proclaim the gospel to the poor. Christ's mission was to proclaim God's kingdom penetrating the culture of his time—and to bear the consequences of its rejection. As practical theologians, ministers of the gospel today question how God's kingdom is activated in today's society. The previous chapter dealt indirectly with this issue. Now we must squarely face the questions: What is Caesar's and what is God's? Does, or how does, Christ want to change our society through us? To answer these questions, we take another look at culture, at Christ, and at Scripture and how it has been interpreted though history.

Culture's very existence and our ability to socialize have come only through the *logos*, the Word of God. Do you take the *logos* (Word) of John 1:1–3 to correspond to the Wisdom by which God made the world in the Old Testament (Ps. 104:24; Prov. 3:19; Jer. 10:12)? However you interpret these verses, it is clear that God created the world and its culture through the Son, described by John as the *logos*. In addition to your necessary relationship to culture, then, you have a relationship with the most important Person in the world. You face two realities: culture and Christ. But how do Christ and culture come together in your practical life? Previous chapters have laid a foundation for cultural understanding, but how are we, in Christ, to relate to, carry on business in, be witnesses to, and enjoy our cultural resources? This is a challenging conundrum.

The Christ-and-culture issue includes the relationship of church and state, but we are asking more generally about the whole relationship between Christians and the world. How do we respond to "come out from them, and be separate . . . and touch nothing unclean; then I will welcome you, . . . says the Lord Almighty" (2 Cor. 6:17–18)? And, at the same time, how are we to follow Christ's instructions to be "the salt of the earth" and "the light of the world" (Matt. 5:13a, 14a)? Light, Jesus says, must not be hidden away but set in the midst of darkness, and salt needs to be dissolved in food to be effective. Jesus often left the temple for parties with sinners. How deeply are we to enter the darkness of this world, and to what extent are we to be dissolved into the stuff of this world? What does it mean to be *in* the world but not *of* it? Such questions take us in the direction of theological ethics: How then should we live? What does the Bible say about this?

We have already considered how much we have to learn from culture.[1] Can we not learn about God and Jesus Christ through popular culture, human arts, and nature, as well as in the Bible and through the church? Doesn't the church need to learn from the world as it tries to heal and reform the world? Isn't it for such healing and reform that we pray, "thy kingdom come, thy will be done on earth"?

God wanted Israel to see their existence based under divine lordship. "I am the Lord your God. As my servants and partners, be holy as I am holy, carry out your relationships in love, do justice and have mercy—among yourselves, and as a witness to all nations."[2] Israel's failure is paradigmatic of universal and continuous

1. See the discussion about two bibles in chap. 10, as we considered John Van Sloten's *The Day Metallica Came to Church: Searching for the Everywhere God in Everything* (Grand Rapids: Square Inch, 2010).

2. This is not a direct quotation but an attempted summary of God's will for Israel in the Old Testament.

human failure. Yet, through prophetic laments and warnings come promises of a great Suffering Servant who will fulfill God's original intent.

Jesus Christ *was* the fulfillment of God's intent; he fulfilled Jewish expectations in a surprising and, for many, disappointing manner. As grand exemplar of godly humanity (and of course full divinity), Christ stands between the Old Covenant and the New, between Israel and the church. We Christians look to him as Lord and Savior, and also as a model of kingdom living. In his teaching and actions Christ embodies a divine ethic. Christ's teachings often seem enigmatic until we come to grips with his life and its context. The sermons, parables, and last discourse in John's Gospel make fuller sense in light of the incarnation, cross, and resurrection. Still, how Jesus would have us living in families, gaining further education, making a living, engaging in public and military service, and viewing popular culture is not clear—at least for most of us. Throughout church history, Christians have taken many different stands on the relationship of Christ and culture. Attending to wisdom of the past is of great value.

Historical Reflections on the Christ-and-Culture Issue

Relating Christ and culture raises questions about the relationship of church to society, faith to reason, theology to philosophy, and Christian lifestyle to worldly lifestyle. As with all such challenges, we want to think as practical theologians. Our practical theology is based on doxological, biblical, and systematic theology—but also on often-neglected historical theology. The latter is a rich source of lessons and examples in dealing with Christ and culture. What an array of different opinions church history shows us on this subject! They demonstrate the relativity of cultural contexts, a healthy array of innovative thinking, and a unity around the revelation of God in Jesus Christ. In briefly highlighting some examples, we are forced to skip fascinating background and profound nuances in the writings of these theologians.

Consider yourself a theological student at different times in church history. We may begin with Tertullian (160–220) of the Western church in Carthage at the turn of the second and third centuries asking, "What indeed has Athens to do with Jerusalem? What concord is there between the Academy and the Church?"[3] From the Eastern side of the Christian world, we hear Clement of Alexandria (150–215) replying:

> Philosophy came into existence, not on its own account, but for the advantages reaped by us from knowledge.[4]

3. Tertullian, *On Prescription against Heretics*, ch. 8.
4. Clement of Alexandria, *The Stromata* 1.2, in *The Ante-Nicene Fathers*, ed. Alexander Roberts and James Donaldson 10 vols. (1885–96; Grand Rapids: Eerdmans, 1986–89), 2:304.

And should one say that it was through human understanding that philosophy was discovered by the Greeks, still I find the Scriptures saying that understanding is sent by God . . . from God . . . that philosophy more especially was given to the Greeks, as a covenant peculiar to them—being, as it is, a stepping-stone to the philosophy which is according to Christ.[5]

Who would you be more inclined to follow: Tertullian or Clement? Would you be more likely to despise the classical philosophers and scientists or to learn from them?

Cultural philosophy was for Clement part of a Christian's first step in knowledge that could lead, through the grace of Christ, to a vision of God. But in terms of the Christian's engagement with culture, as to participation in worldly entertainments, men shaving their beards, women wearing earrings, eating for eating's sake, or drinking fine wine,[6] Clement and Tertullian were both what we might call "moral puritans." This must be understood, however, in terms of their pastoral concern for believers coming out of, and tempted by, the allure of surrounding licentious extremes. As youth leaders, your encouragement to young people will be motivated by your pastoral concern for them in *their* particular context and in light of their faith tradition.

Then, imagine you are living in early fifth-century Rome. You have been shocked by the sack of your great city, center of the long-lasting Empire, by the Visigoths. Christianity is the state religion, but it is coming under attacks from many competing religions and philosophies. Augustine, bishop of Hippo (354–430), tries to distinguish the Christian faith from politics, introducing a concept of two spheres, an idea that would permeate the Western church down through the Reformation. Only a few objected to his view of the tension between the two spheres of our lives, the temple and the marketplace, our faith and our country. Here is Augustine's classic statement of our double, and different, responsibilities to Christ and secular society.

There are two kinds of love; of these the one is holy, the other impure; the one is social, the other selfish.[7]

[These two loves] separate the two "cities" founded among the race of men, under the wonderful and ineffable Providence of God, administering and ordering all things which have been created; the first [city] is that of the just, the second is that

5. Ibid., 6.8, in Roberts and Donaldson, *Ante-Nicene Fathers*, 2:494. Compare Paul telling the Christians in Galatia that the law was a stepping stone or tutor to bring them to Christ (Gal. 3:24).
6. Clement of Alexandria, *The Instructor*, 2.9–10, in Roberts and Donaldson, *Ante-Nicene Fathers*, 2:237–58.
7. Augustine, *On the Literal Interpretation of Genesis* 10.15, 20, in *An Augustine Synthesis*, ed. Erich Przywara (New York: Harper & Bros., 1958), 266.

of the wicked. And though they are now, during the course of time, intermingled, they shall be divided, at the last judgment.[8]

A key in Augustine's practical and pastoral theology is his fascination with two parables of Jesus: the parable of the wheat and weeds (Matt. 13:24–30) and the parable of the net gathering both good and bad fish (Matt. 13:47–50). Both kingdoms or cities, that of man and that of God, are meant to accomplish good on earth, the first for our temporal good and the latter for our eternal welfare. In both spheres there are good and bad, wheat and tares. We cannot separate or even fully discriminate between those who with open hearts are moving toward, and those whose hearts in rebellion are moving away from, God's gracious salvation. In the end evil will be punished and good rewarded (John 5:28–29)—of course by God's grace. How would you have taken Augustine's teaching then . . . and now?

Centuries later in the high Middle Ages, Thomas Aquinas (1225–1274) used three resources—the recovered texts of Aristotle, the learning of his teacher[9] and predecessors, and his brilliant mind—to bring about a synthesis of worldly knowledge and the mysteries of God. Although using Aristotle's rational dialectic, Aquinas follows those who "believe in order to understand," rather than "I must understand so as to believe." His theological treatises[10] present a magnificent synthesis of Augustine's two kingdoms, grand medieval cathedrals with Gothic art and architecture reflecting heavenly beauty and reality. I was touched to read how tears would flow down the face of this large-bodied priest as he celebrated the Eucharist.[11] Having mastered the learning of his age, he abruptly ended work on his *Summa Theologica* after a mystical vision of God. Do you sense a need for a heavenly vision of God as you work out your relationship to the world and its knowledge?

Struggling for personal peace and salvation, Martin Luther (1483–1546) discovered "justification through faith alone." Deeply disturbed by the commercialization of indulgences, he sought to reform the church, but ended up being condemned and starting a new one. Troubled by Rome's greedy draining of Germany's financial resources and protected by German princes, he seemed to represent one small aspect in the rise of modern nation-states, what we know as nationalism. So Luther, like the figures mentioned above, was caught up in the cultural changes of his time. Certainly he was influenced by his cultural situation, and, in turn,

---

8. Augustine, *On the Literal Interpretation of Genesis* 10.15. 20, in *Augustine's Quest of Wisdom*, ed. Vernon J. Bourke (Milwaukee: Bruce, 1945), 249.

9. Albertus Magnus, also known as Albert the Great or Albert of Cologne, was a German Dominican monk and bishop and responder to the "naturalism" of the Arabian, Muslim philosopher Averroes.

10. Thomas Aquinas, *Summa Contra Gentiles* and *Summa Theologica*.

11. David Berger, *Thomas Aquinas and the Liturgy* (Naples, FL: Sapientia, 2005), 15.

became an important influence on Germany and the Lutheran church—politically and theologically. His stance toward culture was different than those before him. He carries on the sense of "two spheres" that we saw articulated by Augustine. He has a deep sense of evil in individuals and the church. As to the political sphere, his special guidelines come from Augustine and Paul's instructions about Christian civil responsibility found in Romans 13. In one year, Luther produced three epochal works[12] that, with his other writings, express the paradoxical working out of Christian life in these two spheres.

> There are two kingdoms, one the kingdom of God, the other the kingdom of the world.[13]

> The two powers or governments, God's and Caesar's, or spiritual and temporal kingdoms, must be kept apart, as Christ does here. "Render to Caesar the things that are Caesar's. . . . Render unto God the things that are God's." (Matt. 22:15–22)[14]

> God has established magistracy for the sake of the unbelieving, insomuch that even Christian men might exercise the power of the sword, and come under obligation thereby to serve their neighbor and restrain the bad, so that the good might remain in peace among them. And still the command of Christ abides in force, that we are to resist evil. . . . Thus there are two kinds of government in the world, as there are also two kinds of people—namely believers and unbelievers. Christians yield themselves to the control of God's word; they have no need of civil government. . . . But the unchristian portion (need) another government or the use of the civil sword.[15]

> We must firmly establish secular law and the sword, that no one may doubt it is in the world by God's will and ordinance.[16]

The paradox (regarding Christ and culture) in Luther was therefore not only in the objective working out of Christian and secular society, but within believers themselves: "A Christian is a perfectly free lord of all, subject to none; a Christian

---

12. Martin Luther, *To the Christian Nobility of the German Nation, Babylonian Captivity of the Church*, and *The Freedom of a Christian*.

13. Martin Luther, *An Open Letter Concerning the Hard Book against the Peasant*, as found in Hugh Thomson Kerr Jr., *A Compend of Luther's Theology* (Philadelphia: Westminster, 1943), 213.

14. Martin Luther, *Gospel Sermon, Twenty-third Sunday after Trinity*, in Kerr, *A Compend of Luther's Theology*, 214.

15. Martin Luther, *Commentary on Peter and Jude*, in Kerr, *A Compend of Luther's Theology*, 215–16.

16. Martin Luther, *Secular Authority: To What Extent It Should Be Obeyed*, in Kerr, *A Compend of Luther's Theology*, 216.

is a perfectly dutiful servant of all, subject to all."[17] You might have questioned Luther as to how a believing German prince, a pastor, and a peasant should relate to the government and to questionable festivities in town life. From today's perspective some question whether Germans following Luther's "Two Kingdoms" tradition accepted too easily the doctrine of two governments, spiritual and temporal, during Hitler's rise.

For all Luther's power and popularity, some of those leaving the Catholic Church came to feel he was only a "halfway reformer," settling for a new "nationalist" view of church and society. Although there were harbingers of such beliefs among medieval dissenters, a new surge, in what was considered a more thorough reformation, arose in places such as Zurich, Switzerland. Felix Manx (1498–1527) and Conrad Grebel (1498–1526) questioned the efficacy of infant baptism, were dissatisfied with the Mass or Eucharist, and objected to civil authorities deciding church matters. Because of their practice of re-baptizing, they were dubbed Anabaptists. These believers formed separate communities, instituted believers' baptism, held prayer meetings in homes, and practiced simple observances of the Lord's Supper. They may be seen as the first to articulate a clear belief in the separation of church and state. Furthermore, they refused to take any form of civil oaths or to serve in the military. Such "sectarianism" led to their being called the "Radical Reformation" and being looked upon, by authorities and a majority of citizens, as a seditious sect. But Anabaptists soon spread to other parts of Europe. Although some Anabaptists resorted to violence, most rejected such action even in self-defense. A prevailing pacifism has marked Anabaptist movements through history, and its main precepts are enjoying current interest and influence. Menno Simons (1496–1561), great leader and theologian of Anabaptists who would become the Mennonites, made separation by means of the banning or shunning of unbelievers or apostates very clear:

> Let everyone weigh the words of Christ and of Paul [1 Cor. 5:11] . . . and he will discover . . . everything Paul speaks in regard to separation he generally speaks in the imperative mode, that is, in a commanding manner. *Expurgate*, that is purge, 1 Cor. 5:7. *Profligate*, that is, drive out. *Sejungere*, that is, withdraw from, 1 Tim. 6:5. *Fuge*, that is, flee, Titus 3:9. . . . The Scripture admonishes and commands that we not associate with such, nor eat with them, nor greet, nor receive them into our houses, etc. . . . Now we command you, brethren, in the name of our Lord Jesus Christ, that ye withdraw yourselves from every brother that walketh disorderly, and not after the

17. Martin Luther, *The Freedom of a Christian*, in Williston Walker and Richard A. Norris, David W. Lotz, Robert T. Handy, *A History of the Christian Church* (New York: Scribner, 1985), 430.

tradition which ye have received from us. . . . [I]f any man obey not our word by this epistle, note that man, and have no company with him, that he may be ashamed.[18]

Simons goes on to enforce this ban even for husbands and wives against an erring spouse. It is obvious here that negative attitudes toward worldly culture are being carried on and reinforced.

You might have been attracted to this Radical Reformation and its premise of church as an alternative to culture. In modified forms it is enjoying an important resurgence in this century, you might also check out some of its advocates. One of the authors in *Missional Church* writes: "In our view . . . the contemporary voices of the Radical Reformation have an important contribution to make to the formation of a missional ecclesiology in a post-Christendom context."[19]

John Calvin's "sudden conversion," as he described it, in the early 1530s began to put him at odds with Catholic humanism and religious polity in France. Opposition to French Protestants forced Calvin (1509–1564) to flee and then to begin in 1536 his famous *Institutes of the Christian Religion*, which over time would grow from six to eighty chapters. Political turmoil and a revolution (in 1541) in Geneva, Switzerland, brought friends of Calvin's to power, and Geneva became an independent republic. Calvin comes to Geneva in 1541, in one sense as a noncitizen and a mere pastor. But his influence was great. The Protestants of Geneva were agreed on a break from Rome and renouncing of papal authority, on abolishing the Roman Mass, and in dissolving monasteries and the office of bishop. These Protestants were divided between mild and stricter reformers; the more moderate rejected mandatory church attendance, for instance. Calvin's faction wanted a city clerically controlled. In time, sins against the moral code were treated as crimes— thence the disputed charge that Geneva was being pushed toward a theocratic model. Still, in principle, Calvin believed in some separation of church and state.

In the next century, English Puritans who wanted to remain loyal to the reformed Church of England and purify or further reform it joined a majority of separatists or Pilgrims to establish a colony they called Plymouth in today's Massachusetts. Farther to the north, near today's Salem and Boston, the Puritan Massachusetts Bay Colony was formed beginning in 1628. What do you know

18. Menno Simons, *On the Ban: Questions and Answers* (1550), questions 1 and 2, in George H. Williams and Angel M. Mergal, *Spiritual and Anabaptist Writers* (Philadelphia: Westminster, 1962), 263–64.

19. Lois Barrett, "Missional Witness: The Church as Apostle to the World," in Darrell Guder, ed., *Missional Church: A Vision for the Sending of the Church in North America* (Grand Rapids: Eerdmans, 1998), 124. See also John Howard Yoder's *The Politics of Jesus* (Grand Rapids: Eerdmans, 1994); Stanley Hauerwas and William H. Willimon's *Resident Aliens* (Nashville: Abingdon, 1989); Craig A. Carter's *Rethinking Christ and Culture* (Grand Rapids: Brazos, 2007), and others.

about these Puritans and their colony? Would you have agreed with their ideas about church and state, and about popular culture? Can you imagine a discussion with them about Christ and (popular) culture? How would you have led a youth group in the colony—perhaps when some suggested a holiday dance?

Mainstream theology, Catholic and Protestant, sometimes exhibited ugly ecclesial and dogmatic disputes after the Reformation. The trauma of a major church split and its continued splintering, a growing spirit of individualism, and attention to evangelism and missions can explain the lack of social considerations. The eighteenth-century Enlightenment would gradually produce modernistic biblical studies and theology in the nineteenth century and a focus on changing the world. Attention was brought to the history of social ethics in Ernst Troeltsch's *The Social Teaching of the Christian Churches* (1911, in German). Modernistic or liberal theology would gradually free itself from constraints of the supernatural. Jesus was seen, not as God, but as a powerful teacher of peace and love. God was a distant Father of all, desiring the brotherhood of all ("sisterhood" was not then used), humans were essentially good, and modern science and education were bringing inevitable progress. Their view of Christ was very comfortable within contemporary culture, and the moral teaching of the church compatible with humanistic democracy. By the twentieth century the modernist/fundamentalist split was a contentious divide, in the American church especially.

In the nineteenth century, before this divide, Anglican theologian Frederick Denison Maurice (1805–1872) spoke to the church's neglect of social issues. Brilliant and profoundly spiritual, Maurice's passion was fixed on the name and glory of God. Strongly influenced by Plato and Coleridge, and with a love for the Johannine writings above other biblical writers, he rejected dogmatic rational theology and attempts to convert by threatening people into submission. He wrote and proclaimed an inclusive love of God, revering the historic creeds and believing in the pervasiveness of evil.

> The sin of the Church—the horrible apostasy of the Church—has consisted in denying its own function, which is to proclaim to men their spiritual condition, the eternal foundation on which it rests, the manifestation which has been made of it by the birth, death, resurrection and ascension of the Son of God, and the gift of the Spirit.[20]

Maurice was clearer than most as to what we cannot know: the nature of eternity, the resistance of human free will, the ultimate and eternal conclusion of the clash between divine love and human resistance.

20. F. D. Maurice, *The Life of Frederick Denison Maurice: Chiefly Told in His Letters*, ed. Frederick Maurice (London: MacMillan, 1884), 1:272.

Maurice's godly faith brought him sorrow over divisions in church and society, as well as a deep concern for the poor and oppressed. Distressed by the motivations and exploitations of capitalism, he joined early Christian socialists. Such concern about greed, manipulation of people and profits, and disregard for the poor is something we should all share—though we may not come to a similar conclusion. With two socialist friends Maurice founded a journal, *Politics for the People*, which discussed issues such as extension of suffrage, the relation of the capitalist to the laborer, and what a government can or cannot do to find work or pay for the poor.

Discussing the Lord's Prayer and its petition, "Deliver us from evil," Maurice commented, "How hard when evil is above, beneath, within, when it faces you in the world and scares you in the closet . . . when all schemes of redress seem to make the evil under which the earth is groaning more malignant."[21] As to the coming of the kingdom into society:

> The kingdom of God begins within, but it is to make itself manifest without. . . . It is to penetrate the feelings, habits, thoughts, words, acts, of him who is the subject of it. At last it is to penetrate our whole social existence.[22]

Bringing the Issue into the Twentieth Century

Critical biblical studies and liberal theology, undergirded by antisupernaturalist assumptions, spread from Germany and Britain to the United States and its seminaries by the turn of the nineteenth century. D. L. Moody's evangelistic services, the Scofield Bible, and rise of Bible conferences and Bible institutes furthered dispensational fundamentalism. Not all conservative/orthodox Christians were fundamentalists, and not all fundamentalists were dispensational. There were many Reformed Christians who followed the Reformers and Calvin rather than "new doctrines" from the nineteenth-century Plymouth Brethren in Great Britain, which had such a profound influence on early twentieth-century fundamentalism.

Dispensationalism sees Israel as God's earthly people; Christian believers are a heavenly people making up the invisible church, the bride of Christ, waiting to be raptured at his imminent return—then to reign over the earth with him for a thousand years. The gulf between liberalism and conservatism grew, producing a polarization of Protestant denominations, a great divide between a modernist social gospel and a fundamentalist gospel for individuals.

21. F. D. Maurice, *The Lord's Prayer*, quoted in H. Richard Niebuhr, *Christ and Culture* (New York: Harper and Row, 1951), 223.
22. Ibid., 228.

With roots in the Niagara Bible Conference in the latter nineteenth century and the publishing of a twelve-volume *The Fundamentals*,[23] Williston Walker et al. created "a popular summary of their views [which] became known as the 'five points of fundamentalism': the verbal inerrancy of Scripture, the deity of Jesus, the virgin birth, the substitutionary atonement, and the physical resurrection and bodily return of Christ."[24]

On the side of personal ethics, the code under which some of us grew up in the 1930s and beyond (to some advantage and disadvantage with school peers) were five don'ts:

1. No movies
2. No dancing classes, school dances, jukebox dancing, or ballroom dances
3. No smoking, chewing, or snuffing—though these were allowed in the South
4. No drinking of alcoholic beverages
5. No card playing (although Rook was allowed at my Christian college)

My home added television to the list of popular entertainments denied. The theological and social divide between modernism and fundamentalism could hardly be sustained. Understandably, I grew up with a stunted view of secular and popular culture. A rising generation would break out of such social constraints, and the division between churches and denominations was painful and restrictive. A new movement known as neoevangelicalism evolved from new theological thinking and the ecclesiastically and ethnically integrated Billy Graham Crusades. Carl F. Henry, Harold J. Ockenga, and others described this movement theologically and ecclesiastically. As fundamentalism was broadened, modernist claims of the essential goodness of man and inevitability of human progress were challenged by two world wars, the atomic bomb, and continued global conflicts—and chastened by the theologies of Karl Barth and neo-orthodoxy. The last part of the twentieth century brought about some unity between liberals and conservatives, which sadly has been falling apart in the new century over issues such as homosexuality and biblical inerrancy.

In terms of the social issues underlying the Christ-and-culture discussion, special mention should be made to contributions from the Roman Catholic Church. These do not come so much from one great voice and writer, but from the encyclicals that the church has produced. Ten such major documents are outlined by Thomas Massaro, SJ, in his *Living Justice: Catholic Social Teaching in Action.*

23. See also R. A. Torrey and A. C. Dixon, eds., *The Fundamentals: A Testimony to the Truth* (1917; repr., Grand Rapids: Baker, 1994).

24. Many sources are available, including Williston Walker, *A History of the Christian Church* (New York: Scribner, 1985), 662.

The documents include *Rerum Novarum* (*The Condition of Labor*, 1891, workers' rights and a family wage) and *Centesimus Annus* (*On the Hundreth Anniversary of* Rerum Novarum, 1991, combatting consumerist greed in the new "knowledge economy").[25] More than most parts of the Christian church, Roman Catholicism has applied the example of Christ, Scripture, and natural law to economic and political issues with special attention to the plight of the poor.

All this history and background are helpful for you as today's youth leaders. You are dealing with a broad range of concerns among youth growing up in a global, digital, consumerist culture. There is a tendency for emerging generations to throw away what is seen as the staleness and sterility of past and current religion and to begin all over again—which inevitably repeats the mistakes of the past in different forms. Our hope is that youth ministry will gather wisdom from the ages and demonstrate skill in discerning the currents of our age as well as the cultural dispositions of churches. Christ, whom we present to each rising generation, is a Person, an idea, and an event. The Son of God has entered human culture to be understood from within the context of culture. As culture mediates Christ, the eternal Christ challenges culture—and does so through his faithful followers.

The Current Challenge

Two factors influence all of us as we learn to discern with young friends. In the first place, prevailing tensions in culture place us and students on one side or another—or caught in the middle—of a serious conflict of values. Cultural wars about immigration and multiculturalism, about abortion and marriage, about the growing gap between rich and poor, about guns, about government spending and budgets, about violence and sex in media are raging across the face of the globe. Terrorist attacks from Islamic extremists are just one part of the picture.[26] Second, we are witnessing a changing religious scene (which includes a resurgence of Islam). The center of Christianity has shifted to the southern hemisphere where conservative evangelical and Pentecostal revivals are growing the church at unprecedented rates.[27]

As conservatism moved from fundamentalism to neoevangelicalism in the second half of the twentieth century, so in the twenty-first century we are witnessing a splintering of evangelicalism and a moving past the modern into something more

25. Thomas Massaro, SJ, *Living Justice: Catholic Social Teaching in Action* (Lanham, MD: Rowman & Littlefield, 2000), 78–79.

26. Samuel P. Huntington, *The Clash of Civilizations and the Remaking of the World Order* (New York: Touchstone, 1996).

27. Philip Jenkins, *The Next Christendom: The Coming of Global Christianity* (New York: Oxford University Press, 2002).

postmodern. Several writers and thinkers have noted these shifts. Sociologist James Davison Hunter used surveys of students from sixteen evangelical colleges and seminaries to break down stereotypes of conservative Christians and demonstrate important shifts in their manner of thinking and openness to threats against traditional boundaries.[28] Iain Murray describes the history and current division of evangelicalism in Great Britain and North America. He records the history of evangelicalism in Great Britain and North America during the second half of the twentieth century—and its sad divide.[29] Christian churches today are strikingly divided as to theology, society, and politics.

As biblical and cultural hermeneutics shift, it is important to understand the changing church scene. Just what are Fresh Expressions in Great Britain and Emergent churches in the United States about? Dave Tomlinson, whose *The Post-Evangelical* was published in Great Britain in 1995 (2003 in the enlarged US edition[30]), considers himself a postevangelical church planter. He has ministered to those uncomfortable within the rational style, dogmatic boundaries, and set structures of traditional evangelicalism. Brian McLaren's *A New Kind of Christian*[31] and other works argue that postmodern thinking and approaches are necessary and will provide a bridge between liberal and conservative thinkers and churches. Writers like Eddie Gibbs and Ryan Bolger,[32] and Phyllis Tickle[33] describe this movement. Carrying on the British debate over Dave Tomlinson's book, Graham Cray, Maggie Dawn, Nick Mercer, Michael Saward, Pete Ward, and Nigel Wright contribute essays regarding the present and future state of evangelicalism and/or postevangelicalism. Of special interest are Ward's sociological and theological reflections on the various tribes of evangelicalism and his observations as to how these social networks flourish with economic, spiritual, and social capital.

Meanwhile a new critique of evangelicalism has come from Soong-Chan Rah. His *The Next Evangelicalism: Freeing the Church from Western Cultural Captivity* challenges the ethnocentric captivity of the white, North American church. There are many ways of illustrating how cultural values affect our theological questions

---

28. James Davison Hunter, *Evangelicalism: The Coming Generation* (Chicago: University of Chicago Press, 1993).

29. Iain H. Murray, *Evangelicalism Divided: A Record of Crucial Change in the Years 1950 to 2000* (Edinburgh, Scotland: Banner of Truth, 2000).

30. Dave Tomlinson, *The Post-Evangelical* (1995; Grand Rapids: Zondervan/Youth Specialties, 2003).

31. Brian McLaren, *A New Kind of Christian: A Tale of Two Friends on a Spiritual Journey* (San Francisco: Jossey-Bass, 2001).

32. Eddie Gibbs and Ryan K. Bolger, *Emerging Churches: Creating Christian Community in Postmodern Cultures* (Grand Rapids: Baker Academic, 2005).

33. Phyllis Tickle, *The Great Emergence: How Christianity Is Changing and Why* (Grand Rapids: Baker Books, 2008). See also Steven Croft et al., *Ancient Faith, Future Mission: Fresh Expressions in the Sacramental Tradition* (New York: Seabury Books, 2010).

and emphases. Rah cautions against an individualistic reduction of our sense of sin and salvation:

> Our reduction of sin to a personal issue means that we are unwilling to deal with social structural evils and this reduction prevents us from understanding the full expression of human sinfulness and fallenness. We have reduced the power of redemption to a personal salvation from personal sin.
>
> Our approach to evangelism is shaped by an individualized . . . perspective on salvation. . . . Sin, therefore, is found only in the individual, not in structures and systems. The possibility of redemption, therefore, is limited exclusively to the individual.[34]

This example is not original with Rah, but it illustrates how Western European and North American churches need to learn from the East and South.

Christianity's shift from North to South, from West to East, from modern to postmodern (or a combination of both), all affect our interpretation of culture and Scripture. Our histories and social ties must be acknowledged as we locate ourselves in regard to the cultural issues of our times and work out genuine Christian identities in ourselves and with those among whom we minister.

Theological Critiques of H. Richard Niebuhr's *Christ and Culture*

Worship and the internet, Bible studies and a dance, Christ and culture—how do they come together? In 1951, H. Richard Niebuhr started the modern discussion of Christ and culture in a new and deeper way. Recent criticisms of his work *Christ and Culture* have greatly enlarged discussion about how Christians and the church should relate to the world. Taking both Niebuhr and his detractors seriously, our thinking will be expanded in the dialogue. Niebuhr's chapter 1, "The Enduring Problem," and his "Concluding Unscientific Postscript" have been neglected. The suggested fivefold schema—"Christ against Culture" to the far right and "Christ of Culture" to the extreme left, with the aesthetic, medieval synthesis, "Christ above Culture," surrounded by in-between positions of "Christ Transforming Culture" and "Christ and Culture in Paradox"—helpfully suggests approaches adopted by certain figures and movements in church history. Certainly, as fixed paradigms these typologies prove to be forced and somewhat arbitrary; Niebuhr misses nuances and at points is caught in discrepancies or contradictions. But what his detractors miss is that, in 1950, he was pointing out some significant historic trends. For Niebuhr,

---

34. Soong-Chan Rah, *The Next Evangelicalism: Freeing the Church from Western Cultural Captivity* (Downers Grove, IL: InterVarsity, 2009), 40.

the question of Christianity and civilization is by no means a new one. . . . It is helpful also to recall that the repeated struggles of Christians with this problem have yielded no single Christian answer, but only a series of typical answers which together, for faith, represent phases of the strategy of the militant church in the world. . . . Christ's answer to the problem of human culture is one thing. Christian answers are another; yet his followers are assured that he uses their various works in accomplishing his own.[35]

So Niebuhr[36] proceeds to establish his five types of theological responses to the issue of culture. And, as if anticipating his critics, he admits:

When the answers to the enduring problem are stated in this (schematic) manner, it is apparent that a construction has been set up that is partially artificial. A type is something of a construct. . . . When one returns from the hypothetical scheme to the rich complexity of individual events, it is evident at once that no person or group ever conforms completely to a type. . . . The method of typology, however, though historically inadequate, has the advantage of calling to attention the continuity and significance of the great *motifs* that appear and reappear in the long wrestling of Christians with their enduring problem. Hence also it may help us to gain orientation as we in our time seek to answer the question of Christ and culture.[37]

Besides defects in the typologies themselves, Niebuhr's detractors object to his leaving the solution hanging in the end—though he is negative toward those considered in the position of "Christ against Culture," and tilted toward "Christ Transforming Culture." Niebuhr's neo-orthodox or neoliberal stance may also be seen as missing the mark of true orthodoxy.

Dietrich Bonhoeffer found himself abandoned by the compromising impotence of the state Lutheran Church of Germany, which capitulated to Hitler and the Nazis. With courageous confessing Lutheran Christians, Bonhoeffer saw the failure of ethical theologies in

the conception of a juxtaposition and conflict between two spheres, the one divine, holy, supernatural and Christian, and the other worldly, profane, natural and un-Christian. . . . There are not two realities, but only one reality, and that is the reality of God, which has become manifest in Christ in the reality of the world. . . . There are, therefore, not two spheres but only the one sphere of the realization of Christ, in which the reality of God and the reality of the world are united.[38]

35. Niebuhr, *Christ and Culture*, 2.
36. Here and following, I will be referring to H. Richard Niebuhr of Yale University and not his also distinguished brother, Reinhold Niebuhr of Union Theological Seminary.
37. Niebuhr, *Christ and Culture*, 43–44.
38. Dietrich Bonhoeffer, *Ethics* (New York: MacMillan, 1965), 196–97 (written in the early 1940s, published in Germany in 1949 and in the United States in 1955 and 1965).

Others may be able to explain how Bonhoeffer, whom we all so greatly admire, squares this denial of two spheres with reality and how he explains Luther's teaching of "two kingdoms" as not originally intended to mark out two spheres of Christian experience. At any rate, the denial of two spheres of reality attempts to refute at least four of Niebuhr's types—and Niebuhr's theology in general. Yet it fails to explain how Bonhoeffer, ideally a pacifist, entered into a bomb plot against Hitler in the real world. In the end, Bonhoeffer, caught in the paradox of Christian pacifism and real politics, was willing to sacrifice his life.

Chief among Niebuhr's critics are today's Anabaptist and radical reformational theologians. John Howard Yoder, a Mennonite and broadly respected theologian, is esteemed as a Christian theologian and ethicist. Yoder (and Bonhoeffer would agree) faults Niebuhr for separating ethics from New Testament studies (especially the Synoptic Gospels), for one thing, and in the process, relativizing gospel principles in social ethics. Yoder also finds in Niebuhr a "distributive epistemological understanding of the Trinity"[39] that might allow for separate social ethical emphases from God the Father (perhaps more conservative as found in the Old Testament), from the radical Jesus in the New, and from the Holy Spirit as gathered by the church throughout the ages.[40] Yoder objects to the contrast and separation of "the pure and pacifist ethic of Jesus" and the need for power compromises in the real world of politics, a view accepted by both Niebuhrs and most social ethicists. Yoder especially takes exception to Niebuhr's characterization of a "Christ against Culture" perspective as being a "withdrawn" or "purist" position, arguing that this characterization comes from Niebuhr's polemical "stance."[41]

In place of Niebuhr's fivefold typology, Yoder has suggested (and others like Hauerwas and Willimon concur) three kinds of churches: the *activist church*, the *conversionist church*, and the *confessing church*.[42] The activist church is concerned chiefly with changing society rather than reforming the church or saving souls. The conversionist church, believing society can be changed only by changed hearts and lives, gives itself to preaching a gospel of forgiveness to sinners. The confessing church is not something between or a combination of the two but an entirely different view of the church, seeking not to change society or merely transform personal lives but to bring the church to worship and faithfulness to Christ above

---

39. John Howard Yoder, *The Politics of Jesus* (Grand Rapids: Eerdmans, 1972, 1994), 17, 100–101, 144n.

40. These parenthetical interpretations of Yoder are mine.

41. Yoder, *Politics of Jesus*, 154n.

42. John Howard Yoder, "A People in the World: Theological Interpretation," in James Leo Garrett Jr., *The Concept of the Believer's Church* (Scottdale, PA: Herald, 1969), 252–53, noted in Hauerwas and Willimon, *Resident Aliens*, 44–46.

and in all. One limitation with Yoder's first two types is they don't seem to describe churches I know historically before the modernist-fundamentalist debates of the nineteenth and twentieth centuries. But this threefold typology does describe some churches today. Hauerwas and Willimon note Martin Marty's description of the first two types as the "private church," concerned mostly with saving souls and an individualistic piety, and the "public church," mainline denominations trying to achieve justice through politics.[43]

For Yoder, pacifism is central to the Sermon on the Mount and the Christian gospel. Peaceful reconciliation is not just nice when it can work; it is the essential attitude for Christians; it is the cross under which, in confronting culture, we suffer and die in following Jesus Christ. Pacifism and principles of the jubilee should not be quaint doctrines held by small fringe denominations; they are God's mandate for the whole church in faithful witness against the powers of this world.

Yoder's typology is picked up in Hauerwas's and Willimon's powerful little book *Resident Aliens*. Simply put, I believe these theologians are objecting to what they view as Niebuhr's liberal accommodation to secular culture in explaining the mission of the church. These authors rather see mission as nothing less than believing and living out the message of Jesus Christ, and in this, making no allowance for the flesh or for compromises with secular society.

The problem, as *Resident Aliens* sees it, stems from the Constantinian compromise. The persecuted, or at least minority, church of the first four centuries of Christianity was forced to become the established church, a godly example to majority culture. Once Christianity was officially tolerated, and then became the state religion, it found itself with a different mission: to shape culture as effectively as possible. Worse, it became engaged in embellishing itself as an organization with wealth and power. "We believe," Hauerwas and Willimon say, "both the conservative and liberal church, the so-called private and public church, are basically accommodationist (that is, Constantinian) in their social ethic."[44]

To escape its Constantinian captivity, the church, according to these authors, must stop trying to change the world and start transforming the church into a countercultural colony that takes the Sermon on the Mount, not as an abstract ideal or mere subjective personal goal, but as an actual social manifesto lived out by the church. A church living up to the actual teachings of Jesus Christ and its apostolic mandate will be sending peaceful missionaries into troubled war zones, will be lifting up the cross, suffering and perhaps dying, as an alternative to drone attacks. "Failing at such truthfulness, we acquiesce to the sentimentality of a

43. Hauerwas and Willimon, *Resident Aliens*, 31.
44. Ibid., 32.

culture which assumes we have nothing more to offer empty people than to make their lives a little less miserable."[45]

The implications of this interpretation of Scripture and church history are radical indeed. They call into question how, or indeed whether, Christians may enter politics and military service. Are the efforts of those committed to transforming the culture of Hollywood or music in vain? How should individual Christians, churches, and governments have responded to the slaughter of Hutus in Rwanda? The authors' call to take the Sermon on the Mount seriously is a needed challenge, but their criticism of Augustine's suggestion to live out the Sermon as an "inward disposition" rather than as a literal guide to bodily action[46] seems to leave unanswered questions. Nobody is suggesting that people pluck out offending eyes or cut off offending hands, but applying the Sermon to matters such as asking civil authorities for a restraining order, taking someone to court, fighting for political rights and defensive military actions, resisting rape, or using violence to protect a family, remain for most of us complicated yet necessary matters.[47]

Still, another important contribution of the continuing radical reformation is its emphasis on the church, in contrast to individualistic ways of approaching culture and social ethics. Only in community and as the church can we fulfill God's mandates as covenant people. We are led to wonder what church we are talking about; where, these days, is this confessional church acting as a powerful rebuke to principalities and powers, to the ruling institutions of this world?

Given the widespread popularity of this "post-Christendom" teaching, it is worth noting orthodox writing from other perspectives. Besides Norman Geisler's *Christian Ethics*[48] and John J. Davis's *Evangelical Ethics*,[49] such a broader perspective may be gained from Dennis Hollinger's *Choosing the Good*,[50] Wyndy Corbin Reuschling's *Reviving Evangelical Ethics*,[51] and Stephen Mott's *Biblical Ethics and Social Change*.[52]

---

45. Ibid., 143.

46. Ibid., 82.

47. For further study from a post-Christendom, radical reformation perspective, see chaps. 1 and 5 in Guder, ed., *Missional Church*; Craig A. Carter, *The Politics of the Cross: The Theology and Social Ethics of John Howard Yoder* (Grand Rapids: Brazos, 2001) and *Rethinking Christ and Culture: A Post-Christendom Perspective* (Grand Rapids: Brazos, 2006); and Angus J. L. Menuge, ed., *Christ and Culture in Dialogue* (St. Louis: Concordia Academic, 1999).

48. Norman L. Geisler, *Christian Ethics: Contemporary Issues and Options* (Grand Rapids: Baker Academic, 2010).

49. John Jefferson Davis, *Evangelical Ethics: Issues Facing the Church Today* (Phillipsburg, NJ: P&R, 2004).

50. Dennis P. Hollinger, *Choosing the Good: Christian Ethics in a Complex World* (Grand Rapids: Baker Academic, 2002).

51. Wyndy Corbin Reuschling, *Reviving Evangelical Ethics: The Promises and Pitfalls of Classic Models of Morality* (Grand Rapids: Brazos, 2008).

52. Stephen Charles Mott, *Biblical Ethics and Social Change*, 2nd ed. (New York: Oxford University Press, 2011).

Ethics is not just an important discipline alongside practical theology; it is part of practical theology and vital to our ministering among young people—perhaps today more than ever. An excellent beginning review or study would be reading two articles in the *Global Dictionary of Theology*: "Social Ethics" and "Catholic Social Teaching."[53] Protestants are helpfully reminded of the breadth and richness of Catholic social teaching and encouraged to examine a work like Thomas Massaro's *Living Justice*.

Conclusion

We hope to confront the mystery and paradox of living faithfully in a fallen world with confident humility—passing such faith and confidence on to the young people we serve. The mighty and profound mystery of being Christ in the world today is seen in a variety of Scriptures already quoted in this chapter and in the following:

You have made [humans] a little lower than God and . . . given them dominion over the works of your hands. (Ps. 8:5–6)

The god of this world has blinded the minds of unbelievers. (2 Cor. 4:4)

Our struggle is . . . against the rulers, against the authorities, against the cosmic powers of this present darkness. (Eph. 6:12)

Let every person be subject to the governing authorities; for there is no authority except from God, and those authorities that exist have been instituted by God. . . . The authority does not bear the sword in vain! (Rom. 13:1, 4b)

Let your light shine before others, so that they may see your good works and give glory to your Father in heaven . . . so that you may be blameless and innocent, children of God without blemish in the midst of a crooked and perverse generation, in which you shine like stars in the world. (Matt. 5:16; Phil. 2:15)

In trying to digest these Scriptures, we find much mystery and paradox. Some have worked this out in a coherent system of a "countercultural church" or a "separated church," while others struggle to change culture for the better under God's authority.

The complexity of living in the world without being of the world, of engaging culture without submitting to its ungodly powers, can easily diminish our fervor in

---

53. William Dyrness and Veli-Matti Kärkkäinen, *Global Dictionary of Theology* (Downers Grove, IL: InterVarsity, 2008).

following Christ into everyday life. In scanning the internet and following popular culture, I need the power of the Father, the Son, and the Holy Spirit. To have a political opinion about foreign affairs or domestic policies, I need to weigh the contexts and particular issues of specific matters—and listen to those who know more than myself.

Personally, I take some exception to, and gain some important insights from, every thinker and movement mentioned in this chapter—seeking humble insight and confidence for my life and my teaching. Convinced that we cannot solve such complicated issues alone, or live out Christ's high standards on our own, we submit to kingdom thinking and study in a spiritual community. Our challenge, then, is to find and help the church be what it is meant to be in today's world. Christ says to us, "Very truly, I tell you, the one who believes in me will also do the works that I do and, in fact, will do greater works than these, because I am going to the Father" (John 14:12). These words, in regard to our individual lives and witness in today's world, can leave us in shameful despair—unless we hear them, not just as individuals, but as church. So ecclesiology (the study of the church) must be joined to ethics. And our study of church and justice needs subordination to our worship of God.

We all know churches and pastors (bishops and church leaders) ignoring culture. Church, for them, is a church thing, its own separate culture and institution. In such places we often find a sterile gospel and a church fighting for retention of members. We are also aware of churches and youth ministries accepting uncritically a large measure of cultural substance—usually on the basis of attracting outsiders. Here the personalities and styles of the pastor, leaders, worship leader, and musicians with clever use of media can become overly important. As Christians in culture, we are being called to a clear understanding of our culture and the counterclaims of the gospel of Jesus Christ. We are called to courageous Christ-following.

Questions for Reflection and Discussion

1. Please take a quick look back at the Bible verses at the start of this chapter and the Scriptures in its first two paragraphs. How did you respond to the tension in these biblical verses when you first saw them? Do you have any further insights about them now?
2. To what extent are you willing to learn from history?
3. Has the discussion of this chapter pushed you to consider your own identity in church and society?
4. Do you feel a bit humbled by the challenge of being a faithful witness of Christ in complicated cultures?

5. What person or idea in this chapter most impressed you or left you with further questions?

6. What practical relevance can you see in all the history and ethical discussions of this chapter?

7. What principles from this chapter might be of help to high school students headed for a job or college? How might such discussions be started?

—12—

Practical Theology in a Digital Age

> Many shall be running back and forth, and evil [or knowledge, KJV] shall increase.
>
> DANIEL 12:4B

A Cultural State of Flux

Consider the possible meanings of the above partial text about the end times from the last chapter of the book of Daniel.

> Some think it suggests perplexity at the strangeness of such a book of visions whose significance none could see. Others think it means "perusing," that men's eyes will run to and fro rapidly as they eagerly read this strange document. . . . Others think we are to take the words literally, and that the reference is to days of commotion, turmoil, and rushing around.[1]

I like to see this conclusion of the book of Daniel as describing the latter days in which the possibilities of human mobility and communication are incredibly expanded.

Whether or not we are closing in on the end times, and whatever this text means, we are living in an age of global hustle and confusion, with an overload of information, knowledge, opportunities, and evil. How much of the benefits and

1. Arthur Jefferey, exegesis of Daniel in *The Interpreter's Bible* (Nashville: Abingdon, 2000), 6:544.

distractions of the digital age have come from us and how much from the Sovereign of all? This chapter will consider different opinions about change, learning, and thinking in our digital age.

In 1844, the first telegraph message in the United States asked, across fifteen miles of wire, as if by proclamation: "What hath God wrought?"[2] In 1964, a computer in California connected to another by telephone received the first two letters of *LOGON*: "LO . . . !" before it crashed. There was little sense that God had a part in computer technology. So, just how is God involved in our technological innovations? And to what extent does our involvement with this technology point to our need for God? Is God the grand and fundamental communicator? Such questions are the stuff of practical theology in youth ministry.

Did the Holy Spirit, in 1961, inspire electrical engineers Jack Kilby and Robert Noyce to develop the silicon chip, or guide the move from analog to digital,[3] or help Tim Berners-Lee and his assistant develop the World Wide Web in 1991?

Did God's common grace help Shawn Fanning, a freshman at Northeastern University in Boston, create Napster for MP3 music file sharing in 1998? Or Chad Hurley and colleagues come up with YouTube in 2005? Or Mark Zuckerberg (with friends?) develop Facebook in 2007?[4]

Does God provide a means for Sergeant Hernandez to Skype his back-home family from a battle zone? Or the missionary Joneses to follow video of a family wedding they had to miss? Does God care about lonely teens or seniors connecting with someone close, but far away?

Does Jesus Christ see himself, in some sense, as Lord of cyberspace? How might Christ reveal himself to a pastor, a college student, or a middle schooler who each, at the same time, are viewing a pornographic site? How might Jesus intervene when a couple of girls are engaged in vicious cyber bullying, or warn a lonely teen of a predator?

These questions illustrate some of the ways we deal with digital issues in youth ministry—and look for answers in practical theology. Its main questions, remember,

2. It seemed as if Samuel Morse's proposed bill for a first telegraph line between Washington and Baltimore in 1843 would fail. But late at night it was passed by Congress, and a Miss Annie Ellsworth, daughter of the US commissioner of patents, brought Morse the news the next morning. Pleased, Morse gave Miss Annie the opportunity to choose the first message to be transmitted. She chose words from Num. 23:23 KJV, "What hath God wrought!"—with an exclamation point rather than a question mark, as in the biblical text.

3. *Digital* refers to communication signals transmitted in codes of ones and zeroes (meaning, the electricity is either on or off), thus a binary system, as opposed to an analog system—especially notable in transforming the music industry in the 1980s. Screens of phones, video games, television, and computers all work off digital systems—thus our term *digital age*.

4. See David Kirkpatrick, *The Facebook Effect: The Inside Story of the Company That Is Connecting the World* (New York: Simon & Schuster, 2010), which describes how a hacker culture produced a multi-billion-dollar company.

are "What is God doing in the world today?" and "What is God's perspective on what I and others are encountering these days?" We do well to ask, What, in a digital world, are righteousness and justice? For such are the foundation of God's throne (see Ps. 89:14).

The Bible doesn't explain positive benefits or dangers of gaming, the effect of violent or erotic video games on young boys and girls, or the consequences of information overload and multitasking. Biblical principles need information from social-science research.

We face two striking features in the twenty-first century. First, we are entering a digital age (comparable to social changes after the inventions of writing, the printing press, the telephone, and television). Second, we are being offered a whole new picture of the human brain and our learning, thinking process.

No one will deny the significant cultural changes brought about by the internet. But is this change revolutionary or evolutionary, and is it a cause for optimism or pessimism? These are issues we need to explore in this chapter, but not the only ones. A majority of youth in developed nations are, since the 1990s—and from a younger age in this century—using digital devices. As we saw in chapter 6, brain research is demonstrating the plasticity and malleability of human brains. Particularly in the first few years, and then around puberty, children and teenagers are pruning brain circuitry through their use of digital gadgets. Research has also revealed the slow development of the prefrontal cortex (an area of the brain providing discernment and judgment) that continues into the mid-twenties.

We face several basic questions. To what extent are the internet and digital screens changing youthful brains? And, to what extent is this technology changing society? Are young people, whom some are calling the NetGeneration or Digital Natives, a more or less homogeneous new generation, strikingly different from all past generations? How, we next ask, is this digital era affecting families and general lifestyles? Two more questions are of particular importance to us. How are digital activity and life in a digital culture affecting the identities of young people and their relationships and view of the world? And finally, what does the digital world mean for practical theology and for youth ministry?

The Issue of Technology

As students of universal human connectedness, Nicholas Christakis and James Fowler note the way relationships to the third degree and beyond influence our values, beliefs, and behavior. They see the human tendency to connect (in order to survive) increasing with the invention of the telephone and especially the internet. It is as if "these [human] networks were ready-made to put us online. . . . Networks are under our skin. . . . [And] changes in technology may be altering the way we live in our social networks and may have profound effects on the way we govern ourselves."[5]

Our digital devices are one aspect of human technology; the digital age enters a long history of technological evolution.[6] From the use of fire, to the making of tools, to the invention of the wheel and written languages, technology has brought great changes to human culture and civilization.

Plato seems to have opposed the technology of writing and educating people to read. Similarly, the printing press, pencil erasers, television, and the internet have raised grave objections for various reasons from thoughtful critics.

Technology's benefits are enjoyed by all and admitted by most. Even life on a primitive, self-sustaining farm uses many forms of technology. Technologies benefit most of us from morning to night, at home, school, or work, in leisure and social relations—even in places of worship if there are lights in the sanctuary. Still we are frightened by the destructive power of weapons of unthinkable power, their use by terrorists, the possibilities of cyber warfare, pollutions, and the melting of the Arctic ice-cap. Besides possible world devastation, we also wonder what digital and other technologies are doing to our quality of life. Questions must be asked: To what extent are we shaped by the tools we create? To what extent have our servant technologies enslaved us?

Robert Wauzzinski provides us with a classification of attitudes toward technology. Like H. Richard Niebuhr's disputed classification, it can prove helpful when we don't use the categories as rigid and airtight designations.[7] Wauzzinski describes perspectives regarding technology by four types or metaphors. The first three are optimism, pessimism, and realism.

> [Optimists] think of technology as the universal liberator . . . without being sufficiently aware of technology's long-term inherent dangers. . . . Pessimists . . . understand all too well the evils inherent in technology . . . [and] think of technology as a kind of modern Frankenstein's monster. . . . Realists . . . attempt to maximize utilities and reduce the potential or real harms presented by technology. . . . However, they do not care about the meaning of technology . . . [its purpose, intent, identity]. They see their job as pragmatically measuring the good and the bad in, and levels of happiness from, technology.[8]

5. Nicholas A. Christakis and James H. Fowler, *Connected: The Surprising Power of Our Social Networks and How They Shape Our Lives* (New York: Little, Brown, 2009), 209.

6. *Technology*, from the Greek *techne* and *logos* refers to human use and modification of natural resources to produce tools, machines, crafts, and systems of information and organization.

7. Referring to previously cited Niebuhr's *Christ and Culture* (New York: Harper and Row, 1951).

8. Robert Wauzzinski, *Discerning Prometheus: The Cry for Wisdom in Our Technological Society* (Madison, NJ: Fairleigh Dickenson, 2001), 11–16.

All three types are based on the assumption of human autonomy and limit their thinking to naturalistic investigation. Wauzzinski constructs a fourth alternative, a form of structuralism that looks for principles and rules "that do not originate in the autonomy of humanity. . . . I am arguing that any practical technology is formed on the foundation of foundational assumptions. These assumptions I will call 'religious,' only in the sense that they are the preconditions for reflection and practice."[9]

Accepting assumptions of structural reality that originate beyond the material world or from divine ordering allows Wauzzinski to critique naturalistic responses to technology and to provide freedom from natural determinism.[10] Using some general classification of theoretical responses to technology helps us examine the extraordinary technological advances of the digital era.

Digital Revolution or Evolution?

Something big has happened. To highlight the magnitude of the internet, John Palfrey and Urs Gasser ask us to imagine:

> In 2007 alone . . . content created, stored and replaced around the world [on the internet equaled] 3 million times the amount of information in all the books ever written or twelve stacks of books reaching from the Earth to the Sun, or six tons of books for every living person.[11]

Some experts are saying something like this: Everything has changed, and there is no going back. Children and youth are ahead of us, and we must catch up. Business, politics, education, and by implication ministry, must be revolutionized to meet these emerging citizens and the needs of a new age. Many of these experts see digital innovation as a deterministic evolutionary change leading toward a democratic, utopian era of peace and happiness. At the same time, a variety of differing opinions express caution or even deep concern. We now turn to the first question and issue: How big and what kind of change?

Poet, essayist, "cyber-libertarian," and fellow at Harvard University's Berkman Center for Internet and Society, John Berry Barlow issued, in 1996, "A Declaration of the Independence of Cyberspace." It proclaimed cyberspace to be a "new home of Mind," a place not of bodies and material things, a space free

9. Ibid., 16–17.
10. If human life is just an extension of the physical universe, then we may be subject to physical laws we cannot change by human will.
11. John Palfrey and Urs Gasser, *Born Digital: Understanding the First Generation of Digital Natives* (New York: Basic Books, 2008), 185.

from the tyrannies of contemporary governments and powers, a world without discrimination, of complete freedom of speech, a new "civilization of the mind in cyberspace."[12]

In the spirit of cyborg[13] theory, cyber educator Marc Prensky goes further, speaking of a blending of natural reason with digital enhancements:

> Within the lifetimes of our children, more powerful digital mental enhancements—the embedded chip and brain manipulation of science fiction—will become a reality, just as gene manipulation, long considered a far-off dream, is with us now. Just as we have begun to confront the ethical, moral and scientific challenges presented by genetic medicine, we will have to confront the issue of digital wisdom sooner or later, and we will be better off doing it sooner. . . . Nobody suggests that people should stop using and improving their unaided minds, but I am opposed to those who claim the unenhanced mind and unaided thinking are somehow superior to the enhanced mind.[14]

Prensky sees digital technological advance as a clear revolution in human history:

> A really big *discontinuity* has taken place. One might even call it a "singularity"—an event which changes things so fundamentally . . . there is no going back. This so-called "singularity" is the arrival and rapid dissemination of digital technology in the last decades of the 20th century.[15]

Prominent neurologist Gary Small (with Gigi Vorgan) seems to agree: "These Digital Natives have defined a new culture of communication—no longer dictated by time, place, or even how one looks at the moment unless they're video chatting or posting photographs of themselves."[16] These experts see this change as revolutionary rather than incremental. They acknowledge some dangers but generally see these technological advances as being for the good of humankind.

In answer to these optimists (such as Prensky with his prognostication of digitally enhanced humans and utopian hopes for this human-techno revolution), Mark Helprin responds "that man need not model himself after machines."

12. John Berry Barlow, "A Declaration of the Independence of Cyberspace," 1996, www.projects .eff.org/~barlow/Declaration-Final.html.

13. *Cyborg* refers to the theory and scientific experiments of providing biological humans with digital enhancements. See experiments of Manfred Clynes and Nathan Kline.

14. Marc Prensky, "Digital Wisdom and Homo Sapiens Digital," in *Deconstructing Digital Natives*, ed. Michael Thomas (New York: Routledge, 2011), 26–27.

15. Marc Prensky, "Digital Natives, Digital Immigrants," *On the Horizon* 9, no. 5 (October 2001): 1, emphasis original.

16. Gary Small and Gigi Vorgan, *iBrain: Surviving the Technological Alteration of the Modern Mind* (New York: HarperCollins, 2008), 20.

In its complexity, mystery, intelligence, and beauty, humanity is unexcelled as a masterwork of God and nature . . . think of the most complex and extraordinary machines mankind has yet devised, take ten of them, and combine their virtues. This tenfold construction—in terms of exactitude, critical timing, coordination, variety, miniaturization, adaptability, calculation, sensory function, integration, and balletic precision down to the atomic level—is neither a billionth as complex nor a billionth as wondrous as the very least among us.[17]

This is more than disagreement between science and theology—or even technology and the humanities. There are scientists who agree with Helprin's caution. It illustrates rather strikingly different interpretations and forecasting of digital phenomena.

Small sees a seismic change in our brains and culture: "The fact that it has taken so long for the human brain to evolve such complexity makes the current single-generation, high tech brain evolution so phenomenal."[18] Another writer and cultural critic, Lee Siegel, while being no Luddite,[19] agrees that the internet is shaping our minds and cultures but contends we have a choice in its future and ours.

The Internet has its destructive side just as the automobile does, and both technologies entered the world behind a curtain of triumphalism hiding the dangers from critical view. . . . The Internet as technical innovation is the answer to our contemporary condition of hectic, disconnected, fragmented activity. . . . It is as much a question of investigating the influences on the Web as of thinking about the Web's influences on us. . . . The choice is ours. Things really don't have to be the way they are.[20]

As God put Adam and Eve in charge of the earth and its creatures, so God expects humans to control their cultures and technological innovations. Human culture is the passing on of learned behaviors—whether writing, the printing press, the telegraph, or the web—to the next generation. We are, then, responsible for the way rising generations interact with the environment and technology.

Digital Natives: A New Breed or Gradually Changing Youth?

A corollary of this debate—especially as it affects students and the educational institution—is whether or not we have a new kind of students for whom schools

17. Mark Helprin, *Digital Barbarism* (New York: Harper, 2009), xi.
18. Small and Vorgan, *iBrain*, 5.
19. *Luddite* is a term coming from an anonymous King Ludd and supporters who were destroying machines that had taken their jobs. Today it refers to anyone who wants to turn back industrial and technological advances.
20. Lee Siegel, *Against the Machine: Being Human in the Age of the Electronic Mob* (New York: Spiegel & Grau, 2008), 3, 5, 10–11.

(and therefore youth ministry) must be reformed, or perhaps transformed. Prensky again states his case:

> Today's students are no longer the people our educational system was designed to teach. Today's students have not just changed *incrementally* from those of the past, nor simply changed their slang, clothes, body adornments, or styles, as has happened between generations previously. A really big *discontinuity* has taken place. One might even call it a "singularity."[21]

Prensky is challenged by many on this point. Do you, in youth ministry, see yourself dealing with an entirely new "breed" of adolescent? Or do you find the fundamental issues of transition from childhood to adulthood and the consistency of human nature overriding the opinion that young people today are unlike any before?

A strong debate also prevails about the stereotypes commonly used describing GenX and GenY (the Net Generation, Millennials, or Digital Natives). The latter are identified as having been born from about 1980 to 1994.[22] Despite the differences in exact dating, "digital native" theorists agree there is a clear temporal boundary—and that a specific time period makes a significant difference in youthful attitudes. This generation, it is claimed, has grown up with digital tools, a reality that has given them sophisticated technical skills and a learning style that present pedagogical methods are unfit to serve.

From their international studies, Palfrey and Gasser describe this generation. These Digital Natives

> live most of their lives online, without distinguishing between online and offline. Instead of thinking of their digital identity and their real-space identity as separate things, they just have an identity (with representation in two, or three, or more different spaces). . . . They don't think of their hybrid lives as anything remarkable.[23]

While discussing this digital generation, our sense of justice reminds us we are talking about only one-third of the world's population; the digital divide excludes more than two-thirds of our neighbors. (Even in Europe, some 40 percent, and in

---

21. Marc Prensky, "Digital Natives," 1, emphases original.

22. Don Tapscott (*Grown Up Digital: How the Net Generation is Changing Your World* [New York: McGraw-Hill, 2009]), dates the new generation with precision as being born in or after January 1977. Prensky does not specify a year. Palfrey and Gasser (*Born Digital*) use 1980 as the key date. Neil Howe and William Strauss (*Millennials Rising: The Next Great Generation* [New York: Vintage, 2000]); and Diana Oblinger ("Boomers, Gen-Xers, and Millennials," *EDUCAUSE Review* (July/August 2003): 36–47) date Millennials as being born in or after 1982—Oblinger also dates the end of that generation's birth as 1991.

23. Palfrey and Gasser, *Born Digital*, 4–5.

North America more than 30 percent, are excluded from our discussion of privileged internet connection.)[24]

Many have taken exception to designating special characteristics to specific young generations. Have such labels (GenX, GenY, or Millennials) been helpful or detrimental for you in discussing change among young people? Generalizations about a generation's predominant moods and styles, excesses and potential dangers to society, have often been used in the literature. But Sue Bennett and Karl Maton, for instance, take Howe and Strauss, Marc Prensky, and Palfrey and Gasser to task for creating moral panic with theories they see as having inadequate empirical evidence. Their chapter in *Deconstructing Digital Natives* concludes with three key reservations:

> First, the notion of "Digital Native" is a misrepresentation of young people's technology use that idealizes and homogenizes their skills and interests. . . . Second, the impact of these overgeneralizations has been to generate an academic form of moral panic that disregards the past and encourages intellectual complacency. . . . Finally, the implications for education and educational research are likely to be better understood by establishing a more sophisticated footing for discussion and expanding the research effort. . . . The consequences of *not* developing a better understanding . . . [bring] the risk that we will ignore subtle digital divides that do threaten the quality of our educational systems.[25]

Youth ministers and educators are not immune to accepting popular theories and neglecting nuances behind various interpretations of empirical data. Popular speeches, literature, and curricula may begin to reflect undisciplined conclusions. We help one another from our different roles as we discuss what we are observing, researching, hearing, and reading. We might do so by discussing with students and one another some of the controversies covered in a little text called *The Future of the Internet*[26] with chapters like: "The Internet Will Enhance Human Life" and "The Emerging Wireless Internet Will Both Improve and Degrade Human Life," "Internet Dating Will Lead to the Commodification of People," "Internet Dating Could Improve Relationships and Marriage," "The Internet Could Exacerbate the Gap between Rich and Poor Nations," and "The Internet Will Speed Up Human Evolution." Such discussions are part of the way we need to do theology and church and youth ministry. Let's look deeper, then, into the lives of students (and dropouts) these days.

24. See "Internet Users in the World Distributed by World Regions–2012 Q2," *Internet World Stats*, www.internetworldstats.com/stats.htm.

25. Sue Bennett and Karl Maton, "Intellectual Field or Faith-based Religion: Moving on from the Idea of 'Digital Natives,'" in *Deconstructing Digital Natives*, ed. Michael Thomas (New York: Routledge, 2011), 181.

26. Tom Head, ed., *The Future of the Internet* (San Diego: Greenhaven, 2005).

Digital Culture, Families, and General Lifestyles

Too often we've considered youth apart from their families and the other primary (or micro-) systems that surround and support, or fail to support, them. All microsystems are important—family, neighborhood and community, schools (including extracurricular activities), media, peers, and maybe church. In most cases, though, family—for positive or negative reasons—remains most influential, so we will begin our discussion with the family.

Family mealtimes are important. Young people may not eat together with their families for various reasons, including their desire for independence, conflicting schedules, desire for a different menu, and unhappiness with family relations. Studies show a positive relationship between frequent family meals and positive behavioral outcomes in teenagers.

> Teens who regularly have meals with their family are less likely to get into fights, think about suicide, smoke, drink, use drugs, and are more likely to have later initiation of sexual activity, and better academic performance than teens who do not.[27]

> In 2003 42 percent of adolescents ages 12 to 17 ate a meal as a family six to seven days a week, 27 percent ate a meal as a family four or five days a week, and 31 percent ate meals as a family zero to three days a week.[28]

Whether or not, and to what degree, family mealtime discussions enhance family and adolescent growth and well-being is difficult to determine. We know that during meals, the television is on for almost two-thirds (64 percent) of families with eight- to eighteen-year-olds. The number of households in the United States with internet access has risen from 47 percent in 1999 to 84 percent in 2009. Among families with internet access, 36 percent of families with children, age eight to eighteen, have rules about computer use, 30 percent for playing video games, 28 percent for TV consumption, and 10 percent for music.[29]

Are families and all of us being seduced into a culture of efficiency, of immediate information and instant gratification? Are brains being trained to surf and

27. US Council of Economic Advisors, "Teens and Their Parents in the 21st Century: An Examination of Trends in Teen Behavior and the Role of Parental Involvement," Council of Economic Advisors White Paper, 2000; and National Center on Addiction and Substance Abuse at Columbia University, "The Importance of Family Dinners," 2003, both quoted in Child Trends DataBank, "Family Meals," 1, childtrendsdatabank.org/pdf/96_PDF.pdf.

28. Ibid., 1.

29. Kaiser Family Foundation, "Generation M2: Media in the Lives of 8- to 18-Year-Olds," kff.org/entmedia/mh012010pkg.cfm?RenderForPrint=1. For a good presentation of its findings, see "The Amazing Media Habits of 8-18 Year Olds," *Business Insider*, www.businessinsider .com/how-kids-consume-media-2011-4#tv-still-rules-1.

browse rather than focus, concentrate, reflect, and contemplate? Is the internet robbing us of face-to-face skills and conversation? Is the pressure of it all flattening us into robotic conformity? Some critical thinkers are worried about such tendencies.[30] Small and Vorgan write, "Our high-tech revolution has plunged us into a state of *continuous partial attention* which software executive Linda Stone describes as continually staying busy—keeping tabs on everything while never truly focusing on anything."[31]

No generation has yet lived from cradle to grave with digital expertise, and no description of the possibilities and perils of a digital world is complete. We are not, therefore, able to judge the complete perils and possibilities of life in a digital age.

Brain Growth through Adolescence

We should continue consideration of the extraordinary advances in brain research.[32]

A new field of study called neuroinfomatics has emerged. Neuroinfomatics involves the digital analysis of brain processes by means of neural scanning and imaging using the incredible number-crunching power of computers and our growing understanding of the chemistry and biology of the brain.

For the first time, using powerful brain scanners and imaging techniques, including functional magnetic resonance imaging (fMRIs), positron emission tomography (PET) scans, and optical topography (OT), we can get inside the black box and examine the function of normal and impaired living brains noninvasively while they are involved in cognitive tasks. . . . We can give a book to a child who has dyslexia and ask him or her to read as we watch the patterns in the brain.

Recently . . . scientists announced the development of a new imaging technology called Brainbow (Lichtman & Sanes, 2007). The Brainbow allows researchers to color code different neural pathways the same way we color code house wiring. . . . The Brainbow will eventually allow researchers to determine specific neural pathways that are used during specific thought processes.[33]

30. For instance, Nicholas Carr, *The Shallows: What the Internet Is Doing to Our Brains* (New York: Norton, 2011); besides Siegel, *Against the Machine*; Mark Helprin, *Digital Barbarism*; Quentin Schultze, *Habits of the High Tech Heart: Living Virtuously in the Information Age* (Grand Rapids: Baker Academic, 2002); and Jesse Rice, *The Church of Facebook: How the Hyperconnected Are Redefining Community* (Elgin, IL: David C. Cook, 2009). See also a Christian critique from Douglas Groothuis, *The Soul in Cyberspace* (Eugene, OR: Wipf & Stock, 1997).

31. Small and Vorgan, *iBrain*, 18.

32. This section will continue our discussion of brain development from chapter 6.

33. Ian Jukes, Ted McCain, and Lee Crockett, *Understanding the Digital Generation: Teaching and Learning in the New Digital Landscape* (Kelowna, BC: 21st Century Fluency Project and Corwin, 2010), 25–26.

This new information allows us to assess the impact of digital screen life on children and adolescents. Most scientists believe that evolution, or God working through evolution (though some Christian scientists dismiss evolution entirely), has brought the human brain to its present capacities. While genetics (inheritance) determines some of the brain's potential, the way it is used appears even more consequential in determining its abilities. Physical brain development takes place in two stages: first around the time of birth and later at puberty. The first stage, in utero and during the first few months after birth, develops an approximately three-pound human brain containing some hundred billion cells (each with a gray matter cortex and white matter extensions or axons connecting to dendrites, their means of cell-to-cell communication). Brain cell communication takes place through connections of dendrites called synapses (established by use or dismissed by disuse).

Our brains contain an estimated and unimaginable quadrillion synaptic sites! Neuroscientists have identified regions of the brain controlling its various imaging, thinking, judging, decision-making, and feeling functions.[34] (Not being neuroscientists, biblical writers used terms such as body, mind, soul, spirit, and heart—but not in the sense of entirely separate functions. We are also reminded of the King James Version's translation of the Greek *splagehnon* as "bowels of mercy or compassion."[35] Scripture and neuroscience caution us not to "over-intellectualize" or categorize the deep and mysterious workings of the human soul.)

Born with instincts to grasp and to suck, a newborn infant begins to develop ear, eye, and hand coordination. Its brain is processing images to satisfy its curiosity and needs. The infant and toddler's brain cells are all there, but the connections are undifferentiated. As the child experiences patterns, new shortcuts are developed. The brain's neural pathways are developed, which enable the child to distinguish, grasp, and bring objects to the mouth, and then slowly to communicate (infants begin to understand, partly by tone and gesture, long before they can speak). Proper childhood stimulation allows the brain to prune its excess capacity into functional order. Understimulation, an overload of a single kind of stimulation, or overstimulation can be detrimental to childhood development.

Most of a baby's brain synapses are formed during the first six months of life, when the brain consumes more than 60 percent of the body's total caloric intake. Too little

34. Here and in the following we will be primarily following the work of developmental molecular biologist John Medina, *Brain Rules: 12 Principles for Surviving and Thriving at Work, Home, and School* (Seattle: Pear, 2008); and especially Small and Vorgan, *iBrain*.

35. Found in Paul's letters: 2 Cor. 6:12; Phil. 1:8; 2:1; Col. 3:12; Philem. 7, 12, 20; and from the apostle John in 1 John 3:17.

brain stimulation during this period will lead to the formation of fewer synapses; too much could lay down faulty synapses and maladaptive neural circuits. . . .

Reading to a child daily, expressing affection frequently, and other nurturing interactions stimulate the young child's brain so that new dendrites grow and branch out toward one another. . . .

Too many extracurricular activities, too much tutoring, or a home environment that is extremely chaotic can overwhelm a child's developing neural circuitry, leading to low self-esteem, anxiety, and distractibility. When a child's brain is exposed to excessive levels of television, computer, video, and other digital stimulation, it can lead to hyperactivity, irritability, and attention deficit disorders.[36]

The research of neural scientist Jay Giedd points to another spurt of brain cell overproduction, roughly between the ages of ten and thirteen—followed by another stage of pruning in the early teenage years. Giedd speaks of a "use it or lose it" principle: "If a teen is doing music or sports or academics, those are the cells and connections that will be hardwired. If they're lying on the couch or playing video games or [watching] MTV, those are the cells and connections that are going to survive."[37]

An important additional factor is the development of the brain's frontal lobe. Using fMRI scanning, scientists concluded that when teenagers are faced with decisions such as when to eat, or whether or not to go to a movie, attend a drinking party, or have sex, consequent brain activity appears in their temporal lobes rather than frontal lobes. When developed, the frontal lobes allow for greater empathy, the power of delayed satisfaction and risk assessment, and realization of how decisions will affect others and the future. Development of the frontal lobes and their prefrontal cortex is considered to continue until the middle twenties. To put all this in perspective, we need to look at the extent to which young people are using digital media.

Adolescent Media and Digital Use

Almost half the teenagers in the United Kingdom owned a smartphone in 2011, and 60 percent of them admitted they might be addicted to their phone; 23 percent say they lowered their television viewing and 15 percent admitted reading fewer books because of the phone, according to OfCom.[38] In the United States,

---

36. Small and Vorgan, *iBrain*, 27.
37. PBS *Frontline* Special: "Inside the Teenage Brain," Synopsis, January 31, 2002, www.pbs.org/wgbh/pages/frontline/shows/teenbrain/etc/synopsis.html.
38. "The Communications Market Report: United Kingdom," *OfCom*, 2011, stakeholders.ofcom.org.uk/market-data-research/market-data/communications-market-reports/cmr11/uk/.

25 percent of toddlers under age two use digital devices. GenY moms are leading the way as one-third are allowing their toddlers to use a laptop, cell phone, or smartphone. "The sweet spots for majority-usage looks like this: Mobile phone, age 11; smartphones, age 16; laptop/PC, age 4; digital camera, age 5."[39]

According to the respected Kaiser Family Foundation (2010 report):

> Today, 8–18-year-olds devote an average of 7 hours and 38 minutes to using entertainment media across a typical day (more than 53 hours a week). And because they spend so much of that time "media multitasking" (using more than one medium at a time), they actually manage to pack in a total of 10 hours and 45 minutes worth of media content into those 7 and 1/2 hours.[40]

In other words, eight- to eighteen-year-olds in the United States spend one-quarter of their media time using multiple media, and according to this report, 24 percent of eight- to eighteen-year-olds usually use another media while watching TV. Are they using entertainment media while doing their homework? Thirty-one percent say most of the time; 25 percent, some of the time; 22 percent, little of the time; 19 percent, never.

A seventeen-year-old boy describes his scattered attention: "I multi-task every single second I am on line. At this very moment I am watching TV, checking my e-mail every two minutes, reading a news group about who shot JFK, burning some music to a CD and writing this message."[41]

Total media exposure (for eight- to eighteen-year-olds) has risen from 7 hours, 29 minutes on a typical day in 1999, to 8:33 in 2004, and 10:45 in 2009. As to separate medium per typical day: TV content, 4:29; music/audio, 2:31; computers, 1:29; video games, 1:13; print, :38, and movies, :25.

What personal digital devices does this age group own? iPod/MP3 players: 18 percent in 2004; 76 percent in 2009. Cell phones: 39 percent in 2004; 66 percent in 2009. Personal laptops: 12 percent in 2004; 29 percent in 2009. Reading print media declined from 43 minutes in 1999 and 2004 to 38 minutes in 2009. As to print reading, this age group is reading books first of all, then magazines (much less than in earlier decades). Only a quarter glance at a newspaper on a typical day—on overall average, spending just 3 minutes per day with a newspaper.

Total media consumption (in hours per day) is higher among Hispanic youth (13:00) and black youth (12:59) than among white youth (8:36). Among "light"

39. Matt Carmichael, "Stat of the Day: 25% of Toddlers Have a Smart Phone," *AdAge*, August 4, 2011, from an annual survey from Parenting Group, www.adage.com/print/229082.

40. Kaiser Family Foundation, "Generation M2."

41. A. Lenhart, L. Rainie, and O. Lewis, "Teenage Life Online: The Rise of Instant-Message Generation and the Internet's Impact on Friendships and Family Relations," 2001, Pew Internet and American Life Project, available from pewinternet.org.

media users, 66 percent say they are getting good grades, 23 percent, fair or poor grades. For moderate media users, these percentages change to 65 percent and 31 percent. But of those admitting to be heavy media users, 51 percent report good grades and 47 percent report fair or poor grades.[42]

Apart from the benefits and pitfalls of internet usage, it is important to acknowledge differences in this new generation. As previously noted, they do not see their hybrid online/offline identities as unusual, and their sense of privacy is different than older generations, as is their conception of friendship. Their sense of entitlement is heightened; their multitasking abilities and shortened attention spans to offline realities are additional differences. They have a new sense of power in shaping markets and making an impact on industries, education, and even global politics.

As to benefits accrued to this generation from their use of digital technology, they are more tech savvy, have developed digital dexterity and peripheral vision, have a sense of control over their environment, can find any type of information more quickly, are more connected to a greater variety of friends, and have been stimulated in creative activities and sometimes political activism (this has been popularly overrated). The physically confined or emotionally introverted have been able to express themselves in new ways and have been able to explore a greater variety of life possibilities.

Palfrey and Gasser, however, caution youth to guard their identities and private matters in their lives, be aware of manipulation by marketers, be careful about breaking copyright laws, beware of cyber bullying, and be careful about the tendency toward digital and informational overload. Experts like Small and Vorgan explain limitations of the youthful brain in protecting young users from immediate gratification, dangerous short- and long-term risks, and even internet addiction (be it shopping, gaming, pornography, or just over-connection). Most experts are suggesting neither giving up nor overindulging in digital devices but rather establishing discipline of proper limitations and balance. Youth and family ministries involve collaborating with parents, children, and youth in setting limits and developing self-control.[43]

Ian Jukes, Ted McCain, and Lee Crockett are generally positive in their description of this digital generation, seeing them as different than any previous generation and advocating a revamping of school and pedagogy using digital media and fluency. Yet they see a dangerous imbalance in the lives of digital natives:

42. Kaiser Family Foundation, "Generation M2."
43. See the article on childhood self-control and the thirty-year study of New Zealanders by Terrie Moffitt and her team at Duke University, in Aimee Cunningham, "Kids' Self-Control Is Crucial for Their Future Success," *Scientific American*, July 25, 2011, www.scientificamerican .com/article.cfm?id=where-theres-a-will.

1. One important skill area that is underdeveloped in a digital culture is face-to-face interpersonal interaction. . . .

2. Another concern has arisen over one of the most noticeable traits of the digital generation—multitasking. They are always performing multiple digital tasks simultaneously. . . . The problem arises when someone has to do a task that is new to them and requires concentration. . . . *Research shows that we can't multitask. We are biologically incapable of processing attention-rich inputs simultaneously.*

3. There are concerns over the ability of the digital generation to stay with and follow a long and complex argument.

4. There is great concern that young people are not getting enough exercise. . . .

5. . . . there is legitimate concern that they are not gaining an appreciation for nature and being in the outdoors.

6. Many parents and teachers worry that young people are not getting enough time reading for pleasure or reading at all for that matter.

7. There are concerns that the highly addictive nature of computer games . . . and interactive nature of most digital activities are creating such obsessive behavior in kids that it meets the definition of a clinical addiction.[44]

These educational reformers are concerned about finding a balance for this digital generation and especially a balance of traditional and new methods of teaching them. The realization that this age group is on the cusp of technological innovation and a new kind of culture makes it more important than ever that we learn with, rather than teach at, a dynamic youthful generation. We can provide a healthy balance to unbalanced lives.

Youthful Identities in a Digital Age

Caring about young people and relations among people calls for consideration of individual, family, clan, and national identity. Samuel Huntington in his study of American identity reflects:

> The "concept of identity," it has been said, "is as indispensable as it is unclear." It "is manifold, hard to define and evades many ordinary methods of measurement." The twentieth century's leading scholar of identity, Erik Erikson, termed the concept, "all-pervasive" but also "vague" and "unfathomable."[45]

44. Jukes, McCain, and Crockett, *Understanding the Digital Generation*, 3–4, emphasis added.
45. Samuel P. Huntington, *Who Are We? The Challenges to America's National Identity* (New York: Simon & Schuster, 2004), 21.

Scripture was bound to deal with this mysterious, yet crucial, concept—but without modern terminology or psycho-sociological research. It did so, first of all, in terms of names, which held more significance to ancient Middle Eastern people than they do to most moderns. Biblical writers often paused to explain the meanings behind names; God significantly gives new names to Abram, Sarai, and Jacob. More important to us is God's emphasis on shaping individuals and a nation. "Before I formed you in the womb I knew you," God says to Jeremiah (Jer. 1:5). And to Isaiah about the nation Israel, "now thus says the LORD, he who created you, O Jacob, he who formed you, O Israel" (Isa. 43:1). Of course divine initiative is always accompanied by necessary human response; we are also responsible for our identities. So, we often hear, "you have been rebellious" (Deut. 9:7). In Romans 6, Paul describes the Christian's identity as being transformed in baptism to a crucified and resurrected identity in Christ. Then, after reviewing Israel's identity and that of a new people, the apostle urges Roman Christians, and all of us, not to be conformed to this world's character but to be transformed by the renewing of our minds (Rom. 12:2a). We're elsewhere described as being creatures of dust moving toward the glorious image of Christ (1 Cor. 15:48–49; 2 Cor. 3:18). Taken as a whole, Scripture makes it clear that we are to work out unique identities according to God's will and Christ's example. In biblical times this took place in various contexts, as different as poverty or riches, from prison to slavery to freedom, whether in a Persian harem or a thriving faith community.

A natural and central task of adolescence is identity formation. With new consciousness of self and others and vast hypothetical possibilities, a young woman or man seeks to define self as a son or daughter, as a friend and perhaps lover, as a student and possibly employee, or even young celebrity or entrepreneur. The definition must also include the increasingly ambiguous idea of gender, as well as age, race, class, and religion or faith. We both discover and work out our identities. Identity clarification involves clarifying one's purpose and vocation in life.

Teenagers use digital media for several reasons. They love and use their devices for entertainment and diversion from the pressures and boredom of life—gaming, in particular, is a big part of this. They also want to stay current with popular culture and what is happening in the world—an important part of keeping up with friends and feeling informed. Critically important for most is social connection with concentric circles of "friends," with a few real friends at the core, then a larger number of other friends, and finally the teenage crowd whose general attitudes and behaviors they share. Sometimes a young person may just want to withdraw into a solitary world—away from it all. In all this they are working out their special identities, seeking social acceptance, growing in self-confidence, and clarifying their opinions and values—perhaps even their purpose in life.

Palfrey and Gasser consider two different "forms of identity: a personal identity and a social identity."[46] *Personal identity*, they explain, gathers all the attributes that make a person unique—appearance, characteristics, interests, and so forth. A person's *social identity* is the way we are seen and defined by family, friends, and neighbors. They go on to compare the process of changing personal and social identities in agrarian times, in the industrial age, and now in the digital age. In past times a girl might not be able to change her personal identity but by moving to a new town might change her social identity. They conclude that a girl in this digital age,

> can change many aspects of her personal identity quickly and easily [but] she may not be able to change certain aspects of her social identity. The net effect of the digital age—paradoxically—is to decrease her ability to control her social identity and how others perceive her . . . while she can experiment with multiple identities online, she may be more bound to a unitary identity than she would have been in a previous era.[47]

Palfrey and Gasser's distinction of personal and social identities may or may not be helpful to you. I look at identity as something persons work out with the aid of "social mirrors"—those whose opinions they value—but as an identity they own themselves. There are, of course, a variety of social responses to one's identity, and adolescents may feel external attempts to force a particular social identity upon them, with exaggerated feelings of rejection, misunderstanding, or wild adulation. Models of ever-changing celebrity personas and the endless possibilities in a virtual world seem to make identity issues in the digital age an even greater challenge than in the past. As young persons are helped to appreciate the preciousness of their identities, they begin to see the importance of discernment and digital discipline, habit-forming character, values and boundaries, goals and priorities, and choices with long-term consequences. Discovering their special purpose in life is within their grasp.

Shakespeare's extraordinary portrayal of young Hamlet reminds us that the transition from childhood to adulthood is quite universal and time-enduring. This great play defies simple analysis and explanation, and likewise Hamlet's youthful quest remains just beyond our comprehension. His relationship to his mother and to Ophelia, his memory of his father, his moral values and personal boundaries, his very reason for living, are mysteries to us, even with our psychological

46. Palfrey and Gasser, *Born Digital*, 17.
47. Ibid., 19–20.

understanding. These parts of his struggles were also mysteries to his fellow characters in the play—and strikingly to himself as well. Bright high school and college students become intrigued with Hamlet's identity crisis.

We are privileged to enter into the mysterious challenge with young people. What is it all about? Why are we here? Who am I? "To be or not to be?"[48] "Break on through to the other side."[49] Today's world seems all the more difficult. Serving as models, facilitators, and coaches for young people is a special challenge in our digital age.

Of the many studies of youth in the digital age,[50] Sherry Turkle's significant trilogy must be highlighted. Beginning in the late 1970s, as a psychoanalytically trained psychologist and anthropologist, she has studied the impact of the internet and cell phones—especially on young people and students. Early on, a statement from thirteen-year-old Deborah, who was working on a computer, caught her attention, "there's a little piece of your mind and now it's a little piece of the computer's mind."[51] This was part of the inspiration for *The Second Self: Computers and the Human Spirit* (1984). In the 1990s, Turkle watched people moving from one-on-one relationships with computers to connecting with a *world of friends* through the open portals of social networks—leading her to write *Life on the Screen: Identity in the Age of the Internet* in 1997. The new century brought a new emphasis on artificial intelligence and robots, growing popularity of social networking, and expanded use of texting with cell phones—always present and usually turned on. Children are growing up with parents talking on a phone while swinging them in a park, or picking them up at school without a "hello"—which would interrupt a cell phone conversation. A young boy complains that a robot would at least remember what he said, which was more than his father did when multitasking on his BlackBerry. In a Twitter and texting era, many teenagers are

48. Several lines from *Hamlet* could point to adolescent issues: for example, "The time is out of joint: O cursed spite, That ever I was born to set it right"—adolescent sense of making the world or family situation right; "To be or not to be: that is the question. . . . To die, to sleep . . . and by a sleep to say we end the heartache"—consideration of suicide as the only way out (so prevalent among youth). See William Shakespeare, *Hamlet*, act 1, sc. 5, and act 3, sc. 1.

49. Jim Morrison and The Doors, "Break On Through," on *The Doors*, produced by Paul A. Rothchild, Elektra, 1967. Morrison, with brilliance of thought and voice, stuck in adolescent immaturity and drugs, dreams of breaking through to ultimate reality—with strong appeal over the years for youth who claim feelings of alienation.

50. Besides those already mentioned, two books stand out: Anastasia Goodstein, *Totally Wired: What Teens and Tweens Are Really Doing Online* (New York: St. Martin's Griffin, 2007); and Mizuko Ito et al., *Hanging Out, Messing Around, and Geeking Out: Kids Living and Learning with New Media* (Cambridge, MA: MIT Press, 2010).

51. Sherry Turkle, *Alone Together: Why We Expect More from Technology and Less from Each Other* (New York: Basic Books, 2011), x. The other books in Turkle's series are *Life on the Screen: Identity in the Age of the Internet* (New York: Simon & Schuster, 1997) and *The Second Self: Computers and the Human Spirit* (Cambridge, MA: MIT Press, 2005), first published in 1984.

longing for a real phone call or a written letter, even an email, expressing *someone's full attention.*[52]

Alone Together describes online *connected disconnect* and how teenagers are substituting perceptions of others online for real self-exploration in shaping their identities. It should be read for its many quotations, especially from youth, describing the shift from human face-to-face relationships to quick, efficient, less personal, and continuous digital connections. As constructive as experimenting with identities online can be, Turkle found many young people confused between their virtually constructed identities and their real ones.[53]

Practical Theology and Youth Ministry in the Digital Age

Over the world wide web we would write, "What Hath God Wrought!" If the telegraph was worthy of such a quotation (as mentioned at the beginning of this chapter), how much more might practical theologians be wondering about God's perspective on the internet and digital age. If Jesus were here today, would he be on Twitter and Facebook? Along with our optimism about the internet's potential, we recognize the enemy bent on polluting God's and our best intentions. Those the devil cannot pollute, he will try to dilute—goading us to attempt too much good or become distracted by too many demands. The internet can speed up what is dragging, it can connect what is disconnected, it can enable much that is disabled—and much more. But it can also become a masterful distraction—contributing to a tyranny of trivialities. Email can become a constant taskmaster.[54]

Rather than seeing the internet as the devil's deception or just part of human technology's natural evolution, it can be viewed as an extension of *logos*, the Word of God, and as a preview of heavenly eternal communication. God is the Great Communicator and author of cosmic communication. We're not meant to spend a great deal of time contemplating our heavenly and eternal existence, but I assume when we get to our eternal goal, this whole world's history and our infinitesimally short span of life (which now seems forever) will be reckoned as a passing cloud, a single Facebook posting. Then, the deepest virtual hope, the strongest fantasy of intimacy, the greatest desire for friends, the highest dreams

52. Ibid., 266–67.
53. Ibid., 273.
54. See Mike Song, Viki Halsey, and Tim Burress, *The Hamster Revolution: How to Manage Your Email Before It Manages You* (San Francisco: Berrett-Koehler, 2008); John Freeman, *The Tyranny of E-mail: The Four-Thousand-Year Journey to Your Inbox* (New York: Scribner, 2009); and especially William Powers, *Hamlet's Blackberry: A Practical Philosophy for Building a Good Life in the Digital Age* (New York: HarperCollins, 2010).

of achievement, will all be fulfilled. Then we may see the internet, along with telephones and printing presses, automobiles and commercial flight, as harbingers of God's ultimate reality.

Dealing with questions about the morality of digital life in the here and now begs reference to prophets like Jacques Ellul who saw technology (he preferred the term *technique*) as something more than machines and technology per se, but as, in a technological society, "the *totality of methods rationally arrived at and having absolute efficiency*."[55] For Ellul, technique is neither bad nor good in itself but has, in our modern life, caused us to lose sight of any end. In losing sight of God as our end or purpose, we've allowed technological efficiency to become our end—our idol or god. Efficiency for the sake of profits and power has replaced the good of humanity as our end. Rather than products and profit being ends for the good of people, people have become the means to the end of products and profit. And technique does this with irrefutable rationality and efficiency. It is therefore irreversible. As to moral and spiritual restraints, Ellul concludes: "Technique never observes the distinction between moral and immoral use. It tends, on the contrary, to create a completely independent technical morality."[56]

Part of what the secular digital world promises is an easier, fuller life. In the nineteenth century, Søren Kierkegaard reacted against a life of ease and comfort condoned by a church compromising with culture. In place of such intellectual and theological conformity to culture, Kierkegaard called for a radical life of Christlike suffering. Ellul, a twentieth-century French Christian anarchist,[57] called Christians to freedom (from technical domination and this culture's values) in submission to a higher authority in Jesus Christ, and for the purpose of holiness in God.

Most of the world appreciates the Ten Commandments: it is best for clans, tribes, and nations to acknowledge a power greater than themselves; and societies are better off with a minimum of murder, adultery, stealing, and cheating. Strangely, the world does not acknowledge the commandment against idolatry. But people of faith can recognize idolatrous power in a technology promising the good life, demanding our constant attention, and tending to enslave us. We cannot fully engage our cultures without sensing some oppressive effects. In such situations the apostle Paul reminds us that our Lord Jesus Christ has "set us free from this present evil age," and prays for us "grace . . . and peace from God our Father" (Gal. 1:4, 3).

---

55. Jacques Ellul, *The Technological Society* (New York: Vintage Books, 1964), xxv, emphasis original.
56. Ibid., 97.
57. Not to be confused with secular anarchism.

At a convocation of Amsterdam's Free University in 1880, Abraham Kuyper voiced his famous proclamation: "There is not a square inch in the whole domain of our human existence over which Christ, who is sovereign over all, does not cry, 'Mine!'"[58] As servants of Christ we work with young people and their families to establish his lordship over the internet and all digital devices. It is a difficult, ongoing task.

Quentin Schultze is an acknowledged Christian media critic. His *Habits of the High-Tech Heart: Living Virtuously in the Information Age* raises provocative questions about today's digital world. He challenges some of the secular writers referred to in this chapter: "If human life is not intrinsically meaningful, we are all machines with no moral compass and no responsibility."[59] His book raises helpful questions about the digital world:

1. The internet has made our lives easier; but what is the price of this convenience, and what is lost?
2. There seems to be a technical solution for every issue; what does this point of view miss?
3. The internet provides information, but does "informationism" then become a quasi-religion?
4. Are traditional religion and values being devalued?
5. Are technical goals and changes missing deeper human needs?
6. Cyberculture is seemingly providing technical solutions for all human problems; is it not thereby breeding further individualism at the cost of deeper human values and community?
7. Has cyberculture encouraged cowboy capitalism and casino banking?

Schultze is also concerned with social crises exacerbated in digital culture: the growing gap between rich and poor, the plight of poor children and homeless families, the gap between educational systems, political superficiality, and polarization. In conclusion, he suggests six habits to be cultivated for the good of the global digital community and its inhabitants: (1) critical discernment (based on intimate knowledge of the web); (2) moderation (using but not succumbing to technology); (3) wisdom (especially moral wisdom from our religious traditions); (4) humility (avoiding the arrogant power of technique); (5) authenticity (against disingenuous communication); (6) cultivating cosmic diversity (appreciating our diversity while finding responsible unity, for Christians, based on the doctrine/

58. Abraham Kuyper, "Sphere Sovereignty," in *Abraham Kuyper: A Centennial Reader*, ed. James D. Bratt (Grand Rapids: Eerdmans, 1998), 488.
59. Quentin J. Schultze, *Habits of the High-Tech Heart: Living Virtuously in the Information Age* (Grand Rapids: Baker Academic, 2004), 43.

reality of the Triune God). Such virtues and habits require "organic community life . . . [counter to] consumptive communities."[60] Christian integrity in the cyber world requires worship, study of Scripture, and contemplation.[61]

As salt and light, we face challenges in speaking to those who will not accept God's Word. For such secular and agnostic friends, there is ageless wisdom outside the Christian faith. In a busy digital world the centered life is crucial. Socrates, through Plato, urges all to consider the worthlessness of an unexamined life.[62] David Foster Wallace's commencement speech marvelously contemporizes this aphorism, "It is about simple awareness—awareness of what is so real and essential, so hidden in plain sight all around us. . . . It is unimaginably hard to do this, to stay conscious and alive, day in and day out."[63]

The examined life understands *harmonia*, peaceful balance in life and work. It understands things as simple as when to use and when to turn off. Plato and Aristotle also pointed us toward the Good, the good life. Rather than pursuing happiness and never finding the good, they encourage humans to pursue the good with a virtuous life—for this is happiness.

Palfrey and Gasser sum up some of the challenging potential for youth ministry in the digital age when they comment: "Young people have been creative since the dawn of time. . . . The desire to express one's own beliefs and opinions—to share them with others—is central to human nature."[64] With young students we have a wonderful opportunity to face the crises and challenges of digital culture together. Collaboration with emerging generations is necessary in order to discover, discuss, and grow as digital Christians. The Father's love, the grace of Jesus Christ, the enlightenment of the Holy Spirit and the faith community are needed as we examine our culture and God's Word in attempting to find balance and peace in the midst of technological change.

Questions for Reflection and Discussion

1. What main benefits does the internet bring to you? Does it also bring any negative distractions into your life?
2. What have been your main impressions from this chapter?
3. What criticisms of, or comments and questions about, this chapter do you have?

60. Ibid., table of contents and 21–23.
61. Ibid., chap. 8, "Sojourning with Heart."
62. Plato, *Apology* 38a.
63. "David Foster Wallace on Life and Work" (Kenyon College Commencement, 2005), *Wall Street Journal*, September 19, 2008, www.online.wsj.com/article/SB122178211966454607.html.
64. Palfrey and Gasser, *Born Digital*, 124.

4. In your opinion, has this chapter brought together information about the digital age, its challenges and controversies, in a way that helps you move toward practical theology and ministry among so-called digital youth?

5. What further reading and study do you hope to do around the subject of this chapter?

6. To what particular discussion with students are you looking forward?

—13—

Theology and Ministry in a Consumerist Age

I said to myself, "Come now, I will make a test of pleasure. . . . I . . . had great possessions . . . gathered for myself silver and gold and treasure. . . . All was vanity and a chasing after wind, and there was nothing to be gained under the sun.

SOLOMON IN ECCLESIASTES 2:1, 7–8, 11

[Jesus said,] Do not store up for yourselves treasures on earth, . . . but store up for yourselves treasure in heaven. . . . Therefore I tell you, do not worry about your life, what you will eat or . . . what you will wear. Is not life more than food and the body more than clothing?

MATTHEW 6:19–20, 25

Theological and Sociological Prologue

God's nature and activity provide a proper foundation for considering consumerism's deep imprint on the identity of youth today. God's revelation to us is as the great I AM, the beginning and end, the source of all being and meaning, the grand Relationship, the only satisfying end and repose for human life. God created us to be sovereigns over all nature and enjoy what it would produce. Culture and goods were meant to serve people and amplify their relationships, while glorifying the Creator.

230

If I didn't teach practical theology, I'd like to be an economist (if only I were better in math). For apart from God's providence, it is economics that makes the world go around. "Under the sun," as the writer of Ecclesiastes put it, and apart from spiritual powers, it is money, and consequent possessions, pleasure, prestige, and power that make the system go—and keep it going. Rather remarkably, in our consumptive society the desires of children and youth push a big part of market economy. So it seems a bit strange that in the great flood of youth ministry books published in the last couple of decades, there is little concern for economics.[1] This chapter asserts that economics should be part of our catechesis or discipleship training. And if that is so, we leaders need an awareness that God's heart is set on economic justice (rightness or righteousness) for the young and the poor.

To the verses above we might add the biblical paradox regarding wealth, poverty, and justice. "The blessing of the LORD makes rich, and he adds no sorrow with it" (Prov. 10:22). Yet, "the love of money is a root of all kinds of evil" (1 Tim. 6:10). And as to economic justice: "I am the LORD; I act with steadfast love, justice and righteousness in the earth" (Jer. 9:24b) and "the LORD maintains the cause of the needy, and executes justice for the poor" (Ps. 140:12). We grapple profitably with the interpretation of these verses and their implications in consumerist societies. The idea of justice is much neglected. In a consumerist society, what is just (or its biblical synonym, righteousness) from God's perspective?

The American Bible Society has published a Bible highlighting two thousand passages revealing "God's sorrow over poverty and injustice, and His command to believers to eradicate them." Here is more about this Bible edition:

> The Rt. Rev. Dr. Tom Wright, bishop of Durham and Bible Society's president, said, "Poverty and injustice are two of the biggest issues of our day, challenging the minds of politicians and social activists around the world. The imbalance of global wealth, famine, water shortages, exploitation and corruption are all issues that invoke outrage—and demand attention. . . . The Bible connects with the fabric of today's world, with all its problems and messiness—and has something powerful to say."[2]

The Lord our God is concerned about how we tend the earth, how we develop its resources, how we distribute the products we make (distributive justice or righteousness), and how our consumption shapes our identities and brings glory to our

---

1. John Bernard, James Penner, and Rick Bartlett, *Consuming Youth: Leading Teens Through Consumer Culture* (Grand Rapids: Zondervan/Youth Specialties, 2010), is a good exception.

2. Anne Thomas, "New Bible Reveals God's Heart Towards Poverty, Injustice," *Christian Post*, March 2, 2008, www.christianpost.com/news/new-bible-reveals-gods-heart-towards-poverty -injustice-31390/.

Creator's Name. Consumption is a necessary and godly activity; *consumerism*, however, puts us in control, bringing profits and glory to humans.

Consumerism and Identity

Consumerism may denote the protection of consumers' rights or the belief that the buying and selling of large quantities of goods are beneficial to society. The term may also connote the deification or idolization of material goods and wealth. It is in this sense of raising material consumption to the highest good (as well as the bottom line of our lives) that we consider consumerism here.

We have already reflected on the importance of identity formation in the lives of youth. Identity has to do with our purpose for being, our core values, the basis of decision making, the way we think of our physical, emotional, intellectual, social, and spiritual lives. It interprets our relationships to families, our ethnicity or race, our nationality, as it also locates a person spiritually, theologically, and ecclesiastically (church preference).

Identity has to do with the boundaries we draw between our selves and others. This is a complex matter because as humans we are interdependent. As we differentiate and assert ourselves, we determine appropriate limits in our relationships with others.[3]

Society suggests defining the self in terms of negative reference points. To gain self-confidence and reward our efforts, subtly and perhaps subconsciously, we think of ourselves as gaining on, or being superior to, what we were, or others are, in regard to education, class, age, or appearance. We study and work hard so as to be more able, successful, educated, and maybe more affluent or privileged than others. What we've accomplished educationally, athletically, or professionally can become of supreme importance.

We are also subtly induced to judge our in-group in terms of another out-group. This is why racism, classism, and tribalism seem unconquerable for fallen humankind.[4] It is natural, evolutionary thinking as opposed to a God-centered, Christ-following mind-set.[5]

You can see how positive identity is a fragile achievement in a secular world. We judge ourselves in terms of movement on a ladder of upward mobility. Each and

3. Miroslav Volf takes this point much deeper in *Exclusion and Embrace: A Theological Exploration of Identity, Otherness, and Reconciliation* (Nashville: Abingdon, 1996), esp. 90–91.
4. See Gordon Allport, *The Nature of Prejudice* (Cambridge, MA: Addison-Wesley, 1954); James Tillman, *Why America Needs Racism and Poverty* (New York: Four Winds, 1969).
5. Apologetic material, discussed briefly at the end of this book, is scattered throughout the text. Naturalism, as opposed to theism, is a dead end. Though we can't prove it, we can suggest the idea that issues such as love, evil, and destiny have no place to go apart from divine revelation.

every commercial somehow questions our "making it" or being "cool enough." Physical looks and material wealth are generally accepted signs of success, bolstering our fragile identities.

This is how identity is linked with consumerism in basic and powerful ways. I define and see myself in terms of gender, age, race, how I look, and my material possessions. *I have therefore I am.* Without this latest thing, I am diminished or perhaps (for the young) feel like nothing at all. I am never more alive than when I am buying.

Consumerism, especially through advertising, also conditions us to see others as objectified products. Boys/men, and now girls/women, view the opposite sex as appealing or unappealing parts before they are seen as whole persons. Body parts are desired or mentally rejected in terms of their potential for our personal satisfaction. Finally, consumerism begins to make us see ourselves as commodities, valued in terms of what we buy, and therefore, stimulating others to notice and be interested in us. We allow our clothes to become billboards for our favorite brands and our bodies to project notions of constructed uniqueness. The internet can become our extended personal billboard.

We can hardly find true happiness and significant relationships in such ways. Only a radical revolt against false gods can turn us toward healthy self-confidence, wholesome relationships, and a vibrant spirituality. Blessed are they who are able to love themselves because God loved them—and who can therefore genuinely love their neighbors. The great commandments are antidotes for all false creeds and dysfunctional lifestyles. The good life comes in loving God first with all our hearts, souls, and minds, and loving our neighbors as ourselves. These commandments are the basis for healthy relationships, stable families, and just societies.

How then are young people finding their identities in a world that worships at the altar of consumerism?

Economic Manipulation of Children

It is important for youth workers to take an interest in children. Youth ministry is properly "family, children, and youth ministry." Too many youth leaders and teachers are so busy with adolescent issues at the high school level, they forget to ask important questions about teenagers: "How did they get this way?" and "Where are they headed?"

The preface to *Children and Consumer Culture in American Society* begins with this paragraph:

> By all accounts, children play a crucial role in today's economy. According to some estimates, children spend or influence the spending of up to $500 billion annually.

Children's expanding role in consumer spending even prompted an August, 6, 2001 *Time* magazine cover story to ask, "Do Kids Have Too Much Power?"[6]

Here again, we will meet debate. Many argue that marketers and industries are seducing children into materialistic consumerism, leaving "children too little room, too little space, within which to grow and develop their own identities . . . [while others see] consumer culture as a creative and liberating realm in which children forge identities, cement relationships, and assert their independence."[7]

In the United Kingdom, the average child watches an estimated ten thousand television commercials per year. For the average American child, the estimate is from twenty-five to forty thousand TV ads per year.[8] Mary Pipher, author of *Reviving Ophelia*, introduces a book by Juliet Schor (*Born to Buy*) this way:

> Plato defined education as teaching our children to find pleasure in the right things. Most parents do their best, but they are fighting a culture that educates our children to value all the wrong things. Children are suffering mentally, physically, and spiritually. Schor's book can put us on a path toward once again protecting our children.[9]

Schor is an economist who understands marketing. Her book relies on two types of primary research: qualitative interviews and observation, and quantitative surveys and data analysis. Its aim is to "understand how children are being marketed to and how that has changed over time."[10] She notes refusal or resistance in attempts to interview many companies and networks. Her conclusions are significant:

> The United States is the most consumer-oriented society in the world. . . . The architects of this culture—the companies that make, market and advertise consumer products—have now set their sites on children. Although children have long participated in the consumer marketplace, until recently they were bit players, purchasers of cheap goods. They attracted little of the industry's talent and resources and were approached primarily through their mothers. That has changed. Kids and teens are now the epicenter of American consumer culture. They command the attention,

---

6. Lisa Jacobson, *Children and Consumer Culture in American Society: A Historical Handbook and Guide* (Westport, CT: Praeger, 2008), xiii.

7. Enola Aird, quoted in ibid., xiii.

8. Anup Shah, "Children as Consumers," *Global Issues*, November 21, 2010, globalissues.org/article/237/children-as-consumers.

9. Mary Pipher, quoted on the back cover of Juliet B. Schor, *Born to Buy: The Commercialized Child and the New Consumer Culture* (New York: Scribner, 2004).

10. Schor, *Born to Buy*, 1.

creativity, and dollars of advertisers. Their tastes drive market trends. Their opinions shape brand strategies.[11]

There is a general, vague awareness of Schor's conclusions. But parents and youth leaders have not paid adequate attention to their implications. She concludes her book by suggesting ways that we can combat "the prevalence of harmful and addictive products, the imperative to keep up, and the growth of materialist attitudes [that are] harming kids."[12]

Psychologist and educator Susan Linn has also researched the exploitation of child consumers and provides helpful background and examples.

Children have been the targets for some kinds of advertising for a long, long time—from carnival barkers hawking freak shows to ads in comic books and, since their early days, radio and television. But it's not the same today. Comparing the advertising of two or three decades ago to the commercialism that permeates our children's world is like comparing a BB gun to a smart bomb. The explosion of marketing aimed at kids today is precisely targeted, refined by scientific method, and honed by child psychologists—in short, it is more pervasive and intrusive than ever before.

Today's children are assaulted by advertising everywhere—at home, in school, on sports fields, in playgrounds, and on the street. They spend almost 40 hours a week engaged with the media—radio, television, movies, magazines, the Internet—most of which are commercially driven.[13] The average child sees about 40,000 commercials a year on television alone.[14]

The insidiousness of some advertisers may be inferred from their study of the nagging factor in the late 1990s. A few headlines from ad magazines will give you the gist of their research on directing children's nagging to profitable advantage:

Western Media International (now Initiative Media Worldwide), "The Nag Factor, 1998. How to Exploit Nagging to Boost Sales." The report of this study was entitled, "The Fine Art of Whining: Why Nagging Is a Kid's Best Friend."[15]

Selling to Kids, a marketing newsletter, reported on a study conducted with the aid of 150 mothers who were asked to keep a careful diary for two weeks.

11. Ibid., 9.
12. Ibid., 211.
13. We've seen that this is a conservative number, which has increased since the time of Linn's research.
14. Susan Linn, *Consuming Kids: The Hostile Takeover of Childhood* (New York: New Press, 2004), 4–5.
15. Ibid., 33.

In that time "the mothers reported a total of 10,000 nags—an average of 66 nags per mother and 4.7 nags per day."[16]

In *Brand Strategy*: "Kids' Brands Must Exercise Pest Control," by Linda Neville.[17]

These researchers go further by dividing parents into groups according to their vulnerability to such nagging. How public-spirited can this institution be when it seeks to drive further wedges into already fragile family systems? Neville is a research consultant for the ad agency New Solutions who, in an article about Kraft Lunchables, concluded: "Parents do not fully approve—they would rather their child ate a more traditional lunch (more nutritious, less packaging, and less costly)—but this adds to the brand's appeal among children because it reinforces their need to feel in control."[18]

How would marketers respond to our objections (or moral protests)? Lucy Hughes (of Initiative Media Worldwide) is interviewed in the film *The Corporation*. There she justifies the nag factor in this way:

> If we understand what motivates a parent to buy a product . . . if we could develop a creative commercial—you know, a thirty-second commercial that encourages the child to whine . . . that the child understands and is able to reiterate to the parents, then we're successful.[19]

Imagine now, that hearing this we exclaim to Lucy, "But is this right, for parents, for society, and for all of us?" To such a query she responds the way many advertisers (and entertainers and media people) think and argue:

> Is it ethical? I don't know. But . . . our role at Initiative is to move products. And if we know you move products with a certain creative execution placed in a certain type of media vehicle, then we've done our job.[20]

Linn comes to this conclusion:

> Marketing and advertising have been influential in transforming children into autonomous and empowered consumers. . . . Today, the partnership is between children and marketers, who are sometimes implicitly, sometimes explicitly, allied against parents. . . . My research shows that those who are more involved in consumer culture fare far worse in psychological and social terms.[21]

16. Ibid., 34.

17. Ibid., 35. See Neville's article at www.highbeam.com/doc/1G1-80056855.html.

18. Ibid., 36–37.

19. Ibid., 35. From *The Corporation*, a film by Mark Achbar, Jennifer Abbott, and Joel Bakan (Big Picture Media Corporation, 2005).

20. Linn, *Consuming Kids*, 39.

21. Ibid., 16–17.

As we saw in our last chapter, the technological power of marketing not only analyzes children's and adolescents' past in order to meet them in the present; but advertisers use complicated records of past purchases and even communications to friends to anticipate future needs and desires of young people. "Wow, that's pretty cool," a young person may think; "I hadn't even thought about wanting that!"

Social critic William Deresiewicz finds a rising generation, in contrast to former youth cultures, to be a non-rebellious, nice generation (others see this rather as a characteristic of all generations these days). Christian Smith and other researchers have similarly noted such characteristics among youth in the early twentieth century. Deresiewicz's twist is to explain the nice and entrepreneurial tendencies of this generation as a feature of consumerism—a rising generation determined to be nice in order to sell themselves and their wares. The consumptive direction of our society, according to this writer, is producing "polite, pleasant, moderate, earnest, friendly . . . low-key, self-deprecating, post-ironic, eco-friendly" salespersons, selling themselves and their latest production.[22] Acquisition of money and things is seen by most as a primary contemporary goal.

Positive Consumption: Marketing and Mass Production

Our discussion of advertising has been mostly from a negative perspective, which is hardly fair. We have attempted to expose consumerism as a belief and practice rather than discuss society's need for consumption. God surely intends advertising to inform, to inspire healthy competition and creativity, and to stimulate the economy.

Apart from theology, the secular world has much to say about advertising's proper role. Jerry Kirkpatrick's *In Defense of Advertising: Arguments from Reason, Ethical Egoism, and Laissez-Faire Capitalism*[23] provides a crisp, rational, theoretical defense on the basis of the self-interest of the consumer. *Advertising Ethics* by Edward Spence and others is a more balanced and thorough pursuit of ethical practice for those in the profession.[24] A surprisingly sharp little book, *The Brand Gap*,[25] in the style of Marshall McLuhan, offers the industry insightful suggestions in the spirit of truth, trust, and collaboration.

22. William Deresiewicz, "Generation Sell: We're All Peddling Ourselves and Managing Our Own Brands," *New York Times*, Sunday Review, November 13, 2011, 1, 7.

23. Jerry Kirkpatrick, *In Defense of Advertising: Arguments from Reason, Ethical Egoism, and Laissez-Faire Capitalism* (Claremont, CA: TLJ Books, 2007).

24. Edward Spence, Brett Van Heekeren, and Michael Boylan, *Advertising Ethics* (Upper Saddle River, NJ: Prentice Hall, 2004).

25. Marty Neumeier, *The Brand Gap: How to Bridge the Distance between Business Strategy and Design* (New York: New Riders, AIGA, 2006).

Opposing Viewpoints series' *Advertising*[26] provides a good selection of different opinions to discuss. From a faith and theological perspective, Catholic social teaching offers a well-balanced article on "Ethics in Advertising." It sees the increasing importance of advertising in modern society, views advertising as "extremely broad and diverse," and affirms that advertising does not just "mirror the attitudes and values of surrounding culture" but also "helps shape the reality it reflects." This article helpfully outlines both "the benefits of advertising" and "the harm done by advertising."[27]

Beyond marketing, we also want to consider carefully the difference between consumption and consumerism. We need emphasis on the benefits of positive free-market production. This chapter is mainly about consumerism, which we take to be an extreme form of materialism, even obsession, an idolatry of goods and services. Humans were put on earth to bring forth harvests and products to serve the common good. To be fair, let's pause and reflect on three men whose material products we need and treasure.

Henry Ford introduced industrial mass production leading to US power in two world wars. He revolutionized transportation and changed the way we live by lifting our standard of living and putting even the working class on the road. Ford described his goal in these words:

> I will build a motor car for the *great multitude*. It will be large enough for the family but small enough for the individual to run and care for. It will be constructed of the best materials, by the best men to be hired, after the simplest designs that modern engineering can devise. But it will be low in price that no man making a good salary will be unable to own one—and enjoy with his family the blessing of hours of pleasure in God's open spaces.[28]

Ford paid his workers five dollars a day, twice what they would make elsewhere, but they worked under difficult conditions (there is much that is controversial in the life of Henry Ford). Such salaries allowed many of his workers, and other Americans, to buy the Model T (which came out in 1908) for $825. Ford is also known as one of the great philanthropists.

Bill Gates has been called a modern-day Henry Ford. According to Rob Horwitz and Mary-Jo Foley:

> Gates took an arcane technology that was accessible to few and figured out how to re-engineer, extend, package and market it so that it was relevant and affordable to

---

26. Roman Espejo, ed., *Advertising*, Opposing Viewpoints series (Detroit: Greenhaven, 2010).

27. Pontifical Council for Social Communications, "Ethics in Advertising," www.vatican.va/roman_curia/pontifical_councils/pccs/documents/rc_pc_pccs_doc_22021997_ethics-in-ad_en.html.

28. "Henry Ford: The Individual in History," www.ford.chizeng.com/individual.html. Emphasis added.

the masses. . . . Henry Ford didn't invent the automobile, and Gates didn't invent the computer but the brilliance of both was in figuring out how to make their respective products ubiquitous.

On the tech front, I'd say Gates will be remembered for making good on his goal of helping to popularize personal computing. Microsoft did end up enabling consumer and business users to deploy—almost—a PC on every desk.[29]

Not only did Bill Gates become one of the wealthiest men in the world (according to *Forbes*), but he has also given away more than anyone else. The Bill and Melinda Gates Foundation has given billions to health care for the poor, AIDS prevention, and other neglected causes.

One more creative mind can be added to the above innovators and entrepreneurs. "Steve Jobs's Vision, Leadership Are Models for US Businesses," headlines a *Boston Globe* editorial. "Jobs is the rare celebrity CEO whose achievements match up to his reputation. He is one of the handful of truly major leaders of the high-tech revolution."[30] Cofounding what would become Apple out of a garage in the Silicon Valley, then forced out of the company in 1985, Jobs was brought back to rescue Apple in 1997 and brought us a string of beautiful and beneficial products: the iMac, iPod, iPhone, and iPad.

Imagine your life without a car, computer, and iPhone, iPod, or iPad. We should be grateful and congratulate those who have produced what we consume to our benefit—even while acknowledging some of their questionable business practices.

Teenage America

When we reflect on struggles of adolescents ages thirteen to twenty-one, several key books come to mind. The titles sum up a dominant feature of their lives—that of detachment. They have been left adrift by adults they need.[31] We recognize an actual expectation on the part of many adults that teenagers will just go their

29. Tim Ferguson, "Bill Gates' Legacy: A Modern Day Henry Ford," *ZDNet*, June 25, 2008, www.zdnet.com/news/bill-gates-legacy-a-modern-day-henry-ford/208193.
30. "Steve Jobs's Vision, Leadership Are Models for US Businesses," *Boston Globe* editorial, August 26, 2011, A10.
31. David Elkind, *All Grown Up and No Place to Go* (Reading, MA: Perseus Books, 1998); Thomas French, *South of Heaven: Welcome to High School at the End of the Twentieth Century* (New York: Doubleday, 1993); Patricia Hersch, *A Tribe Apart: A Journey into the Heart of American Adolescence* (New York: Ballantine Books, 1998); Mary Pipher, *Reviving Ophelia: Saving the Selves of Adolescent Girls* (New York: Ballantine Books, 1994); Rachel Simmons, *Odd Girl Out: The Hidden Culture of Aggression in Girls* (New York: Mariner Books, 2011); and Chap Clark, *Hurt: Inside the World of Today's Teenagers* (Grand Rapids: Baker Academic, 2004), all speak to the abandonment and isolation of teenagers in our society.

own way, separate from family, from community, from church, and temporarily from the values and strengths of their society. It is difficult to value someone with whom you've lost contact—and many key adults have little real awareness of what young people are thinking. Other writers put it this way: "a large part of the argument in this book [is that] teenagers are valued not for their potential to contribute, but for their ability to consume and, more broadly, for what they achieve."[32]

Another America, Another World

We realize at some point that most of this research has been done with middle-class adolescents. We again tend to neglect a most important and interconnected population—the urban poor.[33] A consideration of inner-city black consumption, for instance, will help us in two ways: it reinforces our emphasis on context, the various social systems among which we grow and operate, *and* it forces us to reconsider the ongoing prevalence of racism. Elizabeth Chin's research is reported in *Purchasing Power: Black Kids and American Consumer Culture.*[34]

What is the enduring effect of the more-than-two-hundred-year period of slavery upon African Americans and the rest of us? Some would say that that epoch is far behind and best forgotten. But in that era the slave was treated *as* a commodity—him or herself—*and* the meager commodities accessible to slaves were quite rigidly controlled. It was important, if the institution of slavery was to be sustained, that striking differences in the consumption of slave and white families be rigidly enforced. Beyond such oppression was the studding of black male slaves, the separation of families, the auction block: "The direct buying and selling of human beings was . . . the most hideous form of consumption."[35] And through peonage and Jim Crow, slavery continued in new forms after the Emancipation Proclamation. Sustained injustice is bound to create enduring images and symbols expressing, for all parties, underlying anger, fear, guilt, fantasies, and desires. All this feeds into our corporate and individual identities in America today.

As a graduate student, Chin studied research on black consumption while doing her own ethnographic research in a poor section of her hometown of New

32. Bernard, Penner, and Bartlett, *Consuming Youth*, 28.

33. LeAlan Jones and Lloyd Newman with David Isay, *Our America: Life and Death on the South Side of Chicago* (New York: Washington Square, 1997). Two young boys poignantly remind us that "we live in two different Americas," 199.

34. Elizabeth Chin, *Purchasing Power: Black Kids and American Consumer Culture* (Minneapolis: University of Minnesota Press, 2001).

35. Ibid., 41.

Haven, Connecticut. (In 1990, Connecticut was judged the wealthiest state in the United States, while three of its cities, including New Haven, were among the poorest of their size in the country.) While one may raise questions about her Chinese American/white identity or some of her reasoning and conclusions in *Purchasing Power*, she must be credited for a fine study that brings this important but neglected matter to national attention. Following her historical analyses, she says,

> Disparities of race, class and gender continue to be enforced and maintained through consumption. In the 1980s, the Michael Douglas character Gordon Gecko declared that "greed is good" in the film *Wall Street*, an apt summary of an economic period that saw unprecedented widening of the gap between rich and poor in the United States, a gap that has since developed into a chasm of alarming size.
>
> At the same time, images of the welfare queen and streetcorner drug dealer have become more ubiquitous. These images purposefully describe a kind of anti-consumer: the welfare mom has amassed several Cadillacs, while the drug dealer loads himself down with ill-gotten gold chains. In other words they spend money they haven't earned on things they shouldn't have.[36]

Chin's study of relevant consumer research and her ethnographic work in the Newhallville section of New Haven led to counter-conclusions. What she found among a majority of the community and of her young friends in particular was that

> children's shopping trips only *begin* with the act of shopping. Newhallville children's reasons for seeking out particular items and their capacity for "spending their money wisely" are socially rooted in attempts to please caretakers, efforts to avoid the disappointment or anger of parents, the desire to share with siblings, and the anticipation of the pleasures of gift-giving.[37]

An important contribution of Chin's work is to show how urban children not only buy into consumerism, not only choose dolls that reflect their ethnicity, but often bring white Barbies into their culture and use creative ingenuity to re-present a Barbie who fits into their world and life by adapting her hair to their styles.[38] These consumers are not just passive; they are continually manipulating ads and products to fit their own scene. Of course, marketers are aware of this and try to make use of such creativity. The interplay of youthful creativity and marketing creativity is a main source of constant change in the youth and pop cultures.

36. Ibid., 43.
37. Ibid., 176.
38. Ibid., chap. 6, "Ethnically Correct Dolls: Toying with the Race Industry."

Consumerism's Ultimate Effect: Existential Emptiness

When driven by materialism a culture may lose its soul. For individuals, the ultimate effects of consumptive materialism are loss of purpose, emptiness, isolation, and loneliness. You can hear this implied or clearly articulated in the cries of many voices. In one of his many spiritually reflective and challenging books, Henri Nouwen describes a New York City subway ride and the notes he made to himself at that time.

> Sitting in the subway, I am surrounded by silent people hidden behind their newspapers or staring away in the world of their own fantasies. Nobody speaks with a stranger, and a patrolling policeman keeps reminding me that people are not all out to help each other. But when my eyes wander over the walls of the train covered with invitations to buy more or new products, I see young, beautiful people enjoying each other in a gentle embrace, playful men and women smiling at each other in fast sailboats, proud explorers on horseback encouraging each other to take brave risks, fearless children dancing on a sunny beach, and charming girls always ready to serve me in airplanes and ocean liners. While the subway train runs from one dark tunnel into the other and I am nervously aware where I keep my money, [yet] the words and images decorating my fearful world speak about love, gentleness, tenderness and about a joyful togetherness of spontaneous people.[39]

Commercial promises are often vacuous. Nouwen goes on to describe consumerism as an idolatry breeding emptiness and loneliness:

> The contemporary society in which we find ourselves makes us acutely aware of our loneliness. We become increasingly aware that we are living in a world where even the most intimate relationships have become part of competition and rivalry.
>
> Pornography seems one of the logical results. It is intimacy for sale . . . hundreds of lonely young and old men, full of fear that anyone will recognize them, gaze silently at pictures of nude girls. . . . Loneliness is one of the most universal sources of human suffering today.[40]

As we buy into consumerism, we compromise our true identities (just as Esau sold his birthright for a bowl of porridge). Our branded identities seek to obtain and promote things *before* personal relationships. Or we are enticed to get things (like cosmetics and cars) to attract "cool" friends. We may settle for virtual rather than real relationships, conversations, and community. We are drawn to sex as a

---

39. Henri Nouwen, *Reaching Out: The Three Movements of the Spiritual Life* (New York: Doubleday, 1975), 24.
    40. Ibid., 24–25.

commodity on sale without the high cost of love and commitment. We may then be lured into pornography without responsibility or even real contact. But more deeply than all this, we lose the real meaning of life; without genuine identities, we become spiritually empty and lonely.

A fifteen-year-old girl comes to see West Coast psychotherapist Madeline Levine, who has treated many wealthy, at-risk youth. Levine describes the girl as bright, personable, highly pressured by her adoring, but frequently preoccupied, affluent parents, and very angry.

> She used a razor blade to incise the word EMPTY on her left forearm, showing it to me when I commented on her typical cutter disguise—a long-sleeve T-shirt pulled half way over her hand, with an opening torn in the cuff for her thumb. . . . I realized that I had been so profoundly affected by my cutter, with her oozing, desperate message, because with that single, raw word EMPTY she had captured the dilemma of many of my teenage patients.[41]

As therapist for affluent teens and families, Levine is on to something—that some adolescents today are overprotected, overindulged, and pressured by too-high expectations from so-called helicopter parents. She is holding such parents responsible for the troubles plaguing many of her young clients. But what initially attracted me to Levine's article and book[42] was a young person's response to her work. Here is the girl's significant insight:

> As a teenager with friends in the demographic discussed, I found Levine's observations correspond to my own experience. While I agree with her conclusions about the harm of [parental] over-involvement and intrusions, I would argue that the problem goes beyond the way parents relate to their children; unhappy teens are not the product of poor parenting techniques as much as they are troubled by the lifestyle that places its highest values on material wealth and financial success. Upper-middle class suburban teens often feel "empty" because the lifestyle they find themselves part of is "empty," the values they are taught to aspire to, are "empty."[43]

Illustrating what we can learn from teenagers, this profound critique of Levine's article and book agrees with its warnings about the psychic dangers of consumerism but places primary blame on advertising and the larger consumerist society.

41. Madeline Levine, "What Price Privilege?," *SFGate* (online) of the *San Francisco Chronicle*, June 25, 2006.

42. Madeline Levine, *The Price of Privilege: How Parental Pressure and Material Advantage Are Creating a Generation of Disconnected and Unhappy Kids* (New York: Harper Paperbacks, 2008).

43. Nick Ross-Rhudy, "Teens, Pressure, and Privilege," Letters, *SFGate* (online) of the *San Francisco Chronicle*, Sunday Magazine, July 30, 2006.

Parents and other protective, indulging, and pressuring adults may be blamed, but they themselves are also victims of social pressures. (Can you see possibilities for discussing the opinions of Levine and her teen critic with your students in youth ministry?)

Branded Adolescents Breaking Free

Youth (and even children) are not passive recipients of media messages and commercials. As we have considered in previous chapters, the relationship between messenger and receiver is much more complicated than that, and humans are both resilient and creative. In reality, our responses to commercial messages and the creative strategies of marketers are unpredictable. Young people appropriate commercial messages in their own way. They establish changing standards of "cool" and make use of logos with particular meanings. Still, we are all caught within the framework of a consuming process. Our various groups and niches, even our individual styles, are worked out in a consumerist culture.

There is obvious pragmatism in the way children today accept consumerism as cool. Kalle Lasn and others deal with *cool* as an essential ingredient of consumerism. He discusses "American cool as a global pandemic" and adds, "The Earth can no longer support the lifestyle of the cool-hunting American-style consumer."[44]

But is there more to it than "being cool"? Throughout life we are all engaged in defining ourselves, in determining the values that underlie our relationships and choices. These values also give meaning and purpose to our lives. We all know that the struggle for identity is particularly prominent in the transition from childhood to adulthood. Identity has been an important theme in the work of Kenda Creasy Dean, and she explains its importance:

> Without a coherent identity, adolescents feel constantly at risk of disintegrating, of becoming non-existent—literally, of becoming a "nobody." . . . They resort to myriad anesthetics to numb the pain of falling apart: achievement, substance abuse, consumerism, serial relationships. . . . Every salve eventually wears off, revealing the fragile self anew.[45]

Dean goes on to point to a positive, "recentered" alternative to be found "in the light of the cross." Instead of being branded by consumerism, "divided by

44. Kalle Lasn, *Culture Jam: How to Reverse America's Suicidal Consumer Binge—and Why We Must* (New York: Eagle Brook, 1999), xiv. See also the startling documentary *Merchants of Cool*, directed by Barak Goodman (Frontline, 2001).

45. Kenda Creasy Dean, *Practicing Passion: Youth and the Quest for a Passionate Church* (Grand Rapids: Eerdmans, 2004), 16. This is a highly recommended book.

unconverted 'passions,' the new self identifies with Christ's Passion. . . . When this happens, adolescents find themselves in a new place; the new self is 'in Christ'" (see Eph. 1:4–11).[46]

Further Practical and Theological Response to Consumerism

There's been a lot of bad news about today's cultures in this chapter. But there is also good news, globally and locally. This summer while researching and writing this chapter, I have seen families and groups of kids having wonderful times along ocean beaches and lakes. Vacation spots often provide better communities than normal home neighborhoods.

God has given the human spirit amazing resilience against domination by any power. We see that in children who refuse to be taken in by commercial hype. A grassy knoll, low-tide beach, or even a driveway can replace video games and organized children's sports. Urban youth have their own street games and can organize tournaments in parks. Friendship groups can replace chat rooms, and local talent shows are often more real than media extravaganzas. Many young people are working on identities counter to consumptive values.

Other counterforces to consumptive emptiness are rising in the secular world. Lasn, quoted earlier (along with similar social critics such as Jerry Mander, *Four Arguments for the Elimination of Television*, 1977), sees the desperateness of our situation but also the hope of necessary change:

> Two generations of chronic over-consumption, decadence and denial have weakened America. American cool is now every bit as vulnerable as the Soviet Utopia was ten years ago, A revolution couldn't happen there, but it did. It can't happen here, but it will.[47]

President Clinton's treasury secretary Larry Summers, once president of Harvard University and chief economic adviser to President Obama, said the following: "We cannot and will not accept any 'speed limit' on American economic growth. It is the task of economic policy to grow the economy as rapidly, sustainably, and inclusively as possible."[48] In response to such sentiments, economist E. F. Schumacher has written a classic call for an end to excessive consumption. After proving, to the satisfaction of many, the folly of blind growth, Schumacher concludes his book with these words: "The guidance we need for this work cannot be found in

46. Ibid., 16.
47. Kalle Lasn, *Culture Jam*, 215.
48. Quoted in E. F. Schumacher, *Small Is Beautiful: Economics As If People Mattered* (New York: Harper Perennial, 1973, 2010), xi.

science or technology, the value of which utterly depends on the ends they serve; but it can still be found in the traditional wisdom of mankind."[49]

To engage consumption, whether beneficial, indulgent, or in between, Christians have been given a deep antidote and abiding hope. First of all we understand the reality of spiritual warfare.[50] The social systems and institutions discussed here are manifestations of a transcendent battle between good and evil, the true God and many idols. And we are given resources for that battle in prayer and godly wisdom. (Read again the closing encouragement of Paul's Epistle to the Ephesians in 5:10–18, in light of this chapter.) We boldly pray the extraordinary and neglected vision, "Thy will be done on earth as in heaven."

Jesus (as recorded in Luke 16:8b–9) seems to imply that, as his followers, we need to learn from those in the secular world. We can make use of the many counter-strategies against the negative impact of consumerism and advertising, some of which are mentioned in this chapter. We can and ought to be engaged with culture and changing our societies.

Above all, this chapter calls youth workers (and parents) to process the electronic barrage. Young people are the final experts as to the effect of this materialistic media onslaught. And they must discover the best ways to overcome sophisticated strategies of branding and brainwashing. Of course, they best do so in partnership with youth leaders, parents, and experts.

As Dean and others have pointed out, young people need to pursue something passionately, and they want a genuine identity; real, honest relationships; and the opportunity for challenging service that can make a difference.

Believing in the human tendency toward selfish indulgence and powerful manipulation and domination in cultural systems, we are meant to confront evil and injustice, in our own personal lifestyles, in sacrificial relationships with young people, and in powerful teaching and discussions.

Finally, we have eschatological[51] hope for the future and present. God is ultimately in charge; God is going to win. And we already see small signs of God's kingdom coming, and God's will being done. Still, it often seems so futile; for the one step we take forward, evil seems to force us two steps back. The newest and most exciting invention, business, and product are so easily corrupted. But the kingdom will come, completely, fully, to the satisfaction of the most marginalized and impoverished! We need to know that, and youth need to ponder its implications for their lives and identity. We need to be moving, the best we can,

---

49. Ibid., 318.

50. See Volf, *Exclusion and Embrace*, 87, as he quotes Walter Wink, *Engaging the Powers* (Minneapolis: Fortress Press, 1992).

51. *Eschatology* describes the end of the story, God's conclusion. God is coming, and Christ will make everything right (just). Future hope gives us courage and tenacity in the present.

from being part of the problem to being a part of the solution. That is what our worship, our gospel, and our ministry are about.

Questions for Reflection and Discussion

1. How have commercials induced you to buy something? What influence has the spirit of consumerism had on you?
2. Do you consider this an effective chapter? Why or why not? What most impressed you in reading this chapter? With what did you disagree, or what suggestions would you offer?
3. What dangers, in your opinion, does consumerism pose to your society? What more would you say about consumerism in its present form?
4. Do you think it is important to discuss the issues of this chapter with young people? Why or why not, and if so how would you do so?
5. Will the resources mentioned in the text and footnotes of this chapter be of use to you?
6. How did you read the two verses at the beginning of this chapter? Do you read them any differently now?
7. Has your consideration of this topic led to any changes you want to make or resolutions about your future lifestyle? Is so, what are they?

—14—

Funny Theology?

> He who sits in the heavens laughs.
>
> PSALM 2:4A

> [Jesus was] a man of sorrows, and acquainted with grief.
>
> ISAIAH 53:3 ESV

Introduction

Just as effective communication of truth is facilitated by stories, so strenuous intellectual effort needs a break for humor. Admitting our need for comic relief, we look for its theological foundations. Does God have a sense of humor? Is it inappropriate, if not blasphemous, to imagine the divine Trinity joking together? Was Jesus just a man of sorrows, or did he, like all of us, do some real laughing, and if so, about what kinds of things did he laugh? Will there be humor in heaven? What if angels are preparing a grand comedy of human foibles for us to enjoy while putting all earthly mysteries into cosmic perspective?

When and how do you enjoy and use humor? We will consider humor as a break in the normal course of things, rather like a brief "sabbath" from our regular work, thinking, and duties. It brings relief, catches our attention, or pushes us to think more deeply. We will see humor, therefore, as both amusing *and* serious in intent. We seek a humor that heals individuals, that binds people together, that frees people to look for brighter hopes. We seek humor, like good drama, to unify and inspire. Our world cannot be preserved without comedy.

Philosophy of Humor

Humor is usually quite easy to identify but difficult to explain, though philosophers have attempted to do so. "Almost every major figure in the history of philosophy has proposed a theory [of humor], but after 2500 years of discussion there is little consensus about what constitutes humor."[1] As deep, thoughtful, and often solitary thinkers, philosophers certainly ought to be able to help us. It has been asked, "How can you tell when a philosopher is an extrovert? . . . . When he stares at *someone else's* shoes." Does this suggest a definition or theory?

Thomas Hobbes illustrates the superiority theory of humor: "the passion of laughter is nothing else but sudden glory arising from some sudden conception of some eminency in ourselves, by comparison with the infirmity of others, or with our own formerly."[2] Students at all levels are familiar with mocking humor from "superiors." Herbert Spencer and Sigmund Freud held to a relief theory—and relief certainly is a function of humor. Spencer explains that a body needs relief from the nervous energy it can generate, which makes some sense but fails to explain quick witticisms. Freud considered humor a defense mechanism and a "liberating release from reality."[3]

Immanuel Kant follows Aristotle in the direction of an incongruity theory. "In everything that is to excite a lively laugh there must be something absurd (in which the understanding, therefore, can find no satisfaction). Laughter is an affection arising from the sudden transformation of a strained expectation into nothing (*Critique of Judgment* I, I, 54)."[4] Drawing on the pre-humorous actions in animals, the tickling of chimps and wagging of a dog's tail, Max Eastman "considers humor as a form of play—the opposite of seriousness. . . . [The Play Theory, though,] is problematic since 'in itself play is not comical for either the player or public.'"[5]

There is a philosophical joke I will try to embellish here to make a point. A certain philosopher attended a great philosophical festival where he ate and drank a little too much. That night he had a dream in which the great Aristotle appeared to him. The dreamer asked Aristotle, "Please give me a fifteen-minute exposition of your entire philosophy." With amazing clarity, the Greek philosopher complied. The dreamer then raised a certain objection, which Aristotle couldn't answer. Confounded, Aristotle disappeared. Then Plato appeared, couldn't answer our philosopher's refutation, and disappeared. Descartes, Immanuel Kant, and

1. "Humor," *Internet Encyclopedia of Philosophy*, iep.utm.edu/humor.
2. Thomas Hobbes, *Human Nature*, chap. 8, quoted in ibid.
3. Sigmund Freud, "Humor," in *The Complete Works of Sigmund Freud*, trans. James Strachey, 24 vols. (London: Hogarth, 1993), 40.
4. Immanuel Kant, quoted in "Humor," *Internet Encyclopedia of Philosophy*.
5. Ibid.

others came and went in the same way! Amazed, our philosopher said to himself, "I know I'm asleep and dreaming all this, but I must force myself over to my desk to write down this universal refutation of all philosophic systems. By morning I will have forgotten, and the world will suffer from lack of its wisdom." So with iron determination, he forced himself to get it down and jumped back into bed with a sigh of relief. Waking the next morning, he rushed over to his table to find what he had written. There it was. "That's what *you* say."[6] This chapter is not trying to make you smile or laugh as much as it is begging consideration as to why you consider something humorous or not, and how important you consider humor to be.

Norman Cousins discovered the importance of humor through a serious illness. He considered the nature of humor in the following way:

> The response to incongruities is one of the highest manifestations of the cerebral process. We smile broadly or even break out into open laugher when we come across Eugene Field's remark about a friend "who was so mean he wouldn't let his son have more than one measle at a time." Or Leo Rosten's reply to a question asking whether he trusted a certain person: "I'd rather trust a rabbit to deliver a head of lettuce." Or as Rosten also said, "Let's go somewhere where I can be alone." These examples of word play illustrate the ability of the human mind to jump across gaps in logic and find delight in the process.
>
> Surprise is certainly a major ingredient of humor. Babies will laugh at sudden movements or changes in expression, indicating that breaks in the sequences of behavior can tickle the risibilities. During the days of silent films, Hollywood built an empire out of the surprise antics of its voiceless comedians—Harold Lloyd swinging from the hands of a giant clock, Charlie Chaplin caught up in the bowels of an assembly belt, or Buster Keaton chasing a zebra.
>
> It has always seemed to me that laughter is the human mind's way of dealing with the incongruous. Our train of thought will be running in one direction and then is derailed suddenly by running into absurdity. The sudden wreckage of logical flow demands release. Hence the physical reaction known as laughter.[7]

Overanalyzing humor can, of course, be self-defeating; with too much questioning as to why something was humorous, it may no longer be funny. Art, literature, and our emotional lives are to be enjoyed before we pause to analyze, yet they beg subsequent reflection. A profound analyst of humor, Nancy Walker quotes E. B.

---

6. Raymond Smullyan, *5000 BC and Other Philosophical Fantasies* (New York: St. Martin's Press, 1983) quoted at David Chalmers, "A Universal Philosophical Refutation," www.consc.net/misc/univ-joke.html.

7. Norman Cousins, *Head First: The Biology of Hope and Healing Power of the Human Spirit* (New York: Penguin, 1989), 127–28.

White: "Humor can be dissected, as a frog can, but the thing dies in the process and the innards are discouraging to any but the pure scientific mind."[8] Although music and sports can be overanalyzed to the point of losing their joy, a deep understanding of music and the strategies of sports can also serve to increase our appreciation and delight. I hope that you are finding theological joy in grappling with the theological incongruities suggested in this book. The apostle Paul deals clearly with the disappointments of life while asking us to rejoice, "again I will say, rejoice" (Phil. 4:4). God doesn't answer every prayer for deliverance or healing—at least in our time and way. We sometimes need to deal with disappointments and impossibilities with a smile or even a laugh.

Importance of Context in Humor

Humor, then, is elusive, difficult to define, and of many varieties. It usually involves some kind of physical (tickling) or mental incongruity (this isn't what I was expecting). Humor is also age-specific. While writing this chapter, we've been joined in our home by four grandchildren (plus their parents and a dog). My silliness with two-year-old Linden is different from the way I try to entertain Cashel (5) and Tobin (8). Attempts to relieve any tensions felt by the four of us parenting this high-powered brood rely on a different level of humor.

Humor is not only age-specific but also culture-specific. Humor like music is universal, but although all cultures need and enjoy laughter, they may enjoy different kinds of incongruities in different ways. When in the 1960s I went from teaching at New York City Community College to Cuttington College in Liberia, I was struck by how differently humor is expressed in different cultures. Students on the two continents laughed at strikingly different situations. What is sad or embarrassing to one culture may be uproariously funny in another.

Like music, humor is universally enjoyed but locally adapted. All cultures tap, hum, and giggle. Most enjoy the best of another culture's music but keep distinct tastes of their own. Since H. R. Haweis lectured at the Royal Institution in London (in 1881) on "American Humorists," there have been many studies and books written about American comedy (that is, humor of the colonies and United States).[9] It is interesting how the various perspectives of these works reflect differences regarding American character and amusement. The same could be said of British humor—and that of other countries. Along with national style, we find

8. E. B. White and Katharine S. White, eds., *A Subtreasury of American Humor* (New York: Modern Library, 1941), xiii, as quoted by Nancy Walker, ed., *What's So Funny? Humor in American Culture* (Wilmington, DE: Scholarly Resources, 1998), 5.
9. See Nancy Walker's fine introduction in Walker, ed., *What's So Funny?* ·

distinctive humor among regions or groups within a society. Women humorists throughout US history have understood their humor to be in contrast to that of men.[10] Southern humor has been notably different from that of New England, and the humor of slaves and African Americans from that of mainstream whites. Many of us appreciate the often wise and refreshing style of Jewish-American comedy.[11] Various groups have created humor from the values, styles, and pain of their own situations. Some scholars come down on the side of the unitary nature of North American character and humor; others discredit that notion with evidence from the above distinctions. The best resolution of the debate may be a "both/and" middle position. It is possible to see strong and unique national characteristics while recognizing distinct contrasts and contributions among various regional, gender, and subcultural divides—including the changing humor of youthful cultures.

The youth culture has its own sense of humor. It is an important and distinctive aspect of the social life and culture of youth. Youthful cultures and humor change rapidly, perhaps faster than that of the dominant culture. Like many aspects of adolescent life, youthful humor can attempt to shock and confuse adult society, providing relief from adult authority and its pressures to perform. As humor serves to unite any culture, it provides adhesive for youthful cultures and particular groups of friends.

Youth cultures (and their humor) exhibit "globality." Some youthful humor is universal, while various national localities develop their own styles. Similarly, various subcultures of youth have their own particular brands of humor. An inner-city team plays a largely white suburban team; the jokes in the two locker rooms will bear some resemblance, but with strikingly different nuances and emphases. At your high school, what is funny among the "druggies" out in the woods behind the school, or male athletes after a hard workout on the nicely groomed football field, or young women playing field hockey, or those practicing in the band room, or the "nerds" in the computer lab, is all quite different. The humor of gang members you know is not the same as that among youth moving toward college. In any of these cases, youth leaders must pay attention to the nuances of humor and, without copying it, be ready to make mild, humorous defense in any of these contexts, when young persons' banter is directed at you a leader—sometimes with a self-deprecating jibe.

As with fashion and dress, youth leaders ought not try to copy youthful humor or act inappropriately "hip." Being aware of youthful humor and that of society at

---

10. See, for example, Kate Sanborn, *The Wit of Women* (New York: Funk & Wagnalls,1885); and Martha Bruère and Mary Ritter Beard, *Laughing Their Way* (New York: Macmillan,1937).

11. Noted by Walker, *What's So Funny?*, 59.

large, we contrive our own sense of Christ-honoring, youth-encouraging laughter. We might say we are called to model a higher style of humor that honors God and preserves the dignity of all persons.

Many comics come from an oppressed class or race; a comic's life has often been touched with some special form of pain. The comedy of Lenny Bruce reflected his being Jewish American, a child of divorced parents, discharged from the Navy for being homosexual, and other life difficulties. For many comedians, humor has enabled a profitable and satisfying career—and helped in a healing process. We also know of battlefield humor, mortuary humor, and the jokes of an operating room; such humor is needed to take us through extraordinarily difficult human situations. Without faith in Jesus Christ, I would be "without God and without hope in this world."[12] Missing a spiritual and eternal dimension in my life, I imagine I could only survive banal small talk or thoughts of old age, terminal illness and death, with a strong dose of humor. Humor must be God's gracious gift to the ungodly and to all of us.

You may be asking, what in the world does all this have to do with practical theology and youth ministry? Well, have you ever noticed an expression on the face of someone in your class or group—perhaps even audibly expressed: "Please . . . give me a break!" Sometimes, caught up in enthusiasm for our topic, we may miss an underlying sigh from someone drifting off: "This person is taking his or her teaching, or self, way too seriously." This is where, I believe, God's gift of humor comes into play. A quick flash of jocularity or whimsical self-deprecation can lighten the moment, give the group a break, or bring speaker and audience together—as the limited and confused humans we are.

Comedy in Everyday Life

Dogs are funny to us when they act human; children are funny when they come out with profoundly adult statements. We make others and ourselves laugh when we "lose it," do something entirely out of character or inappropriate. These examples point to intriguing aspects of humor.

Everybody likes to laugh, even though we can't explain the exact nature of funniness. To see their children laughing delights parents. Youth leaders beam when young people let down their defenses, let tension go, and laugh spontaneously. We all enjoy good humor. Yet surprisingly, we may think of humor dismissively even while it is helping us survive the hardships of life. A serious consideration of humor and its vital role in the lives of children and young people can profit

12. A rough paraphrase of Eph. 2:12b. Read this whole chapter in which the apostle is imagining what life is like for anyone outside of Christ.

youth leaders (as well as parents, teachers, and others). Youth ministry needs a psychology and theology of humor.

Research has shown the physical benefits of mirth and fun.[13] In his illness, noted earlier, Norman Cousins discovered the power of laughter, "that ten minutes of solid belly laughter would give me two hours of pain-free sleep. . . . Of all the benefits bestowed by nature on human beings, hearty laughter must be close to the top."[14] A biblical proverb puts it this way: "A cheerful heart is a good medicine, but a downcast spirit dries up the bones" (Prov. 17:22). Laughter, then, is medicine for body and soul—a relief from various tyrannies of the mind.

I remember, as a boy, lying in a hospital bed after a hernia operation, back in the dark ages, listening to a radio playing Red Skelton. My belly laughs were killing me, but I couldn't turn it off. I just held my stomach so the stitches wouldn't split. I also remember cracking up the first time I saw Lucille Ball in the candy factory! The humor of the Great Depression through World War II seemed to evolve, from vaudeville slapstick characters like Jimmy Durante or Joe Weber and Lew Fields to famous pairs like Fibber Magee and Molly, George Burns and Gracie Allen, into variety shows such as "The Jack Benny Program," "I Love Lucy," and sitcoms from the 1960s and on. How do you and young people respond to yesterday's humor?

In the 1960s, I enjoyed and was struck by the satirical humor in Dick Gregory's *The Light Side: the Dark Side* and Bill Cosby's *Black History: Lost, Stolen or Strayed*. They were funny—and starkly serious. How would different groups and ethnicities respond to them today? Different listeners found Richard Pryor and the early Eddie Murphy highly entertaining, revolutionary, or revolting. Comedians like Steve Martin, Robin Williams, and even Rodney Dangerfield can make one laugh—despite some of their extreme raunchiness. Will Farrell's creative impressions and humor on Saturday Night Live, in movies, on television, and on YouTube made him a favorite of many. But in considering all this, we must ask: How does crossing the line of decency enhance humor, and what do we lose when we clean it up?

The celebration of debauchery in the humor of many comedians, even though tongue-in-cheek, would seem to be condemned by the apostle Paul and leaders throughout church history.

13. Lee Berk and Stanley Tan et al., "Neuroendocrine and Stress Hormone Changes During Mirthful Laughter," *American Journal of Medical Sciences* 298, no. 6 (1989): 390–96. Berk has even developed a software program for doctors, hospitals, clinics, and rehabilitation centers for customized laughter prescriptions, allowing doctors to create individualized humor reports for patients. These Christian doctors from Loma Linda University Medical Center, Department of Pathology, base their work on Prov. 17:22. See also Norman Cousins, *Head First*.
14. Norman Cousins, *Head First*, 126–27. See also his *Anatomy of an Illness as Perceived by the Patient* (New York: Norton, 1979).

But fornication and impurity of any kind, or greed, must not even be mentioned among you, as is proper among saints. Entirely out of place is obscene, silly, and vulgar talk; but instead, let there be thanksgiving. . . . Let no one deceive you with empty words, for because of these things the wrath of God comes on those who are disobedient. (Eph. 5:3–4, 6)

How does practical theology interpret this tension between godly admonition and cultural realities? My "adolescent" heart can feel trapped between narrow and hypocritical religious legalism, on the one hand, and the apparent freedom, or license, of wild entertainment on the other. Consider a teenager subject to continuous negative preaching against "sins of the flesh." Contrast the no of his church to the yes of the comedian. Let's further imagine a young fan asking Robin Williams or Richard Pryor, who have been extolling the wild pleasure of cocaine, whether or not he or she should begin to experiment. I really think the comedians would probably answer, "Don't do as I laugh or as I do, but do the right thing for you—stay away from it."

To what extent can we compete with the raunchy humor of popular media? One of my favorite comedians is Bob Newhart. His comedy acts, "Abe Lincoln vs. Madison Avenue," "Bus Driver Training," and "Hairpiece" with Dean Martin, strike me as laughable without dirty language or lewd insinuations. We might also find inspiration from shows like Garrison Keillor's "Lake Wobegon" in *Prairie Home Companion*. Pete Holmes is a graduate of a Christian liberal arts college, with a kind of college humor appreciated by Conan O'Brien.[15] Holmes is bringing attention to serious issues in our digital culture while making us smile or laugh. Such a combination of comedy and serious issues seems to me a kind of prophetic humor. Mark Lowry is a more "churchy" comedian who brings genuine laughs.

As youth leaders, our ability to analyze humor and comedy helps us equip young people in making their own judgments about humor—how it is affecting them, and whether it is helping or hindering their growth. Without some skills of comic analysis and a theology of humor, we will either avoid or confuse the issue. With a little effort, though, we may even help some become comedians.

Jokes about body parts and bodily functions all point to the human insecurity felt supremely in adolescent years. Idealistic and self-conscious young people may feel the powerlessness, the incongruity of life, and the need for comic relief much more than adults do. No one feels more intensely the twin passions of desiring to be a celebrity and fearing being a loser than does a teenager. Humor may relieve what is felt in adolescence—the awful fear of failure, terrible embarrassment, and

15. For a shorter version of his Conan performance on March 21, 2011, see "Pete Holmes— Google (Not Knowing)," YouTube, March 29, 2011, www.youtube.com/watch?v=PQ4o1N4ksyQ.

ultimate rejection. Humor can also unite the members of a group when they laugh together in friendly relief at their many anxieties. Still, there are some occasions when we do not want to forget or be relieved. For example, humor should be only selectively and carefully used at funerals—what might possibly be appropriate in one case could exhibit extremely bad taste at another.

Humor: Limits and Cautions

Remember that humor, like any other form of communication, is always a means to an end. Such ends may be a deepening of relationship, healing or growth, and ultimately the glory of God. The Bible praises joy and laughter but admits the importance of contrasting sorrow: "Then our mouth was filled with laughter, and our tongue with shouts of joy" (Ps. 126:2a). Yet, "Sorrow is better than laughter, for by sadness of countenance the heart is made glad" (Eccl. 7:3 RSV).

Scripture, then, suggests there is a time to move from laughter and joy to seriousness or even sorrow: "Lament and mourn and weep. Let your laughter be turned into mourning and your joy into dejection" (James 4:9).

Many of the ancient church fathers went further, discouraging humor for humor's sake: "Prefer moderation in speech and speak no foolish chatter, nothing just to provoke laughter; do not love immoderate or boisterous laughter."[16] Another caution comes from the wisdom of Ben Sirach: "Fools raise their voices when they laugh, but the wise smile quietly" (Ecclesiasticus 21:20 RSV). So there is much to discuss regarding humor in our lives and ministries.

Young people and all of us can be laughing on the outside and crying on the inside—as an old song puts it. A wise writer of the Proverbs recognizes life's underlying melancholy. "Even in laughter the heart is sad, and the end of joy is grief" (Prov. 14:13). Another Jewish proverb adds, "Not every heart that laughs is really cheerful."[17] Sometimes humor is a necessary coping mechanism; then it may become an ambivalent cover for inner confusion or pain—begging further healing.

Some seem to possess an almost masochistic willingness to be mocked. Consider those who pay to enter a nightclub or comedy club and are then humiliated by a comic who objectifies women and emotionally attacks the privacy and vulnerability of those in the audience. Superficial smiles try to prove they are "cool with it"—even though their manhood or womanhood has been impugned

16. Quoted by Joan Chittister, *The Rule of St. Benedict: Insights for the Ages* (New York: Crossroad, 1992), 53.

17. Kehillat Israel Reconstructionist Synagogue, "Yiddish Sayings, Proverbs . . . ," www.kehillat israel.net/docs/yiddish/yiddish_pr.htm, accessed February 12, 2013.

or their sexual privacy violated. In our society it is very difficult to restrain (with government censorship) those who exploit humor for personal gain at the expense of personal injury and social pollution. The public's recourse (since economics is the most immediate restraint) lies in refusing to patronize such humor. Thoughtful youth workers should acquire a skill in comic analysis so they can guide youth and determine when drama and humor aid ministerial goals and when they subvert our overall intention by crossing lines of respect and decency.

Discussing smutty jokes, Sigmund Freud seems to have linked negative and injurious humor to our present understanding of bullying. We often discuss bullying using a triangle to illustrate the three necessary parties in the act: the perpetrator or bully, the victim, and the bystander. Similarly Freud noted three people involved in smut: the first is the teller of the joke, the second is the object of the joke's hostile or sexual aggressiveness, and the third is the listener, who is supposed to receive some kind of pleasure in hearing and laughing.

> It is not the person who makes the joke who laughs at it and who therefore enjoys its pleasurable effect, but the inactive listener. . . . When the first person finds his libidinal impulse inhibited by the woman, he develops a hostile trend against that second person and calls on the . . . third person as his ally. Through the first person's smutty speech the woman is exposed before the third, who, as listener has now been bribed by the effortless satisfaction of his own libido. It is remarkable how universally popular a smutty interchange of this kind is.[18]

Do you agree that bullying and sexually degrading humor are related? Consider a young man (or woman) who has been rejected by someone he desired. He may taunt her in public (a school bus or a public web space); we call that bullying. Or he may tell his friends an insinuating, often dirty, joke about her. Negative humor may be directed at someone of the opposite sex or someone of another race or ethnicity, someone with a disability, a younger or older person. Such jokes come not from strength but from the weakness of human nature fueled by frustration, fear, annoyance, or ignorance.

Standard sarcasm among children and adolescents often masks pain of one kind or another. Our relationships with youth are tested by the way we are able to share that pain with them. As leaders, we have opportunities to ground or absorb the negative power of hurtful sarcasm before it injures others or possibly leads to violence. This much thought about the broad scope of humor probably raises questions about the unique function of its many varieties.

18. Sigmund Freud, *Jokes and Their Relationship to the Unconscious* (New York: W. W. Norton, 1990), 100.

Types of Humor

From wit, puns, and sarcasm, to fuller and more elaborate forms of comedy and dramatic irony, society needs healthy humor. Through literature and psychology courses we have become familiar with basic literary, spoken, and acted forms of humor.

Our lives and conversations are full of wit. Wit includes any quick and clever twisting of words that strikes the mind of a listener with pleasant surprise. The repartee of Winston Churchill, G. K. Chesterton, and Jon Stewart offer striking examples. Related to it is the play on words called a *pun* (expressed sometimes to the annoyance of listeners). "Calves take well to bottle feeding because one nipple is as good as an udder."[19] The pun has been called the lowest form of humor. But used selectively and judiciously a clever pun can still bring smiles and good will.

Careful readers of the classics and Scripture are familiar with the deeper humor of *irony*. When Socrates tells stories with surreptitious or pretended ignorance in order to provoke thoughtful response, he is teaching ironically— from which we get the term *Socratic irony*. In Sophocles's tragic play, Oedipus is searching for the murderer of his father, while it is actually he himself who has killed his father. The famous line in Samuel Coleridge's *The Rime of the Ancient Mariner*, "Water, water, everywhere, nor any drop to drink," is another example of irony. Irony comes from the incongruity of two ideas with an unexpected meaning. Our first reaction is, there's nothing funny about irony. It is classified as humorous because of the way it plays tricks with our minds and souls. A paradox of humor is that it can serve either a funny or a serious purpose. Its intent may be to lighten the spirit, or, contrariwise, to deepen the mood and focus attention.

Sarcasm may be somewhat ironic. There is a great deal of sarcasm in the Bible, but I would avoid it in youth ministry—except in extreme cases when used with caution. Sarcasm is ironic, mocking, or deriding humor. The way many young people and popular media use sarcasm is often damaging, but it has potentially profitable effects when someone in clear authority uses it to catch the attention of inattentive and offending followers. Groucho Marx's "I never forget a face, but in your case I'll be glad to make an exception," is an example of mocking sarcasm.[20]

Stories designed to expose the gap between what we are and what we ought to be are called *satire*. Satire may be aimed at those who take themselves too seriously,

---

19. Puns are easy to find on the internet. For example, see *Pun of the Day*, www.punoftheday.com.
20. *The Quotations Page*, www.quotationspage.com/quote/115.html.

or at the careless and apathetic who haven't taken time to examine reality. Satire may also be a cry for justice. It uses exaggeration and ridicule, in a humorous way, as an exposé of human foibles, a critique of society's pretentiousness, ignorance, lack of empathy, corruption, or injustice. We might say satire uses ironic wit or derision to expose social dysfunction. Then too, it can sometimes be satire for satire's sake—entertainment merely to amuse. Satire has been used throughout history. In *Gulliver's Travels* Jonathan Swift made English society ask themselves, "Why do we act that way?" Mark Twain's *Huckleberry Finn* humorously encouraged Americans to consider the cruelty and hypocrisy of slavery. C. S. Lewis takes us behind the scenes of our sins and vices in *The Screwtape Letters* to wonder why we are taken in by demonic strategies. Monty Python's brilliant work seems to sway between funny entertainment and serious criticism, between simple parody and deeper satire. Cervantes's *Don Quixote* is a classic example of the fantastic idealism that can grip our hearts.

The best satire, even while it is mocking, cares deeply about its theme. Our present political, economic, and educational systems, apart from God, call for satirical rebuke. Pop culture often does this exceedingly well. Can we marshal student creativity to provoke, with satire, adult conversation in church and society about issues too easily dismissed?

Slapstick comedy is another kind of humor, and one that can have a place in youth ministry. *Film Reference* provides helpful commentary:

> Slapstick is both a genre in its own right, belonging mostly to the years of silent cinema, and an element in other comedies (persisting) from the early years of film till now, when it seems to be an indispensable element of the teen or "gross-out" comedy typified by such films as the *American Pie* trilogy (1999, 2001, 2003) and movies directed by the Farrelly Brothers. . . . *There's Something About Mary* (1998), *Shallow Hal* (2001), *Stuck on You* (2003), *Hall Pass* (2011), and *The Three Stooges* (2012).
>
> Comedy in slapstick lies in the basic tension between control and its loss. Both the verbal outbursts of the wordier comics (the Marx Brothers, Zeppo, W. C. Fields) and the physical eruptions of those who use extreme body comedy (Charlie Chaplin, Jerry Lewis) are predicated on the delicate balance between resistance and inevitable surrender—indeed, the resistance serves to make the surrender even funnier. Slapstick's classic moment, the pie in the face, is funny only if the recipient is not already covered in pie but is first clean and neat; slipping on a banana skin provides humor only when the *before*—the dignified march—is contrasted with the *after*—the flat-out splayed pratfall on the sidewalk.[21]

21. "Slapstick Comedy," *Film Reference*, www.filmreference.com/encyclopedia/Romantic -Comedy-Yugoslavia/Slapstick-Comedy.html.

Is what you are reading about the various types of humor stretching your understanding of its varieties and their purposes? Do you appreciate comedy's various contexts and intentions? Do you see how humor can reflect and relieve a culture—and perhaps encourage greater social authenticity? And finally, are you relating the whole idea and practice of humor to ministry?

Humor in the Bible and Theology

We have already referenced Scripture, but we want to be thoroughly biblical in suggesting a theology of humor. A Christian psychologist once came to help in a training program for urban youth leaders. He took the dogmatic position that humor was a result of the fall and human sin—that there would be no humor in heaven or any need for laughter in the spiritual life. He tended to depreciate humor and encouraged alternatives to making people laugh. I was not sure why he singled out humor. Money, games, recreation, sex, and popular music are all gifts from God that will pass away or be radically altered in our heavenly state. Like humor, they can be used the wrong way, but that does not make them valueless in our earthly lives.

That psychologist didn't know his Bible well enough, because many biblical passages address humor.

> [God] will yet fill your mouth with laughter, and your lips with shouts of joy. (Bildad's opinion, which finally turned true, Job 8:21)

> Then our mouth was filled with laughter, and our tongue with shouts of joy. (Joy in getting close to the temple, Ps. 126:2)

The Bible, as the Word of God, is a serious text, using humor for sheer delight and serious intent. Its humorous elements were appreciated and remembered by ancient oriental hearers more than most modern readers realize. In an essay pointing out the didactic or moralistic purpose of humor, W. F. Stinespring elaborates: "One of the most common kinds of humor (or rather, wit) in the Bible (and perhaps everywhere) is the pun, a form of wordplay or paronomasia. Paronomasia . . . goes far beyond humor in the Bible, because of the oriental fondness for this sort of thing."[22]

Casanowicz and Russell count seven hundred instances of such wordplay in the Bible.[23] Scripture reflects many instances in which serious matters are sprinkled with puns and wit.

---

22. W. F. Stinespring, "Humor," in *The Interpreter's Dictionary of the Bible*, vol. 2 (New York: Abingdon, 1962), 660.
23. I. M. Casanowicz, *Paronomasia in the Old Testament* (Boston: J. S. Cushing, 1894); and E. Russell, *Paronomasia and Kindred Phenomena in the New Testament* (Leipzig: W. Drugulin, 1920), cited in Stinespring, "Humor," 660.

The Gospels invite us to smile at Jesus's picture of children not keeping the rules of their cute little game of weddings and funerals in the marketplace (Luke 7:32).[24] Jesus's words about specks and beams in an eye (Matt. 7:3–5) and straining out a gnat and swallowing a camel (Matt. 23:24) use levity to deal with serious issues.

Humor makes biblical stories, and therefore Scripture as a whole, more memorable. This was especially true in an oral, narrative culture, and continues to be true for us today. Elton Trueblood was having family devotions with his family one evening. Their oldest son was only four years old at the time. In the midst of a solemn reading of Matthew 7, the boy began to laugh out loud. His parents at first were perturbed and asked him what was the matter. He continued laughing at the thought of a human eye with a beam in it! The boy caught the original humor we usually miss.[25] The Bible is a funnier book than we realize, and we miss many lessons without appreciation of ancient Middle Eastern humor. Jesus found himself in many very difficult situations—and with some very slow learners. We'd do well to study and learn from his masterful use of humor.

Biblical irony suggests something far different—and often greater—than the statement itself.[26] The incongruity of two ideas provides the humorous element. Many readers miss the ancient Middle Eastern humor in Genesis 11. Humans said, "Come, let us make bricks. . . . Come, let us build . . . a tower with its top in the heavens" (Gen. 11:3–4). But no matter how high that tower got to be, God had to say, "Come, let us go down" (v. 7). Nathan comes to confront his king about a most heinous sin and does so by telling a story rich with dramatic irony that brought David to his knees (2 Sam. 12). Irony is not necessarily funny, but its element of mental surprise classifies it as humor. The irony in God's final question to Jonah is meant to strike us a little funny—though it was not at all humorous to the angry prophet: Are you really more concerned about a bush dying, God asks, than about a great city with a hundred and twenty thousand infants besides many animals (see Jonah 4:11)? The irony of the chief priests' and scribes' taunts at the crucified Christ is understood but not funny to people of faith. ("He saved others; himself he cannot save," Mark 15:31b KJV.)

God uses sarcasm to catch the attention of, and chastise, his idolatrous followers or the unscrupulous tyrants of this world. "He who sits in the heavens laughs; the LORD has them in derision" (Ps. 2:4). Throughout Scripture, God mocks human attempts to play God, or to make idols in human image. God's prophet Elijah derides the licentious prophets of Baal:

24. See S. MacLean Gilmour and John Knox, "The Gospel According to St. Luke," in *The Interpreter's Bible*, ed. G. A. Buttrick, vol. 8 (New York: Abingdon-Cokesbury, 1952), 140.
25. Elton Trueblood, *The Humor of Christ* (New York: Harper & Row, 1964), 9.
26. Jesus's words in Matt. 23:32 and Paul's in 1 Cor. 4:8 are examples of irony.

At noon Elijah mocked [the prophets of Baal, whose loud petitions had been going up to their god all morning]: "Cry aloud! [louder, for they had already been scream-ing] Surely he is a god; either he is meditating [daydreaming], or he has wandered away [to relieve himself physically], or he is on a journey, or perhaps he is asleep and must be awakened." Then they cried [louder] and, as was their custom, they cut themselves. (1 Kings 18:27–28a)

Jesus also had the authority and skill to use sarcasm effectively (although some want to "protect" Jesus by refusing to see any of his words as sarcastic). Christ sarcastically asks his critics if it is right to do good things on the Sabbath—drawing attention to their disregard for the needy. In answer to the grumbling of Pharisees and scribes about his welcoming of sinners in Luke 15, Jesus uses that special trilogy of parables—the lost sheep, lost coin, and lost son—to confound their arrogant and stubborn religious intolerance. He concludes each story with a lesson; the first with the sarcastic remark: "Just so, I tell you, there will be more joy in heaven over one sinner who repents than over ninety-nine righteous persons [like you guys] who [feel no] need [for] repentance" (Luke 15:7). Other examples of our Lord's sarcasm will probably come to mind.

The taunts of Elijah are examples of sarcasm, but the whole scene may be viewed as a satire on Israel's proclivity to idolatry and its licentious orgies. Similarly, when we take the Tower of Babel beyond its immediate context and think of the symbol of Babylon throughout the Bible, we begin to see divine satire exposing human achievement apart from God. Jonah, also, can be seen as a symbol of exclusive and ingrown religiosity resisting God's call to the un-reached world.

As already noted, biblical humor was sometimes funny to ancient hearers, and even to us. But it had serious moral and spiritual intent. If God is the great communicator, and if humor is a necessary aspect to powerful holistic human communication, then we thank God for humor and ask God's grace and guidance in using it effectively. Smiles and seriousness, laughter and chagrin or weeping, are not necessarily opposites in our theology and ministry.

Humor in Youth Ministry

Some might never have listened to a sermon had the preacher not had a good laugh with them first. Jesus reached such people in a way few would have expected from the divine. When we think about all the incongruities of God becoming human, our imagination cannot refrain from picturing Jesus smiling over the whole idea of what he was doing. I can also conceive of Christ laughing with those who needed to laugh, just as he wept with those who wept (Luke 19:41–44; John 11:33–35;

and Rom. 12:15). We have all seen many pictures of Jesus; I have seen only one of him laughing or smiling.

Those in charge of church or camp programs are often expected to provide comedy, frequently in the form of skits. These can be an important complement to our proclamation of the gospel. Providing comedic skits, or introductions to the next program event, is serious business. It takes a certain talent, the development of skill, and practice. The internet can steer you to several resources for developing skill in creating and presenting skits.[27] Then, as did the early comedians in youth ministry (positively hilarious in the 1940s and on), you are encouraged to copy the best comedy from television (or YouTube) and improve on it. Make sure you use the help of young students in this endeavor. They can provide us with a clearer understanding of this important part of their lives and culture. Humor surrounds them—in television and movies, in their music, and sprinkled throughout their conversations.

Phil McDonald was a great youth leader and master humorist out of Minneapolis for more than a half century. What got him started in setting the standard for humor in Young Life was a 1950s survey asking high school students what they considered to be the most important criteria for a good teacher. Their number one criterion was mastery of the subject; their second, a good sense of humor. As important as humor is, Phil also understands how risky intentional humor before audiences can be. He is struck by how forgiving people can be of speakers or singers, yet how unforgiving they are when it comes to humor. Nightclub audiences, for instance, can become mean when a comedian fails to deliver. And failed humor is a terrible introduction to speeches before young people.

Michael Ashburn, whose "backwoods" humor has brought hearty laughs over many decades, finds it easy to be funny. The challenge for him is to be godly and funny. High standards for humor get compromised when one is unprepared; nervousness can produce inappropriate jokes. Humor is the great mixer, according to Ashburn, and he often thinks of its effect in terms of being as "good and pleasant" as the precious oil running down Aaron's beard (Ps. 133:2). When humor makes anyone feel put down, it has strayed off the mark. Humor can either lift up and confirm or tear down a person's sense of dignity and acceptance.

Jack Carpenter is a much loved and respected youth minister. He is one of those to be honored as having spent an entire lifetime serving young people. Literally

27. See the Skit Guys, www.skitguys.com, and on YouTube. Their training sessions provide important tips for acting. For comedy and drama, you might also adapt some of the ideas from Fred Passmore, www.christianskitscripts.com/scriptpage1.htm, or Chris and Sue Chapman's *Top 20 Skits for Youth Ministry* (Loveland, CO: Group, 2006).

thousands have been touched by his personal concern for them, and even more have laughed themselves silly at his outrageous comic performances. Along with his sense of humor, Jack is a deeply spiritual person. His personal journal reveals some precious insights into humor.

> God, we believe, accepts us all, unconditionally, warts and all. Laughter is a pure form of response to God. . . . When I laugh with other people in genuine mirth, I accept them. So in laughing at myself I accept myself. Laughter is opposite to self-satisfaction in pride. For in laughter I accept myself not because I'm some sort of super-person, but precisely because I'm not. There is nothing funny *in* a super-person. There is everything funny *about* a super-person—seeing a person who thinks he or she has reached such a state. In laughing at my own claims to importance, I receive myself in a sort of loving forgiveness . . . an echo of God's forgiveness of me. Selfishness and pride can be found in much conventional contrition; it can scarcely be hidden. In our desperate self-concern, we blame ourselves. But in laughter we sit lightly on ourselves. That is why laughter is a very pure response to God. In this regard I further pictured myself in a yoke with Jesus, "Come to me all you who are weary and over-burdened. . . . Put on my yoke and learn from me" (Matt. 11:29, PME). At one point Jesus looked at me with a smiling, knowing wink. As I continued to reflect on this image, a new picture came to me. Jesus and I had gone from exchanging smiles to grimaces from the exceptionally heavy load, then broke out in hysterical laughter (as when a bunch of guys on a tough and seemingly impossible project look so ridiculous to each other that all break into uncontrolled laughter).[28]

If you are going to communicate with young people, you must be willing to see yourself and your life as somewhat funny. I hope you can imagine yourself, when very discouraged, taking a walk with Jesus. Along the way he might make a point that puts your difficulties in eternal perspective—perhaps in an ironic way that provokes a smile or even a laugh. And as our Lord touches you and winks, smiles, or laughs, he really does seem to be one of us, your special friend.

Laughing at ourselves can either bolster or undermine our self-confidence and effectiveness in ministry. If we are laughing with our Lord, it will be healthy laughter and will help us laugh with others. Our impromptu and improvisational forms of humor are communicated with words, phrases, and gestures. Humor depends on keen observance and quick and intelligent response or repartee—with an instinctual sense of appropriateness. In communicating to young people, jokes (unless they are spontaneous to that situation) almost always fall flat, but quick wit in the natural flow of conversation or teaching is welcomed. Because humor is a staple of the youth culture, any successful

---

28. Private journal of John B. Carpenter, Founder and Director of Youth Forum Maine.

ministry must allow opportunity for laughter—spontaneous and planned, individual and group.

Let us be honest about our continued need to develop comedic skills. The authors of *The Laughing Classroom* offer some important insights based on their study of humor and its application to education.

> Humor is a mysterious phenomenon. Ask most teachers if they have a good sense of humor, and 99 percent will respond affirmatively. Moore Colby wrote, "Men will confess to treason, murder, arson, false teeth or a wig, but how many will own up to a lack of humor?" . . . Steven Allen wrote, "We will accept almost any allegation of our deficiencies—cosmetic, intellectual, virtuous—save one, the charge that we have no sense of humor." To do so would cause great embarrassment . . . which, if discovered, could lead to social ostracism.[29]

Loomans and Kolberg go on to suggest four styles (one mostly positive, two positive and negative, and a fourth mostly negative) to help us identify our own style and then to develop further our use of humor. Offering general encouragement for a more joyful and pleasant style of life and communication, the book is full of specific ideas for teaching and discussion.

A high view of our Lord Jesus Christ and the holy mysteries creates a setting where healthy humor can flourish, where our lives and ministries can be brought into proper perspective. Young people, as we have said, are often longing—sometimes even crying—for adults and the adult church to "lighten up." Youth ministry without humor may thrive under charismatic leadership, but it suffers something in the long run. Young people, who with their peers have seemingly thrived solely on serious Bible study, may unconsciously feel relief in an atmosphere of relaxed college frivolity—and miss the necessary balance between focus and levity. As leaders we use humor to keep proper perspective and balance in our own personal lives, and to help students do so as well.

Is it possible that church and youth ministry have been missing a great apologetic and prophetic tool in this postmodern era? Have the funnier ones of us used humor uncritically just because it seems to work? Have we neglected the challenge of seeing humor as a creative art form that needs as much study and practice as music, preaching, and teaching? Have we missed the theological prophetic dimensions of humor? If humor is a gift from God, an ability that can be misused, neglected, or profitably channeled, then we ought to give it the honor and encouragement it needs. Like any other art, humor is not to be taken for granted; it must be pondered and practiced.

29. Diane Loomans and Karen Kolberg, *The Laughing Classroom: Everyone's Guide to Teaching with Humor and Play* (Tiburon, CA: H. J. Kramer, 1993), 13.

Let us hope there will be more good comedians than greedy comics for young folks who need to laugh. May we not take ourselves too seriously! Let swelling laughter begin with us and spread to the tense fringes of our ministries.

Questions for Reflection and Discussion

1. About what do you currently hear teenagers laughing?
2. How have you seen people hurt by humor? Has any of this been in youth ministry?
3. What is the best use of humor you have seen in youth ministry? What is the poorest? What would you suggest as the best sources for humor these days?
4. What standards do you suggest for humor in youth ministry?
5. How has your sense of humor changed or developed over the course of your life? How do things considered hilarious to you ten or twenty years ago affect you now? What more than anything else makes you really laugh these days?
6. How does, or might, humor help your emotional and spiritual life these days?
7. Have you ever imagined yourself laughing with God or joking with Jesus Christ? What does your response to this question suggest about your sense of humor and your emotional and spiritual life? Could it reveal a weakness in your practical theology?
8. What was most surprising to you in this chapter? What most helpful? With what did you disagree? What questions about, or what suggestions for, this chapter do you have?

PART 4

Practical Theology for Holistic Youth Ministry

—15—

Where Practical Theology
Meets Holistic Ministry

Our Father . . . Thy will be done in earth, as it is in heaven.
MATTHEW 6:9–10 KJV

Even as the Son of man came not to be ministered unto, but to minister,
and to give his life a ransom for many.
MATTHEW 20:28 KJV

Then said Jesus to them again, Peace be unto you: as my Father hath
sent me, even so send I you. . . . He that believeth on me, the works
that I do shall he do also; and greater works than these shall he do.
JOHN 20:21; 14:12 KJV

Christ-Centered Ministry

Although we have throughout this book tried to apply theological ideas to your
life and ministry, it is time now to sum up our implications. Where and how does
practical theology intersect with our ministries? Worship, we have said, must precede our theology; even so our ministries are to be conceived in, and surrounded by,

serious prayer. It takes patience, persistence, and hard work for prayer to become an awesome and powerful mystery rather than a neglected or formal routine.[1]

Take another look at the verses above. The first verse is from our Lord's Prayer; it sums up the way Jesus saw his world and his God-given mission. In this (sometimes too-familiar) prayer Christ passed his style of prayer on to his disciples and the rest of us believers. The next verse above describes the Son of Man, our mandated model. The last verse is Jesus's words to his disciples (and us today): "As my Father hath sent me, even so I send you . . . and greater works than these shall [you] do." This is far more than we can imagine for ourselves. The works signify the power of the Spirit in collaborative ministry. Taking these verses seriously, we feel we are in way over our heads.

Each of us responds to the calling of Jesus and the Father alone, but alone we can accomplish nothing. In the stillness of our hearts we do not pray, "My Father in heaven," but "Our Father." Ministry kills "lone rangers" who attempt to minister out of their own calling and vision.

The incarnation of God the Son in the Middle East is a dividing point in history (BC and AD are being changed to BCE and CE, but the significance remains). Jesus Christ changed the world, and many or most young people, deep in their hearts, would like to change the world too. Youth and youth ministry are meant to be prophetic challenges to church and society. The Scriptures above imply that Jesus Christ continues his incarnation in the church. We as Christians, together as church, provide for the world a "God-with-us" presence of the kingdom. What does this mean and where do we go from here?

The heart of youth ministry is Christ in us. Youth ministry is a critical mission of the church when leaders are possessed by the love of Christ and the great potential of youth following Christ.

Francis Clark was leader of the great Christian Endeavor Movement in the late nineteenth and early twentieth centuries. Young people by the hundreds of thousands came to Christ and a deeper walk with God through Christian Endeavor. The evident power of this movement popularized the idea of church youth groups. Pivotal was Clark's belief: "the life of Christ and His teachings appeal especially to the young: how natural, almost inevitable, it is for a young person to be drawn to Christ and to accept Him as Pattern and Guide when he is winsomely presented."[2]

Jim Rayburn was arguably the most influential figure in modern American youth ministry. He and those he trained have been significant in my life and ministry. Jim's life passion was finding young people who had never really been introduced

---

1. Jim Rayburn, the great founder of Young Life, had, as some have pointed out, certain blind spots, even flaws. And he was a person often racked with pain. Still he prayed, alone and with friends, for hours at a time, sometimes an all-day session with staff, or even all night.
2. Francis E. Clark, *Christ and the Young People* (New York: Revell, 1916), 14.

to the dynamic person named Jesus Christ. Hearing of Jim's death in 1970, Billy Graham sent a telegram to the Rayburn family: "Jim Rayburn was one of the greatest Christians I ever knew. Jim had a profound influence on my life when I was a student at Wheaton and later when I was a pastor and leader of Youth for Christ. It is up to us to carry the torch that he so courageously carried for so many years."[3]

Beginning in 1940, Rayburn's ministry was about only one thing:

> Young Life Campaign is in the business of presenting Jesus Christ to the high school gang. We believe that He is the most fascinating Person in the Universe. We believe He will completely captivate the heart of any young person that knows Him. . . . Jesus Christ is everything that kids want most, if they just knew it. . . . That's not just all that Young Life's all about; that's all that Young Life is all about—Jesus Christ.[4]

In 1983, Jesuit Charles Shelton described adolescent spirituality as "above all Christ-centered."[5] Rick Lawrence published *Jesus-Centered Youth Ministry* in 2007,[6] which compellingly urges us to be Christ-centered in all aspects of our ministry, to "make a bee-line for Jesus" in all that we do. Here is the key to bringing the keenest insights from our experience and the social sciences together with biblical principles. Christ must be our example; our ministry is done only in his name. One key to effectively reaching all kinds of youth is having leaders who passionately believe that young people will always be captivated by a genuine presentation of Jesus Christ from someone they trust. To have a faith that lasts beyond high school years, young people need a deep personal relationship with Christ our Lord and communion with Christ's followers.

Paul, the apostle, left a mark on churches and society, and on the world ever since, because for him living was Christ and dying (in Christ) was gain (see Phil. 1:21). The Christ-centered person also lives a Spirit-filled life; such is a lifelong pursuit and the key to powerful ministry.

---

3. *The Diaries of Jim Rayburn, Founder of Young Life*, selected and edited by Kit Sublett (Colorado: Morningstar, 2008). Quotation found on front page and 115–16.

4. The first three sentences are from the first issue of the *Young Life* magazine (February 1944). This description of Young Life can be found at several websites, such as "Young Life Alumni and Friend eNewsletter," October 2011, www.alumniandfriends.younglife.org/site/c .mjJVJ3MNIwE/b.7778289/k.F6FE/Alumni_and_Friends_eNewsletter__October_2011.htm. The next short sentence is from *Say Gang*, November 1953. The last sentence comes from Jim Rayburn's final talk to Young Life staff, Asilomar, California, January 1970, in Kit Sublett, ed., *The Diaries of Jim Rayburn* (Colorado Springs: Morningstar, 2008), 528.

5. Charles M. Shelton, SJ, *Adolescent Spirituality: Pastoral Ministry for High School and College Youth* (Chicago: Loyola University Press, 1983), 9.

6. Rick Lawrence, *Jesus-Centered Youth Ministry* (Loveland, CO: Group, 2007).

Theologies, Philosophies, and Models of Youth Ministry

This book may or may not be successful in presenting a theology palatable to Eastern Orthodox, Roman Catholic, liberal Protestant, conservative evangelical, Pentecostal, and other Christian leaders. It does attempt to acknowledge commonalities in theological thinking within the one holy catholic and apostolic church, to recognize differences, and to suggest that no one theology is wholly adequate. That is why we speak of *theologies* in the plural.

With theology as our base, we proceed to consider philosophies of youth ministry. This is not a how-to-do-youth-ministry book; rather it suggests critical ways to think about youth ministry. The best doing of ministry includes thinking systemically about our ministry in its various contexts. Our philosophy of youth ministry guides our approach. Youth ministry, for instance, may be more authoritarian or democratic, more leader-centered or student-centered in structure and style. It may focus on youth outside the church or within it.

Over many years Mark Senter has been a thoughtful professional guide in the discipline of youth ministries. Back in 1968, he wrote a chapter called "Youth Programs" in *Youth Education in the Church*,[7] in which he described six philosophies of youth ministries: (1) the Christian Endeavor Model, with sponsors training team captains to develop the program with team members, (2) the Hero Model, based around relationships formed by a hired, talented youth director, (3) the Evangelism Model, in which group members are encouraged to invite their friends to events and gospel meetings, (4) the Involvement Model, with an emphasis on clarifying the spiritual gifts of young people and "involving them in ministry situations," (5) the Discipleship Model, based on Coleman's *The Masterplan of Evangelism* and Navigator-style Bible study, which disciples young people and trains them to "reproduce their lives in the lives of others," and (6) the Relevancy Model, which "encourages youth to wrestle with the issues which confront them and the church in the midst of a watching world."[8]

Decades later Mark Senter edited a book featuring four philosophies in dialogue.[9] The first philosophy of youth ministry is described by a highly-esteemed South African churchman and professor, Malan Nel. The Inclusive Congregational Approach argues that children and youth should not have separate ministries in

7. Roy B. Zuck and Warren Benson, eds., *Youth Education in the Church* (Chicago: Moody, 1978).

8. Ibid, 271–76. In Warren S. Benson and Mark H. Senter III, eds., *The Complete Book of Youth Ministry* (Chicago: Moody, 1987), Senter has modified these philosophic approaches to Community Model, Competition Model, Discipleship Model, Fundamentalist Model, Gift Development Model, Ministry Model, Urban Model, and Youth Group Model.

9. Mark H. Senter III, ed., *Four Views of Youth Ministry: Inclusive Congregational, Preparatory, Missional, Strategic* (Grand Rapids: Zondervan/Youth Specialties, 2001).

the church but be integrated into the church as a whole—that is, into its preaching, worshiping, fellowship, pastoral care, service, and so forth. "It is more about *finding a place* for children and adolescents than about dreaming up new modes of ministry."[10]

Highly regarded Southern Baptist theologian and professor of Christian education and youth ministry, Wesley Black, argues for a Preparatory Approach to youth ministry. This view recognizes special age traits of students calling for specialized ministry. Such a ministry will attract them, at the point of their pushing away from adults and church, and "prepare them to participate in the life of existing churches as leaders, disciples, or evangelists . . . disciples-in-training, with opportunities for service both in the present and the future."[11]

Chap Clark, well-known professor and author, proposes another perspective: the Missional Approach. It recognizes that "there are cultural barriers that separate adolescents from adults . . . adolescents now represent both a definable culture *as well as* a legitimate phase of the life span. . . . Youth ministry as *mission* is defined as the community of faith corporately committed to caring for and reaching out into the adolescent world (of both churched and unchurched young people) in order to meaningfully assimilate them into that fellowship."[12]

Fourth, Mark Senter calls his approach the Strategic Approach to youth ministry. It is a little more difficult to explain briefly. It acknowledges the complexity of a changing youth culture and the discontinuity experienced in typical parachurch and church youth groups as high school students move on. This philosophy sees youth ministries growing into intergenerational churches. Bill Hybels's youth ministry that grew into the famed Willow Creek Community Church, and Wayne Gordon's urban Fellowship of Christian Athletes program that developed into the holistic ministry of Lawnsdale Community Church are cited as examples.[13] This is a church-planting philosophy.

From a theological base, a church or initiative will consider its philosophy and then develop a model. To build a successful model of youth ministry takes time, careful thought, and planning.[14] Such discussions will consider the group's theology (core beliefs), their philosophy (core values and goals), and finally the methodology of their chosen model—that is, the program itself. Clear and explicit core beliefs and core values help produce a mission or purpose statement (who

10. Ibid., 6.
11. Ibid., 40.
12. Ibid., 80.
13. Ibid., 117–24.
14. The cost and investment for successful youth ministries is made very clear in Mark DeVries, *Sustainable Youth Ministry: Why Most Youth Ministry Doesn't Last and What Your Church Can Do about It* (Downers Grove, IL: InterVarsity, 2008).

we are as distinct from all others), then a vision statement (where we want to go in five, ten years), and finally a strategy statement (how we plan to get there). Strategy connects goals or clear outcomes with activities. Outcomes should be measured or evaluated as to how agreed-upon goals, under the umbrella of a purpose statement, are fulfilled.

The challenge of such discussions often calls for consultants to help groups through this process. Mark DeVries, founder of a consulting agency, Youth Ministry Architects, insists that youth ministry is not sustained by flashy leaders but by a sound investment of a church in youth ministry as one of its primary missions. He suggests critically needed "Control Documents": directories of names and vital information (of students, parents, leaders), an annual events calendar, job descriptions (for all paid and volunteer staff), a master recruiting list (for future needs and a pool of volunteers) along with a mission statement, measureable three-year goals, a statement of values, and an organizational chart.[15] By now we see why we have spoken of theology, philosophy, and models in the plural. Each model will be unique because of its different place, situation, constituency, and leadership.

Each item above is important for successful long-term ministry, and yet few youth programs have a written mission or purpose statement and list of annual outcomes or goals. Very few volunteer youth leaders have written job descriptions and, more sadly, even some paid staff may suffer lack of clear written and agreed-upon expectations.

Case Study from an Attack on Modern Youth Ministry

Over the years many criticisms of the youth ministry profession have surfaced, and serious challenges are being raised against youth ministry in the twenty-first century. Back in the 1990s, a theological trend among some in our seminaries attempted to discredit parachurch (or paraparochial) ministries. All youth ministry belonged in local churches, they said. Their critique of organizations doing ministry without ecclesial[16] reference or support was justified, but their theological arguments were weak. They lacked an understanding of biblical or historical missiology. And they didn't observe and evaluate the young people being reached by Kids Across America, Campus Crusade's Student Ventures, Youth for Christ's Campus Life, Youth Guidance, and Young Life in the United States and around the world. These organizations were reaching young people that many fine Christian families and churches weren't even noticing. These critics failed to remember

15. Ibid., 60–64.
16. *Ecclesial* means pertaining to the church; ecclesiology, the study of the church. Our belief: "We believe in one holy catholic and apostolic church" (the Nicene Creed).

Jesus leaving synagogues and the righteous to seek out the lost. They didn't track Frontier Youth Trust or the Oxford Youth Works in Great Britain, The Atlantic Bridge in the Netherlands, Contact Jeunes in Switzerland, Scripture Union in South Africa, or Breakthrough in Hong Kong. In these organizations staff and volunteers were reaching those untouched, and sometimes avoided, by strong churches. Still, the critique of parachurch organizations operating on their own without vital connection to a church or ecclesial denomination is valid. Young Life used to call itself "an arm of the church"; yet an arm detached from a body is bizarre. And ministries striving for efficiency in attracting and extracting superficial commitments to Jesus that are satisfied with nominal discipleship ought to be challenged. Superficiality in outreach ministries and this conflict between churches and faith-based organizations surely brings delight to the enemy.

The second decade of the twenty-first century brought another critique and a movement calling for the total abolition of Sunday school and youth ministries within local churches themselves.[17] Again, their criticisms of superficial youth ministries, shallow preaching, and neglectful families who relinquish spiritual responsibilities toward their children to youth leaders, are not only justified, but critically needed. Too many parents are satisfied to let youth groups supplant their own spiritual responsibilities. Some pastors, too, fail to challenge parental negligence and preach only to please their comfortable congregations. The challenge of the gospel, the cost of discipleship, and full parental responsibility can also be weakened in seeker-friendly churches. It is easy for churches and pastors to overlook the difficult challenge to hold parents accountable for the spiritual growth and welfare of their children and youth in our digital, consumerist age. And many youth ministries have *entertained* more effectively than they have *challenged* and *instructed* young lives. We are faced with enormous fallout from youth ministry alumni who forsake their faith and church in their late teens and twenties.[18]

Scott T. Brown, spokesperson for this call to abolish youth ministry, and a leader of the National Center for Family-Integrated Churches, issues this stinging critique of weak youth ministries and calls for drastic action:

> Almost everyone involved in youth ministry agrees that something is wrong. . . . The public collapse of modern youth ministry is reaching such legendary proportions that people involved in various functions of church life want to talk about how to repair it.[19]

17. *Divided*, a film by the Leclerc brothers (2011), www.dividedthemovie.com.

18. Christian Smith, *Lost in Transition: The Dark Side of Emerging Adulthood* (New York: Oxford University Press, 2011); and David Kinnaman, *You Lost Me: Why Young Christians Are Leaving Church* (Grand Rapids: Baker Books, 2011).

19. Scott T. Brown, *A Weed in the Church: How a Culture of Age Segregation Is Harming the Young Generation, Fragmenting the Family, and Dividing the Church* (Wake Forest, NC: National Center for Family-Integrated Churches, 2010), 33.

The thesis of this book is that the modern church has been overrun by an aggressively reproducing, non-native species that excludes or injures the desired crop. That weed is systematic, age-segregated ministry, and it has a profound impact on what God desires. . . . Bring the children into the worship service; eliminate youth programs, cancel Sunday school, children's church, and the nursery.[20]

We should, I believe, be chastened and humble enough to consider this rebuke— for reasons already admitted. As a professor of youth ministries for almost forty years, I decided to watch the movie *Divided* and read *A Weed in the Church* with an open mind and heart—even if it meant revoking my calling and professional career. I hope I did that honestly. We prayerfully watched the movie in one of my classes, broke up into small groups to discuss it, and came back to share our responses. Although we had a range of opinions, here is a general consensus from a group of US and international students along with my own judgment. Besides the following rebuttal, this whole chapter presents a solid case for a renewed youth and family ministry.

The film *Divided* creates, as has been noted by many, a straw man of youth ministry's greatest weaknesses and failures. There is no acknowledgment of youth ministry's effective ministries. Over the decades, a good percentage of seminarians have told me they are Christians and in seminary because of youth ministries. It is my experience that most believers have made their faith commitment, first of all, as children in their homes, and, second, as adolescents through some form of youth ministry. The film and book correctly view weaknesses of youth ministry that stem from churches and families who want a youth leader to take over their responsibility, to entertain and instruct their children. It will take time before we are able to compare the vitality and spirituality of exclusively family-integrated churches (FIC) with those churches that mix special-age ministries and age integration (most churches gather together at some time). Only after decades and generations will we be able to observe how this new movement will mature and probably suffer the dysfunction of all human organizations.

FIC's main argument against youth ministry and Sunday school is that these are modern inventions not found in the Bible. Brown's own journey away from youth ministry and age-segregated ministries "was fueled by a return to a cardinal tenet of the Protestant faith, *sola scriptura*, which argues that God's Word alone is sufficient for faith and practice. Such an interpretation of *sola scriptura* makes the Bible the exclusive foundation for all that we do."[21] Brown's interpretation of *sola scriptura* contrasts modern youth ministry with their model of "biblical youth ministry."[22]

20. Ibid., 19, 260.
21. Brown, *A Weed in the Church*, 28.
22. Ibid., 23, 50, 82–83, 169.

The idea and term *sola scriptura* was used in the Reformation to regain what the Reformers saw as a loss of biblical authority and to deal with the extravagances of church tradition (particularly in the matter of indulgences). It was meant to establish scriptural primacy and the notion of salvation by faith through grace. Its meaning and nuances were contested from the beginning. Ulrich Zwingli (considered to be more radical than Luther and Calvin) was yet challenged by Conrad Grebel for allowing unbiblical practices of infant baptism and links between church and magistrates. The Protestant Reformation had no intention of using *sola scriptura* to prevent the writing of a Heidelberg or Westminster Catechism, or a theological tome such as Calvin's *Institutes of the Christian Religion*. The Bible does not explain the doctrine of the Trinity or even tell us what books should be in the New Testament, or how the New Testament canon should be declared. All in all, the biblical/theological argument against youth ministries is weaker than an argument from silence.

There is reason to belabor our response to those calling for the demise of church nurseries, Sunday school classes, youth groups, and teenage mission trips. Observing the movie *Divided*, and reading its online promotion and *A Weed in the Church*, leads one to assume that the theological base of this movement, rather than being historically christocentric and emphasizing the incarnation and blessed Trinity, highlights instead the Bible, the family, and the church—in that order. Besides tending toward bibliolatry, overemphasis on *sola scriptura* can diminish the person and work of Christ and the power of the Holy Spirit. Only two short sections of *A Weed in the Church* deal with the person of Jesus Christ. Rather than the written Word deferring to the living Word, the reverse seems to be the case.

Further argument stresses how Christ did not segregate youth or hold special meetings for them.[23] Not mentioned is the fact that Jesus was dealing with traditional society before adolescence emerged, or that Jesus called at least one father (Peter) away from his family, or, more problematic for this position, the fact that Jesus gives more cautions regarding family ties than encouragement for family life.[24] We have no references to his telling someone to go home and be a good father—although we assume his full acceptance of Old Testament precepts for parental responsibility. Of course we are not using such texts to advocate sacrificing one's family for ministry, but we are showing the weakness of selective exegesis and dogmatic argumentation.

Every church, I think, benefits from a specialist in adolescence and the rapidly changing youth (and pop) culture. Such leaders have opportunity to listen as young people, apart from their parents, express real feelings and doubts that they do

23. Ibid., 164.
24. See Matt. 12:46–50; 19:29.

not share at home. Youth "experts" in a church study the benefits and dangers of technology, digital life, advertising, and music more deeply than the average pastor or parent. They can provide family workshops such as: "Learning to Discern Right from Wrong (and In-between) in Today's Culture."

Finally, in considering the FIC movement, we worry about individualistic separatism—a negative view of culture, the gospel, Christian life, and church in a cocoon separated from the world and other churches. Can such tendencies create a vibrant missiology? Having been pushed by widespread attention to consider the challenge of exclusive biblical youth ministry and family-integrated churches, we offer this response as a case study in practical theology. Isn't it possible to sit down together, admit our weaknesses, and learn from one another?

Malan Nel's Inclusive Congregational Approach[25] to youth ministry shares the same basic philosophy but is less dogmatic and attacking—in person he is gracious and open to dialogue. His writing is also deeper and broader theologically. In the midst of theological and philosophical differences and arguments regarding models, we can remain committed to dialogue and benefit from differing points of view.

Timothy Paul Jones edited a very helpful volume discussing three views of family ministries.[26] All three models of family ministry are distinguished from age-segregated, or what they call programmatic, traditional youth ministry. Further distinguished are the three views: Family-Integrated Ministry: Family Driven Faith (Paul Renfro), Family-Based Ministry: Separated Contexts, Shared Focus (Brandon Shields), and Family-Equipping Ministry: Church and Home as Co-Champions (Jay Strother).

The youth ministry profession generally acknowledges that long-lasting Christian commitment is best established with parents and youth specialists together helping young people make their way into a world of broader friendships and new families.

A position many of us share is that the local church or parish ministry and the youth ministry are the warp and woof of the universal church. Cloth is made by warp and woof, horizontal and vertical threads being woven together. Youth ministry, whether within the church looking out, or from outside the church moving in, is part of the mission of the church. It is important that we not neglect training those who seek to minister to the lost.[27] Sam Shoemaker felt the perspective from outside looking in with his powerful "I Stand at the Door":

25. See Malan Nel's chapter and responses in Senter, ed., *Four Views of Youth Ministry*.

26. Timothy Paul Jones, ed., *Perspectives on Family Ministries: Three Views* (Nashville: B&H Academic, 2009).

27. We enjoy the stories of Jesus—the lost sheep, lost coin, lost son—but inadequately accept the priority of his challenge. Note also the phrase used by Paul and so loved by Jim Rayburn: "Walk in wisdom toward them that are without" (Col. 4:5 KJV).

> I stand by the door. I neither go too far in, nor stay too far out.
> The door is the most important door in the world—
> It is the door through which folks walk when they find God.
> There is no use my going way inside and staying there,
> When so many are still outside and they as much as I,
> Crave to know where the door is.
> And all that so many ever find is only a wall where the door ought to be.
> They creep along the wall like blind men, with outstretched, groping hands,
> Feeling for a door, knowing there must be a door,
> Yet they never find it. So, I stand by the door.
> Go in great saints; go all the way in—
> It is a vast, roomy house, the house where God is.
> Folks die outside the door, as starving beggars die
> On cold nights in cruel cities in the dead of winter
> Die for want of what is within their grasp.
> They live on the other side of it—live there because they have not found it.
> Nothing else matters compared to helping them find it,
> And open it, and walk in, and find Him. So, I stand by the door.[28]

Some are called to evangelize those farthest out or least interested, and these should be commended for their work. Others are called to disciple those who might otherwise be complacent Christians, and they too are heroes in the cause of Christ.

Practical Theology That Is Broad, Honest, and Inclusive

This text strives for a generous[29] and modest[30] orthodoxy among many theologies (Eastern Orthodox, Roman Catholic, Protestant, Pentecostal, and independent). Similarly, it embraces many philosophies and different models of youth ministry. As such it should even include churches advocating the elimination of youth groups and Sunday school—hoping they can tolerate our inclusions of all orthodox theologies and philosophies of ministry. Our Lord Jesus Christ's high priestly prayer in John 17 prays for unity among all his followers. When John asked condemnation

---

28. You will be blessed by finding and reading the Rev. Sam Shoemaker's "I Stand at the Door, An Apology for My Life." Mine is an abbreviated selection with different variations of the whole poem in the public domain, www.thejaywalker.com/pages/shoemaker.html.

29. "Generous orthodoxy" is not meant to steal or endorse Brian McLaren's use of the term but to use the adjective in its generally accepted sense—generous without losing one's own or a church's theological identity.

30. Many might be surprised that Karl Barth described his theology this way: "Evangelical theology is *modest* theology, because it is determined to be so by its object, that is, by him who is its object." *Evangelical Theology: An Introduction* (Grand Rapids: Eerdmans, 1963), 7.

and exclusion of one outside their circle, Christ responded, "Do not stop him; for whoever is not against you is for you" (Luke 9:49–50).

Paul, first theologian of the Christian church, was disturbed by those undermining his ministry in the church of Philippi and yet he observed, "Some proclaim Christ from envy and rivalry . . . out of selfish ambition, not sincerely. . . . What does it matter? Just this, that Christ is proclaimed in every way, whether out of false motive or true; and in that I rejoice" (Phil. 1:15, 17a, 18).

Such examples encourage us to be humble and gracious in the way we respond to the theologies of other Christian churches. Throughout history many have created divisions in the "one holy catholic and apostolic church," questioning the motives and doctrinal emphases of rival factions. So we remember the spirit of our Lord Jesus Christ and the model set by the apostle Paul. The unity of the first church was judged by affirmation of its earliest creed: "Christ is Lord." Beyond that we accept those who, by our standards, err in secondary motives and beliefs: Paul's "What does it matter?" rings in our minds.

To the Corinthian church on the brink of fragmentation, Paul pleaded, "I appeal to you, brothers and sisters, by the name of our Lord Jesus Christ, that . . . there should be no divisions among you, but that you should be united. . . . Has Christ been divided?" (1 Cor. 1:10, 13a). We might also be reminded that, in the midst of all kinds of error, God never suggests starting a new Israel; nor do the apostles call for a separation of any New Testament church—even those that are heretical and dead.[31] Truth, of course, has boundaries. Denying the divinely ordained all-sufficient sacrifice and lordship of Christ, as revealed in authoritative Holy Scripture, or promoting ungodly immorality in the body of Christ, were issues demanding Paul's condemnation and exclusion. We strive to follow this paradox of truthful fidelity to the unity of the church and necessary condemnation of those who spoil its holy witness.

Holistic Youth Ministry to Change the World

Holistic youth ministry flows out of holistic practical theology. Truncated theology creates superficial ministry and one-dimensional disciples. Holistic theology and ministry entail an understanding of context. Jesus Christ has come into the world to save sinners and the systems that influence them negatively. As sinners we interact dynamically with our sinful systemic environment. There are critical cleavages in Christendom between those who seek redemption of individual sinners or families

---

31. Notice the immorality in the Corinthian church, and Christ's words to the heretical church of Thyatira and his description of the church at Sardis as "dead" (Rev. 2:18–3:6) yet without any hint of separation or starting a new church—only "repent" and "hold fast."

and those who would redeem our systemic environment. Both emphases of the gospel are scriptural and necessary.

According to the best research,[32] those who care about emerging generations (high school teenagers, thirteen to eighteen years old, and college age, eighteen to twenty-four years old) face two huge problems. First, high school students are quite ready to acquiesce to a watered-down version of the Christian faith. Such a superficial faith tends not to last through the college-age years, and the loss of faith makes them vulnerable to the subtle and pernicious lies of our culture. Second, many of the world's youth in developing countries and urban cores in and around large cities are being left in social vacuums, which systematically push them toward antisocial behavior, violence and incarceration, or even terrorism.

Holistic ministry challenges us to face all the needs of individual youth—and also the needs of their culture. Ministry always has a context. How are we to engage not only individuals but also the world and those systems by which they are being shaped and to which, at the same time, they contribute? To what extent are we to proclaim—does our gospel proclaim—the coming of the kingdom? Are we honestly praying and working for God's will to be done on earth? How much difference are we meant to make as salt and light? Is the Holy Spirit meant to save souls *and* change the world through us?

Many have undertaken to answer these questions.[33] James Davison Hunter cautions against possible romanticism and naivete about changing the world. But his wisdom does not abrogate instruction for Christians to make a difference in the world. Hunter draws on the often-quoted prophetic advice to the Hebrew exiles in Babylon found in Jeremiah 29.[34]

> Thus says the LORD of hosts, the God of Israel, to all the exiles whom I have sent into exile from Jerusalem to Babylon: Build houses and live in them; plant gardens and eat their produce.
>
> Take wives and have sons and daughters; take wives for your sons, and give your daughters in marriage, that they may bear sons and daughters; multiply there and do not decrease. But seek the welfare of the city where I have sent you into exile, and pray to the LORD on its behalf, for in its welfare you will find your welfare. (Jer. 29:4–7)

32. Christian Smith with Melinda Lundquist Denton, *Soul Searching: The Religious and Spiritual Lives of American Teenagers* (New York: Oxford University Press, 2005); Smith, *Lost in Transition*; and Kinnaman, *You Lost Me*.

33. Carl F. H. Henry, *The Uneasy Conscience of Modern Fundamentalism* (Grand Rapids: Eerdmans, 1947); Brian D. McLaren, *Everything Must Change: Jesus, Global Crises, and a Revolution of Hope* (Nashville: Thomas Nelson, 2007); Tom Sine, *The New Conspirators: Creating the Future One Mustard Seed at a Time* (Downers Grove, IL: InterVarsity, 2008); Andre Crouch, *Culture Making: Recovering Our Creative Calling* (Downers Grove, IL: InterVarsity, 2008).

34. James Davison Hunter, *To Change the World: The Irony, Tragedy, and Possibility of Christianity in the Late Modern World* (New York: Oxford University Press, 2010), 276–79.

Finding flaws in many Christian world-changing theories, Hunter concludes:

> As to a strategy for engaging the world, perhaps there is no single model for all
> times and places. . . . In opposition to the "defensive against," "relevance to," and
> "purity from" paradigms, . . . I have suggested a model of engagement called "faith-
> ful presence." . . .
>   A premise of this view is a recognition that Christians share a world with others
> and that they must contribute to its overall flourishing. . . . *In short, commitment
> to the new city commons is a commitment of the company of faith to the highest
> ideals and practices of human flourishing in a pluralistic world.*[35]

Youth ministry texts, especially from the evangelical side, have not put enough
emphasis on training students to take the proper Christian influence into their
culture—not just to survive or be a witness, but to affect changes, small as they
may be. To the extent that Jesus of Nazareth produced a gradual, social revolution
in world history, Christ calls us to be perpetual revolutionaries for the kingdom—
realistic and patient with small, often delayed effects.

If 20, or even 10, percent of a nation's youth took a strong stand for justice
(righteousness) in the biblical sense, if they began communicating, voting, and
buying in terms of Christ's kingdom values, there would be some viral effect; and
marketers, who reflect and help shape youth culture, would have to take notice.[36]
Youth are dynamic prophets for church and society. Holistic and relevant youth
ministry faces two challenging implications: understanding its cultural and systemic context and using tools adequate to affect change.

The Systemic Context of Holistic Youth Ministry

Each young person is a marvelous, unique creation. A special combination of
chromosomes and genes has produced in each one of us something never before,
and never hereafter, duplicated. Consider the incredible odds, naturally speaking,
that we even exist—our parents might never have met, or our grandparents . . . and
so forth back to the beginning. And besides, we might have been a miscarriage or
abortion. In addition to our genetic makeup, each person has experienced quite different situations growing up—even siblings in the same family. As leaders, whether
we are considering a group of thirteen, twenty, fifty, or hundreds of young people,
it's a lot to get our minds around. How are we to understand the unique dynamics surrounding each of our students and the dynamic that makes up the whole?

35. Ibid., 276, 279, emphasis original.
36. We might take note of youth in the Arab Spring and the Occupy Movement of 2011
and beyond.

Over several decades family ecology has emerged as an academic discipline. Urie Bronfenbrenner[37] helped me to see how I needed to understand any given youth as part of a family system. It wasn't enough to recognize his or her parents and family. Bronfenbrenner's perspective is developed in masterful form by James Garbarino in a book well worth studying.[38] Many laud the work of Edwin H. Friedman as he describes three families: the family of the minister, the family of individuals he or she serves, and the family of the church. All such families, according to Friedman, operate on the same system principles, and dysfunction in the system is more important to tend than the symptoms of any individual. Some brief minutes on the internet can show you the importance of ecological systems thinking.[39]

A family is a system in itself. But it is also a system interacting with outside systems: its natural environment, its social or neighborhood environment, and larger economic and political systems. In brief, family ecology studies the family as it relates to its environments, understood according to systems thinking. Environments in which families grow and function include their natural and geographical environment, their economic and political situation, their schools and churches, and their particular neighborhoods, as well as their proximity to relatives and extended family. Youth ministry is aware of this as it observes and interacts with the relative functionality or dysfunction of each family. When we approach young people in ministry, we are also approaching families and neighborhoods, schools and churches. Our relational style, activities, gospel, and instruction need to be relevant to youth themselves, along with their families, community, and society at large. By the power of the Holy Spirit, largely unseen, we are affecting change in individuals and their surrounding systems.

Living System Ministry in a Technological Age

This section title is also the subtitle of a book, *The Cat and the Toaster*.[40] It is written by friends of mine whom I call "urban saints." They have given themselves to Boston's South End—and missions around the world—for more than fifty

37. Urie Bronfenbrenner, *The Ecology of Human Development* (Cambridge, MA: Harvard University Press, 1979); and Urie Bronfenbrenner, ed., *Making Human Beings Human: Bioecological Perspectives on Human Development* (Thousand Oaks, CA: Sage, 2004).

38. James Garbarino, *Children and Families in the Social Environment*, 2nd ed. (New Brunswick, NJ: Aldine Transaction, 2009).

39. See Michigan State University College of Social Science, "Human Development and Family Studies," socialscience.msu.edu/degree/Family.html; or "Human Ecology Theory," www.public.iastate.edu/~hd_fs.511/lecture/Sourcebook17.ppt.

40. Douglas A. Hall with Judy Hall and Steve Daman, *The Cat and the Toaster: Living System Ministry in a Technological Age* (Eugene, OR: Wipf & Stock, 2010).

years. Immersing themselves in various ethnic cultures, they saw the importance of relational ministry with face-to-face contacts. Ministry must be carried out in primary cultures before it can affect secondary cultures (where face-to-face relationships become lost or are secondary). And these systems—family, neighborhood, churches, and on up—are living, organic systems that cannot be changed by mechanical technique. You can take a toaster apart and put it back together, but you cannot do the same with a cat!

> The church is the Body of Christ, a living system. Neighborhoods, cities, cultures, too are complex and interrelated living social systems. Why, then, would we try to do God's work in a church or social system using tools and methods designed for non-living systems? We do it because our culture is very organizationally—and technologically—centered. We have grown accustomed to thinking of our social contexts not as living systems, but as things we can easily measure and control.
>
> Embracing both perspective and procedure, Living System Ministry is about doing better ministry by seeing a better picture of what exists in the total system. Like farmers, rather than technicians, we learn to be involved in and to be "in tune with" what causes fruitfulness. We never cause fruit to happen. God does! But as our works becomes better aligned with what God is already doing in his complex, living system environment, there is an explosion of life.[41]

Holistic ministry, then, is genuinely contextual. It sees itself as part of God's mandated and human-partnered cultural systems. Each individual person (an endosystem[42]) lives in dynamic relationship to and in tension with surrounding (micro-, meso- and macro-) systems. We cannot relate to people except in relationship to their familial, communal, educational, social, and religious systems. As bearers of good news to individuals and systems affected by human rebellion, we come to understand how God's will and kingdom seek effectiveness within systems. Redemption always strives for healing of the dysfunction so that God's righteousness or justice can bring well-being and peace. A fragmented gospel and compartmentalized salvation cannot bring true peace; it cannot pray "Thy kingdom come, Thy will be done within and around us all." Theology and ministry that are not holistic can hardly sing: "Glory to God in the highest heaven and on earth peace among those whom He favors."

41. Ibid., back cover.
42. I use this term (see chapter 6) to refer to each unique individual as a system within outer systems but also as a system of subsystems with her or himself. We are beautifully complex!

Questions for Reflection and Discussion

1. Can you remember when your practical theology was less holistic than it is today? How do you describe practical theology that is holistic?

2. From your own experience and that of others, can you remember ministry that is hardly holistic? What were some of its strengths and weaknesses? How could you see it being improved?

3. Does the cat and the toaster metaphor keep you from thinking too mechanically and analytically about persons and organizations? How so?

4. What is your position on Sunday school and youth groups and family-integrated ministries? Do you agree that bringing families into youth ministry and youth ministry into a family-integrated church is a process that will take careful time?

5. How do you define Christ-centered and Spirit-filled ministry? What differences might we notice between programs that are more or less so activated?

6. What is the main thing you take from this chapter? What is your most pressing remaining question?

—16—

The High Calling
of Ministry with Youth

Remember your creator in the days of your youth, before the days of
trouble come, and the years draw near when you will say, "I have no
pleasure in them."

Ecclesiastes 12:1

We were gentle among you, like a nurse tenderly caring for her own
children. So deeply do we care for you. . . . We dealt with each one of
you like a father with his children, urging and encouraging you and
pleading that you should lead a life worthy of God, who calls you into
his own kingdom and glory.

1 Thessalonians 2:7b–8, 11–12

Introduction to the Calling

Ezekiel 22:30 has always impressed me as one of the saddest verses in Scripture:
"And I sought for anyone among them who would repair the wall and stand in the
breach before me on behalf of the land, so that I would not destroy it; but I found
no one." Note the emphasis on the land, our community and environment, as
well as the striking importance of an individual. God's heart is set on individuals
(like Abraham, Joseph, Rahab, Deborah, and Ruth), but our Lord also wants this

earth and its cultures to work right. We begin this final chapter of *Foundations for Youth Ministry* with hearts toward each individual young person.

Hopefully Sam Shoemaker's apology still rings in your mind. It concludes: "I shall take my old accustomed place, near enough to God to hear Him . . . but not so far from people as not to hear them. . . . Where? Outside the door—Thousands of them. Millions of them. But—more important to me—One of them, two of them, ten of them."[1] And hopefully we all remember Jesus's emphasis on outsiders—lost sheep, lost coins, lost sons.[2]

Without doubt, God has you on earth to make a difference in some person's life—maybe two or ten of them. In turn, God has plans, a purpose, for each of those you influence toward Christ and God's kingdom. This is what makes God's complaint at the top of this chapter so dramatic. Imagine the Creator of a vast universe, surrounded by cherubim, seraphim, hosts of angels, and multitudes of faithful departed, being frustrated by the lack of one human to step in the gap and hold out against the enemies of God's kingdom!

We are calling adolescents, who are in the exciting process of determining their identities, vocations, and their purpose on earth, to the only fully satisfying human endeavor. It is a call to lose their worldly, digital, consumptive lives for a higher calling. Such a seemingly ridiculous challenge calls for incredible faith in God's promises to every young heart: "You will seek Me and find Me, when you search for Me with all your heart" (Jer. 29:13 NKJV). And, "Delight yourself also in the LORD, and He shall give you the desires of your heart" (Ps. 37:4 NKJV).

You are indeed called to what might be considered the church's most neglected mission. They are the church's closest and most critical unreached *people group*.[3] We are talking, of course, about teenagers and those in their early twenties who have left, or were never involved with, churches they see as boring and discouraging, youth who are anxious to explore all life has to offer, eager to get their share of life's resources, and hoping to give back and serve in some realistic and fulfilling way. And besides those outside, many young people within our churches are willing to be entertained with their friends, accept some teaching and responsibility but without internalizing a full measure of the faith. Either scene, inside or outside the walls of a church, confronts us with an awesome challenge, a goal often discouraging to youth workers.

1. Sam Shoemaker, "I Stand at the Door, An Apology for My Life," in the public domain: www.thejaywalker.com/pages/shoemaker.html.
2. See Matt. 9:13; Mark 2:17; Luke 5:32; and Luke 15.
3. I am using a term missionaries ordinarily use for those whose cultures have not been penetrated by the gospel, for those in a different kind of cultural isolation, a digital, consumerist, postmodern, post-Christian culture and mind-set in which church and the gospel so familiar and accessible to most of us, is literally strange and foreign territory.

Can we have it any other way, and would we want it to be? God seems to be asking us to help prepare young people, in the context of their families, their church, and other interrelated systems, not only for life, but for a cosmic drama—a culmination of the struggle between God's kingdom and that of the enemy. The epic struggles between good and evil that young people devour in novels, video games, and films are all trifling before the most dramatic conflict of all. It takes a lot for a young person, or any of us, caught up in the everyday struggles of life, to comprehend "the kingdom and the power and the glory" that is God's—and to which our Lord calls us. Once personally introduced to the marvelous (human and divine) person of Jesus Christ, and given a picture of the good news of this kingdom (the dramatic biblical story), young hearts are bound to be thrilled, gladly accepting or sadly rejecting,[4] the high calling from their Creator.

Many young people have given up on a Jesus without any here-and-now kingdom. The Jesus they heard about in Sunday school and youth group was either all-personal (lacking the social) or all-social (lacking personal acceptance and relationship). It seems crucial these days to keep the personal and the social of the gospel together. That's what missionary/evangelist E. Stanley Jones was so passionate about throughout his life and toward its end in writing *The Unshakable Kingdom and the Unchanging Person*.

> If Jesus made the kingdom of God the center of his message and the center of his endeavor, the greatest need . . . as I see it, is to rediscover the kingdom of God. [The] cleavage between the individual and the social emphases fade out if we start at the place Jesus started—the Kingdom. For conversion for the individual and for society is a minimum necessity for both—for all.[5]

Call to the Hard Way

There are two kinds of high school football players and teams: those merely going through the motions and those who have caught a vision of high challenge and harder work than they've ever done before—or thought possible. This may be the difference between winning and losing, but there's a larger lesson here. There are two kinds of students and teachers as well: those who for many reasons are going through the motions, doing enough to get by, and those who strive for something greater.

4. See the story of the rich young ruler in Luke 18:23.
5. E. Stanley Jones, *The Unshakable Kingdom and the Unchanging Person* (Bellingham, WA: McNett Press, 1995), 11, 300.

Two brothers, Alex and Brett, have started a website and webzine, and have written a book about high challenge and hard work: *Do Hard Things: A Teenage Rebellion against Low Expectations*.[6] Schools among disadvantaged children like the KIPP Schools,[7] Geoffrey Canada's Harlem Gems and Promise Academy,[8] and others have adopted this principle: we want teachers ready to demand excellence and students ready for hard, disciplined work. Results are impressive.[9] In fact, every high school (especially thinking of low budget inner-city schools) has heroic teachers, spending their own money on basic classroom supplies and working long hours in remedial tutoring—while other teachers accept chaos and poor work as part of the territory.

In this, as in other ways, youth ministers can, if our eyes are open to what's going on in the culture, learn from the world, from the spirit and techniques being used out there. We can accept the way it's always been done, the status quo, or push passionately toward excellence. And if we are passionately challenging young people with a high vision, many of them will respond passionately. With such spirit and intention, let's consider some of the methods and resources available.

Character Training

Determination to give it all you've got, work hard, and work with integrity for the common good, is a character issue. The highest leaders globally, in politics, finance, business, and even education have shown us some sorry examples. Consequently, business and law schools are instituting new ethics courses in hopes of a higher moral standard.

Primary and secondary schools are offering "Character Education" to prevent bullying and other reckless behaviors. Such curricula deal with moral principles and decision making. Virtues such as honesty, fairness and justice, respect, courage, perseverance, and responsibility are emphasized. You can find verses from Scripture to back up each of these virtues and, perhaps more important, biblical stories and stories of Christian heroes from the past.

Paul Tough spent serious and thoughtful time observing Geoffrey Canada's Harlem Children's Zone. From what he observed he thought it important to scour the country finding out what makes a difference in children's success or failure in education and life. What he found from clinics, educators, and other experts were

6. Alex and Brett Harris, *Do Hard Things: A Teenage Rebellion against Low Expectations* (Colorado Springs: Multnomah, 2008), webzine: *Boundless*, www.therebelution.com.
7. KIPP Schools, kipp.org.
8. Harlem Children's Zone, hcz.org.
9. My goal is not to get into an argument about charter schools.

new conclusions, held by remarkably diverse practitioners and researchers—but hidden from the public at large. The two most important features for children were nurturing attendance from parents and training in overcoming stress through building character. Qualities of character include grit, self-control, perseverance, curiosity, conscientiousness. Character, built from early attachment to parents, Tough found, trumps IQ in predicting academic and especially life success.[10]

New brain studies[11] show that willpower and self-control can be learned and practiced as keys to future success. Such studies have produced numerous resources on the development of self-control and willpower, books and programs for the very young through adolescence. Roy Baumeister's and John Tierney's *Willpower: Rediscovering the Greatest Human Strength*[12] and Kelly McGonigal's *The Willpower Instinct: How Self-Control Works, Why It Matters, and What You Can Do To Get More*[13] are important resources for parents and youth workers.

Interestingly, a rather full article on "character education" in Wikipedia lists some functional and ideological problems with character education, charging it with "an assumption that 'character' is often deficient in some or all children, lack of agreement on what constitutes effectiveness, lack of evidence that it does what it claims, a conflict between what good character is and the way character education proposes to teach it, programs instituted toward ideological and/or religious ends, the pervasive problem of confusing morality with social conformity, few if any common goals among character education programs," and more.[14] Considering these charges carefully, one may see the confusion of contemporary secular society and its need for input and encouragement from people of faith. We can integrate the principles of character education into youth programs and catechesis, furnishing its principles with theistic assumptions and the insights of practical theology. We know that sound character is the will and instruction of God, is modeled by the Son of Man, and is a fruit of the Spirit. The cautions, however, remind us that our considerations in this chapter must be taken in context with

10. Paul Tough, *How Children Succeed: Grit, Curiosity, and the Hidden Power of Character* (Boston, MA: Houghton, Mifflin and Harcourt, 2012).

11. See Deborah Kotz, "Goal-Oriented: Research Indicates That Willpower Can Be Strengthened Like a Muscle—and Is a Key Predictor of Success in Life," *Boston Globe*, November 7, 2011, G12–13. See also the study by Brandon J. Schmeichel, Kathleen D. Vohs, and S. Christina Duke, "Self-Control at High and Low Levels of Mental Construal," *Social Psychological and Personality Science*, October 5, 2010, www.spp.sagepub.com/content/2/2/182.short.

12. Roy F. Baumeister and John Tierney, *Willpower: Rediscovering the Greatest Human Strength* (New York: Penguin, 2011).

13. Kelly McGonigal, *The Willpower Instinct: How Self-Control Works, Why It Matters, and What You Can Do To Get More* (New York: Avery, 2011).

14. "Character education," *Wikipedia*, wikipedia.org/wiki/Character_education.

the whole, moving toward holistic ministry. Too often youth ministry has taken up the latest fad, producing piecemeal programs.

An often-missed part of character education is an emphasis on helping young people find their purpose in life. William Damon's study spotlights the failure to encourage youthful discovery of personal purpose as a basis for sound character.[15] A very important study for youth work comes from the YMCA, Dartmouth Medical School, and the Institute for American Values. This secular report concludes that young people are hardwired to connect with an authoritative community and with transcendent moral and spiritual meaning, two often-missing ingredients in contemporary society.[16]

The "Hardwired to Connect" report recommends Search Institute's forty assets. We should all be using this important guide for and measure of youthful growth and the successfulness of our work.

> The Search Institute of Minneapolis has proposed 40 "assets" that contribute to optimal child and youth development. These include external or community assets, such as "family support" and the availability of "youth programs," as well as internal or characterological assets, such as high "achievement motivation" and a "sense of purpose" in life.[17]

Youth ministry's past weakness in creating a sense of life purpose may be measured by an older generation's turning so eagerly to Rick Warren's best seller, *The Purpose Driven Life*.[18] The widespread neglect of strong parental discipline and community influence (along with other social challenges in past times) makes remedial character education important for schools and youth ministry.

Service Learning

The development or strengthening of personal character, if confined to a classroom or youth-ministry vacuum, could become introspective excessiveness or self-serving achievement. Service learning, in addition to character education, is an effective ingredient for a healthy and productive generation. Few children these days help out on the farm, achieve Scouting honors, or clean up a neighborhood.

15. William Damon, *The Path to Purpose: How Young People Find Their Calling in Life* (New York: Free Press, 2009).

16. YMCA of the USA, Dartmouth Medical School, Institute for American Values, A Report to the Nation from the Commission on Children at Risk, "Hardwired to Connect: The New Scientific Case for Authoritative Communities" (New York: Institute for American Values, 2003).

17. Ibid., 35.

18. Rick Warren, *The Purpose Driven Life: What On Earth Am I Here For?* (Grand Rapids: Zondervan, 2004).

If fairness and justice, helping and learning, are aspects of character education, there is a need to put these virtues into practice. Service learning is a type of learning (and teaching) in which students, skilled professors and trainers, and a community with exceptional needs come together. Professors benefit by coming out of their ivory towers and testing their theories of social change in a real community. Students see how others, often materially less fortunate, are living. Bright students and accomplished academics also see how much they have to learn. Beyond prominent needs, they discover amazing strengths and great resources in a given neighborhood. Residents gradually see beyond the boundaries and long-accepted responses to poverty, learning to trust strangers who become their friends. Professors and students learn that help is not always helpful and sometimes not wanted. Systems thinking demands grassroots discussions that empower and offer new ideas for action.[19] The book *Service Learning: A Movement's Pioneers Reflect on Its Origins, Practice, and Future*[20] provides the historical background of service learning as a discipline, clarifies some of the field's controversies, and outlines the main lessons learned.

Susan Cipolle reminds us that service learning is not magic and does not always work well.

> Service-learning at its best: "Life isn't fair, and people don't always get what they deserve. How far are we going to let people fall before we say this is not acceptable."
>
> Service-learning at its worst: "I don't understand. If unemployment is so high on the reservation, how come we are painting their house."

Cipolle's book, *Service-Learning and Social Justice: Engaging Students in Social Change*, offers "the four essential elements of critical consciousness, the three types of critical-consciousness development, and tools you can use to support students as they embark on the journey" of service learning and praxis. The four elements of social consciousness are:

1. developing a deeper awareness of self,
2. developing a deeper awareness and broader perspective of others,
3. developing a deeper awareness and broader perspective of social issues,
4. seeing one's potential to make change.[21]

19. See Douglas A. Hall with Judy Hall and Steve Daman, *The Cat and the Toaster: Living System Ministry in a Technological Age* (Eugene, OK: Wipf & Stock, 2010).

20. Timothy Stanton, Dwight Giles Jr., and Nadine Cruz, *Service Learning: A Movement's Pioneers Reflect on Its Origins, Practice, and Future* (San Francisco: Jossey-Bass, 1999). (See "service learning" in the encyclopedia of centerforyouth.org.)

21. Susan Benigni Cipolle, *Service-Learning and Social Justice: Engaging Students in Social Change* (Lanham, MD: Rowman & Littlefield, 2010), 7.

Middle-class suburbanites are seen here as moving through three developing stages. First, beginning with *charity* there comes a sense of wanting to help—an emerging consciousness on the part of the more advantaged. The dangers of being stuck in this stage have been mentioned and are evident. But through relationships with the poor can come a more mature compassion—a desire, not just to help or provide, but to work together for a common end and better society. The combination of relationships, study, and service leads to a third stage of understanding and commitment to social justice.[22]

Hopefully these principles from a secular author fit with your understanding of the gospel. I believe they ring true to the messages of Amos, Isaiah, and Luke. If they are not compatible with your philosophy of youth ministry, I urge further study of the biblical prophets and the words of Jesus, and more conversations and relationships across the denominational and economic borders of our faith. If you agree with this but can't see it fitting into your church or organization's particular model of ministry, I would ask you to consider a gradual process of discussion and change.[23]

Experiential Learning in Wilderness and Multicultural Experiences

Along with character education and service learning, holistic ministry benefits from wilderness and multicultural experiences. Experiential learning is a tool facilitating group and personal growth. The Bible provides striking examples of those who spent time in the wilderness. Abraham, David, John the Baptist, Jesus Christ, and Paul all had to get away from routine living into the wilderness where they were able to find God and themselves. Too little emphasis has been placed on the fine wilderness programs available. Skillfully run ropes courses and simulations games, trekking through a forest's underbrush, or climbing a mountain can bring a group together. I visit so many Sunday school classes and youth groups and hear about struggles with disconnected young people; they haven't really bonded. Wilderness experiences bring a group together—as do mission trips, and mission trips are often richer when preceded by a time of challenge together in nature.

In brief, experiential learning is learning from life together—from the highs and lows of lived experiences and sometimes-difficult relationships. Skilled facilitators ask for a commitment to "process" (reflect and discuss) what has been going on. What just happened? What did you feel? How did you respond? What

22. Ibid., 13.

23. For a discussion of theologies, philosophies, and models, see Dean Borgman, "Distinguishing Theologies, Philosophies and Models of Youth Ministries," 2004, under the topic "youth ministry" in the encyclopedia at centerforyouth.org.

can we learn from that? And then: How can we take what we've learned to the next challenge? These are the questions of experiential learning. Whether a day has gone poorly because of an accident or a fight, or whether a day has gone well because of a great group success or spiritual blessing, we can ask: "So what?" and "What's next?" I hope you see that these principles can be used with outsiders to the faith, with fired-up young Christians, with those in between, and with mixed groups.

Without multicultural experiences and learning, we can hardly fulfill the Lord's Prayer, the great commandments, and the instructions of the Gospels. The subtle pride of advantaged youth groups and their nagging apathy can be broken by contact and conversation with those unlike themselves. We favored whites can hardly comprehend the pain and unease of our Latino, black, and Asian sisters and brothers in disadvantaged situations. Nor do they understand our frustrations in awkward attempts to break through the walls. There is no way to fulfill the biblical mandates for justice, forgiveness, and reconciliation without confronting our differences and connecting at a deep level. It is time for Christians to reclaim the term and idea of *beloved community*. Such a community will be just as much "theirs" as "ours."

I am of the strong conviction that holistic and Christ-centered ministry committing itself to the above proven practices will see a rising generation with stronger Christian witness, greater voice, and a faith that sticks.

Measuring Outcomes

For too long denominations and Christian youth organizations have shied away from longitudinal research to evaluate the effectiveness of their missions. I believe there are two reasons for this: it can be a costly process, and it may well produce embarrassing results. As to the first hindrance, I would suggest something less than professional that, with expert advice, could nonetheless produce helpful feedback. As to the second, I would rather admit the limitations of our efforts and receive insight as to how we could do better, than to move ahead with a few favorable reports from alumni.

Practitioners at the grassroots level have also been shoddy in honest evaluation. We give ourselves to the youth at hand, mostly *while* they are at hand. With simple exit interviews with graduating seniors and their parents, with yearly follow-up and focus groups, and by sharing the burden among volunteers, we can gather documentation as to where and how young people go when they leave our group. Honest evaluation and discussions about ministries will take us beyond what's mentioned here. What are we really trying to do? What's working, and what is more "grinding it out"? How are people loving themselves, one another, and their Lord? And how are they turning their faith and love into service?

The already mentioned forty developmental assets for adolescents of the Search Institute describe the internal and external strengths young people need to be successful. Considering the assets as goals, we can measure the effectiveness of our ministries. To further our evaluations, a survey of "measurable outcomes" (using Google and Amazon) will show how the fields of public health and education are measuring tangible outcomes (the fulfillment of goals). Attention to such evaluative resources can bring greater accountability and excellence to youth ministry.

Four Basic Questions

The cultural malaise within youth culture has been different for the different generations and subcultures of each age. By now you are familiar with authors who have brought attention to the abandonment and detachment experienced in this generation. The four basic questions[24] propose an anecdotal process for youth leaders, parents, and other adults. Today's culture has busied young people into conditions of stress, and they have very few adults willing and able to intervene. That's why the first question is simple and casual: *What's happening?* Of course, it can be asked with different words and in a variety of ways. It probably won't get much of an answer at first. But if the spirit of personal inquiry persists and trust gradually builds, someone may reply, "Right now, it sucks!" And then the story may come. Or it may be, "I'm afraid my parents are breaking up," "I'm worried about my little brother," or even, "I've been cutting myself lately." Maybe a young student has never had anyone to tell about her academic worries, or, a guy, about his problems with the football coach. I wish adult church members could be challenged this year to talk to one teenager, to ask a similar question to "What's happening?" until something real is shared. So many adult church members have never said more to the church's youth than "Hi"—if that.

Think about two further issues. In how many ways has our culture and its media trivialized a young person's past? And in what ways have they made youthful dreams difficult? In terms of lost ethnic identities and family histories, many young people have told me they consider their past lives boring, of no special significance. Malcolm X and the Black Studies movement of the 1960s were convinced that "a man without a knowledge of his past is like a tree without roots." I see a generation of young people who have, in different ways, been robbed of their

---

24. For further explanation, see Dean Borgman, "Four Basic Questions for Youth Ministry," 2004, under the topic "youth ministry" in the encyclopedia at centerforyouth.org.

roots. I want young people to regain a confident sense of their past. That is why the second question is, *Where are you coming from?* Or, *What about your story?*

Another question recognizes the struggle for a youthful vision. Having robbed youth of their roots, I see a culture stripping young people of their dreams—and offering illusions instead. Illusions are often fortified by a case of beer or smoking pot. Real dreams are costly (ask the biblical Joseph); they call for hard work. So the question is, *Where are you headed?* Or, *What are your future dreams and goals?* I think we are called to be assistant dream weavers; we are encouraging realists.

Moving from past to future made a lot of sense. But, I began to realize that the pain of so many stories was too much for many young people today. This has led to reversing the order of questions two and three, from logical progression out of the past to the future, to sensitive recognition that sharing the past may at first be too threatening. Many find it easier to talk about next year and later on, than about what has happened "to me" in the past. The questions are not meant to be formulaic at any rate; they express an interest in the whole person.

Finally, with present, past, and future in mind, we move to the final question. We do *not*—this is crucial for all of us people-helpers—ask, *How can I help you get there?* Compassion can lead to impulsive messianic offers. Offering ourselves as rescuers, as the main source of forward momentum, ensnares us in the trap of enabler or codependent in whatever has been defeating the person we wish to help.[25] So, although in crisis situation, we may ask, *How can I help you?* our posture and question in youth ministry is better: *How can we (a community) help you help yourself to get there (to the fulfillment of your goals and dreams)?*

The spirit and inner logic of these questions should permeate our relationships with others. We could then care for ourselves, our families, young people, and the volunteers we interview for a place on our leadership team, in the spirit and logic of these questions.

The Ten Stages of Youth Ministry

We need to, from time to time, step back and find new ways of looking at youth ministry, so that with some distance from specific trees we can catch a view of the forest. Mark DeVries's fine text, *Sustainable Youth Ministry*, has already been mentioned. And although many small rural churches and some urban ethnic churches may not find it entirely applicable, there are solid principles in this book

---

25. All people-helpers need to understand codependence. See the works of Melody Beattie, *Codependent No More: How to Stop Controlling Others and Start Caring for Yourself* (New York: Hazelden, 1986); and *Beyond Codependency: And Getting Better All the Time* (New York: Harper & Row, 1989).

on the seriousness of a church's commitment to youth ministry and the basic control documents needed in any program.

My ten stages of youth ministry[26] fit alongside *Sustainable Youth Ministry* (especially its chap. 5, "Building Right") as a planning and evaluating tool for youth ministries. These are not lock-step, mechanical stages but an outline of central building blocks of ministry. A foundation for any ministry must be laid; its contexts, needs, and resources scouted out; and allies sought; and then we enter the world of those we would reach or more relevantly teach. But before we teach, we must spend time together, and out of that some personal problems will come to light and need attention. In appropriate time the center of it all, Jesus Christ, must be introduced and explained, along with the whole biblical narrative and mission of the church. Whether in group or at a camp, some will decide that Jesus Christ is Lord and Savior and will realize their faith needs nurture— which calls for follow-up attention and preparation for the next steps in their lives. Then, at a new level, these followers of Jesus need opportunity to practice kingdom work, the mission of the church. Finally, though this is happening all along, special time must be devoted to reviewing the strategy and management of the whole enterprise and its relationship to a church or a national organization. Youth work is the ministry of the church; it cannot fruitfully stand alone. And it prospers through the prayers of its leaders and the church. Prayer is not given as one of the ten stages; it is a necessity in all steps. These are offered as ten stages of a relevant youth program:

1. Building a support base (senior pastor or regional director, adult council or committee of advisers, and a carefully selected leadership team of volunteers)
2. Research (community research, topical research, evaluative research)
3. Networking and collaboration (Do community research to find other leaders; avoid the "silo" effect of separate churches and organizations doing similar work in separate ways.)
4. Contact work or hanging out (Getting into the world of your students and others to understand their context and culture makes you a different kind of leader, a more authoritative teacher and friend.)
5. Activities (if games they should be for a purpose, study simulation games, trips to broaden perspective, even the beginning of service learning)
6. Counseling (not deep, formal counseling, but crisis counseling and case management; make sure you know something about these and have professional backup in your work with youth)

26. Dean Borgman, "Ten Stages in the Development and Organization of Youth Ministry" 2006, under "youth ministry" in the encyclopedia at centerforyouth.org.

7. Proclaiming/sharing Christ and the good news (holistic gospel and biblical story, emphasizing both individual and corporate aspects of redemption)

8. Nurturing young disciples (The early church emphasized catechesis or discipling, and so should we. Parachurch organizations should be careful to disciple toward church bodies; the continuing spiritual life of youth must be in a faith community.)

9. Service projects and mission trips (This continues activities in step 5; here is an opportunity to develop mature service learning in the name of Christ.)

10. Management of a growing ministry (These stages overlap. But if this is a new program starting from scratch, by now, perhaps a year or two later, you and your advisory council or committee, under the pastor [or bishop or regional director] need to assess the work and see how it can be better managed. If you are a people-centered activist, you may need special help here.)

Note especially that most churches hire a youth pastor with a job description beginning at stage 4, perhaps even stage 6! That simply cannot be holistic youth ministry. It can even suggest they want you to be a "youth sitter," entertaining and instructing their "children." If youth ministry is to be integrated into the life of families and the church community, we must have a fuller vision. If you want to feel and be seen as a professional and function holistically, you and your church (or organization) together must be committed to being a learning and growing organism.

Conclusion

This has not been a how-to book on the nuts and bolts of youth and family ministries. Hopefully you will take the many theoretical frameworks, experiences, and principles offered here and build them on your and your church's or organization's theological foundation, your particular philosophy of ministry, and your chosen model to see individuals, families, and communities transformed.

I am convinced that God wants us to be as wise as possible about ourselves, young people, families, and the cultures around us. God also wants us to understand both the heavenly, spiritual side of the church and its human, institutional realities. Our hazard is pride, subtle or blatant. All our talents, wisdom, growth, and successes, if they are to count for the kingdom, must, as with the apostle Paul's, be counted as rubbish (Phil. 3:7–8). This is paradoxical living. We can't do this alone; it takes the support and accountability of a well-functioning community of faith.

Your interest in youth ministry, your passion for youth, all that you've gained from experience and study, should not be wasted. Pray that God will put you where your faith will be encouraged, your efforts applauded, and your dreams fulfilled. May we, in a field barely acknowledged as a profession, stick together, encouraging and challenging each other in a humble spirit of collaboration.

> May God, the Father, the Son, and the Holy Spirit, give us a spirit of wisdom as we come to know him, so that the eyes of our hearts may be enlightened to know the hope of his calling, the riches of his kingdom, and the immeasurable greatness of his power working in us. (Eph. 1:17–19, author's paraphrase)

Questions for Reflection and Discussion

1. Do you ever stop over a prayer, such as the above, and just ponder or get lost in the meaning of it all?

2. Much of this book has been about culture and God. What from this final chapter most impressed you? Do you find it a little too much, a bit overwhelming? About what would you like more information or explanation? How can you get that?

3. What specific questions do you have about character education, experiential and service learning, wilderness experiences, the four basic questions, and the ten stages of youth ministry?

4. Do you want to be God's kind of shepherd? How close are you to that? Do you aspire to be Paul's kind of mother/nurse and father to young people? What cautions should we have about mothering and fathering? And, finally, are you willing to be the one God calls to stand in a gap, whatever that may be and whatever the cost?

5. How has this book, if it has, helped you to love God, love yourself, and love your neighbor as yourself a little bit more?

Index

Praise for the First Edition

"Writing with the lens of a theologian, the heart of a pastor, and welcome doctrinal breadth, Dean Borgman has provided a field book of pastoral theologies that take seriously the social systems shaping the lives of adolescents—never mind that Borgman knows more about youth culture than anybody alive. This book is a significant step toward the long-awaited conversation about theology and youth ministry in postmodern culture."

—**Kenda Creasy Dean**, Princeton Theological Seminary

"Dean Borgman has been a wonderful mentor and teacher for hundreds of youth workers throughout the years. In this excellent work he brings theological integrity, depth, and years of wisdom like nothing else I have seen in our field."

—**Jim Burns**, president, HomeWord; executive director, HomeWord Center for Youth and Family, Azusa Pacific University

"In youth ministry it's not enough to know what to do. We must know why we do it. Dean Borgman's book gives us the why with depth. This is practical theology at its best."

—**Tony Campolo**, Eastern University

"Dean Borgman has been around since the early days of Young Life. He started Young Life's suburban ministry in New England in the 1950s and helped begin Young Life's overall urban thrust in the United States in the 1960s. He has been deeply involved in training and research and has taught hundreds of Young Life staff and management personnel on adolescent culture and youth ministry in the last several decades. In the last decade, Dean has been involved in the coordination and expansion of Young Life's ministry in Africa and the Middle East. On the subject of youth ministry Dean brings wisdom, a lifetime of experience, and a great track record. I highly recommend his book."

—**Denny Rydberg**, president, Young Life

"A must for anyone involved in youth ministry. Dean Borgman is a man who has done his homework and paid his dues. This book gives the crucial theological framework necessary for youth ministry. It is relevant and accurate in its understanding of youth culture, particularly of urban youth culture."

—**Allen A. Belton**, senior partner for Reconciliation Ministries, Breakthrough Partners; former vice president of multiethnic and urban affairs, Youth for Christ USA

"This solid foundational book is considered a textbook for youth ministry and training of future leaders. A must read for all who work with youth."

—*Ashland Theological Journal*